Ottmar Ette
Writing-between-Worlds

Mimesis

―

Romanische Literaturen der Welt

Herausgegeben von
Ottmar Ette

Band 64

Ottmar Ette

Writing-between-Worlds

TransArea Studies
and the Literatures-without-a-fixed-Abode

Translated by Vera M. Kutzinski

DE GRUYTER

ISBN 978-3-11-057868-3
e-ISBN (PDF) 978-3-11-046287-6
e-ISBN (EPUB) 978-3-11-046112-1
ISSN 0178-7489

Library of Congress Cataloging-in-Publication Data
A CIP catalog record for this book has been applied for at the Library of Congress.

Bibliographic information published by the Deutsche Nationalbibliothek
The Deutsche Nationalbibliothek lists this publication in the Deutsche Nationalbibliografie; detailed bibliographic data are available on the Internet at http://dnb.dnb.de.

© 2016 Walter de Gruyter GmbH, Berlin/Boston
This volume is text- and page-identical with the hardback published in 2016.
Printing: CPI books GmbH, Leck

♾ Printed on acid-free paper
Printed in Germany

www.degruyter.com

Ithaka gave you a marvelous journey.
Without her you would not have set out.
She has nothing left to give you now.

And if you find her poor, Ithaca won't have fooled you.
Wise as you will have become, so full of experience,
You will have understood by then what these Ithakas mean.
—Constantine P. Cavafy. "Ithaca" (1911)

It is means something else to be without a home at home rather than in a foreign country, where we can find a home in our homelessness.
—Imre Kertész, *Someone Other: The Cronicle of the Changing* (1997)

I was often disgusted by people who were fluent in their mother tongue. They created the impression that they could think and feel nothing else than what their language offers up to them so quickly and readily.
—Yoko Tawada, *Talisman* (1996)

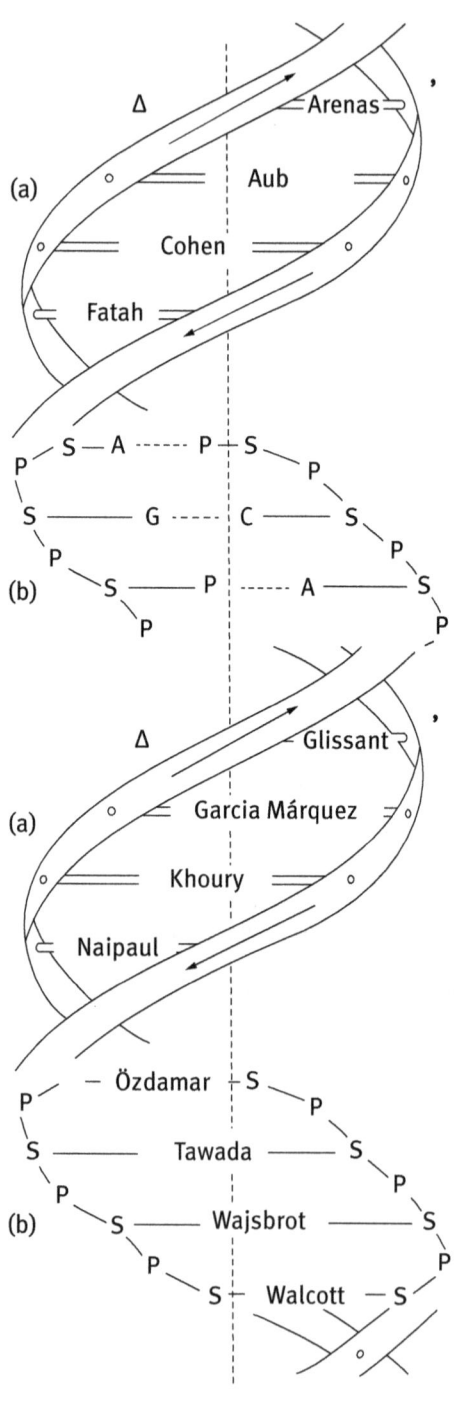

Contents

Translator's Introduction —— IX

Preface: What does literature know? —— XXI

1   Transit —— 1
    Mobile InterWorlds: toward TransAreal (Literary) Scholarship

2   Figurations —— 40
    Odysseus and the Angel of History: The Vectoral Imagination of Shoa Literature

3   Relations —— 84
    Caribbean IslandWorlds: about the fractal geometry of the literary island

4   Incubations —— 126
    A National Literature without a fixed Abode? Fictions and Frictions in Twentieth-Century Cuban Literature

5   Translations —— 157
    In Others' Words: Literary translation as Writing-between-Worlds

6   Oscillations —— 181
    Writing-Other(wise) between Worlds: About translingual writing in contemporary German-speaking Literature

7   Confrontations —— 214
    The Transareal Worlds of the ArabAmericas: Chronicle of a Clash Foretold

8   In(tro)spections —— 255
    Voyages into the realm of the dead: Border experiences of a literature 'after' migration

9   Configurations —— 289
    Literature as Knowledge-for-Living, Literary Scholarship as Science-for-Living

Note on the Text and Acknowledgments —— 313

Bibliography —— 315

Name Index —— 335

Translator's Introduction

Literary studies as LifeStudies

> We are deformed unless we read.
> —William Carlos Williams

Why, then, should we read Ottmar Ette? A passage from Vandana Singh's short story 'The Tetrahedron' helps explain why I feel strongly that at least a portion of a body of critical-theoretical work written in German merits the attention of a wider audience. Singh offers a visual metaphor that encapsulates how Ottmar Ette reads and writes about literature. When Maya, Singh's protagonist, finds a 'door' into the titular Tetrahedron, an 'object [that] extends in a dimension [...] inaccessible to us,'[1] she undergoes what appears to be a remarkable transformation: suddenly, her hands are no longer singular but multiple, her own and also those of spectral presences from other spatiotemporal realms:

> [Maya] looked at her two hands, the familiar river-valley of lines and tributaries, and she saw that they were the same as before, and not the same. Other hands branched off her hands, fading off into an infinity of hands, young hands, old hands, smooth and wrinkled. She took a deep, sobbing breath.
> 'What has happened to me?'
> 'Nothing. You see yourself as you are in more than three dimensions.'[2]

Maya's transformation is a change in (self)perception that results from her newfound ability to see herself from multiple, and multiplying, perspectives at the same time. Singh's figure for this mode of understanding human connectedness is significantly not a tree but a rhizome.[3] I take Singh's image of the ramifications of Maya's hands as an especially apt fictional equivalent of what Ette describes as the 'vectoral spaces' created in literary texts through multidirectional movements across places and temporalities other than those we typically perceive as our own. Like Singh's 'The Tetrahedron,' Ette's *Writing-between-Worlds* teaches us to see ourselves as we are in more than three dimensions and to read

---

[1] Vandana Singh: 'The Tetrahedron.' In: Singh: *The Woman who Thought She was a Planet: And Other Stories*. New Delhi: Zubaan 2013, p. 152.
[2] Singh, *The Woman*, p. 165.
[3] The figure of the rhizome links Singh's stories to the work of Édouard Glissant, and through him, Gilles Deleuze and Félix Guattari, among others.

literature in this initially disorienting way as well. Reading Ottmar Ette 'unflattens' our minds, which is no small matter.⁴

A specialist in Romance literatures by trade, Ottmar Ette is appreciated for different things in different places: in Spain and the Hispanic Americas for his scholarship on José Martí, Jorge Semprún, Mario Vargas Llosa, and Gabriel García Márquez; in the francophone world for his writings on Roland Barthes, Assia Djebar, Édouard Glissant, and Amin Maalouf; and in his native Germany for his path-breaking work on Alexander von Humboldt.⁵ These are only some of the many different authors whose work that find their way into Ette's prolific critical writings. Yet, presenting his critical writings grouped in accordance with geographies that also coincide with different academic fields does a disservice to what I consider most compelling about Ette's scholarship: its comparative ethos, the fact that his work crosses national, linguistic, and disciplinary borders with impunity. *Writing-between-Worlds* alone immerses readers in the migratory contexts of Shoah, Caribbean, new-German, and Arab-Latin American literatures, which Ette approaches from ever-shifting angles and with diverse methods. While his multi-pronged approach, which he himself calls "TransArea studies,"⁶ has become an increasingly significant factor in all of his work, it is most visible in his more recent writings on literary theory and cultural history, notably in his 'ÜberLebenswissen' trilogy.

The monographs that make up this trilogy consist of *ÜberLebenswissen: Die Aufgabe der Philologie* (Survival-knowledge: the task [or surrender] of philology) from 2004,⁷ *ZwischenWeltenSchreiben: Literaturen ohne festen Wohnsitz* (Writing-between-worlds: literatures without a fixed abode) from 2005, and

---

4 See Nick Sousanis: *Unflattening*. Cambridge, Mass.: Harvard University Press 2015.
5 See, for instance, Ottmar Ette: *Weltbewusstsein: Alexander von Humboldt und das unvollendete Project einer anderen Moderne*. Weilerwist: Velbrück Wissenschaft 2002, and Ette: *Alexander von Humboldt und die Globalisierung: Das Mobile des Wissens*. Frankfurt am Main: Insel 2009.
6 See Ottmar Ette: *TransArea: Eine literarische Globalisierungsgeschichte*. Berlin: De Gruyter 2012; also Ette: 'Unterwegs zu einer Weltwissenschaft?: Alexander von Humboldts Weltbegriffe und die transarealen Studien.' In: *HiN - Alexander von Humboldt im Netz* (Potsdam/Berlin) VII.13 (2006), p. 34–54.
7 *ÜberLebenswissen* focuses on the specific history and practices of the field of Romance literatures in the context of globalization, including chapters on Erich Auerbach, Leo Spitzer, and Roland Barthes alongside readings of Alexander von Humboldt, Hannah Arendt, and Max Aub, among others. The difference of Ette's approach comes into view when one reads his chapter on Spitzer and Auerbach in concert with Emily Apter's 'Global *Translatio*. The "Invention" of Comparative Literature, Istanbul, 1933.' In: Christopher Prendergast (ed.): *Debating world literature*. London: Verso 2004, p. 77–109.

ZusammenLebensWissen: List, Last und Lust literarischer Konvivenz im globalen Massstab (Knowledge-for-living-together: the ploys, cares, and pleasures of literary conviviality on a global scale) from 2010. The concept that links these three books may well be translated as "survival-knowledge," as I have often done in the present volume and elsewhere. At the same time, however, it is important to note that the composite noun *ÜberLebenswissen* harbors an additional meaning that, as Ette's unusual internal capitalization suggests, is indeed the primary one: 'about (*über*) life knowledge' or, as I prefer, 'knowledge-for-living' (in which the notion of knowledge *about* living in always already implicit).[8] *Lebenswissen* – knowledge-for-living – is the root from which other terms quite logically branch off: 'survival-knowledge' (*ÜberlebensWissen*) and 'knowledge-for-living-together' (*ZusammenLebensWissen*). Ette developed the key concepts of 'knowledge-for-living' and 'science-for-living' (*Lebenswissenschaft*) to set them off from the biotechnological discourses of the so-called life sciences and thus (re)claim the term 'life' as a central concern of and an intellectual space for the humanities, and for literary studies in particular.[9] *Writing-between-Worlds* and *ZusammenLebensWissen* build on these fundamental ideas to advance an alternate discourse about life and for living (together) through which the erstwhile philologies, now reinvigorated as what I think of as literary and cultural Life-Studies,[10] would "be opened up, made accessible and relevant, to the larger society.' For the humanities, '[d]oing so is, simply and plainly, a matter of survival."[11]

Put differently, *knowledge-for-living* is the filament that interlaces Ottmar Ette's conceptual terminology into the figure of the open-weave tapestry displayed on the first recto and the last page of each of the three monographs.

---

8 Translations into French (*savoir-vivre*) and Spanish (*saber-vivir*) are less cumbersome.
9 While his first book-length articulation of these two concepts dates back to 2004, Ette also published a widely-noticed polemic on the topic three years later. Given how important these two concepts are to Ette's post-2004 writings, it made good sense to include some of his provocative articulations in this book. See Note on the Text below.
10 The poems in Robert Lowell's *Life Studies*, which serves as my inspiration here, would certainly benefit from being reading along Ette's lines. Lowell: *Life studies*. New York: Farrar 1959; 1968.
11 Ottmar Ette: *ZwischenWeltenSchreiben*, p. 270.

XII —— Translator's Introduction

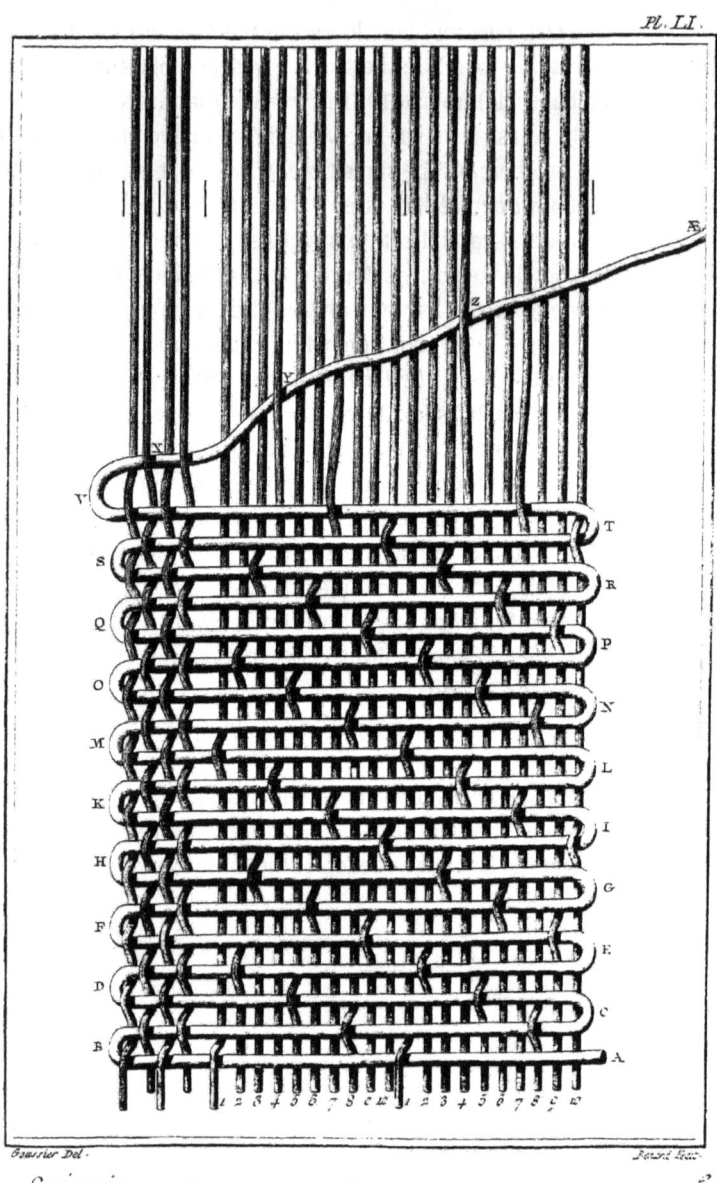

Fig. A: "Soierie. Etoffes en plein. Satin à dix lisses, vu du côté de l'envers," Plate LI, in: *Encyclopédie ou Dictionnaire raisonné des sciences, des arts et des métiers*, Volume Z 373 (1765), © Bibliothèque nationale de France.

In *ZwischenWeltenSchreiben*, four lines from Botho Strauss's 1992 lyric 'Beginninglessness' (*Beginnlosigkeit*) accompany the repeated tapestry image to highlight the fact that this weave has neither a definable beginning nor a foreseeable end. Both are always entangled, even if we cannot always see exactly where, when, and how they intersect and overlap:

> When something is Now, it holds a
> Once-Again and a Nevermore in its folds,
> the Once of promise and the Once of remembrance
> into a double spiral intertwined.[12]

Strauss's entwined double helixes must have been one of the inspirations for the book's emblematic frontispiece, which is also repeated in each of the three volumes but with the names of different writers in each iteration. It immediately conjures up familiar representations of DNA, the matrix of life – hardly a coincidence. The double helixes are thus a fitting motif for Ottmar Ette's very distinctive way of thinking (about) the relations among writers and texts from such diverse provenances. Intricate plays of similarities *and* differences, the relations to which he attends are precisely those that go unnoticed in more linear, static approaches to the literatures of the world and their histories.

In *Writing-between-Worlds*, as in the two books that frame it in the German edition, Ette advances two fundamental hypotheses: One, literature is always in motion. Dynamic rather than emplaced, literature, especially during the twentieth century – which he labels 'the century of migrations' – moves freely across all sorts of borders, including of course national ones. In doing so, literary texts draw attention to the fact that no single nation ever speaks only a single language. Instead, nation-states, as ideological frames, obscure and suppress their own multilingual realities.[13] Two, literary texts artistically encode the patterns of such spatiotemporal movements and store them in the form of 'knowledge(s)-

---

12 'Wenn etwas Jetzt ist, dann trägt es ein / ingefaltetes Abermals und ein Nie-Wieder, / das Einst der Verheissung und das Einst der Erinnerung / in verschlungener Doppelspirale in sich.' Since *Writing-between-Worlds* is, strictly speaking, not part of Ette's trilogy, we decided not to reproduce the image of the weave.

13 Colleen Boggs, whose idea of 'linguistic mobility' is more limited than Ette's, sees nationalism and transnationalism as 'related strategies for negotiating linguistic plurality.' Boggs: *Transnationalism and American literature: Literary translation 1773-1892*. New York: Routledge 2007, p. 3. Ette would no doubt grant that 'reconsidering national formations from a position of estrangement helps us... to illuminate the nation's unconscious assumptions, boundaries, and proscribed areas.' Paul Giles: *Virtual Americas: Transnational Fictions and the transatlantic Imaginary*. Durham, N.C.: Duke University Press, 2002, p. 3.

for-living' in the service of survival and of living-*together*. For Ette, literary texts are largely untapped resources of culturally diverse forms not of knowledge as product, object, or information but of *knowing as process*. Accordingly, *Writing-between-Worlds* traces many different literary projections of 'fundamentally complex' intellectual, emotional, and aesthetic designs that, often unexpectedly, connect worlds otherwise cut up into nation-states and rife with linguistic divisions. Such tracings require critical vocabularies and methodologies capable of describing the various directional movements in (and of) literature in precise ways. They require what Ette terms a 'poetics of movement' in which to bring together different yet overlapping figures of movement – such as processes of writing-other(wise) (*Fremdschreiben*) and taking language(s) elsewhere (*Fortschreiben*) – and analyze the effects their dynamic interrelations have exerted, and continue to do so, on nation-states singly and globally. Such an analysis productively interrogates the worn term 'globalization' from the perspective of the 'Literatures without a fixed Abode.' In these and other ways, *Writing-between-Worlds* challenges the prominence that the nation has enjoyed in literary studies, along with the ingrained distinction between national literary canons and so-called world literatures.

Yet, Ette does not just discard the idea of the nation as useful to literary studies today. Instead, he acknowledges the existence of nation-states and probes their function as the conceptual-discursive frames and political realities in tension with the 'Literatures without a fixed Abode.' The concept of the 'Literatures without a fixed Abode' rejects the exclusionary logic of either national literature or world literature.[14] It is what Franco Moretti might call a 'problem' in search of a 'new critical method.'[15] 'Literatures without a fixed Abode,' that is, literatures that do not belong to a single national context, are a theoretical 'problem' because they 'transect,' 'transverse,' and otherwise worry ideological lines and conceptual borders, be they national or disciplinary. The German verb for this process is 'queren,' which suggests unsystematic, disorderly crossings, actions that unsettle, disturb, and disorient conventions and taxonomies, in literary studies and elsewhere. The point of Ette's critical method is not to construct counternarratives as 'a (territorializable) defense against national literature'

---

14 'Literatures without a fixed Abode' is, for instance, a phenomenon quite distinct from 'world literature' in David Damrosch's sense: 'literary works that circulate beyond their *culture of origin*.' Damrosch: *What is World Literature?* Princeton N.J.: Princeton University Press 2003, p. 4.
15 Franco Moretti: 'Conjectures on World Literature'. In: Christopher Prendergast (ed.): *Debating World Literature*. London: Verso 2004, p. 149.

and other orthodoxies. Rather, he is intent on '[accounting] for geocultural and biopolitical changes, and for the literary-aesthetic developments that accompany those changes. Neither the perspective of national literature nor that of world literature enables us to think through such transformations and describe them fully. My goal is to articulate practices of Writing-between-Worlds that cannot be territorialized in any permanent (or settled) way.'[16] Nor is Ette's method akin to Moretti's 'distant reading.'[17] Ette is very clear that larger patterns perceived at a distance will always have to be re-contextualized, lest they lead to a 'de-localized knowledge' made up of reductive simplifications and generalizations about inherently dynamic locations such as 'home,' 'nation,' 'exile,' or 'world.' It is precisely through close attention to texts – and through (hopefully) increasing collaborations of readers from different specialties – that literary studies can supply the local cultural specifics without which the very idea of knowledge-for-living-(together) cannot but remain a meaningless abstraction.

Ette's theories about vectoral spaces in literature are not a backhanded way of returning to some wobbly concept of 'world literature' that flows from the purported universality of human life.[18] Clearly, neither thematic nor formal similarities alone are the most fertile grounds for literary comparisons. Ette, for one, finds it far more fruitful to pinpoint areas of both divergence and overlap in the literary representations of human ideas and experiences across the planet, representations in which neither universality nor globalization simply spells homogeneity; instead, they refer to a vast, often violent, interplay of myriad mutable cultural, social, and political perspectives. "In no way do I want to misunderstand literature as a mere reflection of society in a vulgar-Marxist or positivistic sense," Ette clarifies. "Such theories of reflection reduce intertextuality to a mere positivistic analysis of sources, recklessly eclipsing, among other things, cultural differences and crossovers in literary writing. At the same time, any inquiry into the uses of literary scholarship, including theory, cannot but raise questions about specific historical, cultural, and socio-economic contexts, not to mention academic politics and educational policies."[19]

---

16 P. 8 below.
17 Moretti, 'Conjectures,' p. 151.
18 According to Haun Saussy, 'universality' is the 'most obvious, and usually undertheorized, candidate for 'trunk' status in the discipline of comparative literature.' Saussy (ed.): *Comparative Literature in an Age of Globalization*. Baltimore, MD: Johns Hopkins University Press 2006, p. 13.
19 See p. 290 below.

To focus on the knowledges necessary for living and surviving, in and beyond our academies, does not mean to build thematic gateways to universality but to "adjust to multiple frames of reference and to attend to relations rather than givens."[20] And terms such as 'life,' 'survival,' and 'knowledge' are never givens in Ette's writings but abstractions that stand for remarkably complicated exchanges and relations, be they historical, social, political, economic, or cultural, especially linguistic. Not taking one's language for granted resounds throughout Ette's lively critical engagement with his own language, which has already yielded a crop of neologisms that test German readers' imaginations no less than they do translators'. An example is 'ZwischenSprachWeltenBereich,' a noun that refers to the areas or spaces that form in the interstices of linguistic worlds, and which may well confound even German-language readers. Mark Twain's famous complaints about long composite nouns in his essay 'The Awful German Language' (1880) come readily to mind here. 'These things are not words,' he wrote with endearing sarcasm, 'but alphabetical processions.'[21] English, of course, rarely accommodates the stacking up of words in the way that German does. That almost all of Ette's key terms qualify as linguistic 'processions' does not exactly facilitate the task of translation; but it does force the translator (and any other reader) to engage with English as intensely as Ette does with German. In this sense, difficulty, even 'untranslatability,' can be quite enabling and, in fact, rather pleasurable.[22]

I began translating excerpts from Ottmar Ette's writings some years ago, but other projects and responsibilities kept getting in the way of completing this particular volume. Thanks to these otherwise frustrating delays, I have had more time than expected to ponder possible ways of bringing Ette's vexing linguistic creations over into USAmerican English and also to reflect on the process having to rethink English via German, my first but now estranged language, in the same way that Ette reworks German, often via French and Spanish. It quickly became clear to me that simply importing Ette's coinages into an English-language environment, as I have provisionally done above, either placing them in quotation marks or italicizing them (or both), was woe-

---

20 Saussy: *Comparative Literature*, p. 34.
21 Mark Twain: *The Writings of Mark Twain*: P. F. Collier & Son Company 1907, p. 277.
22 Ette's critical-theoretical vocabulary would make a fitting addition to the Barbara Cassin's *Dictionary of Untranslatables*. It is somewhat surprising that the entry for 'Life' is very short and that, among the 400 entries included in this *Philosophical Dictionary*, neither 'knowledge' nor 'survival' have found a place. See Cassin et al. (eds): *Dictionary of Untranslatables. A Philosophical Lexicon*. Princeton: Princeton University Press 2014, p. 576.

fully inadequate. For one, it would needlessly clutter an already polylingual text in which words and locutions in French and Spanish have been left intact.[23] For another, such imports would mark the German words as linguistic oddities without necessarily making readers more aware of the need to reconsider their all-too-familiar English usage. I decided that a better way to achieve a measure of translational defamiliarization of English was by resorting visual markers of a different sort – hyphens, parentheses, and unorthodox capitalization – to signal that certain locutions in English (often versions of a single composite term in German) are descriptive phrases that also have distinct conceptual dimensions. The titular 'Writing-between-Worlds' is a good example. That, in contrast to 'ZwischenWeltenSchreiben,' I render the noun 'Zwischenwelten' as 'inter-Worlds' indicates clearly that the additive method Ette uses to create many of his neologisms does not, and cannot, produce the same sort of logic or consistency in English. I found 'InterWorldWriting,' which would have followed more logically from 'interWorlds,' unappealingly static when compared to 'Writing-between-Worlds.' Other prominent examples are the verbs 'fortschreiben' and 'fremdschreiben' – taking-language(s)-elsewhere and writing-other(wise), in my English versions – whose nuances in German quite simply elude English. 'Fortschreiben' can mean 'to continue to write' or 'to add to;' it can also signify 'to write away from,' as in 'to revise' but with an added spatial dimension. 'Fremdschreiben' emphasizes the strangeness of linguistic and cultural differences that accompany acts of spatial and temporal distancing. Both forms of writing are closely related: if one writes-other(wise), one may also take one's (native?) language(s) *elsewhere*, that is, to other times and places.

Ottmar Ette's writing shifts the linguistic and conceptual ground beneath our proverbial feet. Sometimes, he twists our readerly tongues only slightly, almost imperceptibly; at others, we are more fully aware of tectonic shifts that leave us feeling disoriented, contorted, estranged from ourselves. Ette's point, indeed his entire critical and linguistic practice, is to make ideas and experiences thinkable, sayable, and writable that were not so before, or at least not easily. To do so, one has to take one's language elsewhere and, in the process, alienate it from itself. The point is not to hand readers a cache of ready-made critical-theoretical terms – in German or in English – which they can apply without further critical reflection. Following Ette's principles, I have attempted to make my translation a thought-provoking mixture of the familiar and the

---

[23] I have kept all quotations from the original texts (mainly in the footnotes) to render their differences from my own and/or others' English versions palpable without interrupting the flow of the critical narrative.

strange in which intellectual excitement may at times (I hope) spring from linguistic impediments. These impediments include translational inconsistencies designed to keep English as dynamic as possible without risking definitional confusion. Readers of this book will finally decide whether my various choices as a translator are indeed effective in this way.

Like all of Ottmar Ette's work, *Writing-between-Worlds* challenges humanists worldwide to consider carefully how they might reclaim certain terms and discourses – notably on life, living, and living together – as grounds for their own intellectual and political pursuits and responsibilities. Doing so seems particularly urgent in societies where the rhetoric of life has been lionized not only by the biosciences (this is true nearly everywhere) but also, and often even more aggressively, by fundamentalist religious and other likeminded conservative organizations. Similarly, the momentous changes that are underway in Europe and worldwide in a century that is proving to be another 'century of migrations' require a great deal thoughtful knowledge-for-living-together in ways respectful, not just tolerant, of cultural differences, whatever those might be. To survive, a society clearly needs to know more than what it takes to keep its residents breathing. A society, any society, stands to benefit from understanding, for example, the exact differences between a language of mere tolerance and expressions of respectfulness toward other humans. To this end, societies need to cultivate more critical attitudes toward and within language. This is by no means a new idea. '[W]e need to have a habitually critical attitude toward language – our own as well as that of others,' Samuel Ichiye Hayakawa, a professor of English and a former U.S. Senator from California, wrote in the 1990 Preface to the fifth edition of *Language in Thought and Action* (1941). 'Hitler is gone,' he continued,

> but if the majority of our fellow citizens are more susceptible to the slogans of fear and race hatred than those of peaceful accommodation and mutual respect among human beings, our political liberties remain at the mercy of any eloquent and unscrupulous demagogue.'[24]

Xenophobia is all around us, and it is not elsewhere but very much in our own homes, wherever those may be. When 'slogans of fear and race hared' fill the airwaves and the internet almost daily, and when walls are once again being built around nations, it matters enormously that we reflect more carefully on how we think of ourselves in relation to other people and understand better

---

24 S. I. Hayakawa and Alan R. Hayakawa: *Language in Thought and Action*. San Diego, Calif.: Harcourt Brace Jovanovich 1990, p. xi–xii.

how those we 'other' think about us. We live at a time in history when massive waves of migrants from the war-torn Syria and other war-devastated Middle Eastern and African regions are flooding Europe, changing the world as we known it. Reflecting on what these impending changes might mean in the future, and not just in negative ways, involves being more thoughtful than separating migrant populations into political (read: legitimate) 'refugees' and 'economic migrants.' Does it really matter why people fear for their lives enough to leave their homes? Do their lives matter less if they flee their countries for economic reasons rather than political ones? The answer should be self-evident; but self-evidence is always risky because it seems to require from us neither thoughtfulness nor action when both are most needed.

That most of today's media encourage us to approach cultural differences as something to be treated with fear and suspicion stands in stark contrast to what we could read in the literatures of the world, which are filled with many alternatives. I cannot help but wonder if it is mere coincidence that many of the texts Ette analyzes in *Writing-between-Worlds* are not even available in English (yet?). This lack is something I felt compelled to point out in some of the notes I added to this translation, because I find it important that English-language readers of this book realize how little they know about the different perspectives that writers in other parts of the world have to offer, writers who care deeply about mutual respect, survival in the eddies of cultural difference, and knowledge(s)-for-living-together. Ottmar Ette's scholarship points a way for humanists in the English-speaking world to reinvigorate their own disciplines, something that is indeed a matter of professional survival. One way of doing so (and there are many others) is by making available to English-language readers literary and critical texts that can make a substantial difference to how we think and live. These are the primary reasons why I read Ottmar Ette, and why I chose to translate *Writing-between-Worlds*.

Vera M. Kutzinski, Nashville, Tennessee, October 2015

Preface: What does literature know?

The question of what precise knowledge literature creates and delivers has moved closer to the center of current debates in literary studies for some years now. That it has done so seems to follow from the growing trend in the humanities, especially in literary and cultural studies, to replace the thematics of commemoration, dominant for the last quarter of a century, with the problematics of knowledge (production). This tendency may or may not amount to a paradigm shift of some import in the history of the sciences.[1] Commemoration will no doubt remain on the agenda. Particularly in connection with the deregulation of the world that Amin Maalouf has diagnosed,[2] it will, however, become important, in years and decades to come, to develop multi-perspectival approaches whose combination can guide a deepened historical field toward a *prospective* dimension and thus a modelling of the future. A new direction for literary studies? Absolutely, and it is already underway.

The question about knowledge in and through literature is also a question about the social, political, and cultural relevance this knowledge may have for today's differently organized information and (also) knowledge societies.[3] What does literature want? What can it do? And what can it contribute to formulating new, imaginative answers to the challenges of globalization, answers that might get us out of the grooves of our entrenched ways of thinking?

In this book, I propose that there is no better, no more complex way to access a community, a society, an era and its cultures than through literature. For millennia, literature from a wide variety of geocultural areas has gathered knowledge about life, about survival, and about living together, without either falling into discursive or disciplinary specializations or functioning as a regulatory mechanism for cultural knowledge. Literature is able to offer its readers knowledge through direct participation in the form of step-by-step intellectual and affective experiences. Through this ability, it can reach and affect audiences across great spatial and temporal distances. Literature – what different times

---

1 [Ette's term 'Wissenschaftsgeschichte' encompasses both the history of the natural and social sciences and the humanities. TN]
2 See Amin Maalouf: *Disordered World: Setting a new Course for the twenty-first Century*. London: Bloomsbury 2011; see also Tzvetan Todorov: *The New World disorder: Reflections of a European*. Cambridge, UK: Polity 2005.
3 See Manuel Castells: *Das Informationszeitalter; Wirtschaft – Gesellschaft – Kultur*. Opladen: Leske & Budrich 2003.

and cultures have been able to understand as such in a broad sense – has always been characterized by its transareal and transcultural origins and effects. It is the product of many logics, and it teaches us to think *polylogically* rather than monologically. Literature is an experiment in living, and living in a state of experimentation.

In a vital, indeed radical way, literature (or better, the literatures of the world) is designed to be interpreted in many different ways, to release a cosmos of heteroglossia, of whose coordinates we are far more, and more clearly, aware thanks to Mikhail Bakhtin's work. Literature is a playing field of multiple meanings, of polysemousness, insofar as it can, indeed must, employ a variety of different logics at the same time. Through its fundamental polysemy unfold polylogical structures and constructions oriented not toward securing stable ground, in the sense of a single, fixed location, but toward identifying the movements of comprehension in all their permutations. Is not this ability more valuable for us today, in our present world of contradictory socio-globalization,[4] than it has been for any of the generations that have preceded us?

Literature puts into relief the mobility of knowledge. As a mobile of knowledge, it ensures that very different areas of knowledge (production) and the partial knowledges of one, several, or many communities and societies are related in ever-new, experimental ways. Such uninterrupted transfer necessitates transformations. The cultural compression that literature produces always implies more than a simple interweaving;[5] literature creates playing fields that resist and counteract the extermination of culture(s).

It follows, then, that literature is *knowledge in motion*. Its polylogical constructions are vital to human survival in the world of the twenty-first century, whose greatest challenge is the ability to live together in peace and in difference on a global scale. Through a serious experimental play always variously buttressed by the pillars of aesthetics and poetics, literature allows us to rehearse and refine simultaneous thinking in different cultural, social, political, and psycho-

---

4 See Mathias Albert: *Zur Politik der Weltgesellschaft: Identität und Recht im Kontext internationaler Vergesellschaftung*. Weilerswist: Velbrück Wissenschaft 2002. [The German term 'Verweltgesellschaftung' is a combination of globalization and socialization = socio-globalization. See also Matthias Albert and Lothar Brock: *Debordering in the World of States: New Spaces in International Relations*. Frankfurt am Main: World Society Research Group 1995. TN]
5 For the concepts of interweaving and 'histoire croisée,' see Michael Werner and Bénédicte Zimmermann: 'Vergleich, Transfer, Verflechtung. Der Ansatz der 'histoire croisée' und die Herausforderung des Transnationalen'. In: *Geschichte und Gesellschaft: Zeitschrift für historische Sozialwissenschaften* (Göttingen) 28 (2002), p. 607–636.

logical contexts. Literature creates what is yet to come; it models our future from within the traditions of a millennial world consciousness.

This ability accounts for literature's extraordinary importance in the experimental creation of a future under the conditions of globalization. It may be that literature's experimental resourcefulness cannot stamp out the flagrant lack of imagination that marks global relations in political, economic, ideological, and religious areas; but it can fight that lack. With its manifold connections to life, literature reveals its own life force: its ability to acknowledge things as they are, or as they can be thought of, in their being-this-way, at the same time transforming 'how things are' and 'how things should have been' into a movement, indeed a pull, in the direction of 'how things should become.' In other words, the compression of life in literature creates not only a life (and thus a history) of literature but also drives a process of knowledge about life within living that extends across decades, centuries, and indeed millennia. Lodged within literature's systems of transmission, this process transforms life itself, individually and of course collectively.

To be sure, we should not stop examining the phenomena of globalization from the perspectives of economics and politics, finances, law, and medicine, history and geography. But we should be aware of the fact that these perspectives yield only more or less limited, partial views and prospects. By contrast, the literatures of the world enable sensory ways of thinking and experiencing that neither simplify the complexity nor screen out the contradictions of the multiple logics that might explain the life of and on our planet. Literature's knowledge has no substitutes: it is knowledge about life within living.

Since the *Gilgamesh* epic and the earliest narrative traditions of *Arabian Nights*, the literatures of the world have confronted the phenomenon of globalization through an aesthetic of writing and reading. As a result, literature and globalization are hardly strangers to each other, and there is no need to force any connections between them. Marked by transmission, transfer, and transformation, and thus by translation of varying sorts, their relationship could not be more intimate. In literature's world consciousness, there are many responses to the present world disorder and deregulation. They offer no simple guidelines but, rather, LifeSupport, that is, food for living and surviving,[6] inasmuch as such nourishment can be understood as the provision of imaginative test sites or workshops for the future. To understand something anew, however, we al-

---

6 [Ette's composite terms here are 'LebensMittel' and 'ÜberLebensMittel', both pun on the German word for food or victuals, which is 'Lebensmittel,' literally, *means* for living and surviving. TN]

ways need new or newly-defined concepts and terms to render visible in other ways that which cannot be missed but so often is.

1 Transit

Mobile InterWorlds: toward TransAreal (Literary) Scholarship

> Coming Home to a Foreign Country; the Foreign as Home;
> A Return to What Never Was.

A young man stands at the Corniche, Alexandria's famous coastal promenade, and looks, musing, across a Mediterranean Sea already shrouded in deep darkness. Children wave at him, and he responds with a gesture of familiar intimacy, as if this ordinary scene could repeat itself at any time. His hands touch and feel the seawall's rocks roughened by the saltwater but resistant to it. The traffic noise behind him fades from his consciousness more and more. Time and space stand still.

We might be on Havana's Malecón or on the coastal road in Florida's San Augustine, on the old seawalls of Sitges in Cataluña or on the Río de la Plata in Montevideo. The young man, however, is in the city that Alexander the Great founded, a city that houses the Occident's most mythical library and which, today, decades after the scene I just described, seeks to reconnect with the great tradition of a city open to the world under a new name: El-Iskandariya. It is a mild Mediterranean evening during the mid-1960s, and the young man knows that his farewell, his own leave-taking from Egypt is imminent; it is at once very personal and yet suffered jointly with his family. The calm is deceptive: the moment, in the blink of an eye, is interWorldly; it puts him on the brink of historic change.

For the last time, he looks across the bay, over which once towered the Lighthouse of Pharos, one of Antiquity's Seven World Wonders. It was here that Euclid once conducted some of the experiments that became the basis for the geometry that bears his name and thus for 'the entire standard geometry' that was to dominate the West's spatial imagination for centuries to come.[1] As if to prove the point, the bay pushes its semi-circle out into the sea.

Those days seem long past, even if their weave still remains tangled up with the bay and creates more complex room for movement between waves, worlds, and cultures. King Faruq of Egypt, with whom a member of the young man's family had enjoyed cordial relations, has long been deposed by Egypt's second

---

[1] Benoît Mandelbrot: *The Fractal Geometry of Nature*. Rev. ed. New York: H. Freeman 1983, p. 13.

president, Gamal Abdel Nasser. Land reforms and nationalizations followed quickly, and the decisive military conflicts of the Suez War against Great Britain, France, and Israel were won. What began then was a process of building a nation-state, with all of its requisite mechanisms of inclusion and exclusion, which was to catapult Egypt out of its old Levantine dependence and its post-Osmanian faux-independence and into modernity – another modernity. The space yielded a bit of the future, for others.

Soon the pressure on the Jewish populations would grow to such an extent that the young man's family, like so many others, left the country: Exodus from Egypt. The world that the Bay of Alexandria connects geometrically becomes the world in the I's mind. By tomorrow, this bay will have become – in Stefan Zweig's sense – 'yesterday's world,' and not only for the first-person narrator. It is evening; it becomes night.

At the same time, however, the narrator's long gaze across the Bay of Alexandria is already infused with what is to come, with the imminent exodus, and thus with the presence of future memories of a waning world:

> And suddenly I knew, as I touched the damp, grainy surface of the seawall, that I would always remember this night, that in years to come I would remember sitting here, swept with confused longing as I listened to the water lapping the giant boulders beneath the promenade and watched the children head toward the shore in a winding, lambent procession. I wanted to come back tomorrow night, and the night after, and the night after that as well, sensing that what made leaving so fiercely painful was the knowledge that there would never be another night like this, that I would never eat soggy cakes along the coast road in the evening, not this year or any other year, not feel the baffling, sudden beauty of that moment when, if only for an instant, I had caught myself longing for a city I never knew I loved.
>
> Exactly a year from now on, I vowed, I would sit outside at night wherever I was, someone in Europe, or in America, and turn my face to Egypt, as Moslems do when they pray and face Mecca, and remember this very night, and how I had thought these things and made this vow.²

In this passage of his memoir, first published in 1994 under the title *Out of Egypt*, André Aciman – a native of Alexandria from where he emigrated with his family in 1965, first to Italy, then to France, and finally to the US – opens up an archetypal scene of migration. Here, spaces and times crisscross and overlap, as do natural and cultural contexts, past remembrances and future projections. The overlap is the permanence of a future that has already become past. Time does not stand still, does not stop: it offers up its knowledge of eternity. In the

---

2 André Aciman: *Out of Egypt: A Memoir*. New York: Riverhead Books 1994, p. 339.

blink of an eye, without beginning and yet not timeless, the transitory and the trans-historical become inextricably interwoven without, however, being completely indistinguishable. Alexandria: once, always.

Not long after the publication of his Alexandria memoir, André Aciman, who already lived in New York then, tried to describe the spatial feeling of exiles in his Preface to *Letters of Transit*. In this essay, the Arab world is as strangely distant and backgrounded as it is in the old photograph in which the Egyptian domestics appear only by accident and at the outer margins of the centered wedding picture of a well-off Jewish family in Alexandria. As the camera captures this fleeting moment, photography's luminous languages bring out both the familiar and the repressed, as if by accident:

> In the back of the assemblage, peeping ever so furtively from behind the veranda's French windows, are the faces of three Egyptians. The maid, Zeinab, no older than twenty and already in the family for a decade, is smiling mischievously. Ahmed, the cook, who is from Khartoum, bashfully attempts to avert his eyes from the photographer, covering his face with his right palm. His younger sister Latifa, a mere child of ten, stares with impish dark eyes into the lens.[3]

As Aciman comments in *Letters of Transit*, '[w]ith their memories perpetually on overload, exiles see double, feel double, are double. When exiles see one place they're also seeing – or looking for – another behind it. Everything bears two faces, everything is shifty because everything is mobile, the point being that exile, like love, is not just a condition of pain, it's a condition of deceit.'[4]

Already in *Out of Egypt*, mobile dynamics emerge from behind the doubled locales, places, and spaces. These dynamics transform fixed structures anew and turn them into the kind of open, arrow-like structures that I call vectorized or vectoral. A mobile system of coordinates is sketched out in the memoir, one in which past experience creates places, where spaces grow out of movement, where the past grows out of having been lived and the present out of the process of becoming future. They form a mobile network in which – as in the case of the Egyptian domestics in the yellowing photograph – the movements in and of the past cannot be separated from the movements in and of the future. Castaway time, as José F.A. Oliver traces it out precisely in the Bay of Alexandria in the opening stanza of the poem 'strandgut. El Iskandariya' [beach treasures] from his Alexandria cycle:

---
3 Aciman: *Out of Egypt*, p. 19.
4 André Aciman (ed.): *Letters of Transit: Reflections on Exile, Identity, Language, and Loss*. New York: The New Press 1999, p. 13.

> floating in an old wooden box
> sand & seastrained / 1 sandswept 1 fluid
> mosaic 1 sandmemory 1 afternoon
> out of the loudspeaker
> 1 flute play [nai] 1 wave-
> cradling for the singer
> 'who sang for everyone.'[5]

The *vectorization*, the storing of old (and even future) patterns of movement that resurface in present movements, there to be experienced anew, goes far beyond individual experience in the past and future. Vectorization encompasses an area of collective history whose patterns of movement it stores in a post-Euclidean field of discontinuous and multiply refracted vectors. Below the surface of present movements – and it is at this that the concept of vectorization aims – old movements can be felt and made present again: literature store them *as* movements and as knowledge *about* movements.

Vectorization in literature refers back not only to (collective) history but also to myth: to a reservoir of myths whose historically accumulated movements, the stuff of tradition, literature 'translates' into present processes of movement. Only in this way do many earlier dynamic patterns become even noticeable in a protagonist's movements. For instance, the exodus from Egypt and the wanderings of Odysseus add potential meanings to the migrations of the twentieth century, meanings that semantically charges and densely poeticizes even the simplest of choreographies. Not only the words underneath the words, or the places below the places, but especially the movements on the underside of movements point precisely to the knowledge-for-living and for surviving that literature, as an interactive storage medium, holds in store for each reader. Literature is an extremely dense weave of *ways* of knowing.

In Aciman's *Out of Egypt*, an Italian migrant, Signore Dall'Abaco, who had fled 'from his native city Siena during Mussolini's regime,' reminds the protagonist of the figure of Odysseus at a time when the twentieth-century Jewish exodus from Egypt was already well underway.[6] The first-person narrator's governess Roxane – lovely but quite ignorant of Greek history – is a young Per-

---

[5] '[I]n einer alten holzkiste antreibend / sand & meergesiebt / 1 versanden 1 fließ- / mosaik 1 sandgedächtnis 1 nachmittag / aus dem lautsprecher / 1 flötenspiel [nai] 1 wellen- / wiegen dem sänger / der für jeden sang.' José F.A. Oliver: *finnisher wintervorrat: Gedichte*. Frankfurt am Main: Suhrkamp 2005, p. 63. Oliver also translated into Spanish the Alexandria cycle by Joachim Sartorius: *Alexandria. Ein Zyklus / Alejandria. Un ciclo*. Huelva: Deputación Provincial de Huelva 1999–2000.

[6] Aciman: *Out of Egypt*, p. 272.

sian woman, who came to Spain to study dance and, due to unfortunate circumstances, 'landed in Alexandria,' where she lives with a British journalist who writes for the English-language newspapers.[7] Roxane immediately feels sorry for this Odysseus, as if he 'were a contemporary whose unresolved fate was still a source of concern.' Because, having been far from home for a whole twenty years can surely not be trivial: 'Twenty years, that's something.'[8] But to the Sienese scholar, who would not return to Italy until the end of the 1930s, twenty years in a foreign country seems a rather manageable period of time. He systematically inculcates in the narrator a love for Homer, 'the most sunlit author of antiquity,' as well as for his hero Odysseus, whose servant Eurycleia knew him because of his scar 'when her master returned to Ithaca after a twenty years' absence.'[9] From the perspective of a person in exile, how could this scene (and the anagnorisis associated with it) not have become the primal scene in the representation of reality in Western literature? At the beginning of the first chapter of *Mimesis*, the foundational text he wrote during his Istanbul exile, Erich Auerbach opened this scene up for literary analysis in more impressive ways than any scholars who followed after him.[10]

For a version of Odysseus's return, Dall'Abaco prefers the modern Greek poet Constantine Cavafy (aka Konstantinos Kavafis), who was born in Alexandria, to Homer and Dante. In Cavafy, Odysseus does not return to Penelope and to his native isle of Ithaca but, rather, chooses the goddess Calypso's island and his own immortality. In *Out of Egypt*, the Italian exile Dall'Abaco quotes to the Egyptian refugee Aciman lines that the poet Cavafy, writing in Alexandria in modern Greek, put in Calypso's mouth:

Why spurn my home when exile is your home?
The Ithaca you want you'll have in not having.
...
Your home's in the rubblehouse of time now,
And you're made thus, to yearn for what you lose.[11]

---

7 Aciman: *Out of Egypt*, p. 271.
8 Aciman: *Out of Egypt*, p. 288.
9 Aciman: *Out of Egypt*, p. 289, p. 287.
10 See Erich Auerbach: *Mimesis: The Representation of Reality in Western Literature*. Princeton. NJ: Princeton University Press 2003, p. 3; see also Ottmar Ette: *ÜberLebenswissen: Die Aufgabe der Philologie*. Berlin: Kulturverlag Kadmos 2004, p. 51–96.
11 Aciman: *Out of Egypt*, p. 290. In her extensive study *Booking Passage. Exile and Homecoming in the Modern Jewish Imagination*. Berkeley: University of California Press 2000, Sidra deKoven Ezrahi presents a pattern of movement that focuses on Jerusalem and does not even shy

Dall'Abaco becomes the narrator's Greek teacher in Alexandria and remains so even after his pupil has long left Egypt and made his home in a foreign country. In the end, three possibilities open up in Dall'Abaco's speech, possibilities that arise from the convergence of all these migrant biographies: the homecoming to a (former) home and thus the return to a place that has long become strange; the desire to transform a foreign place into a (new) home; and, finally, the attempt at a complete temporal and spatial reordering of home and motherland. Botho Strauss's 'Beginninglessness' (*Beginnlosigkeit*, 1992), a fragmented text characterized by continual 'derivations, allusions, repetitions, resemblances,' accomplishes such a reordering through a reference to the poem 'Return' (Ritorno) by the Italian lyricist Giorgio Caproni. It is a return to something that never was:

> Again, I am here,
> where I never was.
> Nothing is different from how it was not.
> On the halved table, the checkered
> wax cloth the glass,
> that never held anything.
> Everything remains just
> as I had never left it.[12]

Home as a foreign place, the foreign as home, return to something that never was (there). This book offers numerous examples of these and other figures of the vectoral imagination from different cultural, historical, and sociopolitical perspectives. What role the dynamic figure of Odysseus plays in all this will have already become apparent and, with the help of literary voices, will become audible in the following chapter on the dialectics of homelessness.

---

away from putting Jerusalem in place of the name of Odysseus's home island in Konstantinos Cavafy's famous poem 'Ithaka': 'Jerusalem gave you the marvelous journey' (p. 235). See also Konstantinos Cavafy: *Collected Poems*. Edited by George Savidis. Princeton, NJ: Princeton University Press 1992, p. 37.

12 'Ich bin wieder da, / wo ich niemals war. / Nichts ist anders als es nicht war. / Auf dem halbierten Tisch, dem karierten / Wachstuch das Glas, / darin nie etwas war. / Alles geblieben, wie / ich es niemals verließ.' Botho Strauss: *Beginnlosigkeit: Reflexionen über Fleck und Linie*. Munich: Carl Hanser Verlag 1992, p. 18–19. For the Italian original of this 1971 poem see Giorgio Caproni: *L'opera in versi*. Critical edition by Luca Zuliani. Milan: Mondadori 1989, p. 392.

In addition to the figure of wily Odysseus, Shoah literature gives us the dynamic figure of being swept away which also echoes in Aciman's contemplations of the Bay of Alexandria. The protagonist in *Out of Egypt* is someone swept away by Benjamin's angel of history, who moves to Italy, to France, and finally to the USA. In place of Odysseus's circular movement, we find here a discontinuous movement shot through with breaks. One might call it, in Botho Strauss's words, 'a kinetic pattern of aimless, erratic changes.'[13] Key, however, is how, much like in the kinetic figure of the Angel of History, the eyes reverse their gaze. Measured out in terms of Euclidian geometry, that brief glance across the Bay of Alexandria rises to the realm of the transtemporal in which a loss is always yet to be re-presented, again and anew. In this look of being swept away, which doubles the locales it renders placeless, appears what exiles 'fear most: that my feet are never quite solidly on the ground, but also that soil beneath is equally weak, that the graft didn't take.'[14] Our own view here opens onto a Literature without a fixed Abode whose experiential and conceptual spaces are characterized precisely by an absence of euphoria.[15]

Not literature without borders

To prevent imaginable, even plausible, misunderstandings that might arise in the context of my reading of André Aciman's *Out of Egypt*, let me be clear that the concept of *Literature without a fixed Abode* is not the same as 'migration literature' or, even more narrowly conceived, 'literature of exile;' nor can it be retranslated into either. The transareal, transcultural, and translingual dynamics I introduce in this book point to the pervasiveness and vital importance of the literatures without fixed abode. A never-ending bouncing back and forth between places and times, societies and cultures, Literatures without a fixed Abode is a concept that insists on being off-center and running against the

---

13 Strauss: *Beginnlosigkeit*, p. 128.
14 Aciman: *Letters of Transit*, p. 22.
15 See also Edward Said's self-portrait as a young man: 'A Palestinian going to school in Egypt, with an English first name, and American passport, has no certain identity at all. To make matters worse, Arabic, my native language, and English, my school language, were inextricably mixed: I have never known which was my first language, and have felt fully at home in neither, although I dream in both. Every time I speak an English sentence, I find myself echoing it in Arabic, and vice versa' (Edward Said: 'No Reconciliation Allowed.' In: Aciman: *Letters of Transit*, p. 96).

grain. It is not an easy fit for categories such as 'national literature,' 'migration literature,' or even 'world literature.'

In this book, I focus on phenomena of displacement and heterotopia, that is, on different, yet often overlapping figures of movement and processes of writing-other(wise) and taking language(s) elsewhere. All of them point toward a larger concept that queers the familiar distinction between national literature (the province of the still-dominant national philologies) and world literature (the domain of comparative literary studies), and which envisions a highly complex interWorld structured by countless border markings and erasures. No longer is the existence of the literatures-without-a-fixed-abode an exception – with national literatures as the rule – even if nationally anchored literary histories usually ignore them and have no place for them in their canons. As I will show, the Literatures without a fixed Abode are always a plurality, permeating and thwarting the binary of national vs. world literature without having to yield to and reproduce the exclusive, and exclusionary, logic of either.

More or less broad areas of overlap and exchange exist among the Literatures without a fixed Abode on the one hand and national/world literature on the other. One result, as the example of Cuba will illustrate in Chapter 4, is that the dynamic perspectives of the Literatures without a fixed Abode illumate a rich tradition of national literatures and define it as such. The point, then, is not to deploy a (territorializable) counter-concept to the idea of national literature but, rather, to account for geocultural and biopolitical changes, and for the literary-aesthetic developments that accompany those changes. Neither the perspective of national literature nor that of world literature enables us to think through such transformations and describe them fully. My goal is to articulate practices of Writing-between-Worlds that cannot be territorialized in any permanent (or settled) way, that are, in Aciman's sense, foreign grafts that did not fully 'take.'

There can be no question about the rapid growth of many varied forms of the Literatures without a fixed Abode during the second half of the twentieth century, a development that continues in the twenty-first. Because the concept of Literatures without a fixed Abode that I will flesh out in the following chapters points to *and* transgresses national *and* national-literary borders, it renders dynamic the often static idea of migration literature. It is no longer the (biographical) event of migration alone that defines migration literature; nor can migration serve as a convenient excuse for expatriating texts in this category from supposedly national literatures for being 'strange' or 'not quite' German,

French, English, or Spanish.¹⁶ An in-depth analysis of the Literatures without a fixed Abode also disrupts the homogenizing concept of world literature, especially because such systematic scrutiny renders visible how new borders – oblique, crossable, and translatable – are constantly being drawn and re-drawn. It would thus be a serious error to define the Literatures without a fixed Abode as a 'literature without borders.' An analytical view of the phenomena that run transverse to national literatures is precisely not one that is boundless and boundary-less: not literature without borders.

It would also be misleading to attempt to assign to the Literatures without a fixed Abode a firmly bounded space and to anchor them in that cultural location. Even Homi Bhabha's 'third space,' from *The Location of Culture*, would not do justice to a modus of literary writing that oscillates among different worlds. My goal is not to produce a new literary cartography by defining new literary spaces but to identify transcultural, translingual, and transareal patterns of movement that exist beyond the worn distinction between national and world literatures.¹⁷

Drawing upon a host of diverse examples of Writing-between-Worlds, I concentrate in this book on dynamic space-time configurations that render visible, in transit, overlapping interWorlds characterized by an extraordinarily intricate array of borders. The literary scholarship connected with this analytical method understands itself as a transareal form of inquiry interested in the vectorization of different points of origin. One may reasonably call this kind of scholarship, which is itself in perpetual motion, '*literary*-studies-without-a-fixed-abode.'¹⁸

What exactly are the traditions and developmental lines that sustain the Literatures without a fixed Abode? The filaments of tradition and the formal shapes of the Literatures without a fixed Abode are no less numerous and varied than the knowledges for living and surviving that these literatures store in all their lived and imagined specificities. My individual chapters address a broad panorama of questions. In Chapter 2, 'Figurations: Odysseus and the Angel of

---

16 Just how problematic this discourse of expatriation is becomes clear in a special issue of the German journal *Literaturen* (Berlin) on 'Foreigners. Living in Other Worlds.' Already the title of an interview with Terézia Mora, Imran Ayata, Wladimir Kaminer, and Navid Kermani identifies these four writers as 'not quite German authors': 'I am part of German Literature, as German as Kafka.' How each of these writers responds to such imposed classifications, and each responds very differently, is very much worth reading. See 'Ich bin ein Teil der deutschen Literatur, so deutsch wie Kafka.' Interview with Terézia Mora, Imran Ayata, Wladimir Kaminer and Navid Kermani. In: *Literaturen* 4 (April 2005), p. 26–31.
17 See Homi Bhabha: *The Location of Culture*. New York: Routledge 1994.
18 See Ette: *ÜberLebenswissen*, p. 88–96.

History,' I connect the Literatures without a fixed Abode with Shoa literature. My analysis of the pre- and post-figurations of the *univers concentrationnaire*, the concentrationary universe, uses two key figures of the vectoral imagination in order to trace what remains of Auschwitz in the *literatures sans domicile fixe*. Travel is an especially prominent structural feature of the Literatures without a fixed Abode. Without travel literature and the twentieth- and twenty-first-century offshoots of that tradition, the Literatures without a fixed Abode would lack the key components and connectors that make both readable and re-imaginable the full complexity of the inter- and transcultural exchanges inscribed in patterns of movement. I discuss the fractal dimensions of travel literature in Chapter 3, 'Relations: Caribbean IslandWorlds,' arguing that multiple overlapping travel movements create transecting spaces that belong to a post-Euclidian fractal geometry of culture. Chapter 4, 'Incubations: A National Literature without a fixed Abode?' poses the question of whether Cuba's national literature is (also) a Literature without a fixed Abode. Here, I use the dynamic space of the Caribbean IslandWorlds to reconcile the specificity of national-literary gestations with the idea of the Literatures without a fixed Abode. To focus on national literatures while at the same time engaging in a transareal scholarly practice is not necessarily contradictory; rather, I see both as cross-pollinating perspectives. How else, after all, could one grasp processes of transculturation and nation building both as they relate to each other and in correlation to territorial inclusion and exclusion? Transareal (literary) studies cannot do without the traditions of national literatures and the results of regional (that is, area) studies research any more than transdisciplinary scholarship can neglect disciplinary and interdisciplinary research. Chapter 5, 'Translations: In Others' Words,' takes a playfully serious turn toward literary translation as a form of Writing-between-Worlds whose importance is often either not acknowledged at all or, at best, undervalued. This chapter seeks to work through the significance that intra-, inter-, and translingual processes of translation have for literary studies and for contemporary literary production. Chapter 6, 'Oscillations: Writing-other(wise) between Worlds,' and Chapter 7, 'Confrontations: The Transareal Worlds of the ArabAmericas,' explore individual areas and translingual practices of writing that transgress the linguistic borders of native tongues. How can we grasp literary practices that move back and forth between, say, Turkey and Germany, or Japan and Germany? Writing-other(wise), taking a language (and a whole literature) elsewhere, and writing languages into each other, that is, crosshatching them, are advanced forms of Writing-between-Worlds that, as in the cases of Yoko Tawada and Emine Sevgi Özdamar, avails itself of innovative patterns of movement that reach beyond native tongues toward a transareal horizon, that it, a space beyond individual areas. Chapter 8, 'In(tro)spections: Journey into the Realm of the Dead,' fleshes out these ideas through additional models of transareal kinetic spaces that interrogate the *spiritus vector* about further forms of vectorization.

In an attempt to offer the reader as wide-ranging and diverse an array of perspectives as possible on the Literatures without a fixed Abode, I vary my critical emphasis and method in each chapter. My priority in reading Shoa literature (chapter 2) is thematic. When my field of analysis is the Caribbean, my method is area-specific (chapter 3). It is philological when I address the issue of national literature (chapter 4) and theoretical in the context of translation (chapter 5). When I discuss textual production in a foreign language, my approach is aesthetic (chapter 6) and intertextual in a transareal context (chapter 7). Finally, my analysis focuses on movement when I examine the work of the children of migration (chapter 8).

Globalization and TransArea studies: What does globalization mean?

Because the Literatures without a fixed Abode exist within the networks of globalization, it is necessary to dwell on that term before proceeding. Regardless of the undisputed fact that the term 'globalization' is a recent invention whose ubiquitousness dates back only to the 1990s, the awareness that one can adequately describe processes of globalization only from a long-term viewpoint began to surface much earlier, right after the turn of the nineteenth century, especially in the cultural sciences. We can trace this insight back to Alexander von Humboldt, perhaps the first theoretician of globalization. Globalization, I argue, is not a recent phenomenon but a lengthy process that has sustained itself for several centuries now. It can be divided into four phases of accelerated globalization and, via several diverging international modernities, connects the early modern of European historiography with our present.[19] Distinguishing among different phases of *acceleration*, which is necessary because of the multi-

---

19 For an initial sketch of the four-phase model, see Ottmar Ette: *Weltbewusstsein: Alexander von Humboldt oder das unvollendete Project einer anderen Moderne*. Weilerswist: Velbrueck Wissenschaft 2002, p. 26–27. From a specifically historiographical perspective, see also Jürgen Osterhammel and Niels P. Petersson: *Geschichte der Globalisierung: Dimensionen, Prozesse, Epochen*. Munich: Beck 2003. [For an English version, see Osterhammel and Petersson: *Globalization: A short History*. Princeton, N.J.: Princeton University Press 2005. TN].

tude of complex, and often opposing, developments, should keep us from either dehistoricizing an actual phrase of globalization or from detaching it from a sort of 'pre-history' that presumably began in 1492, 'coincided with European expansion,' and concluded 'at the beginning of the twentieth century.'[20] Each of the four phases of acceleration has its own centers and practices, its own strategies of legitimation and global-historical consequences; without them, the phases I describe in this section cannot be understood sufficiently. Each of these main phases has unique traits that distinguish it from the earlier and later phases of globalization. To comprehend the current fourth phase of accelerated globalization– and thus what Maalouf has dubbed world disorder or deregulation – we cannot do without historical *and* cultural depth, nor without an understanding of the continuities with the preceding phases. In many respects, today's push toward globalization still moves along the same trajectories that brought about an epochal change at the end of the fifteenth century.

The fact that the trajectories I trace here are significantly influenced by Europe need not translate into a Eurocentric explanatory model. Even during the first phase of accelerated globalization, there were systems of power and cultures, such as the Inca domain *Tawantinsuyu* in the Andes and the Aztec empire in North America, in the process of expanding rapidly at the time when the first Spanish caravels appeared on the horizon. These expansions, however, did not occur on a global scale, and they were readily pulled into the vortex that the worldwide spread of Spanish power created. Spain very deliberately used the provincially limited exploits of the Incas and the Aztecs to realize its own goals, that is, its own lust for power, all the more effectively and swiftly.

A multi-perspectival approach brings into relief even more clearly the central role that the so-called Old World played in providing the impulses toward globalization that either were European or else originated in Europe. This role should not be dissolved in an image of history in which everything is perceived as relative. It is important *not* to relativize Europe's involvement in the century-long, and still ongoing, process of the *longue durée* and the ensuing responsibility it has for it, especially when one wants to study and highlight the brutality and enduring consequences of such actions. Once translated into different cultural configurations and economic formats, the *conquista* surely continues.

---

20 Ulfried Reinhardt: *Globalisierung: Literaturen und Kulturen des Globalen*. Berlin: Akademie Verlag 2010, p. 29.

Phases of acceleration

One

European colonial expansion stands at the beginning of the sequence of events that left an indelible imprint on early modernity; it is the first phase of accelerated globalization. The Iberian powers of Spain and Portugal largely dominated this phase initiated by developments across the Mediterranean. The plan to reach the East by sailing to the west had momentous effects on history, notwithstanding the fact that Christopher Columbus's project, as is well known, was based on erroneous and overly optimistic assumptions and calculations. The only reason why the Genovese's ships, long past the point of return, did not shipwreck and vanish in the ocean was that the American continent halted their voyage at the halfway point. Important was, for one, that the overland route, largely controlled by Arabic powers, could be now bypassed and direct trade relations could be established with the spice islands to the east of Europe and the large Asiatic kingdoms. For another, and perhaps even more significantly, the rivaling Iberian kingdoms, with active help from the Pope, were dividing up the world between them, starting, at the latest, by the time of the Treaty of Tordesillas in 1494. From Europe, they practiced an expansionist global politics in the truest sense of the term.

Columbus's caravels quickly paved the waves to a potent and ruthless world politics that was conceived on a planetary scale for the first time. After the conquest of the Nasrid dominion of Granada, the last remaining Arabic strongholds on Iberian territory, a Spain only recently unified under the Catholic kings, now directed the movement of the *Reconquista* not to the south, that is, to North Africa, but instead concentrated all its power on the new conquest, the *conquista* of the immense territories it swiftly tore from several indigenous cultures beyond even the Aztec and Inca spheres of influence. Both Spain and Portugal worked overtime to build up empires that spanned the globe.

Until the middle of the sixteenth century, the Europeans' so-called discovery of the 'New World' led to vast territorial acquisitions hardly limited to the Americas. Put in place with astonishing speed, colonial institutions and apparatuses of power, together with the circulation of knowledge,[21] spawned trade relations that could be called global for the first time in history, and for good rea-

---

21 See Arndt Brendecke: *Imperium und Empirie: Funktionen des Wissens in der spanischen Kolonialherrschaft*. Cologne: Böhlau 2009.

son. The means of transport emblematic of this period was the caravel, the product of the most advanced feats in European shipbuilding.

Compared to the might and momentum of these greatly accelerated colonizing processes, which were of course accompanied by genocides and massacres, all prior expansions on which European and non-European powers had ever embarked would seem pre-historical; nothing had even come close to the scope of a movement that literally spanned the globe.[22] From today's vantage, we assume that there were no reasons why even risky circumnavigations à la Magellan and Elcano could not succeed, even if the collateral damage was massive. By then, Europeans had empirical knowledge of the dimensions of the Earth whose surface could, therefore, be conquered and controlled.

Within a short period of time, Europe amassed immense riches,[23] start-up funds for a new era, a modern age that would, for centuries to come, remain deeply marked by a colonial power structure that moved erratically and was controlled from different centers. The asymmetrical power structures that divided 'the civilized' from 'the savages,' 'Christians' from 'heretics,' and the 'West' from the 'rest,' appeared to be cut in stone. Europe employed these binaries for a long time to deal with the problem of otherness, discursively and otherwise.[24] The age of what one might call a world economy in an actually rounded, global, sense, had begun – and well before the conquest of the Philippines and their attachment to a colonial economy controlled from Spain would close the final link in the Iberian chain around the globe. The asymmetry of European and non-European relations that emerges during the first phase of accelerated globalization became the launching pad for subsequent phases. It left ineradicable marks on the structures of uneven and unequal relations that developed in the areas of the military, economics, politics, technology, and culture. In this phase, the routes on which knowledge about the 'New World' traveled were typically one-way roads, as is clear from Columbus's logbook and, even more so, from the letters and chronicles of sixteenth-century Spanish or European conquerors and historians, not to mention countless missionaries' observations and speculations. The names of such different historical figures as Hernán Cortés, and Ber-

---

22 See Serge Gruzinski: *Les quatre parties du monde: Histoire d'une mondialisation*. Paris: La Martinière 2004.
23 Stephen Greenblatt: *Marvelous Possessions: The Wonder of the New World*. Chicago: University of Chicago Press 1991.
24 See Urs Bitterli: *Die 'Wilden' und die 'Zivilisierten': Grundzüge einer Geistes- und Kulturgeschichte der europäisch-überseeischen Begegnung*. Munich: Beck 2004; see also Tzvetan Todorov: *The Conquest of America. The Question of the Other*. Translated by Richard Howard. New York: Harper Perennial 1992.

nal Díaz del Castillo, Francisco López de Gómara and Gonzalo Fernández de Oviedo, Garcilaso de la Vega el Inca and José de Acosta, Bartolomé de las Casas and Bernadino de Sahagún are proxies that stand for the beginnings of a transfer process through which knowledge about the New World was assembled in the Old World and used for the development of global control and exchange.[25] Processes of globalization require not only new rules and regulations, but also ways of disseminating knowledge.

Archipelagic and trans-archipelagic relations are of enormous significance to the first phase of accelerated globalization.[26] In the Old World, the Canary and Cape Verdean Islands, the Azores, and Madeira were of crucial importance to the history of exploration and conquest, while the islands of the Caribbean became virtual beachheads for the takeover of the entire continent. 'These islands were secure(d) bases from which power-islands were created on the continent, and the Iberian invaders' rule over large territories was organized and implemented from the insular structures of cities: an island tactic that was fundamentally different from the continental territorial approach of an advancing frontier, as is would be used so successfully in the north of the continent.'[27]

What also characterized the first phase of accelerated globalization was the targeted implementation of the politics of language within an empire-in-the-making, especially in the Spanish sphere of influence. A total of three European languages were globalized in this way and positioned as world languages: Spanish, Portuguese, and Latin. Scholars have rarely explored the presence of Latin and its role in conquest, colonial administration, and the transatlantic circulation of knowledge.

---

[25] See the research by Birgit Scharlau: 'Beschreiben und beherrschen: Die Informationspolitik der spanischen Krone im 15. und 16. Jahrhundert.' In: Karl-Heinz Kohl et al. (eds.): *Mythen der Neuen Welt: Zur Entdeckungs-geschichte Lateinamerikas*, p. 92–100. Berlin: Frölich & Kaufmann 1982; Birgit Scharlau (ed.): *Bild, Wort, Schrift: Beiträge zur Lateinamerika-Sektion des Freiburger Romanistentages*. Tübingen: Narr 1989; Birgit Scharlau: 'Nuevas tendencias en los estudios de crónicas y documentos del periodo colonial latinoamericano.' In: *Revista de crítica latinoamericana* (Lima) 31–32 (1999), p. 365–375; Birgit Scharlau (ed.): *Übersetzen in Lateinamerika*. Tübingen: Narr 2002.

[26] For the concept of the trans-archipelagic, see Ottmar Ette: 'Le monde transarchipélien de la Caraibe colonial'. In: Ottmar Ette and Gesine Müller (eds): *Caleidoscopios coloniales: Transferencias culturales en el Caribe del siglo XIX / Kaléidoscopes coloniaux*. Madrid/Frankfurt am Main: Vervuert 2010 (Iberoamericana), p. 23-64.

[27] See Walther L. Bernecker: 'Staatliche Grenzen – kontinentale Dynamik: Zur Relativität von Grenzen in Lateinamerika.' In: Marianne Braig et al. (eds.): *Grenzen der Macht – Macht der Grenzen: Lateinamerika im globalen Kontext*. Frankfurt am Main: Vervuert 2005, p. 7-37.

Anxieties about globalization always accompany processes of globalization, and such fears typically manifest themselves at times of crises. The Europeans carried a host of 'new' diseases into the 'New World,' where they significantly accelerated the conquest by weakening the indigenous populations' resistance. At times, the Spanish conquistadors deliberately used these diseases by distributing infected objects. The conquerors, in turn, also contracted diseases previously unknown to them; these infections spread rapidly through the ranks of the Iberian soldiers deployed not only on the American continent but also in various parts of Europe, Africa, and Asia.

Syphilis became the leit-epidemic of the first phase of globalization. It spread rapidly in Spain and Italy and also appeared in various parts of North Africa, as we know from the reports of Giovan Leone l'Africano (aka Leo Africanus). An increasing frequency of plagues and epidemics always attends the phases of acceleration that usually drive the process of *mondialization*. In his cultural history of plagues, Stefan Winkle has pointed out the following from the perspective of the history of medicine:

When, on March 15, 1493, Columbus's returning fleet (after the loss of a ship) arrived at its port of origin in Palos at the southern coast of Spain, it carried, in addition to the products of the new continent, a heretofore unknown sexual plague as a special 'gift': syphilis. From Palos, the sailors traveled first on the Guadalquivir to the nearby Seville, where they stayed for four weeks. Already in Seville, the crew, sexually starved after the long sea voyage, must have frequented bordellos where they infected the whores who worked there with this entirely unknown disease. The process repeated itself in Barcelona, whence Columbus sailed with his two vessels without touching the rest of Spain.[28]

We can take the 'touching' quite literally. And the consequences manifested very quickly, as an eye witness, the physician Ruy Díaz de Isla who then worked in Barcelona, added to his 1539 treatise: 'It pleased divine justice to send us a heretofore unknown illness, which first appeared in the city of Barcelona in 1493. This city was infected first, then the whole of Europe, and finally the entire populated world.'[29] Within a few years, relatives of Spanish military and admin-

---

28 Stefan Winkle: *Geisseln der Menschheit: Kulturgeschichte der Seuchen*. Düsseldorf: Artemis & Winkler 1997, p. 541f.
29 Winkle: *Geisseln der Menschheit*, p. 542; on the spread of the disease, see p. 541–575. A flier from 1496 is reproduced on p. 546.

istrative personnel had indeed made the calamitous connection between America and Europe, Asia and Africa.³⁰

The syphilis plague remains an object of fascination to this day, in part because it is an epidemic whose ravages are very well documented for the first time in history. The real reason why this disease continues to captivate people's imaginations, however, is more likely that syphilis, as Albrecht Dürer's 1496 painting demonstrates (Figure 1), has become inseparable from a (clearly western) imaginary of the global.

Fig. 1: Albrecht Dürer, *Der Syphilitiker (Syphilitic Man)* (1496), © Albertina, Wien, Graphische Sammlung.

---

30 See also Alfred W. Crosby: *The Columbian Exchange: Biological and cultural Consequences of 1492*. Westport Conn.: Greenwood Pub. 1972, p. 122–164.

Together with the Latin text that frames this early woodcut, the year 1484, which Dürer, in this earliest representation of a person infected with syphilis, visibly inscribed in the orb that floats above the mercenary's head,[31] shows how quickly things happened globally and how rapidly this plague – which Dürer himself might have contracted several years later[32] – spread across the Old World. As we can see from this work of art in the tradition of the so-called plague sheets, the contemporaneous reactions to syphilis significantly influenced all later responses to global epidemics, up to the present day. The image of a pain-stricken, pustule-covered man on his journey across the world encapsultes what the introduction of plagues and epidemics, which always came 'from the outside,' from afar, meant for the tranquil landscapes with their quaint church steeples and houses: namely, that the global destroys the seclusion and presumed peacefulness of the local. Globalization, then, always carries fear at its core.

Two

A second phase of accelerated globalization extends from the middle of the eighteenth century to the onset of the nineteenth and is perhaps best represented by the travels of Louis-Antoine, Count of Bougainville, James Cook, and Jean-François de Galaup, Count of Lapérouse. The names of great French and British seafarers connect the early naval exploration with the later forms of the research voyage that James Cook exemplifies. At the end of this period, most of the 'white spaces' on the map of our planet had disappeared. The concurrent transformation of utopias into uchronias, in which the projection of another place turns into projections of another time, provides an important first hint in various literatures that, during the last third of the eighteenth century, new temporalizing approaches were beginning to supplant the spatialized genre represented by Thomas More's *Utopia* (1516).

The Iberian powers, whose colonial possessions are in the midst of numerous reforms, no longer dominate the second phase, which unfolds under the aegis of the rising colonial powers of France and England. Like their forebears, these two leading European powers originated in the western parts of Europe and confronted each other as rivals outside of Europe in various regions of the

---

31 Colin Eisler: 'Who is Dürer's "Syphilitic Man"'? In: *Perspectives in Biology and Medicine* (London) LII.1 (Winter 2009), p. 48–60.
32 Eisler: 'Who is Dürer's "Syphilitic Man," p. 57–59.

world on land and at sea. In England and France alike, the emblematic conveyance for the second phase of accelerated globalization is the frigate.

The development of both British and French systems of trade relies in part on already existing regional and supra-regional trade relations with non-European powers and peoples, which are gradually 'integrated' into a now more complex system of commerce increasingly controlled from London and Paris. Lisbon, Madrid, and their transatlantic ports, along with Amsterdam, lose a significant part of their ambit. (Amsterdam had ascended to power during an interim phase that shared much with the first phase but, at the same time, also anticipated aspects of the second phase in the economic sector.) As in the first phase of accelerated globalization, the European capitals from which worldwide expansionism is directed during the second phase are in close geographical proximity to one another.

The reports of the voyages of exploration and research during the second half of the eighteenth century, with their attention to processing and ordering information in keeping with the special interests of European régimes and sciences, document impressively the swelling of the streams of knowledge that multiplied not only Eurocentric ways of knowing, but also caused profound epistemological changes in the universalism of the European sciences. Vast amounts of new information were not only amassed but also had to be newly organized, which forced the asymmetrical system of knowledge circulation, constructed for exclusively European needs, to create the structures of temporalization analyzed by Michel Foucault and Wolf Lepenies.[33] These structures affected diverse disciplines-in-the making and other areas of knowledge production. The transfer of knowledge thus changed the way in which all knowledge was ordered and organized. Temporalization brought about both the end of nature and the end of a system of thinking in which, as Reinhart Koselleck has shown, *Historia* could still be the *magistra vitae*.[34]

Against the background of a developing understanding of a history open to the future, it strikes me as necessary, and indeed inevitable, to consider not only the *European* dual revolution of the eighteenth century – the industrial revolution initiated in England and the political revolution in France in 1789 – but also to include a dual revolution *outside of Europe* which was highly significant

---

[33] See Michel Foucault: *The Order of Things: An Archaeology of the Human Sciences*. New York: Vintage Books 1971, and Wolf Lepenies: *The End of Natural History*. New York: The Confucian Press 1980.
[34] See Reinhart Koselleck: *Futures Past: On the Semantics of historical Time*. New York: Columbia University Press 2004, p. 26–42.

to the second phase of accelerated globalization: the successful bid for independence that the United States of America won in 1776 from the British colonial powers and the Haitian revolution against France, which culminated with independence in 1804 and was directed, above all, against the slave trade of the Black Atlantic. The fact that the slave revolution of Saint-Domingue, the first to end in the founding of a free state, is often omitted, be it consciously or not, from the 'general' theory of revolution[35] has contributed to the 'Europeanization' of theories of revolution on the one hand and, on the other, to the studious neglect of the vital relations that the Haitian revolution has to the second phase of accelerated globalization.[36]

The great sea voyages of the second half of the eighteenth century, on frigates whose names became imprinted in Europe's collective memory, would surely have been impossible without enormous technological strides in the areas of navigation, transportation, and communication. These voyages did not primarily target the interior of continents but focused on coastlines, straights, possible passages, and archipelagic structures because of their usefulness as fast, secure transatlantic and transpacific transport routes. Especially when it came to the Pacific Ocean, the largest body of water on the planet, archipelagic and trans-archipelagic structures played a major role, and continue to do so. The strategic value of IslandWorlds, important for trade and military control, was crucial in the Atlantic and the Pacific alike, not to mention for sea routes in the Indian Ocean. The importance of the islands of Saint-Domingue, Tahiti, and Mauritius to the French colonial system can hardly be overstated.

The acceleration and intensification of worldwide connections changed the conditions of life not only in the francophone and Anglophone spheres of in-

---

35 See Paul Gilroy: *The Black Atlantic: Modernity and Double Consciousness*. London: Verso 1993.

36 See Gesine Müller: *Die koloniale Karibik: Transferprozesse in hispanophonen und frankophonen Literaturen*. Berlin: De Gruyter 2012, p. 128f. With respect to the predominant Western theory of revolution, the 'case of Haiti' is more than problematic. In her *On Revolution* (New York: Viking 1963), Hannah Arendt preferred not even to mention Haiti. For a long time, colonialism and slavery were only included in theories of modernity – and also theories of revolution – as either marginal phenomena or as nuisance factors. See Sibylle Fischer: *Modernity disavowed: Haiti and the cultures of slavery in the age of revolution*. Durham, NC: Duke University Press 2004, p. 8f. Of late, however, scholarly interest in the Haitian Revolution has been on the rise: see Chris Bongie: *Friends and enemies: The scribal politics of post/colonial literature*. Liverpool: Liverpool University Press 2008; see also Susan Buck-Morss: 'Hegel and Haiti'. In: *Critical Inquiry* (Chicago) 26 (Summer 2000), p. 821–865, and Susan Buck-Morss: *Hegel, Haiti and Universal history*. Pittsburgh, Pa.: University of Pittsburgh Press 2009.

fluence. In fact, most of the still familiar composite nouns that include 'world' – such as world trade, world traffic, world peace, world consciousness, world economy, and world literature, among many others[37] – belong to the second phase of accelerated globalization. These composites and neologisms testify to a changed mindset that mastered a world almost encyclopedically, and of course from Europe. An excellent example is the world we find in colonial encyclopedia entitled *Philosophical and political history of the settlements and trade of the Europeans in the East and West Indies* that Guillaume-Thomas Raynal published anonymously in 1770.[38] These volumes, motivated in the main by Raynal and Denis Didérot, and the work of other, contemporaneous European precursors of a global history, such as ther writings of Cornelius de Pauw, William Robertson, Juan Bautista Muñoz, and Alexander von Humboldt, abound with references to diseases and epidemics, especially the dreaded yellow fever. These mentions substantiate a link between globalization and catastrophic plagues in the second phase. Yellow fever, which had swept mainly across the Caribbean region during the first phase of accelerated globalization,[39] experienced a much faster resurgence in the second. Precautions were soon introduced to British war ships, of which a British naval officer reports in 1761: 'The firing holes were opened daily. If the weather is dry, the lower deck is cleaned with a broom and hosed down; if the weather is wet, it is scoured dry so that the beams from which the beds hang do not grow mold. Dry wood was also burned there, with resin tossed in. The smoke not only killed the insects, but also dispelled foul odors.'[40] The worldwide dread of yellow fever was unfathomable. It stirred inordinate interest even in provincial Berlin, a situation on which no lesser a figure than Heinrich von Kleist – who had good reasons for discussing the especially

---

[37] For more about these 'world terms,' see Ottmar Ette: 'Unterwegs zu einer Weltwissenschaft? Alexander von Humboldts Weltbegriffe und die transarealen Studien.' In: *HiN – Alexander von Humboldt im Netz. Internationale Zeitschrift für Humboldt-Studien* (Potsdam/Berlin) VII.13 (2006), p. 34–54. <www.hin-online.de>

[38] Guillaume-Thomas Raynal: *A philosophical and political history of the settlements and trade of the Europeans in the East and West Indies*. London: Routledge 2007. For studies of this global dimension, see Hans-Jürgen Lüsebrink / Manfred Tietz (eds.): *Lectures de Raynal: L'histoire de deux Indes en Europe et en Amérique au XVIIIe siècle: actes du Colloque de Wolfenbüttel*. Oxford: Voltaire Foundation 1991. See also Gilles Bancarel (ed.): *Raynal et ses réseaux*. Paris: Champion 2011.

[39] See Winkle: *Geisseln der Menschheit*, p. 972–986.

[40] Winkle: *Geisseln der Menschheit*, p. 978.

frightening yellow fever separately[41] – sought to capitalize in 1810 to sell his newspaper *Berliner Abendblätter*. On December 5, 1810, we read there:

> Swiss reports confirm that yellow fever 'is on a rampage' in Cuba. From Copenhagen, we hear about strictest measures adopted by the King's quarantine leaders 'because of the infectious diseases in various regions of the world.' 'The ensuing decree shows that the contagion that has broken out in Otranto and Brindisi features pestilent pustules, whereas the outbreak in the Spanish cities of Malaga and Cartagena seems to be yellow fever.[42]

The actions that followed in the immediate wake of such urgent bulletins, not only aboard warships but also in the colonies and motherlands, demonstrate a high degree of networking, and the world consciousness it brought with in, during the second phase of accelerated globalization. It is no accident that, during this second phase, we can track yellow fever outbreaks all the way back to the first reported case in Africa in 1768.[43]

Not always, however, did government institutions react quickly enough. For instance, the necessary steps Alexander von Humboldt recommended in his reports were not resolutely implemented even for the rest of the nineteenth century. During his travels, Humboldt, who left his mark on the concept of world consciousness, became himself a victim of a yellow fever epidemic that had reportedly spread from the Caribbean to the Mediterranean since the end of the eighteenth century. This bout with illness unavoidably changed the course of his American travels. His own ailment brought home to him with great clarity the vulnerability of the transoceanic connections that he had first experienced during his crossing from Spain to the Caribbean on the frigate *Pizarro*. During his crossing, he had also witnessed repeatedly just how dependent the formerly proud Spanish galleons were on the omnipresent British warships. Thanks to the superiority of their fleet, the British had long won the race of the European powers for control of the world's oceans.

---

41 See Heinrich von Kleist: 'Kurze Geschichte des gelben Fiebers in Europa.' In: *Berliner Abendblätter* 19/20 (January 23 and 24, 1811), p. 73–75 and 77–79.
42 Quoted in Winkle: *Geisseln der Menschheit*, p. 985. He includes an extensive compilation of news reports from 1810 which Kleist had collected.
43 See Jari Vainio and Felicity Cutts: *Yellow Fever: Division of Emerging and Other Communicable Diseases, Surveillance and Control*. Geneva: World Health Organization 1998, p. 16–18.

Three

The *third* phase of accelerated globalization, that is, the last third of the nineteenth century and the opening decade of the twentieth, witnessed the ascent of a non-European power, albeit one under the cultural, political, and economic sway of Western Europe: the United States of America, a country that had thrown off the fetters of colonial dependency during the previous phase. What characterizes the third phase were worldwide neocolonial conflicts over distribution along with processes of dependent and unequal modernization; both reshaped the many different regions of the planet to differing degrees. This period saw the development of the many divergent concepts and practices of modernization that now make it impossible to speak of modernity in the singular.

Neither the uncompleted project of modernity[44] nor the unfinished project of an other modernity[45] alone characterize the third phase of accelerate globalization. A multitude of different modernities vied for attention on the political, economic, and, above all, the cultural stage, such as Hispanic-American *modernismo* in Latin America and, later on, the Brazilian *modernismo* of the avant-gardes. The leading socioeconomic factor in the emergence of a multiplying modernity[46] and divergent modernities was the noticeably accelerated globalization impulse that occurred between 1870 and 1914. With regard to the worldwide webs of trade, this third phase may well be described as a multilaterally modeled 'closed system.'[47]

Modernists such as the Cuban José Martí, probably the first to contemplate the consequences of the third phase, and the Uruguayan José Enrique Rodó warned vociferously against USAmerican hegemony, which developed quickly on the continent in concert with growing sea power. Add to this that the USA's economic power in the Caribbean and Latin America since the end of the nineteenth century also increasingly spawned military interventions. Not only had the United States of America liberated itself from the colonial stranglehold of Great Britain during the second phase; now, owing to its technologically far superior war fleet, the USA also succeeded in asserting its interests against those of the leading powers of the first phase. In 1898, US battle cruisers mercilessly

---

44 See Jürgen Habermas: 'Die Moderne: Ein unvollendetes Projekt' (1980). In: Jürgen Habermas: *Kleinere politische Schriften (I–IV)*. Frankfurt am Main: Suhrkamp 1981, p. 444–446.
45 See Ette: *Weltbewusstsein*.
46 See Shmuel N. Eisenstadt: *Multiple Modernities*. New Brunswick: NJ: Transaction Publishers 2002.
47 Osterhammel/Petersson: *Globalization*, p. 66.

pounced on the Spanish fleet and its allies at Santiago de Cuba and Manila, having laid in wait for the right moment to intervene in Cuba's war of independence. At the same time, the new transoceanic cables, whose installation had commenced in 1857, transformed the conflict between Spain and the USA in the Caribbean and the Philippines, making it the first global media war in history. The news reporting about the war in the media of the countries involved in the war directly affected strategic decisions and respective local tactics.

New, faster communication; vastly improved naval and military technologies; and new interests that were developing in advance of World War I led to a situation in which the building up and expansion of trans-archipelagic naval bases and transportation networks became economic and military priorities. Even Germany, at the time still smarting from the unsuccessful attempts of Brandenburg at the close of the seventeenth century, jumped into the colonial power plays. The naval bases this new American hegemonic power set up in its sphere of influence created an island-based structure suitable for the military reinforcement of political and economic interests across the continent and also in the Pacific area. By then, the steamship, used for civil and military purposes, had become the emblematic global means of transport.

In this third phase of accelerated globalization, no additional idiom joined the European languages that had previously been globalized. All attempts to introduce German, for example, to the militarily upgraded empire's still recent overseas dependencies in Africa and Oceania were doomed to failure because these colonial spaces soon broke up again. Noticeable at the time, however, is a global shift of power in favor of English and Anglo-Saxon culture. There were of course vehement protests against this shift, from Pan-Slavists, Pan-Germanists, and, above all, Pan-Latinists. Though still unquestioned up to this point, the hegemony of French, Spanish, and Portuguese, the languages derived from Latin, had, after all, already been crumbled. But Pan-Latinism, which, during the mid-nineteenth century, tried to counter the encroachment of the Anglo-Saxon world with the 'invention' of *Latin* America,[48] was thrown into a worldwide crisis when France lost the 1870-71 war against Prussia and Spain had to sur-

---

48 See, among others, John Leddy Phelan: 'Pan-Latinism, French Intervention in Mexico (1861-1867) and the Genesis of the Idea of Latin America.' In: Juan Antonio Ortega y Medina (ed.): *Conciencia y autenticidad históricas. Escritos en homenaje a Edmundo O'Gorman*. Mexico: UNAM 1968; Joseph Jurt: 'Entstehung und Entwicklung der LATEINamerika Idee.' In: *Lendemains* (Marburg) 27 (1982), p. 17–26; and Miguel Rojas Mix: 'Bilbao y el hallazgo de América latina: Unión continental, socialista y libertaria.' In: *Caravelle* (Toulouse) 46 (1986), p. 35–47.

render to the USA in 1898. This crisis casts its shadow over the entire third phase.

Plagues and epidemics also flourished during this phase of accelerated globalization, most notably the wave-like spread of smallpox. Born on the island of Lefkas to a Greek mother and a British military doctor, Lafcadio Hearn revealed in his remarkable descriptions just how devastating smallpox could be in the Caribbean, worse by far than the effect the disease had in Europe and the USA.[49] Raised and educated in Ireland and England, Hearn spent long years in the USA and the Caribbean, and he lived in Japan until his death; as a result, he knew much about trans-archipelagic relations.[50] Ignored for a long time, Hearn's demanding literary scenes from the 1880s show how very fragile the dense net of naval traffic really became when ports had to be closed for periods of time due to pandemics. Although smallpox, or small pocks,[51] had already been known and feared during the first globalization phase, the 'epidemiological lightening' of the US Civil War (1861-65)[52] once again raised the destructive power of this plague to the heights of global public awareness.

Literary responses to globalization came especially from the Spanish-speaking areas, from the pens of such authors as José Rizal, who grew up in the Philippines and later lived in Europe, the USA, Hong Kong, and Japan, and his widely traveled Nicaraguan colleague Rubén Darío. They and others responded to the palpable challenges of globalization with original literary works and with concepts of identity that, combining different cultures, pointed to their very own ways into modernity. José Martí's work as a correspondent and founder of journals exemplify the desire to reverse the direction of the knowledge transfer between the New and the Old World and reshape ingrained ways of knowing on a global scale so as to benefit a Latin America increasingly portrayed as 'crisis-torn' and 'sickly.' From the processes of acceleration they both lived and described, these authors deduced that the meridian of political power, and also of artistic energy and potency, would soon shift from Europe to the America. It was necessary, then, to prepare the path (of new, different perspectives and knowl-

---

49 See Lafcadio Hearn and Christopher E. G. Benfey: *American Writings*. New York: Library of America 2009, p. 340.
50 See Lafcadio Hearn: *Two Years in the French West Indies*. Oxford: Signal 2001; Lafcadio Hearn: *In ghostly Japan* (1899). London: Kegan Paul 1907; and Lafcadio Hearn: *A Japanese Miscellany*. Boston: Little, Brown, and Co. 1901.
51 See Winkle: *Geisseln der Menschheit*, p. 853.
52 Winkle: *Geisseln der Menschheit*, p. 892. Winkle also includes statistic data about vaccinations.

edges) for a new world order, one less marred by asymmetrical dependency relations.

Four

The current and as yet incomplete *fourth* phase of accelerated globalization spans the last two decades of the twentieth century and the first two decades of the twenty-first. It is characterized by the increasing globalization of the financial markets, the construction of new, planetary communication systems in real time, and the relinquishment of binary, ideologically motivated bloc systems. As the increasingly conflictual contrast between 'orient' and 'occident,' which often appear in religious disguise, indicates, this does not mean that we are on the verge of a unified global society or that national borders have suddenly become obsolete. Indeed, the number of countries that are still becoming independent grows steadily.

It remains to be seen whether and to what extent these developments, especially in the context of a new (really, an old) contrast between 'East' and 'West,' will provoke increasing military action, and whether this will turn Huntington's infamous theory of the 'clash of the cultures' into a self-fulfilling prophesy.[53] Either way, the can be no question that the rapid advancement of electronic data exchange systems, worldwide digital networks, and mass-media communication in virtually real time is changing perceptions of global political and economic, and, above all, cultural and everydaylife cultural phenomena. The cant about the global village of course only gets traction at certain levels, all of them politically intended. And like the earlier emblems of the caravel, the frigate, and the steamship, the airplane, which first entered the picture during the third globalization phase and became the symbolic vehicle for the fourth phase, is by no means available to all inhabitants of our planet.

Changes in people's mindset, resulting from a multiplication of the rapid traffic in people, goods, and ideas and sped up through communications technology, occur on a global scale in the context of a virtual public and find their expression in the new terminology of globalization. In this is a discursive socio-globalization,[54] we can still detect distinct notes of the structural asymmetries of the preceding phases of globalization. We can only understand the phenomena

---

53 See Samuel P. Huntington: *The Clash of Civilizations*. New York: Simon & Schuster 1996.
54 See also Mathias Albert: *Zur Politik der Weltgesellschaft: Identität und Recht im Kontext internationaler Vergesellschaftung*. Weilerswist: Velbrück Wissenschaft 2002.

of the current phase, then, if we are able to frame the paths and histories of previous globalization phases such that the globalizations behind the globalization come into structural relief. The corresponding literary phenomenon is the rise of the Literatures without a fixed Abode.

As the advent of the internet and GPS easily demonstrate, the new communication and storage technologies are close allies of military needs and strategies. The island approach to the military domination of entire continents have been refined through the use of aircraft carriers and rockets supported by submarines in the creation of mobile 'islands' from which vast territories can be controlled, threatened, or bombed back into the distant past. With the aircraft carrier, which welds the steamship of the third phase to the airplane of the fourth, the island strategies of our present state of technological development reach its perhaps most palpable illustration.

Fears about plagues and epidemics that are comparable to the globalization anxieties of earlier phases also emerged, notably in the form of HIV/AIDS and Ebola. On June 5, 1981, the *Morbidity and Mortality Weekly Report* published by the US Center for Infectious Diseases included an initial report about five homosexual men in Los Angeles who had fallen ill; reports from other parts of the country followed in short order.[55] By 1985, at the latest, the full extent of the catastrophe was deemed inestimable: 'Every time that we learn something new about this virus or the course of the disease,' one US doctor put it in a public appeal, 'our worst fears gain yet another dimension.'[56] The 2010 *Global Report* soberly stated that, by the end of 2009, about 33.3 million persons worldwide are infected with HIV, up by 27% compared to the number in 1999 (26.2 million).[57] Visualizing this development, the WHO world map (see Figure 2) shows that AIDS, like syphilis, yellow fever, and smallpox before it, creates global connections no less intense than the pleasant, 'positive' aspects of globalization people experience. Important is this: the transcontinental means of transport that, thanks to airplanes, have become dramatically faster and more precise in their trajectories, can spread viruses worldwide within a few hours, and the affected areas are no longer located on the margins (in ports or border towns) but right at the interior centers of countries and continents.

---

55 Winkle: *Geisseln der Menschheit*, p. 605; for the beginnings of AIDS in the 1980s, see p. 605–617.
56 Winkle: *Geisseln der Menschheit*, p. 612.
57 See UNAIDS: *Global Report. UNAIDS Report on the Global AIDS Epidemic: 2010*. Geneva: Joint United Nations Programme on HIV/AIDS (UNAIDS) 2010, chapter 2. The world map for the year 2009 is on p. 23.

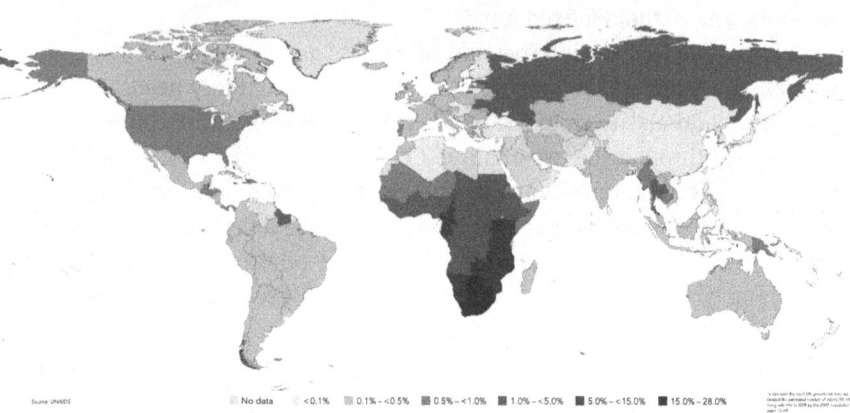

Fig. 2: *UNAIDS Report on the Global AIDS Epidemic* 2010, Source: www.unaids.org

As recent developments in many Arabic countries show, decentralized, rhizomatically structured communication networks can make destabilize autocratic governments. But, as the case of China exemplifies, efficient oppression machines can easily enough obstruct, cripple, and defuse them.

The protagonists of the fourth phase of accelerated globalization are no doubt the USA and, to some extent, the island nation of Japan, with Europe, once again, as an active participant. One may well wonder, with Jürgen Habermas, how Europe has managed to reaffirm its position among the world's powers, since the great empires in world history typically had but a single chance. This rule applies to 'the empires of the Old World as much as it does to the modern nations of Portugal, Spain, England, France, and Russia.'[58] It is, however, Europe *as a whole* that has received this second chance, with the caveat that it use this opportunity 'not in the style of its old power politics' but only for 'the purposes of non-imperial communication' and 'to learn from others.'[59] Amin Maalouf would surely agree with Habermas's analysis, since Maalouf sees the history of the European Union, regardless of all necessary points of criticism, as

---

[58] Jürgen Habermas: 'Staatsbürgerschaft und nationale Identität' (1990). In: Jürgen Habermas: *Faktizität und Geltung: Beiträge zur Diskurstheorie des Rechts und des demokratischen Rechtsstaats*. Frankfurt am Main: Suhrkamp 1992, p. 651.
[59] Habermas: 'Staatsbürgerschaft,' p. 651.

hope for a concrete and realistic possibility that centuries-old enmities and military conflicts might be resolved or set aside permanently. Whether in the current globalization phase, the European Union has indeed managed to neutralize its imperial power aspirations when it comes to world politics is a question that can and will be answered variously. At the same time, the European Union is at least an attempt at defining new, stable frameworks for the creation of a knowledge-for-and-about-living-together. In an effort not to confine such knowledge to EU territory, Amin Maalouf has formulated important guidelines for a more far-sighted politics of conviviality from a literary space and from a position that combines both interior and exterior perspectives.

After this inevitably compacted survey of the four phases of accelerated globalization, it should seem obvious that one needs to know the first phase to understand those shifts in the history of economics, politics, culture, and mindsets which the different historiographical traditions in Europe tend to identify as 'modern times' (*Neuzeit* or *les temps modernes*). The second phase of accelerated globalization may, in turn, be taken a direct precondition for the emergence of a (Western) modernity whose temporalizing structures and altered epistemological bases manifest themselves during the last quarter of the eighteenth century, chiefly after the USAmerican, French, and Haitian revolutions. Phases of accelerated globalization are stages of historical and cultural compression in which long-term currents and trends enter into direct, mutual relation. In such a scenario, oft-neglected questions about multi-, inter-, and transcultural relations assume positions of crucial importance. One simply cannot comprehend the move of Western modernity towards a shared space open to the future, the very idea on which the the internet age was technologically and culturally founded in the last two decades of the twentieth century, without taking into account the practices that characterize the third phase of accelerated globalization. As different modernities emerge, globalization 'from above' (through financial markets and capital investments) is joined by globalization 'from below' (mass migrations and the radical globalization critiques that accompany them) and a 'transverse' globalization (a globally networked information and knowledge society) whose centers continue to be located in the USA and (partly) in Europe, even if it might seem otherwise at times. In the fourth phase, China, India, and possibly Brazil also become global players with future inputs into political, social, economic, and cultural matters. China in particular may currently be in a situation comparable to that of the USA during the third phase. Given the growing significance of Asian markets and powers, it is unlikely that the next phase of globalization, which might be expected for later on in the twenty-first century, would necessary rely largely on English.

While the characteristics of our current phase of accelerated globalization are no doubt very specific, they are no more so than those of the previous phases; nor are they independent of them. Only when we do not insist that today's globalization is something unique and completely new, a creation ex nihilo, can we derive any lessons from the earlier incarnations of this same process. Only then do we have the opportunity to define new directions and new forms of knowing for the routes and vectors that have been observable ever since Europe's initial expansion in the fifteenth century. Such new directions and forms of knowledge can then take the place of world-deregulation; through them, we might articulate models and standards inexorable for a peaceful living together in difference. Literature is of inestimable value in the search for such new paths and models. Rather than being imited to specific regions and nations, literary knowledge is always on the move; it crosses and transgresses cultural areas as a matter of course.

Towards a poetics of movement

In 2003, Karl Schlögel emphasized that historiography needed to foreground the dimension of space more strongly to counterbalance the hegemonic power of time and chronology. There were already indications, so Schlögel, 'that the spatiality and spatialization of human history were becoming the point of reorganization, of a new configuration, of the old disciplines – from geography to semiotics, from history of art, from literature, to politics.'[60] Schögel's optimistic plea for a 'spatial turn, finally,' assumes that the radical changes of space and time in the twentieth century, through the fall of the Berlin Wall and advancing globalization, had contributed to a 'momentum' 'that moved everything to the new track of a *spatial turn.*'[61] Is it important today, then, to encourage a turn to spatiality, toward spatial understanding? One can understand the call for such a turn as a reasonable reaction to all those public fanfares that announced spatial atrophy, the increasing disappearance of space as result of global networks, and worldwide data transfers that would presumably erase space as a perceived barrier to communication. Already in the second half of the 1980s, however, new spatial concepts that had evolved in the context of postmodernism were used to counter such simplifications (and mystifications), and we can easily

---

60 Karl Schlögel: *Im Raum lesen wir die Zeit: Über Zivilisationsgeschichte und Geopolitik.* Munich: Carl Hanser Verlag 2003, p. 12.
61 Schlögel: *Im Raum lesen wir die Zeit*, p. 60, 62.

enough return to them today.⁶² Even if the ghost of the simplified notion of vanishing space continues to haunt the public sphere, talk about a 'spatial turn' is hardly anything new.

The *temporal*, historio-chronological foundations of our thinking and our ability to process reality, which once dominated European modernity, have no doubt weakened during postmodernity. At the same time, spatial concepts and modes of thinking, along with perceptual patterns and experiential modes, have increased in importance. This shift did not occur smoothly, nor without any dissenting voices. At the center of many of the academic debates in the 1980s and 1990s, however, were geocultural and geopolitical questions in no way limited to cyberspace. These debates produced spatializations and mappings as much under the heading of postcolonialism as they did under the auspices of the clash-of-cultures paradigm. Postmodernity clearly is impossible without a re-mapping of frontlines and borders previously believed to be stable.

We have, it seems to me, more than enough spatial concepts. What we are urgently lacking is a sufficiently precise terminology for movement, dynamics, and mobility. One could go so far as to speak of a colonization of the concepts of movement by a flood of spatial models that arrest dynamic processes through obsessive spatialization and reduce them by painstakingly ignoring the dimension of time. The paucity of concepts that relate to movement corresponds to the reduction of spatio-temporal choreographies to spatial still lives and mental maps that filter out dynamic elements, often with disastrous consequences.⁶³ In this way, the sifting out of motion and its semantic reduction to the spatial produces fundamental distortions that we cannot just overlook. Doing so would be akin to dismissing as trivial the loss of one dimension in the transfer of a three-

---

62 See, for example, Edward W. Soja: *Postmodern Geographies: The Reassertion of Space in Critical Social Theory*. London: Verso 1989.
63 These examples, to which more might easily be added, show that the emphasis on space by no means leads to greater analytical complexity but can quickly result in an eclipsing of fundamental historical processes. Already Schlögel's initial concepts for the spaces in question – and this is astonishing for a historian – are somehow temporally hollow and, in an anachronistic way, unable to unfold either temporally or spatiotemporally. For instance, we hear, in the context of turn of the nineteenth-century 'Latin America' and a 'voyage across seven countries in South America, Cuba, and North America,' about the specific vice-royalties and *audiencias* of the Spanish colonial empire in the Americas, when the politico-cultural concept of Latin America had not yet become available. Instead of pre-Columbian civilizations, we repeatedly encounter 'pre-Columbian civilizations,' and geographical terms such as South, Central, and North America are used in highly idiosyncratic ways. Even the border between the USA and Mexico appears as 'an accepted border which no one would see as the forced result of violence and imposition.' See Schlögel: *Im Raum lesen wir die Zeit*, p. 19, 21, and 142.

dimensional globe to a two-dimensional map and thus to disregard the inevitable problems of cartographic projection. Spatialization has its price, especially when it ignores movement. By contrast, Walter Benjamin's arcades – to mention but one example – not only create spaces but in fact construct *mobile spaces*, as the passage ways of the German title of his *Arcades Project* (*Passagen-Werk*) already signals. Benjamin's mobile spaces create interWorlds that function like mobiles and that include passersby.

What is the value of these thoughts for literary analysis? First of all, they draw our attention to migrations and movements of the most varied sort which start to occupy center stage during the twentieth century. Especially the Literatures without a fixed Abode, which came into being during the past century without their existence really being noticed, set all elements and aspects of literary production in motion in far more radical and robust ways than had ever been done before. We witness now a vectorization of all (spatial) relations, including those of national literatures. Our theories and terminologies have to be responsive to this change. To analyze the Literatures without a fixed Abode, we need concepts that can articulate difficult vectoral processes. We still do not have any testable concepts of movement that correlate space and time in sufficiently complex ways to allow us to describe this vectorization with precision. This is why we have as yet no fully articulated *poetics of movement* to help decode the vectoral imagination of today's literatures in all its intricacy and multiplicity, so that we can retrieve from them the knowledge-for-living sedimented there in layers of overlapping movements. This is not to say that a 'vectoral turn' should now replace the spatial turn. Rather, we have to our attune critical analyses of cultural and literary phenomena more to the forms and functions of movement.

Karl Schlögel quips that the Baedeker is 'the basic form of area studies': 'area studies are the scholarly, specialized forms of that same knowledge, which millions of people make their own each year, always with the latest updates.... There is no more convincing evidence of people's interest in the world in which we live.'[64] Such witticisms cannot, however, hide the crisis in regional studies à la Baedeker. The reasons for this crisis are many, but they are no doubt related to the need for serious thinking about movement. What might area (or regional) studies look like after or beyond Baedeker? A response to this question requires some initial conceptual clarifications.

---

64 Schlögel: *Im Raum lesen wir die Zeit*, p. 264–265.

Multi – inter – trans

Disciplines: Traditionally, centers for regional studies have both *multidisciplinary* and *interdisciplinary* foundations. On the one hand, there is the multidisciplinary side-by-side-ness of individual disciplines, with separate disciplinary anchors. On the other hand, there are interdisciplinary conversations among the representatives of various disciplines. This relatively static, indeed 'disciplined,' model should have as its complement a *transdisciplinary* structure, whose goal is not an interdisciplinary exchange among conversation partners who remain firmly rooted in a single discipline but a continual crosshatching of those disciplines. In this way, it becomes possible to render dynamic radically different areas of knowledge and to bind them more strongly and flexibly. It goes without saying that the advancement and the results of this 'nomadic' practice, which is transdisciplinary in the true sense, must be tested out in ongoing disciplinary and interdisciplinary exchanges.[65] In this section, I want to introduce concepts analogous to these terminological demarcations and translate them into the logics of different areas of research. Within each area's analytical framework, the differentiations I propose above can be rendered more precise with the help of three prefixes: 'multi,' 'inter,' and 'trans.'

Cultures: When analyzing cultural phenomena, it is necessary to distinguish between the *multicultural* side-by-side-ness of different cultures that reside, say, in different urban spaces (neighborhoods or districts), and an *intercultural* living-with-one-another. The latter defines encounters of all sorts among the members of cultures who interact with one another without questioning that they belong to a given culture or cultural group. What I call the *trans-cultural* level is a critical extension of the path-breaking writings about *transculturalidad* by the Cuban ethnologist and cultural theorist Fernando Ortiz.[66] This level is distinct from the two previous ones in that it encompasses movements and practices that cross very different cultures: that is, people oscillate between cultures, thus making it impossible to discern stable affiliations with a single culture or cultural group.

Languages: Beyond monolingual situations in which one language clearly dominates the logosphere, one can primarily distinguish between the *multicultural*

---

65 See also Ette: *ÜberLebenswissen*, p. 29–34.
66 See Fernando Ortiz: *Contrapunteo cubano del tabaco y el azúcar*. Caracas: Biblioteca Ayacucho 1978. Originally published in 1940.

side-by-side-ness of different languages and linguistic spaces with little or no overlap and *interlingual* situations in which two or more languages engage intensely with each other. In contrast to an intralingual translation, which might be called, with Roman Jakobson, a 'rewording' within the same language, interlingual translations are transactions between two distinct languages.[67] Different from intra- and interlingual situations are translingual ones which refer to a never-ending process of linguistic transection.[68] In this situation, the high degree of linguistic interpenetration makes it difficult, even impossible, to distinguish one or more languages from each other. In the context of literary writing, a translingual practice would be one in which an author moves back and forth between different languages both in his or her work as a whole and within a single text. In the following chapters, I will further nuance these terms.

Media: Parallel to the above formulations, one might, one might distinguish *multimedial* situations, in which numerous media exist next to each other without any significant overlap or contact, from *intermedial* situation, in which different media come together in an intense dialogue without, however, losing their respective characteristics. In a *transmedial* situation, finally, different media interpenetrate in an incessant process of movement, crossing, and 'trans-lation.' Here, unlike in the previous definitions, it is impossible cleanly to separate multi-, inter-, and transrelational phenomena either spatially or temporally. This sort of transparency and definitional rigor offer ways of analyzing such areas of overlap and intersection more precisely.

Temporalities: Temporal processes can be structured in comparable conceptual ways. If *multi-temporal* processes concern themselves with the side-by-sideness of different temporal levels that exist independently of each other, then *intertemporal* processes define the ongoing communication among different temporal dimensions that neither blend nor fuse. In keeping with this, *transtemporal* processes or structures refer to a ceaseless crisscrossing of different temporal dimensions. Such a movement creates a highly unusual kind of temporality whose transtemporal nature brings to the fore specific transcultural and translingual phenomena. With respect to periodization, suffice it here to refer to the

---

67 See Roman Jakobson: 'On Linguistic Aspects of Translation.' In: Stephen Rudy (ed.): *Roman Jakobson: Selected Writings*. The Hague: De Gruyter Mouton 1971–1985, vol. 2, p. 260.
68 For different use of the term 'translingual' in the context of China see Lydia H. Lui: *Translingual Practice: Literature, National Culture, and Translated Modernity – China, 1900–1937*. Stanford: Stanford University Press 1995.

four phases of accelerated globalization that structure economic, political, social, and, above all, cultural processes under colonialism and postcolonialism.[69] My examples in the previous sections and in the following chapters describe the phases of accelerated globalization from the perspective of different 'areas.'

Spaces: It is hardly surprising that spatial structures can be similarly divided: *multispatial* situations with poor contact coexist with *interspatial* structures with intense interactions. *Transspatial* structures come into being when different kinds of spaces are traversed and characterized by a dynamic pattern that will become conceptually more detailed in later chapters.

(Travel) Movements: In analyzing the writing practices of travel literature,[70] whose texts frequently oscillate between fiction and diction – a movement I call *frictional* – we must first distinguish among the different dimensions of a travelogue. In addition to the three spatial dimensions, there are temporal ones, as well as dimensionalities created by social structure, imagination, literary space, generic relations, and cultural space. Next, it is useful to differentiate among certain overdetermined scenes in a travelogue, notably departures, climaxes, arrivals, and returns. These scenes are part of basic figures of movement – such as circle, pendulum, star, or leaps – which suggest patterns to readers and influence the movement of their own hermeneutics. Especially relevant for the study of the highly complex field of Writing-between-Worlds, these nuances allow for the spatiotemporal exactness of textual analyses.

Why TransArea Studies?

How can one use the conceptual model I outline above for transareal (literary) scholarship? This question is enormously important for the future development of so-called area studies. Following the conceptual nuancing of the relations between culture and language, space and time, medium and discipline, let me try to capture actual spatial movements in detail. To begin with, I want to distinguish among five different levels. Movements on the *translocal* level occur between urban or rural places and spaces of limited expanse – landscapes and cityscapes in Bharati Mukherjee's sense.[71] At the *transregional* level, we find mo-

---

69 See Ette: *Weltbewusstsein*, p. 25–27.
70 See Ette: *Literatur in Bewegung*, p. 21–84.
71 See Aciman: *Letters of Transit*, p. 47.

vements between certain landscapes and/or cultural spaces that are either smaller than nations or constitute manageable units situated between nations. I call *transnational* movements among different nation-spaces or nation-states. *Transareal* movements, by contrast, occur between different areas, such as, for instance, the Caribbean or Eastern Europe. *Transcontinental* movements are passages from one continent, such as Asia, Africa, or the Americas, to another. It is easy to see how the dynamics at each level can be further subdivided according to the type of movement, that is, into *multi-*, *inter-*, and *transnational* models.

Movements contribute decisively to the ways in which (living) spaces are constituted and invested with meaning. The internal relations within a given space are of key significance in connection with an external set of relations that connects one space with another. To give a concrete example: the Caribbean can be understood in its specificity only when one's historical analysis includes the diverse inter-island communications *and* the web of the Caribbean's external relations with different European (colonial) powers, their American possessions, Africa, the USA, China, and India. If a given space is effectively characterized by relevant movements in the past, present, and, prospectively, the future, then the combination of the five different levels I suggest above can tell us much about political, cultural, and particularly literary phenomena.

An initial example, which I will develop more in chapter 6, shows just how multifaceted such a combination can be. In Emine Sevgi Özdamar's novel *The Bridge of the Golden Horn* (*Die Brücke vom Goldenen Horn*, 1998) the cities of Istanbul and Berlin overlap such that, for the protagonist, a translocal urban movement appears in a transnational and, at the same time, transareal context in which both national and areal borders are crossed. But there is more: If we look at the young woman's movements between the European and the Asian parts of Istanbul, which are crucial to the novel's plot, then her daily commute across the Bosporus also appears as a transcontinental movement, even though it remains below the national and even the regional level. The partition of Istanbul also mirrors the partition of Berlin, so that the frequent back and forth between the western and eastern parts of Berlin, in the context of two nations that, prior to 1989, still belonged to antagonistic blocs, turns out, at the local level, to be a transnational *and* a transareal movement. As I demonstrate in chapter 6, these movements have far-reaching consequences for the configuration of space and perception in Özdamar's novel.

Let me dwell on the local level a little longer. Although the migratory, economic, and social relationships between a village in Chiapas and a neighborhood in Los Angeles exist in transnational and transareal contexts, they bring these two levels into focus from the perspective of a translocal pattern of movement that is at once rural and urban. If one considers comparable translocal relations, for instance between Cuban exiles in Miami and their original families in the Cuban province of Oriente, one can already on the translocal level discern a pattern of movement that creates a dynamic interWorld of (North) American and (Latin) American studies. Although this inerWorld is indispensable for understanding these areas and their studies, it tends to be eclipsed for disciplinary reasons as frequently as the fact that such movements constellate the American continents as a hemispheric space.

The constitution of regional spaces often occurs with the help of boundaries, as is the case in Sherko Fatah's novel 'In the borderlands' (*Im Grenzland*, 2001) where a smuggler frequently crosses the borders between Iran, Iraq, and Turkey. Such crossings subvert and *at the same time* solidify existing borders, and they set in motion a complex dialectic of spatial construction through oft-repeated (even if, as in this example, prohibited) patterns of movement.[72] An example from French literature further demonstrates this dynamic of transregional border crossings: Cécile Wajsbrot's *Beaune-la-Rolande* (2004) and *Mémorial* (2005), on which I will comment in chapters 2 and 8. Both texts have transregional settings in which a particular landscape south of Paris and the region around Auschwitz are superimposed upon one another. They connect not only the first-person narrator's train journey but also the train tracks that lead from the internment and concentration camp in France to the extermination camp in today's Poland. The transnational and translocal levels are transregionally interwoven into a single landscape whose physical appearance brings into view the survival of the Shoah. Here, transregionality, as a connection between two landscapes that are at once distant and yet oddly proximate, becomes a powerful literary strategy. In these texts, the transregional patterns of movement transmit an image familiar to an individual's sense of space, which is much more intense than it would have been on the more abstract transnational level.

Transregional relations at a transareal and, at the same time, transcontinental level also characterize the political efforts that then-Brazilian President Lula da Silva initiated in May 2005, and which led to a joint summit of the Latin American countries and the states of the Arab League in Brasilia. While in the political realm, the transcontinental and transnational south-south relation occupied the center of attention, the transareal level was perhaps more important for the strengthening of Arab-American cultural relations.

---

72 See Eva Horn et al. (eds): *Grenzverletzer: Von Schmugglern, Spionen und anderen subversiven Gestalten*. Berlin: Kulturverlag Kadmos 2002, p. 7–22.

Traditional area studies tend either to disregard such transareal patterns of movement or to minimize their importance. For patterns of movement that go beyond a given familiar area often seem less relevant so long as they do not affect centers in either Europe or the USA. The eclipsing of Arab-American relations is a good example here. It is often the case that disciplinary 'jurisdictions' claim that there are deficits in the perceptual pattern either of entire branches of research or of regional studies centers. While Arab-American relations are present in the literatures of Latin America, they do not appear on the radar screen of regional studies that have only disciplinary or at best interdisciplinary moorings. For such centers function much like a Baedeker guide in that they concentrate exclusively on their respective area; beyond that, they may consider how their area relates to their institutions' own locations in Europe or the USA. As chapter 7 seeks to demonstrate through readings of novels by Gabriel García Márquez and Elias Khoury, the transareal interWorlds of the Arab-Americas are of far-reaching interest to transareal research, because the knowledge stored in this literature may very well provide correctives to familiar disciplinary patterns of perception.

This book attempts to sound the depths of the complex combinations of all these different conceptual levels and, in addition to examining transareal relations, determine the transcultural, translingual, and transtemporal patterns of movement connected with them. The future of area studies is not in the Baedeker but lies in an opening onto *TransArea studies* in which area-related competencies connect with transdisciplinary research practices. The Literatures without a fixed Abode, with their fascinating ways of Writing-between-Worlds that national literary studies notice only in passing, offer rich resources for such research and, at the same time, a boundless reservoir of knowledge (for living). It is the responsibility of literary scholarship to recover and protect this treasure. For this reason, a transareal orientation is of great significance for literary studies. If one were to distinguish transareal literary studies, which joins the different disciplines within the framework of TransArea studies, from the traditional approaches of Comparative Literature, one might say that the latter engages in static comparisons of the politics, societies, economies, and symbolic production of countries that it pits against each other. Transregional research, by contrast, focuses more on movement, exchange, and processes of transformation. For TransArea studies, routes and vectors matter more than spaces; shifting borders matter more than static ones; and relations and communication matter more than territories. Our times are times of inter-nets. They demand mobile and relational, transdisciplinary and transareal concepts of knowledge production, along with terminologies and methodologies capable of articulating movements better.

2 Figurations

Odysseus and the Angel of History: The Vectoral Imagination of Shoa Literature

The Literatures of the World and Mobile Specialization

In his 1952 Festschrift essay with the programmatic title 'Philology and Weltliteratur' (Philologie und Weltliteratur), Erich Auerbach – who wrote *Mimesis* between May 1942 and April 1945 in his Istanbul exile – sketched the outlines of a philology that would elucidate the 'radical change in the circumstances of life' in the wake of World War II and that would grant 'that this activity still has relevance for the present and the future' and make 'their [the philologists'] awareness practically operative.'[1] Important for this German-Jewish emigrant, who started to teach Romance literature at different US universities in 1947, was a critical development of Goethe's concept of Weltliteratur, which, as Auerbach well knew, Germany's national poet had conceived in large part as a foil for the dominant concept of national literature. Goethe's remark of January 31, 1827 was paradigmatic: 'National literature does not have much to tell us today. The era of Weltliteratur is imminent, and everyone must do what he can to accelerate its arrival.'[2] There can be no doubt that it was Erich Auerbach's concern, against the backdrop of the historical events of his time, to make his own contribution to a new era of world literature. In doing so, he was conscious of the fact that, historically speaking, the 'period of Goethean humanism'[3] had been very short-lived and that large and perhaps irreconcilable differences existed between what the author of *Faust* personally knew and the state of knowledge that researchers had attained by the mid-twentieth century: 'The world literatures that were available to Goethe at the end of his life were more numerous than those which were known at the time of his birth; compared to what is available to us today, however, the number was small.'[4] But how can any future philology

---

1 Erich Auerbach: 'Philology and Weltliteratur.' In: *Centennial Review* XIII.1 (1969), p. 4. See also Erich Auerbach: *Gesammelte Aufsätze zur romanischen Philologie*. Munich: Francke 1967, p. 302.
2 Johann Peter Eckermann: *Gespräche mit Goethe in den letzten Jahren seines Lebens*. Frankfurt am Main: Insel 1981, vol. 1 p. 211.
3 Auerbach: 'Philology and Weltliteratur,' p. 3.
4 Auerbach: 'Philology and Weltliteratur,' p. 4.

do justice to this steadily growing mountain of facts, to what was a tremendously expanded store of knowledge already in Auerbach's time? This is particularly a problem if philology should wish to treat that which – based on its claim to be a 'historical discipline' – it must recognize as the 'inner history of the last thousand years,' namely, 'the history of mankind [sic] achieving self-expression.'[5] The unmanageable flood of data has long since heightened the pressure toward specialization in the area of philology:

> The scholar who does not consistently limit himself to a narrow field of specialization and to a world of concepts held in common with a small circle of likeminded colleagues, lives in the midst of a tumult of impressions and claims on him: for the scholar to do justice to these is almost impossible. Still, it is becoming increasingly unsatisfactory to limit oneself to only one field of specialization. To be a Provençal specialist in our day and age, for example, and to command only the immediately relevant linguistic, paleological and historical facts, is hardly enough to be a good specialist.[6]

In this passage, Auerbach pinpointed the central dilemma confronting not only philology, the arts, and the humanities but also the natural sciences. He recognized at the same time that if philology did not wish to cede a good bit of its social relevance, then specialization in a single discipline would not be the answer. Auerbach announced the need for what I call a transdisciplinary approach that queers the boundaries of various academic specialties. His remarks also draw attention to the fact that, already in his time, the pressure to specialize was dual in nature. On the one hand, scholars had to engage in research *within* constantly differentiating or – as Auerbach repeatedly called it – 'ramifying' disciplines, while at the same time trying to respond to the pressure to work across disciplinary boundaries and thus specialize in different fields at once. How else could Auerbach himself have been able to tackle so bold, even audacious, and yet so self-evident a project[7] as an investigation into 'The Representation of Reality in Western Literature'?

It follows from Auerbach's 'Philology and Weltliteratur' that specialization is to be understood as a dynamic concept, as a term of movement, and not exclusively as disciplinary 'ramification' and a disciplined one-way street. As Auerbach formulated it during his teaching stint at Yale: 'I am talking about specialization, but not specialization that results from outdated divisions of knowledge. What I mean is specialization that is appropriate to its object of

---

5 Auerbach: 'Philology and Weltliteratur,' p. 5.
6 Auerbach: 'Philology and Weltliteratur,' p. 8–9.
7 See Ette: *ÜberLebenswissen*, p. 57–96.

study and which, therefore, always has to be newly determined.'⁸ Specialization, then, does not just proceed from the 'general' to the 'particular,' from the 'broad' to the 'narrow,' or even from the 'superficial' to the 'deep,' but can perform the most diverse of movements so long as these are adequate to the specific construction of the object of study and are verifiable in their discursive design. The specializations that make for the most creative and innovative scholarship are precisely those that queer the 'outdated divisions of knowledge.' According to brain specialist Wolf Singer, scholarly creativity can be described as the ability 'to see together what has never been seen together before.'⁹ But specialization in an area that has not yet been seen, as it were, together in its entirety demands a high degree of flexibility, or relational mobility, when it comes to the objects of study and to research methods.

Auerbach, who was born in Berlin in 1892 and died in the USA in 1957, deeply regretted that precisely 'what earlier epochs dared to designate man's place in the universe,' was 'very far off' from the research agenda of his time.¹⁰ It is no exaggeration to say that this scholar of Romance literatures was preoccupied with achieving a *world* consciousness in the fullest sense – a world consciousness whose emergence Auerbach's own concept of a philology of world literature would facilitate.¹¹ This also explains why, in the last section of his essay, he issued a programmatic call for a philology not restricted to narrow specialization, or perceived in this way:

> In any event, our philological homeland is the earth: it can no longer be the nation. The most priceless and indispensable part of a philologist's heritage is still his own nation's culture and language. Only when he is first separated from his heritage, however, and then transcends it does it become truly effective. We must return, in admittedly altered circumstances, to the knowledge that pre-national medieval culture already possessed: the knowledge that the spirit [Geist] is not national.¹²

---

8 Auerbach: *Gesammelte Aufsätze*, p. 309.
9 Wolf Singer: *Ein neues Menschenbild? Gespräche über Hirnforschung*. Frankfurt am Main: Suhrkamp 2003, p. 108.
10 Auerbach: 'Philology and Weltliteratur,' p. 17.
11 See Ottmar Ette: *Weltbewusstsein: Alexander von Humboldt und das unvollendete Project einer anderen Moderne*. Weilerwist: Velbrück Wissenschaft 2002, and Ette: *ÜberLebenswissen*. Auerbach was well aware of the semantic multi-layeredness of the concept of 'world' and pointed out that '[t]o make men conscious of themselves in their own history is a great task, yet the task is small – more like renunciation – when one considers that man not only on earth, but that he is in the world and in the universe.' Auerbach: 'Philology and Weltliteratur,' p. 17.
12 Auerbach: 'Philology and Weltliteratur,' p. 17.

Unmistakable in this passage is the degree to which the exile, 'separation,' enters into the concepts and research of a scholar whose major work emerged from the experience of migration and exile and was only successful because his forced change of place in the universe made him particularly sensitive to the world-relevant, worldwide dimensions of literature.[13] Auerbach knew very well the extent to which any philology thus conceived would necessarily have to expose itself to the 'tumult of impressions and claims' he himself conjured up. He also realized that abandoning such a transverse and transdisciplinary reorientation of the task of philology would ultimately bring about implosion, surrender, and descent into meaninglessness. For philology to turn a deaf ear on the clamor of the post-War period could only imply renouncing any claim it might have to exploring humanity's place in the universe and to being heard beyond ever-more narrowly drawn disciplinary parameters. Auerbach felt a responsibility to the 'the passionate commitment to philological and historicist activity of a small number of young people who are distinguished for their talent and originality;' he did not want to doubt their 'relevance for the present and the future.'[14]

We have yet to think fully through the consequences of Auerbach's groundbreaking attempt to plot a new direction for literary scholarship. From today's perspective, its significance can no more be overlooked than his partial miscalculation of a rapidly increasing planetary homogenization in the spheres of literature and culture in which 'our earth, the domain of Weltliteratur,' would become ever 'smaller' and lose its 'diversity.' His mistake was the completely understandable result of a US postwar perspective. The author of *Mimesis* knew himself to be in accord with his contemporaries when he expressed his fear that a global de-differentiation process might level and erase all cultural distinctions and developmental processes. What others greeted as a desirable standardization, Auerbach saw as a fundamental threat to cultural diversity, especially the wealth of world literature. For many reasons known to everyone, wrote Auerbach, 'human life' everywhere on the planet was 'becoming standardized' and marked by the same modern ways of life that had their point of origin in Europe.[15]

But did life and ways of life actually grow ineluctably more uniform on a global scale? The half century since the publication of Auerbach's pioneering

---

13 See the work of Edward Said in connection with his translation of Auerbach, namely Auerbach: 'Philology and Weltliteratur' from 1969.
14 Auerbach: 'Philology and Weltliteratur,' p. 4.
15 Auerbach: 'Philology and Weltliteratur,' p. 2.

essay has shown us to what degree an opposing current of cultural heterogenization accompanies, contrasts, and subverts still observable homogenization processes. This highly complex double movement has made the question about the coexistence of different cultures in the world the survival question of the twenty-first century. Today, there is no real call for us to inure ourselves to Auerbach's vision of 'a single literary culture, only a few literary languages, and perhaps even a single literary language.' If this analysis corresponded to actual historical developments, then, in fact, 'the notion of *Weltliteratur* would at once be realized and destroyed.'[16] The reduction to a singular would take the place of concretely experienced diversity.

Auerbach's perspective falls short here. Against the backdrop of the current fourth phase of accelerated globalization, it is necessary to bring into better view the complexity of the manifold world-literary developments and to focus, above all, on that dynamic processes in which the bipolar and antagonistic distinction between world and national literature has either largely gone unobserved or has been declared irrelevant and *marginal*. The question of what can be preserved of literary diversity should not just be directed at the rather static concept of national literature, whose practices the individual disciplines that specialize in them address and administer in the form of relatively autonomous (national) history. Rather, in the face of an immobile philology that simply administers literary texts, we need to understand as fundamentally complex processes of movement those cultural and literary networks that unsettle linguistic lines and lineages, be they national or disciplinary. Traditional literary scholarship, particularly when it devotes itself to a single language or literature, can no longer adequately represent the complexities of these literary networks, which are greater than the sum of their individual parts,[17] and in which the vectoral component cannot just be 'filtered out.'

Such processes of movement and networking cannot be assigned either to *a* national literature or to world literature.[18] We have to develop dynamic concepts of movement and place them alongside (and sometimes opposite) assumptions of singularity and static identity embedded in the distinction of national from

---

16 Auerbach: 'Philology and Weltliteratur,' p. 3.
17 According to Friedrich Cramer, apart from their relative unpredictability, fundamentally complex systems, and he 'include[s] here the integrated or network system called "life," possess the characteristic that 'the whole is more than the sum of its parts.' Friedrich Cramer: *Chaos and Order: The Complex Structure of Living Systems*. Weinheim: VHC 1993, p. 214.
18 Casanova's carefree francophone work exemplifies the problems of doing so. See Pascale Casanova: *La République mondiale des lettres*. Paris: Seuil 1999.

world literatures. In what follows, then, I am concerned not with a philology of 'world literature' but with a *relational* inquiry within the framework of a philology of the literatures of the world. The literatures of the world, however, cannot be understood either as the sum of national literatures or as a homogenized world literature. While we cannot lose sight of, or altogether ignore, national literary, linguistic, and disciplinary borders, the literatures of the world, in all of their vectoral multidimensionality, must be understood within a discontinuous, post-Euclidean fractal space (see chapters 3 and 5 above). A yet to be configured fractal geometry of the literatures of the world must be aware less of boundaries and borders and more of routes and forms of communication, less of territorialism and more of trajectoral and vectoral dimensions from a transregional, transnational, and transareal perspective. From such a precise, multiple, and simultaneously mobile vantage, it might then be possible to grasp new processes of differentiation alongside ongoing processes of de-differentiation in such a way that the full creative scope of the literatures of the world in their vectoral dimension becomes visible in the space between (and beyond the sharp contrasts of) homogenization and heterogenization. In this way, literary scholarship might go beyond its administrative function and contribute to determining humanity's place and life in the universe, of course in connection with other sciences-of-and-for-living.

Dialectic of Enlightenment as dialectic of homelessness

It is no coincidence that Auerbach, in concluding his reflections on 'Philology and Weltliteratur,' took recourse to Hugo von St. Viktor in order to connect the theme of exile with the concept of 'world': 'mundus totus exilium est.'[19] And it was with great care that, in the opening pages of what is surely his most successful book, he chose to recall the figure of Odysseus in which – particularly considering Auerbach's exile in Istanbul at the time – we glimpse a self-portrait of the Jewish émigré. Odysseus embodies the exile's experience of roaming in a fractal space refracted, broken, in so many places. At the same time, there is still a last glimmer of hope for a possible homecoming, that re-recognition whose trigger is his very wounding and injury. 'The Scar of Odysseus' is also the title of *Mimesis*'s famous first chapter. Auerbach was wise enough at this point in his

---

[19] Auerbach: *Gesammelte Aufsätze*, p. 319. See also the entry 'Exil' in Max Aub: 'Auerbach-Alphabet: Karlheinz (Carlo) Barck zum 70. Geburtstag.' In: *Trajekte* V.9 (2004).

life to understand 'what Ithacas mean,' as Constantine Cavafy's put it in the closing stanzas of his poem 'Ithaka.' [20]

Near-contemporaneous with Erich Auerbach's reflections on the *Representations of Reality in Western Literature* was Max Horkheimer and Theodor Adorno's *Dialectic of Enlightenment*, written between 1941 and 1944. In the latter year, five hundred copies were distributed 'to friends' before the Amsterdam émigré press Querido printed these 'Philosophical Fragments' under its definitive title in 1947.[21] Even beyond the second chapter, 'Odysseus or Myth and Enlightenment,' the travel movements of the Homeric hero permeate *Dialectic of Enlightenment*, where Odysseus often appears where one might have least expected him. Time and again, Odysseus, constantly plunging into new adventures with his companions, pushes to the fore and presents himself – as in 'the encounter with the Sirens' – as a 'pre-sentient allegory of the dialectic of enlightenment.'[22] According to Horkheimer and Adorno, *The Odyssey* 'bears witness to the dialectic of enlightenment.' In its sundering of epic from myth, it denotes a loss: the singing of the 'Wanderings of Odysseus' is the 'wistful stylization of that what can no longer be celebrated,' and the 'hero of the adventures shows himself to be the prototype of the bourgeois individual, a notion originating in the consistent self-affirmation which has its ancient pattern in the figure of the protagonist compelled to wander.' Hence – and here one can find many surprising parallels to Auerbach's reading of the Homeric epic – 'the venerable cosmos of the meaningful Homeric world' is revealed to be 'the achievement of regulative reason, which destroys myth by virtue of the same rational order in which it reflects itself.'[23]

This stimulating new interpretation of the figure of the sly Odysseus, which was likely 'primarily Adorno's,'[24] is of major significance for my own reading. If Auerbach reads *The Odyssey* as at once complement and contrast to the Bible, Horkheimer and Adorno project Odysseus's adventure against a historico-philosophical background that belongs 'to one concept of universal history and its

---

20 Erich Auerbach: *Mimesis: The Representation of Reality in Western Literature*. Fiftieth anniversary edition. Princeton, NJ: Princeton University Press 2003, p. 110.
21 See Jürgen Habermas: 'Nachwort.' In: *Dialektik der Aufklärung: Philosophische Fragmente*. Frankfurt am Main: Fischer 1986, p. 277. For the story of the work's composition from November 1941 to May 1944, see p. 278–281.
22 Max Horkheimer / Theodor W. Adorno: *Dialectic of Enlightenment*. New York: Continuum 1972, p. 34.
23 Horkheimer/Adorno: *Dialectic of Enlightenment*, p. 43–44.
24 Habermas: 'Nachwort,' p. 287.

interpretation' no less than to the Holy Scriptures.[25] Just like the worldwide claims of this philosophy, this is obvious from the fulminating start of the book: 'In the most general sense of progressive thought, the Enlightenment has always aimed at liberating men from fear and establishing their sovereignty. Yet the fully enlightened earth radiates disaster triumphant.'[26] In their foreword dad 'Los Angeles, California, May 1944,' the authors attempt to work out more clearly the 'seed of the regression' within Enlightenment thought itself, which is 'universally apparent today,' against the backdrop of a historical and historico-philosophical situation in which 'not only the pursuit but the meaning of science [Wissenschaft] has become problematical,' part of 'the self-destruction of the Enlightenment.' This germ is the reason why humanity 'is sinking into a new kind of barbarism.'[27]

As work on the regression of the Enlightenment to mythology and of civilization to barbarism, Horkheimer and Adorno's writings on myth[28] is close to Walter Benjamin's ideas in his 'On the Concept of History,' a text that Hannah Arendt saved for posterity and, in 1941, placed in Adorno's hands: 'There is no document of culture which is not at the same time a document of barbarism. And just as such a document is never free of barbarism, so barbarism taints the manner in which it was transmitted from one hand to another.'[29] Adorno and Horkheimer's *Dialectic of Enlightenment* positions itself within 'the theoretical work of German emigrants that continued despite Hitler' and thus blazes the trail for a kind of reading in which *The Odyssey* is not just one of the 'earliest representative testimonies of Western bourgeois civilization.'[30] This thread from

---

25 Auerbach: *Mimesis*, p. 17.
26 Horkheimer/Adorno: *Dialectic of Enlightenment*, p. 3.
27 Horkheimer/Adorno: *Dialectic of Enlightenment*, p. xi–xiii.
28 See Hans Blumenberg: *Arbeit am Mythos*. Frankfurt am Main: Suhrkamp 1979.
29 Walter Benjamin: 'On the Concept of History.' In: *Walter Benjamin: Selected Writings*. Cambridge MA: Harvard University Press 2003, vol. 4, p. 392. In German: 'Es ist niemals ein Dokument der Kultur, ohne zugleich ein solches der Barbarei zu sein. Und wie es selbst nicht frei ist von Barbarei, so ist es auch der Prozeß der Überlieferung nicht, in der es von dem einen an den andern gefallen ist.' Walter Benjamin: 'Über den Begriff der Geschichte.' In: *Benjamin: Gesammelte Schriften*. Frankfurt am Main: Suhrkamp 1980, vol. 7, p. 696. This passage takes on an odd coloring when one applies it to 'Prozess der Überlieferung' (process of tradition) itself, whose historico-philosophical theses played such an important role in the development of the Frankfurt School. For the circumstances surrounding Hannah Arendt's handing over of the suitcase containing Walter Benjamin's manuscripts to the office of the Institute of Social Research (the former Frankfurt School: then established in New York City); see Elisabeth Young-Bruehl: *Hannah Arendt: Leben, Werk und Zeit*. Franfurt am Main: Fischer 2000, p. 241–42.
30 Horkheimer/Adorno: *Dialectic of Enlightenment*, p. xvi–xvii.

The Odyssey is interwoven with writing down their reflections – much like Benjamin's theses – as fragments. The 'inner proximity of the material to the destiny of humanity after two world wars' left its imprint on philologists and philosophers alike.[31]

Horkheimer, born in Stuttgart in 1895 as son of a Jewish industrialist, and Adorno, the son of a Jewish wine wholesaler born in Frankfurt am Main in 1903, left Germany after Hitler's rise to power and eventually reached the USA after having passed through various way-stations. It is no surprise, then, that they, like Auerbach, were attracted to the peripatetic figure of Odysseus as a reference point in a series of ever-changing life-situations. For them, the figure of Odysseus still symbolized a certain hope in the midst of their own peregrinations. The 'trembling' castaway 'anticipates the work of the compass.'[32] Even in his powerlessness, 'no part of the sea remains unknown to him, and so his powerlessness also indicates that the mighty powers will be put down;' it simultaneously aims at the 'disempowerment of power.'[33] These remarks also inscribe in the figure of Odysseus a double self-portrait without reducing it to mere autobiography. For Horkheimer and Adorno, Odysseus embodied a 'knowledge which comprises his identity and which enables him to survive,' so that, as a 'knowing survivor,' he is simultaneously one 'who takes the greatest risks when death threatens, thus becoming strong and unyielding when life continues.'[34] The peripatetic figure of the knowing Odysseus is, above all, a mythic, larger-than-life figure of survival providing a link to the 'Old World.'

The Homeric hero stands not only for knowledge-for-living but also, even more so, for survival knowledge: that is, for a knowledge that life has of itself, which becomes the prerequisite for survival in exile, without surrendering the claim of contributing decisively to the disempowerment of the 'mighty powers.' But no less crucial is the fact that 'homesickness'[35] gives birth to Odysseus's adventures. The idea of a homeland forms in relation to settledness and property. But for Horkheimer and Adorno, it does not fuse with a notion of settledness in contrast to nomadic life. According to them, one's 'homeland is the state of

---

31 'Die innere Nähe des Stoffes zum Schicksal der Menschheit nach zwei Weltkriegen.' Elisabeth Frenzel: *Stoffe der Weltliteratur: Ein Lexikon dichtungsgeschichtlicher Längsschnitte*. Stuttgart: Alfred Kröner 1983, p. 564.
32 Horkheimer/Adorno: *Dialectic of Enlightenment*, p. 46.
33 Horkheimer/Adorno: *Dialectic of Enlightenment*, p. 46.
34 Horkheimer/Adorno: *Dialectic of Enlightenment*, p. 47.
35 'The quintessential paradox of the epic resides in the fact that the notion of homeland is opposed to myth – which the fascist would falsely present as homeland.' Horkheimer/Adorno: *Dialectic of Enlightenment*, p. 78.

having escaped.'[36] Furthermore, '[e]loquent discourse itself, language in contradistinction to mythic song, the possibility of retaining in the memory the disaster that has occurred, is the law of Homeric escape, and the reason why the escaping hero is repeatedly introduced as narrator.'[37] Just as in flight, there is an element of *having* escaped, a homeland is preserved in the endless movement of exile. Even the recitation of gruesome events, which 'represents horror as if it were a conversational topic, also allows the horror,' whose memory it preserves, 'to appear for the first time.'[38] It is only in having escaped that a homeland becomes accessible again; but this access is not to one's initial, prelapsarian condition, to one's 'original' heritage and home. Only by having escaped can Odysseus, marked and identified by his scar, become the homecoming homeless one and the homeless homecomer, that is, the personification of an unending dialectic of homelessness. He becomes the 'model for a modern epic of homelessness as counterweight to the fascist glorification of rootlessness and homeland mythology,' just as exile would become the '*conditio sine qua non* of modern existence.'[39]

To be sure, the exilic experience of the homo migrans is as old as humanity itself, and the *homo sacer* has always been part and parcel of the human experience, the conditio humana.[40] And yet, there are good reasons why we should understand migration and homelessness as specific to human existence and to life knowledge *under modernity*. We may first take recourse to Nietzsche who, in *The Gay Science* and, with reference to European modernity, connected homelessness with the disappearance of ideals and values and with a desired the transvaluation of all values. For Nietzsche, the very notion of the 'European' was inseparable from homelessness and migration:

---

36 Horkheimer/Adorno: *Dialectic of Enlightenment*, p. 78.
37 Horkheimer/Adorno: *Dialectic of Enlightenment*, p. 78.
38 Horkheimer/Adorno: *Dialectic of Enlightenment*, p. 86.
39 '[D]as Modell einer modernen Epik der Heimatlosigkeit als Gegenentwurf zur faschistischen Glorifizierung der Wurzellosigkeit wie der Heimat-Mythologie. Der Held Odysseus, dem es gelingt, der Welt der Magie zu entfliehen, verkörpert das Exil als *conditio sine qua non* moderner Existenz.' In: Silke Segler-Messner: *Archive der Erinnerung: literarische Zeugnisse des Überlebens nach der Shoah in Frankreich.* Cologne: Böhlau 2005, p. 75.
40 In the words of Klaus Bade: 'There has been 'homo migrans' as long as there has been 'homo sapiens;' for wanderings are as much a part of the conditio humana as are birth, procreation, sickness and death.' Klaus Bade: *Europa in Bewegung: Migration vom späten 18. Jahrhundert bis zur Gegenwart.* Munich: C. H. Beck 2000, p. 11. See Giorgio Agamben: *State of Exception.* Chicago: University of Chicago Press 2005.

> Among Europeans of to-day there are not lacking those who may call themselves homeless ones in a way which is at once a distinction and an honour; it is them that my secret wisdom and *gaya scienza* is especially to be laid at heart! For their lot is hard, their hope uncertain; it is a clever feat to devise consolation for them. But what good does it do! We children of the future, how *could* we be at home in the present?[41]

The expatriation from the here and now opens up a temporal dimension that can be linked with the experience of a ruptured, discontinuous time that, in the words of Saxony-born Hugo von St. Viktor who died in Paris, has turned the whole world into an exilic space. Why should this not also apply to the continent beholden to the myth of Europa, an abducted, raped, and finally homeless migrant?

Critical to my discussion is the dialectic of homelessness that runs through *Dialectic of Enlightenment* and which is the unmistakable force behind this book and Auerbach's *Mimesis*. This dialectic stems from the specific experience of two world wars and, above all, from an anti-Semitism whose manifestation as National Socialism pursued the so-called 'Final Solution' of the so-called 'Jewish Question,' and whose depths Horkheimer and Adorno endeavored to sound in their 'concluding' chapter with varying degrees of success. Half a century before Giorgio Agamben, Walter Benjamin unequivocally noted in the eighth of his historico-philosophical theses, that

> [t]he tradition of the oppressed teaches us that the 'state of emergency' in which we live is not the exception but the rule. We must attain to a conception of history that is in keeping with this insight.... The current amazement that the things we are experiencing are 'still' possible in the twentieth century is not philosophical. This amazement is not the beginning of knowledge – unless it is the knowledge that the view of history which gives rise to it is untenable.[42]

But if the concept of a history that declares as a state of exception what has long been the norm must be changed with a view to the far-reaching legal, philosophical, and bio-political consequences that, according to Agamben, charac-

---

41 Friedrich Nietzsche: *The Gay Science*. New York: Dover Philosophical Classics 2006, p. 192. In German: 'Es fehlt unter den Europäern von heute nicht an solchen, die ein Recht haben, sich in einem abhebenden und ehrenden Sinne Heimatlose zu nennen, ihnen gerade sei meine geheime Weisheit und gaya scienza ausdrücklich an's Herz gelegt! Denn ihr Los ist hart, ihre Hoffnung ungewiss, es ist ein Kunststück, ihnen einen Trost zu erfinden, aber was hilft es! Wir Kinder der Zukunft, wie *vermöchten* wir in diesem Heute zu Hause zu sein!' Nietzsche: 'Die fröhliche Wissenschaft.' In: Friedrich Nietzsche: *Kritische Studienausgabe in 15 Einzelbänden*. Berlin: DTV, De Gruyter 1988, vol. 3, p. 628.
42 Walter Benjamin: *Illuminations*. New York: Schocken Books 1969, p. 257.

terize the state of exception paradoxically as a paradigm of political rule in the modern era,⁴³ then it follows logically that any history of literature that defines as a state of exception any text that does not fit the presumably universal schema of national literature must also be fundamentally rethought and altered. Persecution and exile, diaspora and migration, still stubbornly dismissed as states of exception and relegated to those conceptual pigeonholes created especially for them, have long been the rule worldwide, not 'only' in the political, biopolitical, and economic spheres but also in those of culture and more specifically literature. It is no coincidence that the phenomenon of the exception becoming the rule, and of homelessness becoming a primary reference point in life, reading, and writing, appears so clearly in the context of the warring conflicts and the totalitarianism of the twentieth century, of international anti-Semitism and the Shoah. As Horkheimer wrote in 1944, having escaped cannot be separated from the knowledge that, 'actually, anyone might be in a concentration camp.'⁴⁴ Both are products of an epistemological process owing to the awareness of an historical situation which initially represent themselves (in the Benjaminian sense) as a 'picture' that 'flashes up at the instance when it can be recognized' or 'at a moment of danger.'⁴⁵ That this 'flash' occurred almost in the same 'instance' for thinkers as different as Auerbach, Adorno, Benjamin, and Horkheimer⁴⁶ is as little due to chance as the fact that Benjamin chose to depict History by using a soon-to-be famous image that was apposite for a still 'the oppressed humanity': a 'Klee painting named "Angelus Novus."'⁴⁷

> One pictures the Angel of History with his face turned toward the past. Where we perceive a chain of events, he sees a single catastrophe that keeps piling wreckage upon wreckage at his feet. The angel would like to stay, awaken the dead, and make whole what has been destroyed. But a storm is blowing from Paradise. It blows open the Angel's wings with such violence that he can no longer close them. This storm thrusts him into the very future to which his back is turned, while the pile of debris before him grows skyhigh. The storm is what we call progress.⁴⁸

---

43 See Agamben: *State of Exception*, p. 1–2.
44 See Habermas: 'Nachwort,' p. 281.
45 Benjamin: *Illuminations*, p. 255.
46 For the familiarity with and closeness to Walter Benjamin of the authors of *Dialect of Enlightenment*, notably with a view to the historico-philosophical interrelation of myth and the modern era, see Habermas: 'Nachwort,' p. 282f and 286f.
47 Benjamin: *Illuminations*, p. 257.
48 Benjamin: *Illuminations*, p. 257–58.

Like Adorno, Horkheimer, and Auerbach, Benjamin chose a figure in motion. But for his angel of history, unlike for Odysseus, the way back home, the path leading to an original paradise, is barred. And yet, the angel's gaze is no less averted from home than that of the crafty Greek. Storms push both figures; both rove while still having a point of orientation. Yet, whereas the homecoming homeless figure is still granted the possibility of a final homecoming to Penelope's loom, which makes his erratic and disconnected wanderings circular, Klee's angel, in Benjamin's eyes, has only the possibility of moving toward a stormy impending progress. For the Angelus Novus, progress(ion) becomes a regression toward the future without return, erratic yet still perfectly linear. Above all, this figure of movement, and in motion, is estranged from his own will, much like 'science's progress has become almost independent of what we *want* to do,' as Hannah Arendt stressed in her reflections on power and violence.[49]

Auerbach's philological and world-literary reflections; Horkheimer and Adorno's critical philosophical-scientific fragments; and Benjamin's historico-philosophical and progress-critical theses show to what extent the dimension of homelessness pervaded knowledge (production) in the mid-twentieth century. They also demonstrate in how fundamental a way homelessness had imprinted itself on writing, thinking, and even life itself for a long time. Through evermore brutal wars and mass pogroms, anti-Semitism and the Shoah, homelessness had become the rule. When one considers how ineluctably their own life experiences were intertwined with their historical circumstances, it is hardly surprising that the generational experience of authors such as Hannah Arendt, Victor Klemperer, and Werner Krauss would be refracted, in transgenerational ways, in the lens of later reflections on persecution and exile, migration and internments. Homelessness has continued in changed historical and socio-cultural circumstances since the end of the twentieth century, the century of migrations. The dialectic of enlightenment still operates as a dialectic of homelessness. Even as other figures of motion come into being at the end of the twentieth century, Odysseus and the Angel of History by no means disappear. If home is a state of having escaped, then escape is a way to image and imagine one's homeland, to capture it in a (moving) picture. In fact, it is many ways.

If the state of exception is the rule and the concentration camp is a bio-political paradigm of modernity, then homelessness, in a time when the storm continues to blow Benjamin's Angel of History ever farther away from Paradise become as collective experience of living-without-a-fixed-abode. Even though lite-

---

49 Hannah Arendt: *Macht und Gewalt*. Munich: Piper 1970, p. 86.

rary explorations of the supposed state of exception in the era of postcolonial theory increasingly call attention to phenomena such as diaspora and exile, migration and transmigration, it will still be a long while before the literatures of homelessness – or better, the Literatures without a fixed Abode – will be understood and recognized as more than just peripheral parts of global literatures. If we are to attain an adequate understanding of literary writing in the twenty-first century, we have to adjust not only the concept of history but also the concepts of literature and literary history which are connected with history in a fundamentally complex way. There is no doubt that these global literatures will increasingly have to be understood as Literatures without a fixed Abode. The wings of Benjamin's angel are still spread open wide, and the storm has increased in intensity. It may well be that, faced with such forces, neither the present concept of history nor those of literature and literary scholarship are sustainable any longer.

Literatures without a fixed Abode

Within the globalized, but by no means egalitarian, literary networks of the world, the Literatures without a fixed Abode are occupying a large and increasingly important space. At the end of a century marked by migrations on an unprecedented scale, migrations due to war, famine, economic pressures, and ecological catastrophes as well as political, racist, and sexist persecution, developments occurred that have gradually transformed, and continue to do so at an accelerated pacem, the maps of world literatures in transit from the twentieth to the twenty-first century. Planetary systems of communication and transnational labor markets; fundamentalist religious wars and 'ethnic cleansing;' globalized money markets and mounting numbers of economic refugees, along with other phenomena too numerous to mention here have all created a situation in which the previous centers have been pushed out to the periphery and the former margins have moved in toward the centers where they have become culturally active. But in contrast to the globalization of 'disaster triumphant' evoked in *Dialectic of Enlightenment,* the globalization of democracy and justice has yet to arrive in our age of migration and interdependence.[50]

---

50 See the very different approaches of Ottfried von Höffe: *Demokratie im Zeitalter der Globalisierung*. Munich: Beck 1999; Matthias Albert: *Zur Politik der Weltgesellschaft: Identität und Recht im Kontext internationaler Vergesellschaftung*. Weilerswist: Velbrück Wissenschaft 2002;

Our metropolises in particular have become focal points of multicultural, intercultural, and transcultural movements, by which I mean various kinds of cultural side-by-sideness, exchanges among clearly distinguished cultures, and the sort of nomadic interactions that cross different cultures. Even in cases where such phenomena overlap and intersect with each other, it is crucial, and in fact unavoidable, in any study of world literatures that we differentiate conceptually among the movements of cultural side-by-sideness, coexistence, and entanglement or crosshatching. Otherwise, we run the risk of conflating the opposing vectors of cultural homogenization and heterogenization and of underestimating their complexity.

The unavoidable crossing of linguistic boundaries frequently disturbs political and cultural borders. Taking recourse to Hannah Arendt, Giorgio Agamben draws attention to the fact that what has put the 'originary fiction of modern sovereignty' in a crisis in the context of modern nation-building is the rift of the 'continuity between man and citizen, *nativity* and *nationality*.'[51] This fissure became increasingly visible during the twentieth century. Refugees, stateless persons, and migrants destabilize assumptions about processes of identity formation based on the nation state, which are predicated on the 'naturalness' and 'self-evident' character of supposedly homogeneous (cultural, religious, and linguistic) communities. Literature has played an especially vital role in the creation and the discursive subversion of imagined communities.

For quite some time now, the mother tongue into which someone is 'born' has no longer automatically been the same language that a given writer uses as her literary language, either long-term or sporadically. One can migrate to a foreign national literature much like one can migrate to a foreign country. Belonging to two or more national literatures or writing in various languages either serially or simultaneously is no more unusual in our day than changes in citizenship and holding several passports. Even if they differ in degree and kind in the various literary regions of the world, such phenomena are no longer rarities and have not been for some time now. Precisely in zones of dense globalization, these developments are emerging on such a massive scale that the construction of homogeneous 'national' spaces for culture and literature seem not just outdated; they are part of a conscious, deliberate re-nationalization. But what does all

---

and Nancy Fraser: *Justice Interruptus: Critical Reflections on the 'Postsocialist' Condition*. New York: Routledge 1997.
51 Giorgio Agamben: *Homo sacer: Sovereign Power and Bare Life*. Stanford: Stanford University Press 1998, p. 131.

this mean in a world where the nation can no longer be a 'philological homeland?'

These developments give Goethe's concept of 'Weltliteratur' a completely new meaning, one that clearly goes beyond ideas of both the nation state and national literature, even if the latter concept continues to affect important aspects of literary production, reproduction, distribution, and reception. The literatures of the world are less settled and have increasingly adopted nomadic patterns of thinking, writing, and perceiving. To this vectorization of literary production corresponds in literary criticism and scholarship an increased sense of spatial and, at times, intercultural and transcultural mobility. For various reasons, as my examples have shown, the USA have, at least since the mid-twentieth century, become not exactly a *melting pot* but, the most important *meeting point* and platform for developments in the worldwide literary network, and not only in the sense of the famous *salad bowl*. In a sense, the USA have inherited the mantle of France and particularly Paris, which, as Henri Michaux once put it, was 'the homeland for those who did not have a homeland.'[52] Eloquent testimony to this fact is the enormous number of intellectuals, writers, scholars, and scientists from all corners of the world who come to the USA for either short or extended stays or live on both sides of the Atlantic or the Pacific.

Writing-without-a-fixed-abode undermines national borders. Rather than challenge the existence of these borders, it frequently multiplies them. Such writing opens up the concept of national literature through the growing presence of a literature that one often subsumes under that highly unsatisfactory rubric of 'migrant' literature. In an article about the Spanish translation of Emine Sevgi Özdamar's German-language novel *Life is a Caravanserai* (*Das Leben ist eine Karawanserei*, 1999),[53] Juan Goytisolo, who had forsaken his native Barcelona to make his first home in the Arab world, stressed how, for many years, he had been at pains to call attention to the fact that Turks would soon write a significant portion of German literature, writers from the Caribbean and the Maghreb would pen a major part of French literature, and Pakistanis would author a large share of English literature.[54] This fact has been incontrovertible for some

---

52 'La patrie de ceux qui n'ont pas de patrie.' Henri Michaux: 'Lieux lointains.' In: *Mercure de France* 1109 (1956), p. 52.
53 See Emine Sevgi Özdamar: *Life is a Caravanserai, Has Two Doors, I Came in One, I Went Out the Other*. London: Middlesex University Press, 2000. Among other honors, Özdamar received the Austrian Ingeborg Bachmann Prize in 1991.
54 Juan Goytisolo: 'On Emine Sevgi Özdamar.' In: *New York Times Literary Supplement* 12 (1994); see also Ette: *ÜberLebeswissen*, p. 227–52.

time now, even if the general consensus among national academic institutions and the media is still to dismiss such developments as marginal. Goytisolo's prognosis has come true in an astonishingly short period of time. It represents an important, if by no means the only, reality of contemporary writing at the start of the twenty-first century. Özdamar, who grew up in Turkey, said in an interview conducted on the occasion of her being awarded the Kleist Prize that languages 'are like instruments, you make music with them, vary them,' adding: 'National pride gives me hives. It's enough to say that I was born here or there. Nothing more. You would really have to have at least twenty passports; one never knows what country is going to be the enemy of what country next. Or a world passport. Or none at all.'[55] Similarly, the Algerian-born writer Assia Djebar noted in a lecture on her novel 'Strasbourg nights' (*Les nuits de Strasbourg*), which was written in French in Louisiana in 1997 and whose action takes place in two different time frames in French-Alsatian-German Strasbourg:

> Without a place to call home, without the need for an origin: for at least twenty years, I've enjoyed my nomadic existence; I felt comfortable and sometimes even at home in Barcelona, Venice, Freiburg im Breisgau, or in the metropolises of northern Europe, in Paris, where I arrived, which I wanted to discover. [...] When a man or woman comes to Europe from points south and writes European literature, is that not a kind of reverse 'exoticism'? For us, the counterpart or parallel of Europeans' 'Orientalism' would be 'Occidentalism' – a temptation: why not?[56]

As a casual aside, Djebar signals here that European literature is no longer the sole *chasse gardée*, the private preserve, of Europeans. Her remark that her 'writing longed for *other places*' in no way implies a desire to be territorialized as other in the literary terrain, but, rather,the wish to create a literature that cannot *easily* be territorialized. The rebellion against time-honored lines of demarcation is patently obvious here, even though (or especially because) her writing deals intensively with specific places, for example, Strasbourg during the period when the French troops had evacuated it (September 1939 to June 1940), thus tackling a subject that has been largely avoided in both French and German lite-

---

55 'Sprachen sind ja wie Instrumente, man musiziert mit ihnen, kann abwechseln.' 'Von Nationalstolz kriege ich Allergien. Es reicht doch zu sagen, ich bin da oder dort geboren. Mehr nicht. Überhaupt, man müsste mindestens zwanzig Pässe haben, man weiß ja nicht, welches Land sich als nächstes mit welchem verfeindet. Oder einen Weltpass. Oder keinen.' Emine Sevgi Özdamar: 'Wir wohnen in einer weiten Hölle (interview with Nils Minkmar).' In: *Frankfurter Allgemeine Sonntagszeitung* (December 21, 2004), p. 23.
56 Assia Djebar: 'Schreiben in Europa: Über den Roman *Nächte in Straßburg*.' Lecture at the Haus der Kulturen der Welt, Berlin, November 28, 1998.

ratures. The Literatures without a fixed Abode cannot simply be evacuated because they thwart and unsettle traditional territorial lines in literature and philology inherited from the nineteenth century.

The development Goytisolo sketched and Djebar's writing embodies in its own way has picked up its pace since the end of the twentieth century. This acceleration should not, however, deceive us into thinking that national literary categories, ascriptions, and exclusionary mechanisms have either already disappeared or will disappear in the foreseeable future. Readers' outmoded categorical expectations, be they marked by an insistence of 'national' or 'one's own' culture, continue, along with difficulties within the literary industry and academic literary scholarship. As long as they do, Turks will continue not to consider the work of Özdamar part of Turkish literature; José F. A. Oliver's writing will remain on the outside of Spanish literature, as Spaniards see it; and Amin Maalouf's books will not be counted as Arab literature in the Arab world itself. Authors whose work can be classified as Literature without a fixed Abode are the preferred objects of expatriation from national literary (and, at times, nation-state) canons. Examples are legion. Rare exceptions, such as Yoko Tawada, who has published in German and in Japanese and has received awards in both countries, prove rather than disprove the rule of mutual exclusion.

Writers who have no permanent residence in a land that is supposedly their 'own' often have a difficult time escaping such exclusionary mechanisms. Both serial (cultural and literary) border crossers – branded variously as border-*violators*, smugglers, or spies, as vagabonds, nomads, and mercenaries, as freebooters, refugees, and double agents – are borderland dwellers who have always had problems being recognized in those countries where they live at any given point. It comes as no surprise, then, that representatives of the Literatures without a fixed Abode – in contrast to those authors whose work can easily be assigned to a single national literature – tend to be considered suspect and subversive.

And yet, it is increasingly difficult today to dismiss migratory literature and other forms of the Literatures without a fixed Abode as exceptions and to exclude them on that basis. Moreover, national institutes of cultural foreign policy, such as the Goethe Institut and the Instituto Cervantes, have long recognized that literary 'nomads' allow them to score points abroad and publicly exhibit (and aesthetically prove in persuasive ways) the openness of their respective societies. Until now, however, the philologies have not yet articulated concepts that would do justice to phenomena and developments that have been widespread and frequent within the international literary industry for some time now.

The point of my discussion of Auerbach's preliminary reflections on a philology of Weltliteratur was to show that the conceptually contrasting notions of 'national literature' and 'world literature,' which we have inherited from the nineteenth century, are no longer adequate for addressing events that, in the wake of the totalitarianisms, wars, and persecutions of the twentieth century, the Shoah in particular, have fundamentally changed what we consider 'normal' in thinking and writing and have made migratory writing into an international mass phenomenon. The limits of existing concepts, which Auerbach seismographically registered against the background of his own life-experience, demand conceptual changes and flexible academic specializations that can do justice to the vectoral imagination of literary writing and to the dynamic dimension of artistic production on as many levels as possible. What is at stake is not to apply Goethe's famous dictum, that 'national literature has little to tell us today' and that the 'era of Weltliteratur' is dawning, to the changed conditions of the late twentieth and early twenty-first centuries but to adapt that dictum critically and creatively to altered conditions. In light of our fourth phase of accelerated globalization, it is now time to interrelate the diverse literatures of the world in innovative ways, to set them in motion conceptually by including the Literatures without a fixed Abode, and to focus attention on dynamic figures of movement in the context of a fractal, discontinuous and, as it were, post-Euclidean geometry of literary production and reception. The following chapters are devoted to showing how this might be done.

What I mean is that, in the future, we should direct our attention more to phenomena of literary translation and transmission and, from this 'external' perspective, shed light on the entrenched instances of individual (national) literary fields. Simultaneously, we need to understand literary languages and territories as migratory spaces for 'foreign' languages and 'foreign' cultures, as spaces in which we glimpse the 'foreign' as part of 'our own' without, however, losing its 'foreignness' altogether. It is especially important to explore how writing displaced in translocal, transnational, or transareal ways establishes a sense of home in other places and, by doing so, transforms and enriches the host (literary) language, a process on which Walter Benjamin reflects in 'The Task of the Translator.' To see such processes only as signs of either cultural homogenization *or* hybridization is conceptually impoverishing. One of the key tasks of contemporary literary studies should be more precisely to document and analyze the multiple patterns of movement that occur between these two poles.

The Literatures without a fixed Abode increasingly came into their own during the late twentieth century, without everyone actually being aware of this development. Their maturation set in motion all aspects and elements of literary production in a far more radical and enduring ways than ever before. We are now witnessing a broad-based vectorization of all sorts of relations, which also affects the structures of national literatures. Because postmodernity weakened the temporal foundations of our thinking and writing, spatial concepts increased in significance. Today, then, our attention should be focused on movement and migration as distinctive traits of the literatures of the world. We need a fully articulated poetics of movement to help us decode the varied and complex literary figurations of the vectoral imagination behind much of today's writing. Beyond literary themes and content, vectorization comprises various (re)presentational forms of movement; on a global scale, it also extends to a wide spectrum of readers and their movements. That we can, as a result, no longer territorialize cultures in an unreflected, unselfconscious manner by no means applies 'only' to non-European or so-called postcolonial symbolic production. Rather, we must vectorize literary production and reception to understand cultures as always in motion and to be able to discover the historically accumulated coefficients inscribed in actual patterns of movement.

With their varied overlays of space and movement, the literatures of the world allow us to observe, and playfully test, from different, simultaneous perspectives, processes of inclusion and exclusion, traditions and breaks with traditions, along with sequences of multi-, inter-, and transcultural events. The literatures of the world mediate a planetary consciousness that corresponds to the state of affairs of our time. They make available a life knowledge (or biosophia) that reveals reductionist mappings – in which homogeneous cultural blocs stand in hostile opposition suggestive of what Huntington called a 'clash of civilizations' (1996) – to be ideological parts of a hegemonic strategy that persistently pushes politics by other means.

It is no coincidence that Horkheimer and Adorno see in the peripatetic figure of the crafty migrant Odysseus the embodiment of a 'knowledge which comprises his identity and which enables him to survive.'[57] This survival knowledge, which had to reorient itself and incorporate new tactics at a time when the Enlightenment had taken a turn toward totalitarian violence, results from the movements the 'knowing survivor' performs as he is tossed about in a Homeric world of alien, yet familiar powers. In the hermeneutics of this nomadic figure of the migrant, survival knowledge is encoded without necessarily being tied to authorial intent or even consciousness. This knowledge is accessi-

---

57 Horkheimer/Adorno: *Dialectic of Enlightenment*, p. 47.

ble to us even today and can be acquired from outside of its original context. The very figures of movement inscribed in the figure of roving Odysseus facilitate the process of translation and acquisition because they contain a spatiotemporal weave of movements structured as an itinerary. As a spatial model of understanding, this weave can be re-experienced in other spaces and times, and it can be transferred as knowledge-for-living to the narrative structures of one's own life. The Scar of Odysseus may well suggest that such a transfer cannot succeed without loss and injury. The complex processes of which I speak here are, as a rule, painful and, with regard to the Shoa, infinitely agonizing.

The reception and acquisition of knowledge-for-living (and surviving) continues to generate knowledge-for-living that can be injected into a society – and herein lies a good part of literature's political potential. A more intensive engagement with the Literatures without a fixed Abode in the context of the literatures of the world can define new areas of knowledge and spheres of activity for the various philologies. They can be explored once a predominantly static view of academic disciplines gives way to more flexible forms of specialization. Understanding the present phase of accelerated globalization as an extension of the earlier historical sequence of accelerations and decelerations, and recognizing in our ordering of knowledge the history and thus the shape of currents of knowledge, might promote new insights into literary and cultural processes within fractal spaces of movement beyond, among other things, the Goethean dichotomies of national and world literatures. A critical extension of Erich Auerbach's challenging reflections to the twenty-first century, my considerations in this book hope to contribute to such a new understanding from the philological (or literary-critical) perspective of the sciences-of-and-for-living.

Figures of vectoral imagination in Shoah literature

The historical development of the Literatures without a fixed Abode experienced a sharp increase with the rise of Shoah literature in the twentieth century. Shoa literature constitutes one of the most important traditions of the *littératures sans domicile fixe* and *literaturas sin residencia fija* in that it reversed the previously tabooized confluence of anti-Semitism, the Shoah, and totalitarianism even beyond the context of National Socialism.[58] Even the founding of the state of Israel and the associated project of a quasi-global reterritorialization

---

58 Hannah Arendt was the first to break the taboo in her today still fascinating book *Elemente und Ursprünge totaler Herrschaft*. Munich: Piper 1991.

have in no way weakened its importance.⁵⁹ The additional waves of emigration and immigration triggered at the time in the Middle East had worldwide effects that are still with us.

Hannah Arendt's study of the concentrationary universe (univers concentrationnaire) ended with the prognosis that 'concentration camps and gas chambers' would continue to endure far beyond the existence of National Socialism and other totalitarian regimes of the twentieth century: 'Just as in today's world totalitarian tendencies can be found everywhere and not only in those countries with totalitarian rule, these central institutions of total power could very easily survive the toppling of all those totalitarian regimes with which we are familiar.'⁶⁰ The existence and infamy of concentration camps neither began nor ended with the atrocities of Auschwitz, Buchenwald, Dachau, and Mauthausen. Nor did the *univers concentrationnaire* cease to exist with the liberation of these camps. As numerous studies have shown, concentration camps have persisted throughout the twentieth century and even into the present day in many regions of the world. It is for good, though not uncontested, reasons that Giorgio Agamben termed the concentration camp itself a 'biopolitical paradigm of the modern.'⁶¹ Understandably, then, Shoah literature has become not only a transgenerational but also, at the same time, a transcultural and transhistorical phenomenon.

Faced with the imminent deaths of the last survivors of the Nazi concentration and extermination camps, present debates about the Holocaust and the Shoah have increasingly focused on testimony, an area where all discussions and research about concentrationary universe intersect.⁶² Paul Celan's oft-cited verse 'No One Bears Witness to the Witness' has become a major reference point for a debate about the access to and legitimacy of eyewitness accounts that is far from over. Agamben remarks that, 'from a historical perspective, we know, for example, the most minute detail of how the final phase of the extermination

---

59 See Sidra de Koven Ezrahi: *Booking Passage: Exile and Homecoming in the Modern Jewish Imagination*. Berkeley: University of California Press 2000.
60 '[E]s steht zu fürchten, dass die Konzentrationslager und Gaskammern nicht nur eine Warnung, sondern ein Beispiel bleiben werden. So wie in der heutigen Welt totalitäre Tendenzen überall und nicht nur in totalitär regierten Ländern zu finden sind, so könnte diese zentrale Institution der totalen Herrschaft leicht den Sturz aller uns bekannten totalitären Regime überleben.' Arendt: *Elemente und Ursprünge*, p. 942–943.
61 See Agamben: *Homo sacer*, especially Part three, 'The Camp as Biopolitical Paradigm of the Modern,' p. 119–180.
62 For an extensive overview of research on this theme see Segler-Messner: *Archive der Erinnerung*, p. 14–23.

was executed,'⁶³ and contradicts his own reference to the fundamental aporias that open onto the question of the 'Remnants of Auschwitz.' We have confronted these aporias anew for more than sixty years now. Agamben writes: 'The language of testimony is a language that no longer signifies and that, in not signifying, advances into what is without language, to the point of taking on a different insignificance – that of the complete witness, that of he who by definition cannot bear witness.'⁶⁴ As Agamben emphasizes in his foreword, the 'aporia of Auschwitz' is the 'aporia of historical knowledge itself: a non-coincidence between facts and truth, between verification and comprehension.'⁶⁵ It is here that literature and literary scholarship can stand for knowledge and especially survival knowledge, beyond the documentary without relying on the overused pipeline that links facts and truth. Beyond the aporias to which Agamben points, an analysis of figures of movement can throw another, entirely new light on the construction of testimonial discourses in Shoah literature, which renders visible the very dynamics that characterize the Literatures without a fixed Abode. The hermeneutic figures of movement introduce a spatialized model of understanding that, through the aesthetic dimension of these texts, opens the 'impossibility of witnessing' up to a cognitive function that the aporias of witnessing can crossed but not cross out.

In the following sections, I will use four examples to explore the vectoral imagination in different figurations of the concentration camp, which might give us aesthetic access to a testimonial function that lies outside of or beyond referentiality. My brief readings proceed from the conviction that testimonial discourse generates Literatures without a fixed Abode.

Albert Cohen, or the prefiguration of the concentration camp

For brevity's sake, I begin with a short text by Albert Cohen (1895–1981) which has garnered little critical attention thus far.⁶⁶ One of the twentieth century's outstanding Francophone authors, Cohen is, in many respects, difficult to classify. He was born on the small Greek island of Corfu and grew up surrounded by

---

63 Giorgio Agamben: *Remnants of Auschwitz: The witness and the archive.* Homo sacer III. New York: Zone Books 2002, p. 11.
64 Agamben: *Remnants of Auschwitz*, p. 38.
65 Agamben: *Remnants of Auschwitz*, p. 12.
66 See also Ottmar Ette: 'Albert Cohen – 'Jour de dix ans': Räume und Bewegungen interkultureller Begegnung.' In: *Dulce et decorum est philologiam colere. Festschrift für Dietrich Briesemeister zu seinem 65. Geburtstag.* Frankfurt am Main: Domus Editoria Europaea 1999, p. 1295–1322.

the Venetian dialect of the local Jewish community. Driven from the island by the fear of future pogroms, Cohen's parents left for Marseilles. It was only after Cohen completed his university studies in Geneva that he exchanged his Ottoman passport for a Swiss one. Helvetian citizenship enabled him to visit relatives in Alexandria without any problems and to work at the Bureau International du Travail in Geneva. When the British consul in Bordeaux recognized him as the author of the famous novel *Solal*, and thus as a Francophone writer, he could flee the Germans and gain entry to England. Later, as an international diplomat, he created a passport for stateless persons and succeeded in having it internationally recognized. He was no less proud of this passport than he was of the novels he penned in a language other than his native tongue. He wrote his novels under a name into which he had discreetly slipped an 'h' upon acquiring his Swiss passport (a resident of Geneva, he became a citizen of Mellingen in the canton of Aargau).[67]

Cohen's life experience as the progenitor of a stateless passport no doubt left an imprint on his literary work. Similarly complex 'internationalized' biographies populate Cohen's stories, plays, and novels, often grotesquely exaggerated. What makes Cohen's characters so peculiarly readable is not only their language, clothes, and physiognomy but, above all, the spatial dimensions of life histories that could easily be travel accounts. Their movements across space map out their personalities and historical experiences for the reader. This is precisely the case with a 'primal scene' from Cohen's 'Oh you, human brothers' (*Ô vous, frères humains*) from 1972, which is key to his literary oeuvre. Decades earlier, just months after the war's end in 1945, Cohen had published this scene in two parts, under the title 'My tenth birthday' (Jour de mes dix ans) in the prominent exile periodical *La France libre*. An abridged version appeared in September of that year in the journal *Esprit*.

'My tenth birthday' appeared on Cohen's fiftieth birthday. It was the first publication in *La France libre* to carry his own name and not the pseudonym 'Jean Mahan.' The text is divided into thirty-seven short sections, each with a separate heading. The first section is 'Childhood recollections' (Souvenirs d'enfance), a title that subsequently becomes 'Recollections of a Jewish childhood' (Souvenirs d'enfance juive).[68] Without analyzing in detail the text's characteristic divergence of first- and third-person singular voices, I want to note that the solipsistic individual, seated in front of a mirror and reminiscing about his past

---

[67] For a biography of Cohen, see the monograph by his friend Gérard Valbert: *Albert Cohen, le seigneur*. Paris: Grasset 1990.
[68] Albert Cohen: 'Jour de mes dix ans.' In: *La France libre*, 16 July and 15 August 1945, p. 193.

in writing, is hardly all that this text offers. The narrative voice paints a picture not of one but of many Jews. Like the I-narrator on his tenth birthday, they approach a street vendor on their way home from school. The vendor, who is hawking an all-purpose spot remover, carefully inspects the boys' physiognomy and tells them to be on their way: 'You, you are a Jewboy, yeah, ... you are a dirty Jew, you are greedy, yeah, your father works in international finance, yeah, you came here and eat the bread of the French, yeah, but we don't like you dirty Jews, what a dirty race.'[69] This key scene has an individual and a collective dimension. We find much the same in Alain Finkielkraut's writings. Taking recourse to Jean-Paul Sartre's *Reflections on the Jewish Question* (*Réflexions sur la question juive*) Finkielkraut, who was born in Paris in 1949, begin his (self-) critical and at times provocative engagement with the Jewish self-image and Jewish constructions of identity with a similar ascription of an identity from the outside: the *juif imaginaire*, the imaginary Jew, is 'born' only in the gaze of the other and his cursing.[70] The birth scene in Cohen's 'My tenth birthday' works in the much same way. The trap that Finkielkraut, who had read Cohen closely, sets through 'the obligation to think of Judaism in term of myself and of identity' snaps shut.[71]

This key scene of a person's coerced transformation into a Jew takes place in the street among a crowd of onlookers who raise not a single voice in defense of the child. All of them are amply familiar with anti-Semitic propaganda and would appear at least to abide it. In this open, public space, there is no counter-discourse; the I-narrator is defenseless before the blond aggressor's exclusionary mechanisms. The historical background of this episode, which forms the nucleus of 'My tenth birthday,' fades into the text. It conveys the anti-Semitic atmosphere of a Marseilles that, in 1905, was still caught up in the furor of the Dreyfus Affair. Cohen's vendor of spot removers is sure to allude to this amidst the commonplaces of his anti-Semitic discourse. Being expelled from the community without warning marks the beginning of the young boy's 'migration' that, after several short respites, finds its (temporary) end in the parental home in the tale's last section. The approach to the crowd of spectators around the street-vendor prompts a diametrically opposed, non-autonomous movement

---

69 'Toi, tu es un Youpin, hein.... tu es un sale Juif, tu es avare hein, ton père est de la finance internationale hein, tu viens manger le pain des Français hein, eh ben nous, on n'aime pas les sales Juifs par ici, c'est une sale race.' Cohen: 'Jour de mes dix ans,' p. 193.
70 Alain Finkielkraut: *Le Juif imaginaire*. Paris: Seuil 1980, p. 10.
71 '[L]'obligation de penser judaïsme en termes de moi et d'identité.' Cohen: 'Jour de mes dix ans', p. 215.

that casts the boy out of the community and into society at large. The youth roams the streets of Marseilles, following walls that double as his first Wailing Wall. He walks among the indifferent mob aimlessly, like a *juif errant*.

The next section, 'A concentration camp in miniature' (Un camp de concentration en miniature), takes the protagonist to the railroad station. As is often the case in Cohen's work, trains symbolize transportation to the concentration camps, a fate that also threatened the Jews of Marseilles after the German occupation of the *Zone libre*. Here, the locus of the concentration camp in miniature is the train station lavatory, which is eminently unsuitable as a transitory space but to which the boy retreats in his desperation to protect himself from an outside world that has become threatening. The vendor's index finger drives the boy from the community and already assigns him a place in (still virtual) concentration and death camps of whose existence Cohen was first to learn in his exile in Britain and which he himself had been able to escape only narrowly. The adult Cohen's later knowledge of this fact informs the situation of his ten-year-old protagonist, whose transformation into a Jew in Marseilles during the Dreyfus Affair represents the Jewish people in their *errance*. It also *prefigures* the concentration camps in a projection that oscillates between 1905 and 1945, between narrated time and narrative time.

There are several 'reenactments' of this key scene in the text itself. Repetition of the street vendor's accusatory words quickly becomes representation: with the help of his five fingers standing for the five figures in Cohen's novel, the boy stages a private performance that transforms the lavatory, that 'camp de concentration en miniature,' into a place of self-reflection and art. The narrative I lets his fingers dance in the same way that the novelists himself repeatedly makes his protagonists dance through his fictional cycles. In the concentration camp, art is juxtaposed to the unbearable *errance* in a hostile external world and becomes a critical factor in warding off thoughts of suicide. Already implicit in Cohen's prefiguration of the concentration camp is the notion of artistic work as an expression and tool of the enduring will to live and of knowledge for survival. Both create their own spaces in his fictions. The transitory interior space – a transit camp of sorts – offers only momentary refuge. The toilet attendant is annoyed with the boy for having spent so much time in the station's lavatory, and after she drives him out, his aimless wandering resumes. The narrator overdetermines this episode historically, and, as in the case of the 'Wailing Wall,' turns it into a culturally re-coded collective history. The processes of vectorization become quite obvious here as story turns to history: 'I walked. My hereditary roaming [errance] had begun.'[72] For the first time, this wandering jew (juif errant) is able to decipher the words on the city walls that he passes: 'Death to the Jews!' (Mort aux juifs!). In passing, as it were, the protagonist moves from being an outcast to being a member of a Chosen People, truly recognizing himself as he passes by a mirror in jeweler's shop and greets his reflection. The outcast has become the 'prince of exile.'[73]

At the end of the text and of the protagonist's errant, the banished Chosen One returns to his parental home, and thus to the safe haven of inherited history: 'oh sweet ghetto of my dead childhood.'[74] Following the death of childhood is the birth of a Jewish identity as one both ostracized and chosen. The boy's return to his parental home turns his aimless wanderings and his stay in the concentration camp into a circle that makes his transformation into a Jew meaningful. In the dialectic of his homelessness, the Jewish Odysseus does find his way home. At the same time, he also finds a new way: that of his own writing.

Emma Kann, or writing in the concentration camp and coming home to a foreign place

Emma Kann was born in 1914 in Frankfurt am Main. Several months after completing high school, the Jewish Kann left Germany for Britain in September 1933. In 1936, she arrived in Belgium after myriad obstacles and, in 1940, fled to France. In the summer of that same year, she was interned for some four weeks in the concentration camp of Gurs at the foot of the Pyrenees, from which she was able to escape as a result of the chaos that followed in the wake of France's capitulation. After fleeing France in 1942, Kann reached Havana by way of Casablanca, and in March 1945, she gained admittance to the USA, where she lived, mostly in New York, until her return to Germany in 1981. She began to write in English in 1948, and it was only with her return to Germany that she 'returned to her mother tongue.'[75] Emma Kann's biography is inseparable from her numerous lyrics which, so far, have been published only in excerpts in a few volumes

---

[72] 'J'allai. ... Mon héréditaire errance avait commencé.' Cohen: 'Jour de mes dix ans,' p. 287.
[73] Cohen: 'Jour de mes dix ans,' p. 292.
[74] '[Ô] doux ghetto privé de mon enfance morte.' Cohen: 'Jour de mes dix ans,' p. 294. Albert Cohen's Geneva home was secured against the outside world with multiple locks and bolts. As many have testified, it was only with great reluctance that he ever left the seclusion of his house.
[75] 'Seit 1981 kehrte ich wieder zur Muttersprache zurück.' Emma Kann, 'Biographische Notizen.' In: *Exil. Forschung, Erkenntnisse, Ergebnisse* VI.1 (1986), p. 67.

of poetry. Written in the year of her flight from Germany (but published decades later), the 1933 poem 'Homeless' (Heimatlos) is Kann's first literary articulation of the condition of exile:

> The hills are near, and the sea is close to me,
> Yet the homeland is so far from me.
> Not only hills and sea separate us,
> These I would gladly traverse.
>
> We are separated by an abyss much deeper
> Than the orbiting earth knows.
> It is its hatred and its rage
> That keeps me apart from my homeland.
>
> I could go home. It is not so far,
> not so remote on the map.
> Yet my homeland no longer exists at home.
> I am a stranger to the people there.
>
> A stranger there and a stranger here,
> And nowhere am I known;
> And even if I wander across hills and the sea,
> I will not find a homeland.[76]

The frequent recurrence of the central lexemes 'homeland' and 'home,' 'strange' and 'remote' underscores the loss of one's homeland that the poem's title already signals: the loss of a homeland from which one is separated not by natural barriers but by historical experience, not by spatial distance but by an affective distance from hate and rage. The resulting chasm that opens up between 'home' and 'homeland' appears as a process of estrangement on a truly planetary scale: there is no way out of exile. The aimlessness of the wandering self suggests a homelessness that leads to a deterritorialization that makes the entire world into an exile: '*mundus totus exilium est.*'[77] As the triple iteration of the words 'hills' and 'sea' shows, having escaped has not (yet) produced a homeland; it is the

---

76 'Die Hügel sind nah und das Meer ist mir nah, / doch die Heimat ist mir so fern; / es trennt mich von ihr nicht nur Hügel und Meer, das überbrückte ich gern. / Es trennt mich von ihr ein viel tieferer Schlund als die kreisende Erde ihn kennt; / es ist ihr Hass und es ist ihre Wut / was von der Heimat mich trennt. / Ich könnte nach Hause; es ist nicht so weit, auf der Karte nicht so weit fort. / Doch zu Hause ist meine Heimat nicht mehr, / fremd bin ich den Menschen dort. / Fremd bin ich hier und fremd bin ich dort und nirgends bin ich bekannt, / und wandre ich auch über Hügel und Meer, / ich finde kein Heimatland.' Kann, 'Biographische Notizen,' p. 67.
77 Auerbach: 'Philology and Weltliteratur,' p. 17.

point of departure for an errancy in an abstract, interchangeable *landscape of exile*,

In the poems Kann composed in the Gurs concentration camp in 1940, the movement is away a movement that others force.[78] Added to the homeless and aimlessness is, at times, a lack of will power that drives the I forward. The world's vastness, as it already appears in the poem 'Homeless,' stands in contrast to the camp's spatial restrictions: the I's state of siege leads to the creation of spaces of resistance whose refuge, beyond thought, is the I's physical body. In 'To someone far away' (An Jemand Fernes) another poem from Gurs, Kann writes: 'Your name may not enter the brain, / For there it would only produce pain.'[79] The loss of a future follows the loss of a homeland space, as is illustrated in the poem 'Frieden im Krieg' (Peace in war), written shortly after Kann's release from the camp in 1940 and first published in 2004: 'Yesterday died. Tomorrow died. / Sight banished thought, / And between death and death it enjoys / What the hours grant it.'[80]

The second and final stanza of the poem with the characteristic title 'The vagabond' (Der Vagabund), according to Kann 'probably written shortly after [her] release from Gurs,'[81] also stresses the absence of home and homeland. While it underscores the importance of the landscape that fascinates the I, a goal once again comes into view:

> I have no home that comes with me,
> And none that stands far away.
> A high mountain, a green meadow,
> A beautiful view are my world.
> But there is an aim to my journey:
> The freedom that my mind keeps for itself. [82]

---

[78] Ottmar Ette: *ÜberLebenswissen: Die Aufgabe der Philologie*. Berlin: Kulturverlag Kadmos, p. 191.
[79] 'Dein Name darf nicht ins Gehirn, / Dort schüfe er nur Schmerz.' Kann, 'Biographische Notizen,' p. 69.
[80] 'Das Gestern starb. Das Morgen starb. / Das Sehn vertrieb das Denken, / Und zwischen Tod und Tod geniesst / Es was die Stunden schenken.' Quoted in Ette, *ÜberLebenswissen*, p. 193.
[81] Emma Kann to Ottmar Ette, October 16, 2003.
[82] 'Ich hab kein Haus, das mit mir geht, / Und keines, das im Fernen steht. / Ein hoher Berg, ein grünes Feld, / Ein schöner Blick sind meine Welt. / Doch ein Ziel hat auch meine Fahrt: / Die Freiheit, die mein Geist sich wahrt.' Emma Kann: 'Der Vagabund.' In: *Mnemosyne* 15 (1998), p. 15.

In this passage, that we can see clearly how the dialectic of homelessness after a process of de-territorialization has become what one may well call writing without a fixed abode. Flight, deportation, internment, release, and renewed flight, this time not to France but from France and Europe to the New World, open pathways between Kann's poems. In the three-stanza poem 'At sea, I' (Auf dem Meer, I) from 1942, the Atlantic crossing, the I's being-there aboard the ship, is figured as a sinking down of 'yesterday' and 'tomorrow,' which, in 'The vagabond,' surrenders itself entirely to a 'drifting through good fortune and bad' (durch Glück und Unglück treibend) in which 'my I will lose itself in space' (mein Ich im All verliert). Images of drifting on the ocean and through space, through the outer space of an essentially uninhabitable and non-ecumenical world, also appears in the 1941 poem 'We once lived on one earth' (Wir Lebten Einst Auf Einer Erde), where the one world has broken into pieces. Here is the second stanza:

> Until what united us as earth
> broke into pieces. The rind cracked.
> Now we drift among the world's shards
> Alone on fate's path.[83]

'The Land of My Childhood,' the title of an English-language poem that Kann composed in the USA in 1973, is figured as a past made continuously present. But, in contrast to the poem 'Homeless,' this land is now not a geographical entity, one of 'the world's shards;' rather, it is omnipresent in its affective dimension: 'Hatred and fear are always present, / And one wrong step will set them free.'[84] A single false move can unleash the past's (self-)destructive movements and injuries. Breaking open old scars, it can set in motion again, and almost inescapably, both individual and collective trans-historical patterns of movement.

Emma Kann's poems testify to a will to survive that turns into a knowledge for survival to the extent that the act of being moved both in a spatial and an emotional sense can once again change from an aimless errancy to an itinerary whose purpose is to come home. Such homecoming can, of course, no longer be to a distant land of childhood. It is more a matter of coming home in a language that has become foreign to oneself while at the same time offering the habitable and revitalized place of a homeless homeland. The 1981 poem 'Coming home to

---

83 'Bis das, was uns als Erde einte, / In Stücke fiel. Die Rinde sprang. / Nun treiben wir auf Weltenscherben / Allein des Schicksals Weg entlang.' Kann: 'Biographische Notizen,' p. 70.
84 Kann: 'Biographische Notizen,' p. 74.

the German language (Heimkehr zur deutschen Sprache) reflects this coming home to a foreign land as language about language.

> When I return to the German language,
> It is not the language I knew
> When I left this land.
> The words still string together as sentences,
> As they did then, as always.
> Yet the springs from which these words arise,
> The invisible ones, have changed.
> Old rock decomposed.
> Deeds, suffering, thoughts
> Created new scree.
> Rain falls down.
> Water rises once more.
> Through altered strata.[85]

As before, images of hills and the sea, of land and water, appear integrated into a natural life. But the seemingly immutable is exposed to a process of erosion that is as irreversible as life itself. The deterritorialization of the homeland into language shows that even one's mother tongue is closely interwoven with 'The Land of My Childhood' and does not transcend time and place. The author's last name appears at the end of the second line, almost as time's signature, in the past tense of the first person singular: 'ich kannte' (I knew). The homecoming of this female Odysseus is a coming home to a foreign place and, moreover, a coming home to one's self as if it were foreign. Emma Kann's writing is a persistent attempt at tracing the dialectic of homelessness through its 'altered strata,' giving it a linguistic shape in which survival, the state of having escaped, becomes the only thinkable, livable, and writable home.

Max Aub, or the concentration camp lists

Max Aub was born in Paris in 1903 to a German father and a French mother, neither of whom practiced their forebears' Jewish faith. In 1914, the 'boche' and his family were forced to flee France and settled in Valencia, where young Max lear-

---

85 'Wenn ich zur deutschen Sprache zurückkehre, / Ist es nicht die Sprache, die ich kannte, / Als ich dies Land verließ. / Noch fügen sich Worte zu Sätzen / Wie damals, wie immer. / Doch die Quellen, aus denen die Worte steigen, / Die unsichtbaren, haben sich verändert. / Altes Gestein zerfiel. / Taten, Leiden, Gedanken / Schufen ein neues Geröll. / Regen fällt nieder. / Wasser steigt wieder empor / Durch veränderte Schichten.' Kann: 'Biographische Notizen,' p. 75.

ned Catalan and Spanish and adopted the latter as his literary language. Aub was active at various levels on the side of the Spanish republic in the Spanish Civil War.[86] After his flight from France, he was interned twice in the concentration camp Le Vernet d'Ariège (from May 30 to November 30, 1940 and again from September 6 to November 24, 1941)[87] and was later shipped in a cattle transport to the Algerian work camp of Djelfa, from which he successfully escaped to Mexico via Casablanca in 1942. He became a Mexican citizen in 1955. At the center of Aub's entire literary output is a single, ambiguous word that always ties back to his experience of internment: *campo*. The ambiguity of this term, which reflects the camp experience from ever-new perspectives, opens a space for writing that developed within the camp itself and left its imprint on all of Aub's writings in exile.[88] Aub's lyrical diary, *Diario de Djelfa*, underscores the fact that these poems were written in the concentration camp Djelfa on the Atlas plateau.[89] It also makes plain to its readers that this writing was necessary to the survival of an author who otherwise would have been unable to bear and resist the strains of this extreme situation. Here, literature and writing are the forces that prevent the state of exception from taking hold of a human being and pulling him down into a maelstrom that obsessively swirls around a faceless center.[90] At the same time, this writing creates a world that exists at the remove of any aestheticization, a world in which the state of exception has long become the rule.

Max Aub's oeuvre can be understood as a motile writing whose paradoxical focus is the concentration camp's location. After the French consul in Mexico rejected Aub's application for an entry visa into the country where he had been born, the exiled writer appealed to the French president Vincent Auriol in an open letter dated February 22, 1951. Aub's plea was not for help but for justice:

---

[86] For Aub's activities during the Spanish Civil War and especially his friendship with André Malraux see Ottmar Ette / Mercedes Figueras et al. (eds): *Max Aub – André Malraux: Guerrra civil, exilio y literatura*. Madrid: Vervuert 2005 (Iberoamericana).
[87] For the exact circumstances see Ignacio Soldevila Durante, *El compromiso de la imaginación: Vida y obra de Max Aub*. Segorbe: Fundación Max Aub 1999, p. 43.
[88] See Ette: *ÜberLebenswissen*, p. 202ff.
[89] See Max Aub: *Obras Completas: Edición crítica*. Estudio introductorio y notas Arcadio López Casanova et al., vol. 1: *Obra poética completa*. Edited by Joan Oleza Simó. Valencia: Biblioteca Valenciana 2001, p. 93.
[90] See Max Aub: *Hablo como hombre*. Edición, introducción y notas de Gonzalo Sobejano. Segorbe: Fundación Max Aub 2002, p. 112.

> In March of 1940, I was arrested as a Communist because of what I later learned was an anonymous denunciation. I have known concentration camps – Paris, Vernet, Djelfa – and jails – in Marseille, Nice, Algeria. I was led through Toulouse in handcuffs in order to be thrown into a cattle car and sent to forced work in the Sahara desert and other pleasant experiences reserved for antifascists.[91]

A vital point for him was that he was still being treated along the lines of the index cards and lists that the police of the Vichy government had drawn up about him: 'I know that I exist in the files, and that is the only thing that matters.'[92] Aub levels a charge against a nation still caught up with the Vichy regime and the 'archives of the fascist police' (los archivos de una policía fascista).[93] It was high time, he implies, that the country came to grips with its past and distanced itself from the 'monstrous way of understanding the world according to police procedures.'[94]

It was not only in Franco's Spain but also in republican France that Max Aub was forced to experience with his own body that the old lists had survived and retained their power. Consequently, lists had to be a part of his literary engagement with the concentration camp experience. The writing during internment was soon to be followed by a post-internment writing that stood clearly under the aegis of the concentrationary universe and in which camp lists were of special importance. One of the most fascinating twentieth-century literary depictions of life and survival in the concentration camp is Aub's 'The raven manuscript: Jacobo's history' (*Manuscrito Cuervo: Historia de Jacobo*), a *frictional* tale narrated from the perspective of the raven Jacobo.[95] In 1952, a year after his open letter to the French president, the 'Raven manuscript' appeared in Aub's own journal, *Sala de espera,* and was published in its final form in 1955. Without going into the highly complex structure of a text riddled with lists, I want to emphasize the degree to which this raven's report on the world as a concentration

---

91 'En marzo de 1940, por una denuncia, posiblemente anónima, fui detenido, a lo que supe después, por comunista. Conocí campos de concentración – París, Vernet, Djelfa – , cárceles – Marsella, Niza, Argel –, fui conducido esposado a través de Toulouse para ser transportado, en las bodegas de un barco ganadero, a trabajar en el Sahara y otras amenidades reservadas a los antifascistas.' Aub: *Hablo como hombre*, p. 112.
92 'Ya sé que estoy fichado, y que esto es lo que cuenta, lo que vale.' Aub: *Hablo como hombre*, p. 112.
93 Aub: *Hablo como hombre*, p. 115.
94 '[H]ay que enfrentarse con esa monstruosa manera de entender policiacamente al mundo.' Aub: *Hablo como hombre*, p. 116.
95 See Ottmar Ette: *Roland Barthes: Eine intellektuelle Biographie*. Frankfurt am Main: Suhrkamp 1998, p. 308–12.

camp consciously employs the imagery of the 'concentrationary' universe in which the camp becomes the place where all things human (and thus also, and especially, inhuman) concentrate.'[96] Human fates flare up briefly, in highly compressed imagery, before receding again into the darkness of history and of the story itself. In the chapter 'Some men' (Algunos hombres), some of the concentrationists, are torn from the anonymity to which the nameless terror of persecution and extermination had consigned them in the era of twentieth-century totalitarianism. At the very opening of the chapter, the raven Jacobo notes that there are some six thousand internees in the camp, most of whom do not even know why they are being held.[97] Nor do their guards. The raven narrator proceeds to pick out at random certain index cards documenting internees of the concentration camp in southern France during June 1940. This ploy is typical of Aub's strategy to have characters pop up suddenly and then disappear. Aub's telegram-like prose sketches a handful of biographies and outlines the ever-different ways in which individual lives were disrupted. The arbitrary ascriptions of identity, as much as the 'travel movements,' show clearly how the dialectic of Enlightenment with its totalitarianisms also becomes a dialectic of homelessness that is no more strongly concentrated than in the camp. Here are a few excerpts from Jacobo's list, which, in turn, refers to other lists:

> *Julien Altmann*, watchmaker, thirty-five years old, French, previously German. Of average stature, not much hair, long nose, reddened eyes.
> *Jerzy Karpaty*, shoemaker, Hungarian. Short, fat, but not so much any more. Crooked legs. Easy to handle. A chatterer. He also does not know why he is here but suspects that the police found his name on the list of a *Committee of Friends* for Hungarian Interbrigadists.
> *Ludwig Schumacher*, chemist, chemical engineer, German. Young, tall, strong. Since 1933 a refugee in France. All papers in good order, registered with the foreign legion, just passed a health check-up.
> *Gonzalo Rivera Torres*, Spaniard, grump. Raven nose, raven black hair, and raven black fingernails. Mechanic. One of few who do not complain. Communist. Passes his time singing. His most urgent wish: to get hold of a guitar. After he left the concentration camp, he was in Paris for just two days before they arrested him again. He knows how things work.
> *Jan Wisniak*, Czech, ugly face, one-eyed, without profession or wealth, as far as is known, a man of foul moods. Seventy-two years old. Traveled the world in order to see it – in his words.
> *Franz Gutmann*, supposedly from Luxemburg, furrier. His wife denounced him as German. He did want to agree to the divorce even though she cuckolded him.

---

96 Max Aub: *Manuscrito del cuervo: Historia de Jacobo*. Introducción, edición y notas de José Antonio Pérez Bowie, con un Epílogo de José María Naharro-Calderón. Segorbe: Fundación Max Aub / Universidad de Alcalá de Henares 1999, p. 96.
97 See Aub: *Manuscrito del cuervo*, p. 154.

Paul Marchand, painter, Belgian. Personal friend of King Leopold III. He claims. Tall, fat. By bragging about this friendship, he does not find friends at the official places that currently accuse the Belgian Sovereign of treason.
Ettore and Francesco Giardini, Italian, twins, fat, short, bearded, high forehead, glasses, a little like Snow White's dwarfs. Both were arrested because one was not a hundred percent sure which one was the suspect. One of them is supposed to be an anarchist. But they don't say which one.[98]

Faces emerge from facelessness, the light shines on lives for a brief moment before they sink back into formlessness, into the facelessness of a statistic of the phatic. The cunning of this list consists in the fact that it presents to the reader not only the absurdity and caprice of totalitarian rule but also its openendedness: this catalog could include anyone, even the reader, in a movement that – when one considers the internees' individual lives – is highly varied and discontinuous, yet still linear on the whole. This is the movement of history that sweeps everything along with it, no matter what the native lands and the life goals of the various camp detainees in this catalogue of lives. The movement and perspective that emerge here are comparable to those of Benjamin's Angel of History who, as he is being pushed back in time, sees at his feet rubble being heaped upon rubble: destroyed lives caught up in the vortex of a history whose dialectic knows only the homeland of having escaped. Like the Angel of History, the writer has no time to rouse the dead and piece together that which lies in

---

98 '*Julien Altmann*, relojero, treinta y cinco años, francés, después de haber sido alemán. Estatura regular, poco pelo, nariz larga, traje raído, ojos enrojecidos... *Jerzy Karpaty*, zapatero, húngaro. Pequeño, gordo, pero ya no tanto; con las piernas arqueadas. Sin complicaciones. Judío. Parlanchín. Tampoco sabe por qué está aquí, aunque supone que la policía halló su apellido en la lista de una *Amicale* de internacionales húngaros... *Ludwig Schumacher*, químico, ingeniero químico, alemán. Joven, alto, fuerte. Refugiado en Francia desde 1933. Con todos sus papeles en regla, alistado en la Legión Extranjera, en trance de revisión médica... *Gonzalo Rivera Torres*, español, cetrino, nariz corvina, pelo corvino, uñas corvinas. Mecánico. De los pocos que no protestan. Comunista. Se pasa el tiempo cantando. Su única preocupación: conseguir una guitarra. A los dos días de llegar a París, salido de un campo de concentración del sur de Francia, le volvieron a agarrar. Está de vuelta... *Jan Wisniack*, checo, mal encarado, tuerto, sin oficio ni beneficio conocido, hombre de malas pulgas. Setenta y dos años. Andaba por el mundo, para verlo – según dice.... *Franz Gutmann*, dícese luxemburgués; peletero. Denunciado por su mujer como alemán. Él no le quería conceder el divorcio, a pesar de los cuernos... *Paul Marchand*, pintor, belga, a lo que él dice: amigo personal del rey Leopoldo III. Alto, gordo. La amistad que pregona no le favorece con las autoridades, que tildan, actualmente, al soberano belga de traidor... *Héctor y Francisco Girardini* italianos, *hermanos gemelos*, gordos, bajos, con barba, frente despejada, gafas, un poco al estilo de los enanos de Blanca Nieves, los detuvieron a los dos porque no sabían a ciencia cierta quién era el *sospechoso*. Dicen que uno es anarquista. Ellos no dicen cuál.' Aub: *Manuscrito del cuervo*, p. 154–166.

ruins.⁹⁹ For the writer, too, the barely achieved escape is the only homeland that is still conceivable in a world that has become one big concentration camp. This is the real answer to the question as to what remains of the totalitarianism and the wars, the persecutions and the collaborations of the twentieth century.

Cécile Wajsbrot, the post-figuration of the concentration camp, and the voices of the past made present

In her 1999 essay 'For literature' (*Pour la literature*), Cécile Wajsbrot (b. 1954) draws attention in no uncertain terms to the great divide in twentieth-century history, which, though of major significance for French literature, was blithely passed over in France for a long time.

Between Balzac, Flaubert, the Breton of the First Surrealist Manifesto, and Robbe-Grillet, there lies an abyss: there is 1939-2945, the horror of Nazism, the first atomic bomb, the systematic murder of Europe's Jews and the silence that surrounded it; the occupation of France, Vichy, the collaboration, and then the cleansing, especially in literary and artistic circles, what could be said and what not, those who paid and those continued as if nothing had happened.¹⁰⁰

Despite the distance in time and their different perspectives, Wajsbrot's accord with Aub's attestations from 1951 is remarkable. Both agree that '*French society* of the 1950s, 1960s, and 1970, and even to the present day, has chosen to close its eyes and to turn a new page, to turn to other matters.'¹⁰¹ In contrast to the literatures of other countries, such as Germany or Russia, where it was not only contemporary witnesses who came to grips with this period but also those who were born 'in the shadow of its memory,' French literature has studiously glossed over the fact that our world was born from World War II and that everything, including the 'monuments to the dead' (les monuments aux morts) –

---

99 Benjamin: *Illuminations*, p. 257–58.
100 'Entre Balzac, Flaubert, le Breton du *Premier Manifeste* et Robbe-Grillet, il y a un abîme, il y a 1939–1945, l'horreur du nazisme, la première bombe atomique, l'extermination systématique des Juifs d'Europe et le silence autour; l'Occupation en France, Vichy, la collaboration, et puis l'épuration, notamment dans le milieu littéraire et artistique, ce qu'elle a permis de dire et ce qu'elle a permis de taire, ceux qui ont payé et ceux qui ont continué, comme avant, comme si de rien n'était.' Cécile Wajsbrot: *Pour la littérature*. Paris: Zulma 1999, p. 23.
101 'Dans son ensemble, la *société française* des années cinquante, soixante, et soixante-dix – et on pourrait continuer jusqu'à aujourd'hui – a choisi de fermer les yeux, et de tourner la page, pour passer à autre chose.' Wajsbrot: *Pour la littérature*, p. 23.

everything except, of course, literature – reminds us of this fact.[102] In French literature, so Wajsbrot, the inquiry into this past has just begun: 'Our primal scene is Vichy, and, like every primal scene, it resides in the half light of an unconscious that just awaits being able to forget it.'[103] As in all primal scenes, Wajsbrot's psychoanalytic diction suggests, repression is at work; there is a 'refoulement' that reverberates in the sphere of literary theory.

Already in 1990, in his important book on France's collective coming-to-terms with the German occupation and with French collaboration during World War II, Henry Rousso spoke of the trauma of Vichy and of the Vichy 'syndrome.' Silke Segler-Messner notes in her own study that it was 'only decades after more than 70,000 Jewish fellow citizens had died in the concentration camps that they were officially mourned.'[104] Geoffrey Hartman, in turn, interprets this psychological repression as collective self-defense that continued for fifty years after the fact, with many French Jews even today employing the same strategy.[105] It clearly remains a question to what degree such mechanisms of psychological repression were an integral part of the deplorably homogeneous image of a 'Europe without Jews'[106] – and not only in France. Cécile Wajsbrot, for one, has clearly adopted a position in favor of a literature that meets head on the challenge of careful inquiry into the emergence of National Socialism and the inhuman consequences of totalitarianism.

In her plea for literature, the French author emphasizes that, in the final analysis, it is only the literary work that counts: 'L'œuvre est ce qui compte.'[107] Literature's purpose and justification, the 'raison d'être des écrivains' and the 'raison d'être de la littérature,' lie in the uniqueness of what literary writing

---

102 Wajsbrot: *Pour la littérature*, p. 25.
103 'Notre scène originelle, c'est Vichy, et comme toute scène originelle, elle gît dans la pénombre d'un inconscient qui ne demande qu'à oublier.' Wajsbrot, *Pour la littérature*, p. 27.
104 Segler-Messner: *Literatur und Zeugenschaft*, p. 52.
105 See Segler-Messner: *Literatur und Zeugenschaft*, p. 53, and Geoffrey Hartman: *The Longest Shadow: In the Aftermath of the Holocaust*. Bloomington: Indiana University Press 1996, p. 73.
106 Approaching the matter from a completely different perspective, Bernard Wasserstein invokes the spectre of a 'Europe without Jews' in a period that witnessed a *Vanishing Diaspora*, the title of his 1996 book, with the subtitle 'The Jews in Europe since 1945.' In this work, he argues that 'perhaps the most important repercussion of the Holocaust was that postwar Jewish life has been characterized by an obsession with survival. Beyond the borders of Israel, and particularly in the open societies of the West, the strong pressure to assimilate has greatly diminished the chances that there will be any collective survival of the Jews.' See Bernard Wasserstein: *Europa ohne Juden: Das europäische Judentum seit 1945*. Cologne: Kiepenheuer & Witsch 1999, p. 327ff.
107 Wajsbrot: *Pour la littérature*, p. 58.

makes its own vision of the world.[108] It seems to me that such view demands from literature – and for literature – the aesthetic shaping of a knowledge-for-living that, in its multi-dimensionality and polysemousness, develops a vital and socially responsible relationship to the many different aspects of life and of survival.[109] Of critical importance to Wajsbrot, who has been dividing her time between Paris and Berlin for several years now, is the engagement with a historical period that my discussion so far has portrayed as the point of departure and reference for a literary tradition that should be regarded as foundational for the worldwide development of the Literatures without a fixed Abode. What happened in the wake of two world wars and the persecution and murder of the Jews at mid-century has left its mark on the concepts of exile and diaspora in the literatures (and the literary scholarship) that have emerged more strongly since the beginning of the twenty-first century. The Literatures without a fixed Abode are impossible to imagine without due consideration of the Shoah; but they cannot be reduced to this particular tradition and fault line alone.

It is in keeping with the spirit of a poetics that focuses on (the concept of) the literary work that Cécile Wajsbrot, in her search for answers to the question 'what of Auschwitz remains?' did not limit herself to the genre of the essay but also resorted to other narrative and representational forms. In the slim volume *Beaune-la-Rolande* (2004), which appeared at the same time as her novel *Le Tour du lac*, Wajsbrot's narrator, from the very opening paragraph of the first section (of five), leaves no doubt that the ensuing treatment of the theme of concentration camps and Jewish persecution in France will require a wide array of peripatetic figures and both linear and cyclical ideas of time:

The emptiness of the country road prolongs the streets' silence, Sunday is the worst of all days, and this Sunday is the worst of all Sundays, the highway from Chartres to Orléans has become the highway from Nantes to Bordeaux, but this is all that has changed, and the years pass like miles, one like the other, unpalatable, and spring changes and stretches shadowless into summer, is late for winter, one leaves the highway and the country road extends straight on, cuts through a monotonous, flat, mercilessly horizontal landscape.[110]

---

108 Wajsbrot: *Pour la littérature*, p. 59.
109 'Quelque chose, la déportation, l'exil, la guerre, la catastrophe. Et quelqu'un l'a vécu et survécu.' Wajsbrot: *Pour la littérature*, p. 49.
110 'Le vide de la route prolonge le silence des rues, le dimanche est le pire des jours et ce dimanche, le pire des dimanches, l'autoroute Chartres-Orléans est devenue Nantes-Bordeaux mais c'est bien tout ce qui a changé, et les années défilent comme les kilomètres, une à une, fastidieuses, et le printemps varie sans ombre, s'étirant vers l'été, s'attardant en hiver, on

78 —— Figurations

To the inescapability of time's pitiless progress, amplified by the interspersed cycles of weeks and years, corresponds to the no less inexorable horizontality of a two-dimensional topography. The landscape becomes merely transitory; it is a place of passage that takes one along highways congested by vacation traffic toward the south. In this landscape of transit, between the lines that roll along, we can sense another passage, one that temporally recedes further and further into the past: Beaune-la-Rolande, a transit camp 'used' for refugees of the Spanish Civil War. This place takes everything onto itself: 'nothing exists other than memory, remembrance, and commemoration.'[111]

But is Beaune-la-Rolande, as one might assume from the annual ritual of official commemorative speeches, nothing more than a 'lieu de mémoire,' a place for memory? In the hopelessness of her existence 'on the road' (sur la route),[112] the first-person narrator is simultaneously trapped in and complicit with a genealogy that links her with her grandmother. Although she has lost their voice (la voix), she sets out on her journey (sa voie),[113] a journey in the 'shadows of memory' (l'ombre portée du souvenir), as Wajsbrot calls it in *Pour la littérature*.[114] This path is painful both at the individual and the collective level. In *Beaune-la-Rolande*, it leads the narrator to doubt (and despair) whether in France, 'in this country' (dans ce pays), there exists anything like a 'mémoire collective,' a collective memory beyond commemorative plaques.[115]

The imaginary 'voilà,'[116] which her grandmothers perhaps never even uttered, reveals to the first-person narrator her obligation to take a closer look at that from which most others avert their gaze.[117] Above all, the narrator realizes that she must follow the grandmother's voice and her journey, along with the voyage of the grandfather she never knew, who, during the Vichy régime, was taken into custody through a simple green ticket (billet vert), only to be taken away, interned, deported, and murdered. As the search begins, not-knowing and no-longer-being-able-to-know quickly enter the text: 'I know nothing of my

---

quitte l'autoroute puis la route s'étend, droite, coupant un paysage monotone, plat, impitoyablement horizontal.' Wajsbrot: *Beaune-la-Rolande*. Paris: Zulma 2004, p. 7.
111 'Rien n'existe d'autre que la mémoire, le souvenir, la commémoration.' Wajsbrot: *Beaune-la-Rolande*, p. 8.
112 Wajsbrot: *Beaune-la-Rolande*, p. 8.
113 Wajsbrot: *Beaune-la-Rolande*, p. 12.
114 Wajsbrot: *Pour la littérature*, p. 25.
115 Wajsbrot: *Beaune-la-Rolande*, p. 53.
116 Wajsbrot: *Beaune-la Rolande*, p. 8.
117 Wajsbrot: *Pour la littérature*, p. 23.

grandfather, only that he died in Auschwitz.'[118] Memory can no longer reconstruct the words with which the anonymous loudspeaker voice informed the women waiting in front of the barracks of the arrest of their husbands; memory has to it construct this event through multiple meanings: 'What exactly did they say, they will leave, they will be carried along, they will work in a camp, their arrest, detainment, has been temporary, they will be transported, deported, concentrated, which words did they use?'[119] Literature captures all these virtual and, at the same time, very real voices.[120] It knits them together in a fabric that traps history and allows the literary text to take shape. Thus commences the I-narrator's long, endless trip. That the narrative is interlaced with authorial biography lends greater complexity to what, from the beginning, is recognizable as an imbrication of various travel movements and time frames – the days in May of 1941 and the repeating days in May more than half a century later – and travel movements. One entry in the volume's *Journal* is dated Paris, September 12, 1990:

> I was born in 1954 – the war had been over for nine years. My grandmother's husband was dead, deported to Auschwitz. Before he arrived there, he had spent a year in the camp Beaune-la-Rolande near Pithiviers. I did not know this grandfather, but my grandmother told me much – and apparently very early on – about the gas chambers, the camps, the arrest, the police that came to pick up her and the two children, the crossing of the demarcation line, all this, and I carry inside me the images of a different time, of another life, without being able to rid myself of them.[121]

---

118 'De mon grand-père, je ne sais rien, seulement qu'il est mort à Auschwitz.' Wajsbrot: *Beaune-la-Rolande*, p. 14.
119 'Que disaient-ils exactement, ils vont partir, on les emmène, ils vont travailler dans un camp, ils sont momentanément détenus, retenus, transportés, déportés, concentrés, quels mots employèrent-ils?' Wajsbrot: *Beaune-la-Rolande*, p. 10.
120 I can only hint at the importance of these voices; see the successful acoustic staging of an initial draft of this text in a radio play by France Culture ('Atelier de Création Radiophonique'), which was broadcast in July 2003 under the title 'Beaune-la-Rolande: La Cérémonie.' I thank Cécile Wajsbrot for providing me with a recording of it.
121 'Je suis née en 1954—la guerre était finie depuis neuf ans. Le mari de ma grand-mère est mort, déporté à Auschwitz. Avant d'arriver là-bas, il avait passé un an dans le camp de Beaune-la-Rolande, qui se trouve près de Pithiviers. Je n'ai pas connu ce grand-père mais ma grand-mère m'a raconté abondamment, et sans doute très tôt, les chambres à gaz, les camps, l'arrestation, la police venue la chercher avec ses deux enfants, le passage de la ligne de démarcation, tout, et je porte ces images d'un autre temps, d'une autre vie, sans pouvoir m'en débarrasser.' Wajsbrot: *Beaune-la-Rolande*, p. 15–16.

The specification of time and space wraps up the I-narrator in the tale she is telling, but without allowing us to equate the narrative voice with that of the 'real' author external to the text, even though the book's 2004 jacket text refers to the 'author's grandfather' and, in an allusion to the author's own name, notes that in Poland no one requires an explanation as to how to pronounce the name of the unnamed narrator.[122] The narrative voice's *frictionalization*, produced through the oscillation between fiction and diction, turns this voice into a bearer of knowledge-for-living that, in this case, is knowledge about a life whose existence can no longer be directly witnessed but has to mediated by the figure of the grandmother: 'a life that is not mine but whose shadows changes from one hour to the next.'[123] Literature, in its own way, tries to explore this realm of shadows beyond official days of remembrance.

Due to the topographical and climatic similarities that the narrative introduces, the death camp Auschwitz is soon superimposed on the concentration camp Beaune-la-Rolande: 'a piece of central Europe transplanted to one hundred kilometers from Paris.'[124] Auschwitz is everywhere and nowhere: 'Auschwitz is not in Poland; it is an indefinite place that is everywhere and nowhere.'[125] Literature multiplies the places of memory; having become ubiquitous, memory can no longer be emplaced. Everything is set in motion and evades static territorialization. It is hardly surprising, then, that the narrator feels an affinity not to settled persons (sédentaires) but to migrants, those who have been deported, who are refugees: the so-called 'sans-papiers,' without papers.[126] The deportation of the unknown grandfather; the annual pilgrimage of grandmother and granddaughter to the concentration camp of Beaune-la-Rolande; the journey of the granddaughter and narrator to Auschwitz, Krakow, Warsaw, and Vilnius; the deportations, forced migrations, and voluntary journeys – all these combine with erratic and peripatetic figures to produce what one might call a *littérature sans-papiers*, a literature without papers. It is no accident that the preparations of the suffering narrator for her visit to Auschwitz, in the journal entry dated Krakow, 7 May 1990, are linked to a conversation with the Polish poet Baranczak, who emigrated to the USA in 1981 and has now returned to Poland for the

---

122 See Wajsbrot: *Beaune-la-Rolande*, p. 42.
123 '[U]ne vie qui n'est pas la mienne mais dont l'ombre varie avec les heures.' Wajsbrot: *Beaune-la-Rolande*, p. 16
124 '[U]ne portion d'Europe centrale transplantée à cent kilomètres de Paris.' Wajsbrot: *Beaune-la-Rolande*, p. 21
125 'Auschwitz ne se trouve pas en Pologne, c'est un lieu indéfinissable qui est partout et nulle part.' Wajsbrot: *Beaune-la-Rolande*, p. 55.
126 Wajsbrot: *Beaune-la-Rolande*, p. 20.

first time. In this post-figuration of the camp, the camp's prefiguration, through which the ten-year-old boy[127] in Albert Cohen's Marseilles experiences a concentration camp in miniature, connects with the fate of migrants on the turn of the twenty-first century: 'all the refugees, in Sangatte and elsewhere, all those who are turned away, all the Kurds who disembark in Fréjus, the Poles who are thrown in jail because a fire broke out in a small room.'[128] The catalogues of the nation- state's exclusionary mechanisms are long indeed.

Here, the paradigms of movement inherited from Shoah literature join with the vectoral imagination of a literature nourished by mutually overlapping migratory processes. In its post-figuration, the concentration camp becomes a focal point for worldwide movements that intersect and overlap in time and space. In this way, the concentrationary universe becomes a bio-political as well as literary paradigm of a writing that knows itself to be part of the dialectic of homelessness: swept away like Walter Benjamin's Angelus Novus, who cannot and will not close his eyes.

It is a fundamental part of the task of literature and literary scholarship, then, to try to make present the voices of the past, to represent voices (not only of the grandmother) and voyages (not only of the grandfather) and pry them loose from a frozen, distant past. It is not surprising that *Beaune-la-Rolande* cites the famous passage from the 55th chapter of Rabelais's *The Fourth Book* (1694), in which Pantagruel and his companions, on the high seas near the Arctic Sea, suddenly hear voices that horrify many of the travelers. These are, we come to know, the voices of a past battle, a past war, voices frozen in the cold of the Arctic winter until they thaw during springtime and become audible once again.[129] The narrative locates itself in this spatio-temporal echo chamber between being frozen and thawing, between being silent and becoming audible. It situates and temporalizes 'literature's time' (temps de la littérature):[130]

> It is literature that allows us to move from being frozen to thawing and to change the seasons; it is literature that lets us hear the soldiers' voices which they had already thought

---

127 The narrator's mother in *Beaune-la-Rolande* is also ten years old when the French police try to arrest her along with her brother and mother. But, as if by some miracle, these remaining family members are spared, and the family genealogy (the narrator's) remains intact. See Wajsbrot, *Beaune-la-Rolande*, p. 31–32.
128 '[T]ous les réfugiés, à Sangatte ou ailleurs, et tous ceux qu'on refuse, tous les Kurdes débarqués à Fréjus, les Polonais qu'on emprisonne parce qu'un feu s'est déclaré dans une chambre étroite.' Wajsbrot, *Beaune-la-Rolande*, p. 31–32.
129 See Wajsbrot: *Beaune-la-Rolande*, p. 50.
130 See Wajsbrot: *Beaune-la-Rolande*, p. 52.

lost and which, left in limbo, can later, much later, be heard and restored by those who, as writers, also always travel the world's oceans.¹³¹

It is the task both of literature and literary scholarship to make heard that which has long been presumed lost. Such making-heard marks and, at the same time, overcomes frozen distance through travel, by moving through space. The definition, via Rabelais, of the writer as 'navigators of the world' (navigateurs du large) implies that writers are constantly searching for as many (polyphonic) voices as possible, for voices we can (no longer) access in any other way. In the rhythmically and acoustically impressive sounds of Cécile Wajsbrot's prose, the camp's post-figurations offer us the kind of sensual memory space that simultaneously gives us a piece of the future. The acoustic merging of *voix* and *voies* on which *Beaune-la-Rolande* insists also unfolds its creative power in the continuous crossing of our planet's latitudes and longitudes. Voices and voyages are always closely intertwined.

Sound is inseparable from the art of literature. Literature (like its scholarship) takes into itself the voices of the past and revives them by making them an essential part of the knowledges-of-and-for-living and surviving it generates. Literature occupies both a complementary and competitive position vis-à-vis amplifiers, voice recordings, and other storage devices, from loudspeakers to recording machines. Acoustic 'sound carriers' appear at the end of *Beaune-la-Rolande*, and they fail in their task.¹³² The 'microphones, loudspeakers, and sound recordings' will 'fail first.' Even now, we can hardly understand the old recording of a funeral prayer any more, the 'heart rending voice' that always 'moves us to tears' and, 'instead of the names of the disappeared, recited the names of the camps, Auschwitz, Maidanek, Treblinka.' The voice that once uttered the name of the last camp so softly has now become static noise; 'the old recording machine, held up to the microphone, does not help us anymore.'¹³³ The tape re-

---

131 'C'est la littérature qui nous fait passer du gel au dégel et changer de saison, c'est la littérature qui nous fait entendre les paroles des combattants, celles qu'ils croyaient perdues et qui, demeurées en suspens, sont entendues et restituées plus tard, bien plus tard, par les navigateurs du large que sont aussi les écrivains.' Wajsbrot: *Beaune-la-Rolande*, p. 52.
132 See Wajsbrot: *Beaune-la-Rolande*, p. 56.
133 'Peut-être seront-ce eux qui lâcheront les premiers, les micros et les haut-parleurs, les enregistrements – déjà on n'entend plus la prière des morts qui faisait tant pleurer, cette voix déchirante qui, à la place du nom des disparus, récitait le nom des champs, Auschwitz, Maidanek, Treblinka, s'attardant sur ce dernier avec presque douceur, déjà on ne l'entend plus, et le vieux magnétophone porté près du micro ne nous assiste plus.' Wajsbrot: *Beaune-la-Rolande*, p. 56–57.

corders are used up because 'the voices have long fallen silent' (car les voix se sont tués). [134] It is precisely here where we see the power of literature, its artistic ability to keep these voices alive and open not only for the past but also for the future.

The survival of the camp into our present day and, with it, of a homeland characterized by the precarious, conditional state of having-escaped, has spawned Literatures without a fixed Abode, which can be assigned neither to a single national literature nor to a world literature, however defined. This Literature without a fixed Abode, whose imagination is predominantly vectoral, has established itself for some time now in the gray area between national and global literatures. In an unobtrusive yet insistent manner, *Beaune-la-Rolande* marks the point at which a text that always jumps back and forth between France, Germany, and Poland, evades seemingly self-evident national paradigms. It is not only the author's travels but also the movements of her writing that link France with Germany and Poland in a way that connects the literatures of these countries with one another through a shared dialectic of homelessness. In the midst of the silence of the Sunday roads and streets, which bookmarks *Beaune-la-Rolande*, a literature that has overcome its settledness has also succeeded in establishing its homeland in a state of having escaped that (*pace* Erich Auerbach) lies beyond the nation. Shoah literature finds its way into the Literatures without a fixed Abode, whose strength lies not in the attachment to a certain place but in movement. Literature itself, as it searches for the places and movements of human beings in the universe, generates this strength.

---

134 Wajsbrot: *Beaune-la-Rolande*, p. 57.

3 Relations

Caribbean IslandWorlds: about the fractal geometry of the literary island

Worlds of Islands and I(s)land-worlds

Friedrich Cramer's *Chaos and Order*, a fascinating study that combines scholarship and literature to analyze (so the subtitle) 'the Complex Structure of Living Systems,' ends with a short chapter entitled 'We Island Dwellers: The Beautiful Life on the Archipelago.' In this chapter, the author, a biologist and long-time director of the Max Planck Institute for Experimental Medicine in Göttingen, employs a circular structure to liken his book, and indeed (modern) life in general, to living on an island and, in fact, an island world:

> Our world is an island, an island of order, an island of physical laws, an island of ideas, an island of trust. We live on our island... Perhaps there are other islands – maybe even an entire archipelago. Their order could be different. If it is, we must accept it as equal to ours, since we now recognize the plurality of this world. We live in an island world, on islands of order, islands of physical laws, islands of ideas, and islands of trust. We live on our own private island... There may be other islands, an entire archipelago. The structures there may be of another kind, but we must grant their equality, for we now know about the plurality of this world.[1]

Cramer's island metaphor is to represent a way of living characterized by a certain sense of order on a particular island. At the same time, it testifies to a (world) awareness of other islands where other orders prevail. While these other orders obey logics that are fundamentally different, they still have the same rights as one's own logic. In this respect, Friedrich Cramer agrees with Immanuel Kant, the author of *The Critique of Pure Reason*, one of the most important philosophical treatises of the modern age. At the beginning of his discussion of 'Phenomena and Noumena,' Kant emphasized that one had 'now not only traveled throughout the land of pure understanding and carefully inspected its every part, but have also surveyed it throughout, determining for each thing in

---

[1] Friedrich Cramer: *Chaos and Order: The Complex Structure of Living Systems.* Weinheim: VCH 1993, p. 232.

this land its proper place.'² He added: 'This land, however, is an island, and is enclosed by nature itself within unchangeable bounds. It is the land of truth (a charming name), and is surrounded by a vast and stormy ocean, where illusion properly resides and many fog banks and much fast-melting ice feign new-found lands.'³

The island metaphor – Kant uses its Nordic variation, fog and ice included – is deeply embedded in the traditions and imaginaries of a Europe whose namesake Zeus abducted from the coast of Asia Minor (that is, a continent) and transported to an island, if not in Kant's Baltic Sea, then in the Mediterranean, the seat of Western civilization. Both above quotations, then, belong to a centuries-old Western imaginary, but there is also an important difference between them. The Konigsberg philosopher conceived of his island as a completely isolated 'Land of Truth,' its shores changelessly bounded by a (Baltic) sea that produced but illusions and deceptions. Cramer, however, imagines an island-world in which one's own island and its order enter into a pluralistic relationship with other islands that observe their own discreet systems of meaning.

The island metaphor leaves room for at least two interpretations: it can be as symbol of one's remote seclusion on the one hand *and* of one's keen awareness of many-sided relation with others. On the one hand, in the clarity of its seemingly firm borders, the island is a world detached from the other and is, as in the case in Thomas More's Caribbean-inspired utopia, under the sway of a single logic that has taken on material and territorial form. On the other hand, the island is a place that perceives itself as one fragment among many, torn away, separated and at the same time in many ways still linked with a continent whose very etymology alludes to connectedness, be it as the linked *continens* of the Old Worlds – Europe, Asia, and Africa – or as an unbroken land mass, like the Americas or Australia. The semantics of the island in the Western tradition can pivot either way. As a result, it comprises not only the concept of the island as an I(s)land-world in which seclusion encompasses a totality of breaks into

---

2 Immanuel Kant: *Critique of Pure Reason*. Indianapolis, Ind.: Hackett 1996, p. 303. 'Wir haben jetzt das Land des reinen Verstandes nicht allein durchreiset und jeden Theil davon sorgfältig in Augenschein genommen, sondern es auch durchmessen und jedem Dinge auf demselben seine Stelle bestimmt.' Immanuel Kant: *Kritik der reinen Vernunft*. Edited by Wilhelm Weinschedel. Frankfurt am Main: Suhrkamp 1974, vol. 1, p. 267 (B 294, 295 I A 236).
3 Kant: *Critique of Pure Reason*, vol. 1, p. 303. 'Dieses Land aber ist eine Insel und durch die Natur selbst in unveränderliche Gränzen eingeschlossen. Es ist das Land der Wahrheit (ein reizender Name), umgeben von einem weiten und stürmischen Oceane, dem eigentlichen Sitze des Scheins, wo manche Nebelbank und manches bald wegschmelzende Eis neue Länder lügt.' Kant: *Kritik der reinen Vernunft*, vol. 1, p. 267 (B 294, 295 I 236).

various regional, climatic and cultural parts. It is also a world of islands representing that which is fragmentary, splintered and mosaic-like, and which is distinguished by manifold inner connections and constellations. Obviously, this world of islands can also become a self-contained I(s)land-world, or else it can be conceived as an archipelago that communicates with other regions. Both interpretive models can overlap, thereby creating the conditions for the semantic oscillation of which anyone who studies islands should be aware.

Island boundaries and *mise-en-abyme*

In his March 2, 1977 lecture at the Collège de France about the figure of closure (clôture), Roland Barthes emphasized the spatially fixed mental world that attends definitional processes: 'The meaning of 'defining': to draw borders, determine boundaries. Closure – the definition of a territory, and thus of the identity of those who occupy it.'[4] Even though the French semiologist was not primarily concerned with islands but with other self-contained spaces, such as monasteries or multi-storied apartment buildings, what is still valuable to us here is his notion that the all rational definitions are based on territorial demarcations, on the creation of a clearly circumscribed space that excludes the Other. As in Kant's 'land of truth,' definitions create the isolation of an insular structure that also affects the inhabitants or occupants of this territory who are either ascribed an identity marked by bounded space or feel themselves a common identity bound up with territory. They are part of the definitional processes of narrowing, fixing, excluding, and debordering. Island dwellers are subject to these processes to the same degree as that definitionally insulated island. Here, the isolation of the insular joins up with the question about who holds the power to define and, beyond that, about the power either wielded over the islanders or by them. For islands have always been important points of departure for geostrategic considerations and internal power constellations.

But let me first address the problems involved in defining and fixing islands' borders. One only needs to look at a map to realize that island borders in particular are always clearly delineated, a function, it would seem at first

---

4 'C'est le sens de 'définir': tracer les limites, des frontières. Clôture = définition du territoire, et donc de l'identité de son/ses occupants.' Roland Barthes: *Comment vivre ensemble: Simulations romanesques de quelques espaces quotidiens*. Notes de cours et de séminaires au Collège de France, 1976–1977. Edited by Claude Coste. Paris: Seuil/IMEC 2002, p. 94.

glance, of being 'enclosed by nature itself within unchangeable bounds.'[5] But how can one measure these natural borders within Nature?

In 1977, the French mathematician Benoît Mandelbrot published an influential large-scale study in which he tried to replace or, at least, supplement Euclidean geometry with a new, *fractal* geometry of Nature. He took the island as a graphic example of the term fractal. By taking what appeared to be a simple, straightforward question – how long is the British coastline? – Mandelbrot was able to show clearly just how complicated it really is to solve such a seemingly facile problem: 'coastline length runs out to be an elusive notion that slips between the fingers of one who wants to grasp it. All measurement methods ultimately lead to the conclusion that the typical coastline's length is very large and so ill determined that it is best considered infinite.'[6] But what sort of boundary does an endless insular coastline form? It makes perfect sense that the length of a coastline depends on the scalar accuracy with which we map a certain coast and either include or omit bays, inlets, and coves. Mandelbrot himself discusses a variety of different approaches to such measuring. Since classic, whole-number dimensions are no longer adequate to describe this reality and record it scientifically, Mandelbrot introduces broken, fractal measurements. Euclidean geometry no longer suffices to explain the phenomena he chose to study.

Especially relevant for describing the characteristics of fractals is the concept of self-similarity, which is also key to the questions I pursue in this book.[7] Mandelbrot, who gave his book a fractal structure and stressed his 'lifetime involvement' in this 'rich new land [of fractals],' indicated in his epilogue, 'The Path to Fractals,' that self-similarity held in store some 'extraordinary surprises' that helped him 'understand the fabric of nature' in fundamental ways.[8] The self-similarity of the fractal, which becomes almost palpable when viewed through the various 'extensions' of a coastal outline, displays a characteristic in no way limited to the 'fabric of nature,' as the structure of Mandelbrot's books already suggests. We are dealing with a phenomenon that can be found in many cultures and that we can conceptually connect, in the field of anthropology, for

---

5   Kant: *Critique of Pure Reason*, p. 303.
6   Benoît B. Mandelbrot: *The Fractal Geometry of Nature*. New York: W.H. Freeman and Company 1983, p. 25.
7   'The concepts of fractal dimension and self-similarity are essentially mathematical. For real physical and chemical objects, diffusion curves, the surfaces of crystals or of proteins, self-similarity is never satisfied ideally over the entire linear scale... When a surface is broken down ever further into self-similar fragments, they become increasingly fissured and higher-dimensional.' Cramer: *Chaos and Order*, p. 126.
8   Mandelbrot: *Fractal Geometry*, p. 422–423.

instance, with Claude Lévi-Strauss's *modèle réduit* and, in the field of literary studies, with André Gide's *mise-en-abyme*. These concepts refer to structural components that contain a whole structure, and thus also themselves, in a smaller, reduced form. In this way, they also hold the key to an understanding of the structure as a whole. Again, we have here a fractal relation marked by fundamental self-similarity, a structure to which widely divergent functions can be assigned.

Against this background, Mandelbrot's statement becomes even more relevant. In view of the 'irregular and fragmented' patterns of many natural phenomena, it is about assuming 'that, compared with Euclid ... [n]ature exhibits not simply a higher degree ... of complexity.' Rather:

> The existence of these patterns challenges us to study those forms that Euclid leaves aside as being 'formless.'... Responding to this challenge, I conceived and developed a new geometry of nature and implemented its use in a number of diverse fields. It describes many of the irregular and fragmented patterns around us, and leads to full-fledged theories, by identifying a family of shapes I call *fractals*. The most useful fractals involve chance and both their regularities and their irregularities are statistical.[9]

Mandelbrot's thoughts on the irregular, amorphous character of coastlines draw attention to the quasi-double nature of islands which are to be understood as disjointed fragments of bounded coastlines. Islands distinguish themselves through the multiple, irregular brokenness of their fractal dimension; at the same time; they can be understood through an endlessness based on their self-similarity. In this way, the consideration of island boundaries once again points to the double character of the island: it is both fragment and totality; a fragmented, 'irregular,' structure and a *mise-en-abyme* that recedes into eternity and aims at the creation of ever-new totalities. We may say, then, that the island oscillates between states of being a part torn from a coherent world and the continuously self-differentiating wholeness as a world in its own right. The idea that natural space and location have specific consequences for the development of an island as a cultural space is one of the central theoretical starting points for this chapter.

One might argue that the borders of non-insular countries that are not islands can still be compared to insular coastlines, even equated with them. Such borders, which frequently follow the twists and turns of rivers and mountain chains, are indeed also fractal, so that it is hardly surprising that countries such as Spain and Portugal, or Belgium and the Netherlands, assign different lengths

---

9 Mandelbrot: *Fractal Geometry*, p. 1.

to the borders they share. Mandelbrot himself already drew attention to this interesting phenomenon, venturing that smaller countries calculate their borders at twenty percent longer than larger nations because the formers' chosen scale is attuned to smaller proportions. Great differences in border lengths not only illustrate that 'a small country (Portugal) measures its borders more accurately than its big neighbor,' but also that the concept of length is by no means as objective as it would appear. 'The observer inevitably intervenes in its definition.'[10] Even mathematically based, comprehensible definitions become territorialized in their dependence on an observer.

What concerns me in this chapter, however, is not the mathematical calculability of borders but the differences between the boundaries of island and of mainlands or continents. Contrary to continental (national) borders, island borders separate land from water. This fundamental discontinuity, among other things, forces one to change one's mode of transportation when crossing such frontiers. The streets of an island never leave the island; they do not continue on beyond the island. And if they do, they continentalize the island world, as is the case with the Florida Keys, which are literally connected to the mainland by streets, and with myriad consequences. The basic medial discontinuity is a vital prerequisite for the double(d) meaning of the island and its conceptual oscillation between fragment and totality, between being an I(s)land-world and a world of islands. This movement transforms into a life-world and an everyday cultural experience the very fractal dimension that allows us to think together the duality of being split (off) and being self-similar in the image of the island.

Accelerated globalization and island archipelagoes

In an essay that dates back to 1976, Brazilian cultural theorist Darcy Ribeiro asked himself whether Latin America truly exists. By first considering this question from a geographical perspective, he found a revealing tension between the continental and the insular:

> Geographically, Latin America is well known as the product of its continent's continuity. Within this physical foundation, however, there is neither any corresponding unified sociopolitical structure nor any functioning and interactive coexistence. The whole of the vast continent is broken up into single nationalities, some of them scarcely viable as frameworks within which people may realize their potential. Indeed, geographic continuity never functioned here as a unifying factor because for centuries the different colonial

---

10 Mandelbrot: *Fractal Geometry*, p. 27.

establishments from which Latin America's societies were born coexisted without cooperating. Each one would communicate directly with its colonial mother country. Even today, we Latin Americans live as if we were an archipelago of islands linked by sea and air; more often we turn outward to the great economic centers of the world, rather than inward. Indeed, the borders of Latin America, running along the barren mountain ranges through impenetrable jungle, isolate more than they connect, and rarely allow for an intensive coexistence.[11]

Clearly, the culturally defined concept of Latin America is not a suitable geographical term, and South America is not exactly a continent but a subcontinent. It is also unclear what place the Brazilian anthropologist would be willing to grant the Caribbean in relation to Latin America. But despite such difficulties, his portrayal of the continental nations of South America as an archipelago is significant in several ways. For one, he rightfully draws our attention to the age-old continuity of an emphasis on external relations that stemmed from the needs of the colonial powers. For another, he sees the archipelagic situation as a massive obstacle to developing a purposeful internal web of relations. And finally, that the borders run through the 'uninhabited' Cordillera and jungles pose major hindrances to communication. Twentieth-century Latin America, whose actual existence Ribeiro questions in this much-debated essay, is a splintered space that follows an island logic he stigmatizes as negative.

In 1971, the Uruguayan Eduardo Galeano published an essay that inspired debates throughout the 1970s and 1980s. *The Open Veins of Latin America* (*Las venas abiertas de América Latina*, 1973) offers an analysis comparable to Ribeiro's but much more comprehensive than his. Galeano locates the main reason for the vast differences in economic development between the former British and Iberian colonies in the contrast between internal versus external connectivity: 'This also provides the key to the United States' expansion as a national unit and to the fragmentation of Latin America. Our production centers are not interconnected but take the form of a fan with a far-away vertex.'[12] Whereas the agrarian products of the British colonies in America could be compared to those of the mother country and in no way supplemented them, the situation in the Antilles and in the Iberian colonies was entirely different due to the cultivation of sugar, tobacco, cotton, and other colonial goods: 'a small Caribbean island had

---

11 Darcy Ribeiro: 'Does Latin America exist?' In: Mari Carmen Ramírez et al. (eds.): *Critical Documents of 20th Century Latin American and Latino Art. Resisting Categories: Latin American and/or Latino?* New Haven: Yale University Press 2012, p. 156.
12 Eduardo Galeano: *The Open Veins of Latin America*. New York: Monthly Review Press 1997, p. 133.

more economic importance for England than the thirteen colonies that would become the United States.'[13] Galeano thus equated the archipelagic situation with extreme external dependence and a lack of internal forces geared toward setting up autonomous structures within the 'fragmentation' (fracturación) he observed. Indeed, it may be argued that it was the prominent role various Caribbean islands played particularly during the first and second phases of accelerated globalization – after Columbus's so-called discovery and during the second half of the eighteenth century – that created the highly developed external relationality of the Greater and the Lesser Antilles. Neglected, even purposely impeded, by contrast, were the relations *among* these islands, not in the least because of their allegiances to different metropoles and the resulting boundaries between the respective colonial possessions.

It is surely needless to detail the common basis of those at times gradual, at others tumultuous developments that have left their mark on the Caribbean beyond all political borders and diverse processes of cultural hybridization since they entered a globalized and globalizing economic situation. One can point to four basic phases and structural features of an archipelago of islands that play *at once* by shared *and* different rules: one, the histories of conquest, which differ from island to island, causing either subjugation or genocide of the indigenous populations; two, the transition from a fragile extraction economy, including the forced removal of indigenous laborers from neighboring islands, to a plantation economy increasingly oriented towards sugar and based upon the ruthless exploitation of kidnapped Africans within the rapidly created and steadily optimized machine of the Black Atlantic; three, the growing mechanization, intensification, and industrialization of complementary colonial economic structures that led to the progressive replacement of African slaves with predominantly East Indian, Chinese, and Malaysian contract workers, day laborers, and coolies; and, four, the rise of differently directed independence movements since Haitian independence in 1804, which have transformed the entire Caribbean into the most politically heterogeneous region of the world. The plurality of partly contradictory structures and logics, themselves already hybridized, qualifies as the major structural feature of an island group that, geographically, culturally, and politically, breaks apart into several partial and overlapping regions that simultaneously interact with one another. From the very beginning, this island group was much more than just a transit area between Europe and America, and between the northern and southern regions of the hemisphere.

---

13 Galeano: *Open Veins*, p. 133.

These island dynamics were in fact what created the American hemisphere in the first place.

Proto-islands and spheres of power

The dichotomy between Old and New Worlds began to impact European perceptions of America not with Columbus, who had been convinced until his death that he had reached India, China, and Marco Polo's Cipango via the western route. Rather, it started when the Florentine Amerigo Vespucci began to speak of a *Mundus Novus* in his famous 1503 letter to Lorenzo di Pier Francesco de' Medici, a document that was speedily copied and translated:

> In past days I wrote very fully to you of my return from the new countries [ab novis illis regionibus], which have been found and explored with the ships, at the cost, and by the command, of this Most Serene King of Portugal; and it is lawful to call it a new world [novum mundum appellare licet], because none of these countries were known to our ancestors, and to all who hear about them they will be entirely new [novissima res]. For the opinion of the ancients [opinionem nostrorum antiquorum excedit] was, that the greater part of the world beyond the equinoctial line to the south was not land, but only sea, which they have called the Atlantic; and if they have affirmed that any continent is there, they have given many reasons for denying that it is inhabited. But this their opinion is false, and entirely opposed to the truth. My last voyage has proved it, for I have found a continent in that southern part; more populous and more full of animals than our Europe, or Asia, or Africa, and even more temperate and pleasant than any other region known to us, as will be explained further on. I shall write succinctly of the principal things only, and the things most worthy of notice and of being remembered, which I either saw or heard of in this new world [in hoc novo mundo], as presently will become manifest.[14]

I do not wish here to enter into the debate, which still flares up from time to time, about the extent to which the Florentine might have been conscious of having discovered a land mass that was definitively and, by definition (that is, territorially), separate from Asia. None other than Alexander von Humboldt, in his unjustly neglected study 'Critical examination of the history of the geography of the new continent and of the advancement of naval astronomy in the fifteenth and sixteenth centuries' (*Examen critique de l'histoire de la géographie du nouveau continent et des progrès de l'astronomie nautique aux quinzième et seizième*

---

14 Amerigo Vespucci: 'Letter on his Third Voyage from Amerigo Vespucci to Lorenzo Pietro Francesco Di Medici,' March (or April) 1503. In: Clements R. Markham (ed.): *The Letters of Amerigo Vespucci and Other Documents illustrative of his Career*. London: Printed for the Hakluyt Society 1894, p. 42-56.

siècles, 1838), answered this question in the negative. He felt that both Columbus and Vespucci 'had, until death, held consistently to the belief that at various points they had made contact with the Asian continent.'[15] Well known are the errors and misunderstandings that led the young geographer Martin Waldseemüller, in his map *Cosmographiae universalis introductio* (1507), to propose Vespucci's first name for the 'new' continent that the Italian traveler had effectively invented. In 1940, Stefan Zweig, for whom this 'New World,' as distinct from his 'World of yesterday,' would prove fateful, astutely noted that the extent to which the idea of America – the *Mundus Novus* – as cohesive gradually entered Europeans' awareness depended on naming it. Zweig emphasized that the unity of the 'islands' of the two Americas was a linguistic and discursive creation with a cartographic and territorial anchor. He remarked, not without a touch of irony, that in 1538 'Mercator, King of the Cartographers,' drew 'the entire continent as a single unit in his world map' and inscribed 'the name America across both parts. A M E across the north and R 1C A across the south.'[16] The cartographic joining of the two parts (or islands) of America, which had at first not been perceived as connected by an isthmus, through *one* name opened up the possibility of a hemispheric thinking that has spawned diverse perspectives on the so-called New World since the sixteenth century.

It seems important to me that all these European views of the New World should have come *from islands*. Islands were important for Columbus's first and successive expedition. He used the Canaries, where the Guanche had not yet been completely conquered, as a strategic outpost and launching pad. Due to the famous change of course occasioned by the observation that birds were flying to the southwest, he landed not on the coast of a continent but on what he expected to be the coastal islands of the Asian mainland and immediately seized them for the Spanish crown. These proto-islands of the *Antilles*, which, as Spanish expansion advanced, turned into the counter-islands of the Canaries, became the launching pad for a transatlantic and transcontinental power politics that was island-based from the start and relied on the old island connections until its collapse in the nineteenth century.

---

15 'Vespuce, jusqu'à l'époque de sa mort, était fermement persuadé d'avoir abordé aux côtes d'Asie.' Alexander von Humboldt : *Examen critique de l'histoire de la géographie du nouveau continent et des progrès de l'astronomie nautique aux quinzième et seizième siècles*. Tome quatrième. Paris: Librairie de Gide 1838, p. 188.
16 Stefan Zweig: 'Amerigo: Die Geschichte eines historischen Irrtums.' In: Stefan Zweig: *Zeiten und Schicksale: Aufsätze und Vorträge aus den Jahren 1902–1942*. Frankfurt am Main: Fischer 1990, p. 423.

The first map Juan de la Cosa drew in 1500 shows this insular perspective with great clarity (see Figure 3). The islands on this map, at times impressively precise in their outlines, at others more invented than discovered, suggest the image of a circumCaribbean space whose irregular coastlines allow sufficient room for a connected continent. The Azores and the Cape Verde Islands, which de la Cosa also included, but above all the Lesser Antilles, indicate an insular logic of regional reconnaissance, conquest, and acquisition. This logic illustrates how a hemispheric thinking could develop even at a time when knowledge about the existence of a 'New World' was still uncertain. Within such thinking, the Caribbean island world took on a defining role as a marker of territorial borders. The Iberian powers' 1494 Treaty of Tordesillas already laid the foundation for a division of the world into spheres of political influence whose future effects were hardly apparent at the time. This division was not just a conceptual mapping, but a political and military one as well; all of them began to take shape in Juan de la Cosa's daring drawing which was also based on his own experience. As with Columbus and Vespucci, but now in cartographic outlines that resembled geopolitical blueprints, de la Cosa's map suggests the interrelation between (given) topos knowledge, experiential knowledge, and the horizon of expectations that, as my next example will also show, would thread through all (European) ideas about the 'New World.' From the very start, Europeans conceived of the American continent as *trans*continental. The 'invention of America' is thus a transcontinental invention.[17]

Striking about Juan de la Cosa's map is not only his visual suggestion of the enormous length of the insular coastlines but also the interplay between Island-Worlds and continents. This fundamental relation can also be gleaned from two map sketches included in Alessandro Zorzi's codex, which were based on a map from Bartolomé Colón's travel account from 1506. At the center of these maps one can easily make out some of the named Antillean islands, such as 'spagnola,' 'guadalupa,' and even the island of the 'canibali.'[18] On the eastern edge of

---

17 Edmundo O'Gorman was the first to pursue this metaphor systematically. See his *La invención de América*. México D.F.: Fondo de Cultura Económica 1958. For an English translation, see Edmundo O'Gorman: *The Invention of America: An Inquiry into the historical Nature of the New World and the Meaning of its History*. Bloomington: Indiana University Press 1961.
18 See, among others, Carl Ortwin Sauer (1969): *The Early Spanish Main*. Cambridge, Mass.: Cambridge University Press 2008, p. 143–144. See also Carl Ortwin Sauer: *Descubrimiento y dominación española del Caribe*. Mexico D.F.: Fondo de Cultura Económica 1984, p. 220–222 (especially map 18). Also Bernhard Jahn: *Raumkonzepte in der Frühen Neuzeit: Zur Konstruktion von Wirklichkeit in Pilgerberichten, Amerikareisebeschreibungen und Prosaerzählungen*. Frankfurt am Main: Peter Lang 1993, p. 145 and 185.

the map one can glimpse the Iberian Peninsula as well as Africa and its offshore islands, while the land mass situated on western edge bears the name 'Asia' and stretches to northern China. At the bottom of the map's southern edge appear the coastline of Paria and the words 'Mondo Novo.'

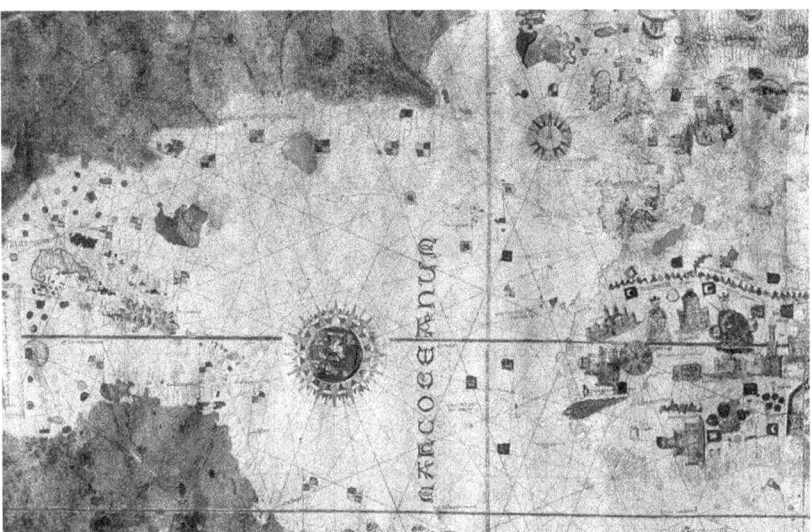

Fig. 3: Section of Juan de la Cosa's map (1500)

My point here is not that a New World can be conceived from a European point of view without necessarily separating it from Asia, but rather that Europeans came to conceive of these largely unknown continents in term of islands. Islands are the actual focal point, and they make up a 'New World' both found and invented by the Europeans. Projected onto this New World, however, is an insular logic. This projection still shines through in Eduardo Galeano's and Darcy Ribeiro's respective studies which emphasize the archipelagic situation of Iberian America and the momentous consequences of 'neglected' internal communications. The invention and configuration of the 'New World' occurred through the Caribbean island world. Especially when conceived as a hemispheric construct, the New World, is unthinkable without the Caribbean.

Island shards and island relations

Nota bene: in the beginning was the island, at least from the perspective of Europe. The maps I mention above, among many others, show this with utmost clarity. Appearances, however, can be deceiving: An island is not a fixed, static object but has to be understood from a *vectoral* perspective as a place. It is a place where diverse, historically cumulative movements intersect and overlap. It is a force field in which these movements are and continue to be stored. An island can thus be defined (and territorialized) as a place in and of motion whose historically stored mobile pattern and vectors are always retrievable.

When the Spanish first landed in America, they already knew much about islands. Their familiarity with island structures as spaces of transit and movement enabled them to develop an island logic that made such a rapid conquest of the mainland possible, not necessarily as an annexation of large areas of land but as occupation and fortification, or provisioning, of singular centers. Independent of the speedy development of a Caribbean colonial economy centered on the sugar plantation, one may speak of an insulin-fueled expansionism whose aim was to establish islands of power that would report back to Madrid. It followed logically that the proverbial insulin injected into the colonial body-in-the-making strengthened external relations, while internal connections between ports and power centers and the 'area' of the hinterland languished. This situation also reinforced the fact that these islands of power and IslandWorlds on the mainland were characterized not by a coherent – that is, continental – territoriality but, rather, by vectorality. It is necessary to emphasize here that the vectors stored, as it were, by the islands do not reside within a continual (one might say Euclidean) geometry but within a multiply refracted space marked by leaps and discontinuities. Not only coastlines but also movements may be understood as fractal pattern.[19] It follows, then, that the stored patterns of movement inhabit a fractal geometry that is not only natural but also, even more so, cultural. They exist within a space that, from a Euclidean perspective, would be deemed amorphous. But when viewed from the standpoint of fractal or quantum geometry, this space exhibits distinct patterns of meaning. In this way, the seeming incoherence of a state of island-ness also becomes characteristic of a geographically continuous and coherent continent. What patterns of movement can we discern there?

'Transitions from periodicity to chaos,' as they are used to describe the 'fundamentally complex' structure of living creatures in nature, make possible a no-

---

19 For the concept of a fractal pattern, see Mandelbrot: *Fractal Geometry*, p. 31.

vel view of the weave of space-time relations within an island world; the separate *location* of each island can be grasped as the result of multiple overlays of, and re-generations among, different patterns of movement.[20] This enables a retrospective understanding of past and also future movements; the latter does not, however, translate into predictability. Rather, what seems static and territorialized can be interpreted as a fundamentally complex pattern of movement in which each location, each island, has its own vectoral history and its own relevance to future movements and developments. That each island has its own sense of (it)self remains imperceptible without a relational analysis of an entire island world.

When he accepted the Nobel Prize for Literature, Derek Walcott voiced legitimate anger about the touristic self-image of the Caribbean islands, claiming that they have lost themselves in the 'high-pitched repetition of the same images of service that cannot distinguish one island from the other.' Instead, each island should develop its own memory:

> All of the Antilles, every island, is an effort of memory; every mind, every racial biography culminating in amnesia and fog. Pieces of sunlight through the fog and sudden rainbows, *arcs-en-ciel*. That is the effort, the labour of the Antillean imagination, rebuilding its gods from bamboo frames, phrase by phrase.'[21]

The task of literature and art, then, is to reconstruct singular island histories that would otherwise dissolve in the shapeless fog. Yet, what Walcott wrote about the poet Saint-John Perse, whom he admired, equally applies to himself: 'Caribbean genius is condemned to contradict itself.'[22] When talking about poetry, Walcott chose an island metaphor not only as characteristic of himself but also aimed at the movement between island and continent: more precisely, at a breaking away of the island as fragment: 'Poetry is an island that breaks away

---

20 Cramer: *Chaos and Order*, p. 142 and 167. For Cramer's concept of fundamentally complex systems, see Cramer: *Chaos and Order*, p. 167–168: 'These systems [i.e. multiparameter systems subject to a high degrees of feedback] are not reducible. I refer to such systems as fundamentally complex; they possess the property that the whole is more than the sum of the parts. There is no reversibility in these systems. Irreversible thermodynamics has to be applied instead of classical, reversible thermodynamics. For this reason it would simply be intellectually negligent to assume that, in sciences such as biochemistry and neurophysiology, the mosaic tiles can be fit back together to obtain the complete picture of a living thing. In quantum theory, overlay or superposition is called "de-coherence."'
21 Derek Walcott. 'The Antilles: Fragments of Epic Memory.' In: Derek Walcott: *What the Twilight Says: Essays*. London: Faber and Faber 1998, p. 82.
22 Walcott: 'The Antilles,' p. 78.

from the main.'[23] Is the poet, then, a lonely islander? Only a few lines earlier, Walcott had set the metaphor of the moving fragment against the static image of a whole to be reconstructed and restored.

> Break a vase, and the love that reassembles the fragments is stronger than that love which took its symmetry for granted when it was whole. The glue that fits the pieces is the sealing of its original shape. It is such a love that reassembles our African and Asiatic fragments, the cracked heirlooms whose restoration shows its white scars. This gathering of broken pieces is the care and pain of the Antilles, and if the pieces are disparate, ill-fitting, they contain more pain than their original sculpture, those icons and sacred vessels taken for granted in their ancestral places. Antillean art is this restoration of our shattered histories, our shards of vocabulary, our archipelago becoming a synonym for pieces broken off from the original continent.[24]

In this poetic sketch of a theoretical landscape, the Antillean archipelago appears as a gathering of shards and fragments that derive from their respective 'originary' continents, including African, Asian, Mediterranean, and European cultures.[25] The fragment is thus closely linked with a global totality, and, in the best case scenario, becomes that totality's poeticized presence. At the same time, however, the image of the broken vase refers to a lost original unity and wholeness that may be recovered in an act of restoration. This image can easily be compared with Walter Benjamin's broken vessel of language, a language that all humans had originally had in common, and whose retrieval falls to the translator concerned with preserving differences.

Fragments of a vessel which are to be glued together must match one another in the smallest details, although they need not be *like* one another. Similarly, instead of resembling the meaning of the original, a translation must lovingly and in detail incorporate the original's mode of signification, thus making both the original and the translation recognizable as fragments of a greater language.[26]

---

23 Walcott: 'The Antilles,' p. 70.
24 Walcott: 'The Antilles,' p. 69.
25 See Walcott: 'The Antilles,' p. 74.
26 Walter Benjamin: 'The Task of the Translator.' In: *Illuminations: Essays and Reflections*. New York: Schocken Books 1969, p. 79. 'Wie nämlich Scherben eines Gefäßes, um sich zusammenfügen zu lassen, in den kleinsten Einzelheiten einander zu folgen, doch nicht so zu gleichen haben, so muß, anstatt dem Sinn des Originals sich ähnlich zu machen, die Übersetzung liebend vielmehr und bis ins Einzelne hinein dessen Art des Meinens in der eigenen Sprache sich anbilden, um so beide wie Scherben als Bruchstück eine Gefäßes, als Bruchstück einer größeren Sprache erkennbar zu machen.' Walter Benjamin, 'Die Aufgabe des Übersetzers.' In:

Inherent in Walcott's concept of restoration, of re-construction, is the idea of an originary and original condition to which one might return, though not without scars. The proximity of Walcott's language to Benjamin's utopia of a 'greater language' is unmistakable. From this point of view, we may see Derek Walcott as representative of an island world in which the island becomes the entire world pieced together. Even if his image of an archipelago always presupposes a multiplicity that can never become uniform, it is still clear that each island as the 'shard' of a broken vessel has its fixed location, from which a totality can then be reassembled. But is this not the way 'back' to cohesion, that is, to the figure of the continent?

Édouard Glissant's island world is different. Unlike an island world that privileges the relationship between 'fragment' and 'vessel,' between island and continent, Glissant's does not focus on the historico-genealogical links with an 'original' but instead develops a 'Poetics of Relation' at the center of which are changeable, mobile, and mutual relations beyond essentialism. Not only does he contrast a territorially rooted concept of identity with that of a mobile 'identité-relation'; by 1981, when he published his influential *Caribbean Discourse*, he had also developed a relational understanding of the Caribbean island world:

> What is the Caribbean in fact? A multiple series of relationships. We all feel it, we express it in all kinds of hidden or twisted ways, or we fiercely deny it. But we sense that this sea exists within us with its weight of now revealed islands. The Caribbean Sea is not an American lake. It is the estuary of the Americas.[27]

This (multi-)relational complexity, logically consistent with the plurality of the Americas, goes beyond an imperial hegemonic power that has long limited the appellation 'America' to the USA. The metaphor of the estuary – of course untenable from a geomorphological perspective – inserts a geographical concept that we have already encountered in connection with Juan de la Cosa's map: an Antillean sea that, fed by the rivers of the surrounding circumCaribbean landmasses, opens onto the Atlantic Ocean. As Glissant makes clear in his *Poetics of Relation*, fixed identities must be set in motion by concepts that radicalize Gilles

---

Rolf Tiedemann / Hermann Schweppenhäuser (eds.): *Walter Benjamin: Gesammelte Schriften*, vol. 4/1. Frankfurt am Main: Suhrkamp 1977–1985, p. 18.

27 Édouard Glissant: *Caribbean discourse: Selected essays*. Translated and with an introduction by J. Michael Dash. Charlottesville: University Press of Virginia 1999, p. 139; and Édouard Glissant: *Le discours antillais*. Paris: Seuil 1981, p. 249.

Deleuze and Félix Guattari's rhizomatics. According to Glissant, every identity must be thought out and invented relationally, in relation to the Other.[28]

It is important for my line of questioning that the island world of the Antilles in its Glissantean multirelationality opens onto an entire hemisphere that is precisely not the *American Hemisphere*. Even though the Guadeloupian poet and cultural theoretician focuses primarily on the part of the New World influenced by Romance languages and cultures, he still underscores the need for a hemispheric perspective on the Caribbean, which also includes a Caribbean perspective on the hemisphere. For the Caribbean, which not only consists of the island world but also includes of the circumCaribbean continental coast, has always served as a geographical and cultural bridge between South and North America. But how does one rethink the relationship between the entire hemisphere and a world of islands, the most sizeable of which (Cuba) is not even counted among the world's ten largest islands? Put differently, what possibilities exist for rethinking the study of the Caribbean in a more holistic fashion, rather than approaching it from an isolating regional perspective or splintering it into individual disciplinary fragments?

'Old World' and 'New World': Hemispheric constructions

On an epistemological and discursive level, the difference between 'Old World' and 'New World' has regulated the asymmetrical exchange of knowledge and material goods such as the implementation of a bio-politics that, like the displacement of indigenous populations into reservations, the introduction of African slaves, and an immigration politics tailored to colonial needs, naturally favored the interests of the Old World, particularly those of the Iberian powers. The categorical distinction between Old and New Worlds has encompassed all aspects and fields of knowledge, from the concept of a continent to be converted and integrated into the salvation narratives of European Christianity, to the development of legal ideas for the non-European regions and peoples, to geognosy and geology. The belief that America was literally a newer, relatively undeveloped world that, as the Orinoco and the Amazon showed, had risen from the waters at a later date lingered throughout the nineteenth century. The long-standing 'Dispute of the New World' substantiates the impact and the explosive power of

---

28 See Édouard Glissant: *Poetics of Relations*. Ann Arbor: University of Michigan Press 2000, p. 18, and Édouard Glissant: *Poétique de la Relation*. Paris: Gallimard 1990, p. 23.

the discursive divorce whose structuring power remains intact even today, and not only in Old Europe.[29]

The beginning of the nineteenth century was witness to the rise of a hemispheric construction that primarily sought to promote the interests of the New World and to eliminate the European colonial nations as powers in America. This construction emerged in the context of the American independence movements and combined secularized narratives of salvation with Bolivarian pan-Americanism and the concepts it drew from the Spanish, especially New Spanish, colonial Enlightenment. In his 'A South American's reply to a gentleman from this island' (*Contestación de un Americano Meridional a un caballero de esta isla*) from September 6, 1815, which, as 'Letter from Jamaica,' became one of the most famous documents of South American independence, Simón Bolívar spoke of his 'limited knowledge about such an immense, varied, and mysterious land as the New World.'[30] The entirety of this New World, to which Bolívar repeatedly referred as 'hemisphere' (hemisferio) or 'new hemisphere' (nuevo hemisferio), had to be free, because freedom was necessary for 'the world equilibrium' and in the interest of a trade-oriented Europe. Instructive is that Bolívar, from the island perspective of Jamaica, also portrayed the New World itself as an island: its inhabitants are in fact 'a small segment of the human race' living in a 'world apart, surrounded by vast seas.'[31] This islandization, indeed Caribbeanization, of at least the Iberian-influenced part of the hemisphere is of course limited. Bolívar saw in the Central-American isthmus, with its 'magnificent' strategic location between two immense oceans, the 'universal emporium' of the future. By connecting the two oceans via a canal, Central America would be able to play a key role as a nexus of Europe, the Americas, and Asia. Consequently, any future 'world capital' (la capital de la tierra) could only be located there.[32] Conceived from an insular Jamaican perspective, this vision of a continentally centered hemisphere opens onto the 'four quarters of the globe' (cuatro partes

---

29 See Antonello Gerbi: *The Dispute of the New World: The History of a Polemic, 1750–1900*. Pittsburgh, Pa: University of Pittsburgh Press 1973; and Antonello Gerbi: *La disputa del nuovo mondo: Storia di una polemica, 1750–1900*. Milan: Riccardo Ricciardi editore 1983.
30 Simón Bolívar / Frederick H. Fornoff / David Bushnell: *El Libertador: Writings of Simón Bolívar*. New York: Oxford University Press 2003, p. 12. For a Spanish version, see Simón Bolívar: 'Contestación de un Americano Meridional a un caballero de esta isla.' In: *Bolívar, Obras completas*, vol. 1. Madrid: Maveco de Ediciones 1984, p. 160–171.
31 Bolívar et al.: *El Libertador*, p. 13, 15, and 18.
32 Bolívar et al.: *El Libertador*, p. 26.

del globo) and thus onto the global perspective characteristic of Bolívar's Pan-American thought.[33]

No less global, but at the same time hegemonic, were the constructions of the hemisphere that came from the north a few years later. The Monroe Doctrine, the millennial salvation narrative of Manifest Destiny, and the growing territorial, political, and economic might of the USA on the American continent signaled the formation of a different kind of pan-Americanism during the course of the nineteenth century. This a pan-Americanism also sought to delimit Europe's power while at the same time doing so very deliberately in the service of US interests. This construction and its underlying understanding of hemispheres as spheres of influence and power recalls the Iberian powers' division of the world in the Treaty of Tordesillas. The main difference was that now the center of power over the continent was shifted to the so-called western hemisphere itself. This theoretical claim to power was translated into practice in 1898 when the USA intervened in the war between Cuban and Spain, successfully expelling the Spanish colonial power from the Caribbean and the Philippines. US Senator and Secretary of State William H. Seward, self-styled 'prophet'[34] of an American expansion based on global trade, had sketched out this development early on and had designated both the Caribbean and Mexico, whose capital, according to Seward, could one day become the 'excellent site for the future American empire,'[35] as direct spheres of influence of the USA. The division of the American hemisphere became an established fact during the nineteenth century, as did the increasing arrogation of the term America by the USA. While, from a European perspective, the Latin South increasingly appeared as a backward region, the USA, as the example of Alexis de Tocqueville shows, came to embody a model for future developments, both positive and negative, for a Europe that seemed deserving of the sobriquet 'old' now more than ever. Even Latin America accepted the notion of a divided hemisphere under the increasingly obvious dominance of the USA.

The separation of the Americas into two continents, resulting as it did from their divergent development, would put a stop to nascent hemispheric thinking

---

33 Bolívar et al.: *El Libertador*, p. 26.
34 See William Appleman Williams: *The Roots of the Modern American Empire: a Study of the Growth and Shaping of social Consciousness in a Marketplace Society*. St. Helens: Wood Westworth & Co. 1970, p. 136. See also Hans-Ulrich Wehler: *Imperialismus: Studien zur Entwicklung des Imperium Americanum, 1865–1900*. Göttingen: Vandenhoeck & Ruprecht 1974, p. 14.
35 Gerard H. Clarfield: *United States Diplomatic History*, vol. 1: Readings for the eighteenth and nineteenth Centuries. Boston: Houghton Mifflin 1973, p. 233.

along egalitarian lines. Throughout the entire twentieth century, discourses on the American Hemisphere maintained their imperial(istic) character. Even José Martí's clearly Caribbean work *Our America* (1891), which continued Bolívar's ideas about the need for a global equilibrium, did nothing to change that. Martí concluded with a plea, as it were, for the blessing of the Indian cultures for 'the new America over the romantic nations of the continent and the sorrowful islands of the sea.'[36] The hemispheric doctrine that ruled the entire twentieth century would henceforth no longer be insular but continental, determined by the contiguous land mass of a great nation and its pervasive economic power. It is only in US military strategy that the island element appeared in the context of concepts of a future 'sea power,' to the extent that it concerned the translation of an initially continental but soon to be global claim to power into artificial, mobile 'islands,' such as battleships and later aircraft carriers that could be rapidly dispatched to the coast of any country where they would serve as floating military bases. In this way, the USA continued and even surpassed the island method that characterized Spanish expansionist politics. Since the third phase of accelerated globalization, which began with the end of the nineteenth century, US hegemony has been supported by the creation of its 'own' islands in the midst of a 'Mare Americanum' that would be worldwide in its scope.

Transareal Caribbean studies and relational logic

Against this background, and in the context of the current fourth phase of acelerated globalization, it is necessary to develop concepts that can be situated between a local and/or national level on the one hand and a planetary one on the other. At the same time, one needs to avoid the intellectual and scholarly buttressing of the static and simplistic territorialized contrasts that would pit the USA and Canada against the Latin American and Caribbean states. Although one can but agree with the notion of a philology of world literature that Erich Auerbach introduced in 1952 – 'our philological home is the earth; it can no longer be the nation'[37] – it still seems necessary that we find ways to mediate be-

---

36 '[L]a América nueva ... por las naciones románticas del continente y por las islas dolorosas del mar.' José Martí: 'Our America.' In: *Critical Documents of 20th Century Latin American and Latino Art. Resisting Categories: Latin American and/or Latino?* New Haven: Yale University Press 2012, p. 215. José Martí: 'Nuestra América.' In: *Martí, Obras Completas*, vol. 6. Havana: Editorial de Ciencias Sociales 1975, p. 23.
37 Erich Auerbach: 'Philology and Weltliteratur.' In: *The Centennial Review* 13.1 (Winter 1969), p. 17.

tween the concept of national literature, oft-challenged but de facto still dominant in academia, and a globally expanded world literature. Similarly, we need to create transareal and transregional frames that would connect nationally oriented historiographies and social analyses with promising research into the forces and factors responsible for creating a global society.[38] The Caribbean is especially suited for developing the transdisciplinary dimensions of such an approach,

Any new hemispheric construction of 'America' as a topic of scholarly research, especially one driven by Latin Americanists, would have to resist reproducing US political and economic hegemony at the level of research, while at the same time of course acknowledging its very existence. It would be especially vital in this context to initiate a conversation between the internal relations among the regions of the different Americas and an external set of relations in ways that would neither revert to the familiar dependencies and hierarchies nor remain caught up in an uncritical view of America from the European (out)side. The networks that exist between America and Africa, and between America and Asia, must move into the foreground of such hemispheric research more than has been the case in the past.

Rather than a new territorialization of regional concepts, the goal of such worldwide networking in transareal and transregional studies is an attempt at rendering spatial concepts dynamic so that we can draw more precise distinctions among the *movements* of the various areas and regions. This includes the movements between and within the Americas, most notably in the Caribbean where cultural relations are uniquely plentiful and intense. The Caribbean island world has been a 'zone of intensified globalization,' of intensified patterns of movement, since the first phase of accelerated globalization.[39] No other place in the world has been witness to the globalizing power and violence of so many European 'mother' countries over a comparably long period of time.

Antagonistic spatial concepts need to be destabilized and rendered dynamic. At the same time, transareal and transregional challenges to specifically European interests and perspectives, which have dominated scholarly work for

---

[38] See Mathias Albert / Lothar Brock: 'Debordering the World of States: New Spaces in International Relations'. In: Mathias Albert et al. (eds.): *Civilizing World Politics: Society and Community beyond the State*. Boston: Rowman & Littlefield 2000, p. 19-43. See also Matthias Albert: *Zur Politik der Weltgesellschaft: Identität und Recht im Kontext internationaler Vergesellschaftung*. Weilerswist: Velbrück Wissenschaft 2002, p. 330-340.

[39] See Günther Maihold: 'Die neue (Ohn-)Macht der Grenze: Mexiko- USA.' In: Marianne Braig et al. (eds.): *Grenzen der Macht – Macht der Grenzen: Lateinamerika im globalen Kontext*. Frankfurt am Main: Vervuert 2005, p. 69.

historical reasons, should not deny the historical asymmetries and dependencies that followed in their wake. Transareal literary analysis would focus neither on Europe-derived ideas of world literature, nor on developments within Latin American literature or any one national literature. Instead, it would concentrate on movements that transect and unsettle these familiar reference points. Rather than with spaces, it would be concerned with routes; it would not draw borders but shift and cross them. The point is not abandon the disciplinary construction of objects of study but to interlink them such that the resulting objects exist beyond traditional area studies and are more than the sum of individual findings.

Conceived as translocal, transregional, transnational, transareal, and transcontinental, American studies would challenge regionalized thought patterns from a comparative perspective. In linking individual regions, specific Latin American(ist) competencies will have to be developed in transdisciplinary fashion. It is not a priority to compare, say, Latin America and Anglo-America but to focus on the fundamentally complex (that is, non-causal) system of interactions within and across a culturally hybrid continent. One cannot reach an adequate understanding of the Caribbean without the transareal and transdisciplinary inclusion of India, China, West Africa, and Western Europe; nor can one, as has often been tried, understand the Caribbean from a single (national) cultural perspective. To see the Caribbean as a space made up of movements requires new concepts of relationality and cultural mobility. Such new concepts and methods use the spatial models of fractal geometry and develop a critical imaginary that allows for discontinuous relations of space, time, and movements marked by numerous rifts and fractures. The goal is not to map out (new) territory but to conceive of a *vectoral* space through the insights of quantum geometry. This peculiar space consists of and contains historically accumulated patterns of movement that we can call upon at any time and in which old patterns appear either 'below' or in the guise of new movements. In this way, the vectoral space functions as a storehouse of movements that constitute fractal patterns and networks broken up in a quantum-geometrical fashion; neither can be explained *fully* through traditional spatiotemporal ideas. The natural sciences can help humanists think (about) the same objects of study differently and from other perspectives, using logics and theories this side of Euclid and Newton.

In the Caribbean, not everything is interconnected with everything else at the same time; but everything does come into contact with everything else, be it sporadically or in the longer term, at one time or another. These leaps and lapses in time and space, these spatial irregularities and specific developmental simultaneities of nonconcurrent events and idea, determine the fundamentally complex structure of the Caribbean. Important is not that the Caribbean is a chaotic structure, as Antonio Benítez Rojo suggests, but that it is a *living* construct that oscillates between chaos and cosmos.⁴⁰

The Caribbean space provides countless examples of how an approach anchored in the hermetic isolation of a single discipline can produce devastating errors of judgment. The restricted vantage point of a single discipline can only inadequately elucidate the complex interplay and high concentration of geopolitical, geocultural, and biopolitical factors in such a region. At issue, then, is a transareal and transregional construction of the American hemisphere, in which researchers do neither separate 'North' from 'South' nor isolate Indo-American, African American, Hispanic American, and Anglo-American aspects from one another. The task of TransArea studies is to analyze hemispheric frameworks, that is, to transcend regional, national, and international thought patterns and explanatory models by bringing into conversation sustained disciplinary expertise with the methodologies of interdisciplinary dialogue and, above all, with transdisciplinary ideas and processes. TransArea studies, then, always rely on the development of multiple logics of mobile relations that, for their part, house singular and particular logics, each in its very own stubborn peculiarity.

At the center of my inquiry are not stable processes of consecutive deterritorialization and reterritorialization but oscillating movements between various regions and areas. I want to understand large-scale migrations, from the 'roving' Caribs to the Caribbean boat people, not as linear processes but primarily as complex interactions that effectuate knowledge transfers between various regions and continents. Beyond bilateral and binomial structures, one cannot assume the existence of stable identities but must attend to configurations of

---

40 See his stimulating but somewhat too binary study: Antonio Benítez Rojo: *La isla que se repite*. Barcelona: Editorial Casiopea 1998, p. 16ff. and 413, and Antonio Benítez Rojo: *The Repeating Island: The Caribbean and the Postmodern Perspective*. Second Edition. Durham/London: Duke University Press 1996, p. 10ff. His borrowings from chaos theory serve merely to dynamize the Caribbean's basic underlying structure, the plantation: 'If I have seized hold of certain models belonging to Chaos, it has not been because I think that these can manage to signify fully what's there in the archipelago; rather it's because they speak of dynamic forms that float, sometimes in unforeseen and scarcely perceptible ways within the Caribbean's huge and heteroclitic archive ... In the case of the Caribbean, I think the most important 'strange attractor' is the Plantation, which allows us to predict the continuation of a literature, a music, and an art having forms similar to those dealt with in this book.' Benítez Rojo: *The Repeating Island*, p. 313. I use the term *living* in the sense of the bioscientifically founded analysis of Friedrich Cramer, whose book illuminates the tension between chaos and cosmos.

mobile identities. It is clearly time for thinking that moves beyond identity and beyond re-centering the spatial models still present, for instance, in Jean Bernabé, Patrick Chamoiseau, and Raphaël Confiant's influential *In Praise of Creoleness* (*Eloge de la Créolité*, 1989) and their focus on 'the chaos of this new humanity that we are.'[41]

Literature plays a large role as the interactive storehouse of knowledge-for-living, for fundamentally complex systems such as literature do not gloss over or even erase contradictions in the same way that disciplinary scholarship can and does. Literary works will thus claim most of my attention in this chapter. Before proceeding, I want to mention that scholarship that deals with the USA from a Latin American point of view, and vice-versa, is to be understood as neither transareal nor hemispheric. Such work proceeds mainly along binary lines that contribute to further cementing fruitless and amply familiar antagonisms. By contrast to such approaches, novel transareal and transregional concepts offer significant potential for innovative interdisciplinary approaches beyond the traditional forms of area studies and regional research.

Fractal Pattern 1: Island House and Island Literature

Following up on George Lamming's remark that there is no more appropriate geographic location for a study of exile than that of the island,[42] Chris Bongie, in *Islands and Exiles* (1998), describes the ambivalence of the island-ness which I have mentioned repeatedly:

> The island is a figure that can and must be read in more than one way: on the one hand, as the absolutely particular, a space complete unto itself and thus an ideal metaphor for a traditionally conceived, unified and unitary, identity; on the other, as a fragment, a part of some greater whole from which it is in exile and to which it must be related -in an act of (never completed) completion that is always also, as it were, an ex-isle, a loss of the particular. The island is thus the site of a double identity – closed and open – and this doubleness perfectly conveys the ambivalences of creole identity that I outlined above.[43]

---

41 Jean Bernabé / Patrick Chamoiseau / Raphaël Confiant / Mohamed B. Taleb Khyar: 'In Praise of Creoleness.' In: *Callaloo* 13.4 (1990), p. 890.
42 George Lamming: *The Pleasures of Exile*. Ann Arbor: University of Michigan Press 1992, p. 96.
43 Chris Bongie: *Islands and Exiles: The Creole Identities of post/colonial Literature*. Stanford, CA: Stanford University Press 1998, p. 18.

The island as materialization of closed or open identities, or, in Edouard Glissant's words, of 'identité-racine' and 'identité-relation,' calls attention to the ambivalent semantics of the island as isolation and exile on the one hand and as openness and relation on the other. Voluntary or forced exile and the tension between *a-isla-miento* and deterritorialization frequently play key roles in Caribbean texts. Consider that even Cuban literature, the (academically) most established of Caribbean literatures, has, from its beginnings in the early nineteenth century to the present day, consistently featured protagonists in motion: José María Heredia's move between Cuba and Mexico; Gertrudis Gómez de Avellaneda's between Cuba and Spain; and Cirilo Villaverde's between Cuba and the USA. On the other side of the insular marginalization of a Julián del Casal or a Juana Borrero, we find the many exiles of José Martí, in Spain, Mexico, Guatemala, Venezuela, and the USA. It is an itinerary that once again brings to light the hemispheric dimension in Cuban literature, a dimension that is also part of Dominican, Puerto Rican, and Haitian literatures. All of them are Literatures without a fixed Abode, in which isolation has a paradoxical relationship to *errance*.[44] A glance at any island map would suggests a territoriality that, in actuality, cannot be reduced to the seemingly stable space within the island's borders.

Because of their self-similarity, the fractal, multiply broken dimensions of these island boundaries relate directly to the technique and processes of the *mise-en-abyme* mainly in longer Caribbean prose narratives but also in some shorter ones. How do Caribbean writers put into practice a method that one might compare to Russian dolls on the one hand and to immensely subtle nestings on the other? What are the thematic, aesthetic, and theoretical specifics that pertain to the Caribbean region?

It comes as no surprise that the figure of the house should play an important role in Caribbean Literatures without a fixed Abode, which, to recall Bongie, comes from the tensions between isolation and exile. The fairly enclosed nature of the domestic space and the possibility for creating multiple, eversmaller spatial subdivisions are features that make the house a world of its own and an inexorable model for an insular situation and a writing that finds its home there. Reinaldo Funes's 2006 painting entitled *The Island* (*La Isla*) is an almost exemplary embodiment of this figure (see Figure 4). In this painting, almost the entire island is taken up by a complex, confusingly build and multiply

---

[44] See Ottmar Ette: 'Una literatura sin residencia fija: Insularidad, historia y dinámica sociocultural en la Cuba del siglo XX.' In: *Revista de Indias* 65, 235 (September–December 2005), p. 729–753.

partitioned house that seems to be at once construction site, dwelling, and Tower of Babel.

Fig. 4: Reinaldo Funes, *The Island* (*La Isla*, 2006), © Reinaldo Funes

Maryse Condé's *Crossing the Mangrove* (*Traversée de la Mangrove*, 1992) is a good literary example of an intricately subdivided area within which the house functions as a *mise-en-abyme* for the structure of the novel, that is, the one spatial arrangement in the novel closely relate to its overall structure. At the displaced center of the novel is the house of the protagonist, who, at the end, is found lying in his coffin. The house, with its multiple layers and tracts, is divided into an inside and an outside and occupies an eccentric position in relation to the microcosm of the hamlet Rivière au Sel. What is more, this hamlet is connected with Petit Bourg, a small, more centrally situated locale that, for its part, is aligned with Pointe-à-Pitre, itself integrated into the bicameral structure of the island of Guadeloupe. The island orients itself first toward the French Antilles and Guyana; then toward the Caribbean island world including, notably, Cuba and Haiti; then toward the circumCaribbean coastline of the South and North American mainlands (*Tierra firme* and Louisiana); then toward the American continent in its hemispheric dimension, toward Europe and especially the French 'motherland,' and finally toward Africa and India.[45]

Rich in representations of overlapping and nested spaces and temporalities, Caribbean literatures abound with expressive and aesthetically effective examples of similarly arranged spatial structures. The house, for instance, plays a central role in V. S. Naipaul's *A House for Mr. Biswas* (1961), where it leaves its imprint on a human life and an entire social group. The book examines the struggle for social advancement of proto-middle-class Trinidadians of Indian descent, a heritage the author himself shares. Already the first part of the novel's prologue lays out the spatial structures of the entire novel in the process of establishing the leading role of the house in Sikkim Street in St. James, Port-of-Spain. Right from the start, *A House for Mr. Biswas* shows us domestic interiors that overlap in the memories of the novel's characters as the text also sketches out the family's past migration from India and its future migration to England. It is in the UK that Anand, thanks to the sacrifices of his father, Mr. Biswas, will begin his university studies, a plot development that also parallels Naipaul's own life. From the very beginning of the novel, the overlapping Trinidadian spatiotemporal structures, embedded as they are in American-Indian-European systems of reference, are lovingly laid out, only to reappear, one last time, in the final chapter, 'The House,' and in the Epilogue, now in an ironic and carefully thought out manner. For Mr. Biswas, the insular situation of a closed and simultaneously differentiated world is impressively 'embodied' in the house of the dying, yet still hopeful, journalist.

> He thought of the house as his own, though for years it had been irretrievably mortgaged. And during these months of illness and despair he was struck again and again by the wonder of being in his own house, the audacity of it: to walk: in through his own front gate, to bar entry to whoever he wished, to close his doors and windows every night, to hear no noises except those of his family, to wander freely from room to room and about his yard, instead of being condemned, as before, to retire the moment he got home to the crowded room in one or the other of Mrs. Tulsi's houses, crowded with Shama's sisters, their husbands, their children. As a boy he had moved from one house of strangers to another; and since his marriage he felt he had lived nowhere but in the house of the Tulsis, at Hanuman House in Arwacas, in the decaying wooden house at Shorthills, in the clumsy concrete house in Port of Spain. And now at the end he found himself in his own house, on his own

---

[45] For a more detailed analysis, see the section 'Romanstruktur und Raumstruktur' in chapter 11 of Ottmar Ette: *Literatur in Bewegung: Raum und Dynamik grenzüberschreitenden Schreibens in Europa und Amerika*. Weilerswist: Velbrück Wissenschaft 2001, p. 479–485.

half-lot of land, his own portion of the earth. That he should have been responsible for this seemed to him, in these last months, stupendous.[46]

This passage is a dense *modèle réduit* of the unmistakable insular trademark of Naipaul's novel: nested spatiotemporal overlaps. After his mother, his siblings, and he himself are evicted from their humble dwelling following his father's death, Mr. Biswas becomes a restless wanderer between houses that do not belong to him but always belong to others, houses that offer him no real abode and in which he cannot feel at home. His life develops in front of the readers' eyes as a life without a fixed abode, characterized by endless changes of place which are part of a long history of migration.

The *mise-en-abyme* structure of the house, then, is one of the key features of Caribbean literatures; it is like a piece of real estate that cannot be sold. In Gisèle Pineau's tale 'Love's torment' ('Tourment d'amour'), the overlapping structures are also tied to an island house, or, more precisely, to the young first-person narrator's initially described project to publish, for the first time, 'an album of the creole dwellings of [her] island' (album inédit sur les cases créoles de mon île).[47] Hidden behind the story's classic frame-and-tale structure, in which an accidental encounter connects external frame with internal tale, is a complex spatiotemporal layering and nesting in which the history of Guadeloupe from the mid-nineteenth century to the end of the twentieth is told through a series of shacks and houses. That history commences with the teller's project of an album with photographs of all kinds of 'creole shacks' (cases creoles). Without being able here to go into detail with respect to the narrative techniques Pineau employs, I still want to stress that the rifts and overlaps that exist between image and writing, between written and oral cultures, and within a genealogy women upon which they have left their distinctive stamp, all proceed from a century-old structure that unites life and death through an 'exalting and morbid vision' (vision exaltante et morbide), 'like a feverish bat that holds on to the side of a verdant rock ledge' (comme une chauve-souris fiévreuse au flanc d'un morne verdoyant).[48] The freedom of movement, stasis, and deportation of the various figures overlap in complex ways in the few pages of the story. In the end, however, the author, who herself grew up in both Paris and Guadeloupe, super-

---

46 Vidiadhar Surajprasad Naipaul: *A House for Mr. Biswas*. London: André Deutsch 1961, p. 8.
47 Gisèle Pineau: 'Tourment d'amour.' In: Ralph Ludwig (ed.): *Écrire la 'parole de nuit': la nouvelle littérature antillaise. Nouvelles, poèmes et réflexions poétiques de Patrick Chamoiseau, Raphaël Confiant, René Depestre, Édouard Glissant, Bertène Juminer, Ernest Pépin, Gisèle Pineau, Hector Poullet et Sylviane Telchid*. Paris: Gallimard 1994, p. 80.
48 Pineau: 'Tourment d'amour,' p. 80.

imposes them in such a way as to allow, on this 'day of the great revelation' (jour de grande revelation), the (literary) recording of a multiply fragmented story in which the isolated island house becomes a shard of a world that her audience and readers are charged with completing.[49] The 'case créole' thus contains a fractal story whose rifts and ruptures, worlds of islands and I(s)land-worlds, create a densely poeticized understanding of a region that does not limit itself to itself but that can only be thought through on a global (and globalized) scale.

Haitian writer Yanick Lahens's 'In the father's house' (*Dans la maison du père*, 2000) will serve as my final example of a fractal pattern embodied in a Caribbean house. The reader sees the titular house right at the outset of the novel. It is a house in which outside and yard, European mass culture and Haitian folk culture, imported body control and traditional body knowledge abruptly and even brutally clash. The novel's fast-moving opening scene, dated January 22, 1942 and narrated in the first person, culminates in an act of violence. From this scene emerges the eventful and affecting image of an entire life in which past, present, and future intersect and overlap: 'There is no beginning that predates this image. The image is central. It is the middle of my life. It summarizes the before and illuminates the after ... I was born from this image. It brought me into the world a second time, just like I myself birthed it.'[50] The origin disappears in the double gestation metaphor of birthing and being born in an interplay of layers that interpenetrate and mirror each other without, however, making individual and collective history disappear in the process. As in Naipaul's *A House for Mr. Biswas*, the image of the house, with its power to render non-concurrent events simultaneous, disorients and skews the whole novel. As in Gisèle Pineau's 'Love's torment,' the fragmented and fractured story of a life and of an island emerges from a single image that has absorbed many other images. And, as in Maryse Condé's novel, the multiply sectioned house orients itself towards an island space that itself opens to the world through the protagonist's peregrination(s) and the always fragile link between body control and body knowledge. Specifically, it opens onto the ex-isle Manhattan, that other dreamed-of and yet foreign island that we also encounter in Reinaldo Arenas's novel *The Doorman* (*El portero*, 1989).

> During all these years I have danced under all the heavens of the earth, and one fine December night I pitched my tents in Manhattan, right next to the crazy dreams of a jazz pia-

---

49 Pineau: 'Tourment d'amour,' p. 87.
50 Yanick Lahens: *Dans la maison du père*. Paris: Le Serpent à Plumes 2000, p. 14.

nist, so as never to take it down again. Far from my island, I often longed for its light, for the steamy boldness of its mornings, for the stands of palms dancing below the wrung-out sky, for the sun-drenched days when the earth has guava eyes, for its gorgeous men and its women; for the dryness of Gonaives; for its strength; for its skies and its torn landscapes. The yearning was as strong as the body's need for food, for air, or for water.

In moments like that, I often swallowed my loneliness, pushed it down my throat and even further down, to a place where the silky mornings of my childhood already live.[51]

This is not the warmed-over island nostalgia, a commonplace in Caribbean literatures but, rather, an image of a dancer's knowledge-for-living which at last embraces the isolated, lonely region of the novel's opening scene. This scene is about the body of the self, the island-body that aches for LifeSupport and creates its own inner interWorld in order to survive. The body knows about the addictions and desires that could not be spoken in the father's house. This *embodiment* of the island, already hinted at in the image of the life-giving newly-born, has both material and literary-theoretical connections with the relation of island and exile. For Yanick Lahens, this relation marks the position of the Haitian writer who finds herself 'Entre l'Ancrage et la Fuite,' between anchorage and flight, in the endless internal space of a literature that no longer has a fixed abode, for reasons that are not only spatial and sociopolitical but also, above all, a function of culture, nation, and language.[52]

Is it possible that Caribbean literatures from Haiti, Cuban, or elsewhere might serve as models for future developments on a transareal and global scale? Lahens's reply to this question was a yes. In an interview held in March 2002 in Berlin, she not only emphasized that Haitian literature is 'a lap ahead' because of its long and painful experience of persecution, exile, and displacement, but also spoke of three generations of Haitian writers, one of whom [Edwidge Danticat], already writes no longer in the mother tongue but in a *langue étrangère*, the foreign tongue of English. One would consequently have to 'rethink the

---

[51] 'Durant ces années j'ai dansé sous tous les cieux du monde et j'ai planté mes pieux un soir de décembre à Manhattan, au plus près des rêves fous d'un pianiste de jazz, pour ne jamais les enlever. Loin de mon île, j'eus souvent envie de sa lumière, de l'iridescence vaporeuse de ses aubes, des palmiers dansant sous son ciel essoré, de ces jours ensoleillés ou la terre a des yeux de goyave, de ses hommes et de ses femmes de foudre, de l'aridité des Gonaïves, de sa force, de son ciel et de ses paysage déchirés. Un besoin aussi fort que celui du corps quand il réclame de la nourriture, de l'air ou de l'eau. Dans ces moment-là, j'enfon ais souvent ma solitude tout au fond de ma gorge et plus loin encore, là où avaient déjà pris place les matinées soyeuses de l'enfance.' Lahens: *Dans la maison*, p. 152f.
[52] See Yanick Lahens: *L'Exil: entre l'ancrage et la faite. L'écrivain haïtien.* Port-au-Prince: Éditions Henri Deschamps 1990.

concept of national literature and cultural heritage: The first generation of exiles and the migrants of later generations will explode the problematics of national literature. We may ask today: What is a national literature when viewed from the perspective of Haitian literature?'[53] It is precisely such questions about the relations between national literature and world literature, about migration and translingual translation, that I will address in the following chapters in the context of the Literatures without a fixed Abode. But first it is necessary to analyze another fractal pattern, one that surprises only at first glance: the pattern of the island as camp.

Fractal Pattern II: Island camp and prison-island

In his often pioneering readings of Caribbean cultures, the Cuban essayist and novelist Antonio Benítez Rojo made the plantation the pivot and crux of his views concerning not only the economic and political but also the cultural and political identity development of the Caribbean. According to his well-argued thesis in *The Repeating Island*, one cannot possibly understand Caribbeanness (lo caribeño) without considering the fundamental structure of the plantation.[54]

The structural matrix of the plantation is also the focus of Cuban Reinaldo Arenas's *El Central (A Cuban Sugar Mill)*, a cycle of poems completed in May 1970 on the Manuel Sanguily sugar plantation and first published, in Spanish and in English, in 1981, when Arenas was already in exile in New Jersey. The late Arenas achieved international fame more through his novels and his posthumously published autobiography, *Before Night Falls: A Memoir (Antes que anochezca*, 1992) than through his poems.

In *El Central*, the transtemporality of the work camps allows for overlapping spatiotemporal nestings: the forced labor of the subjugated, abused Indians; the hard labor of the maltreated enslaved Africans who are used as colonial 'fuel'[55] and the forced labor of the young male convicts who are sexually and politically exploited on the sugar plantations. For none of the groups and individuals is there a way out. It is always the 'slaves' hands' (manos esclavas) that have powered Cuban history, from the Conquest and the time of Christian missionary

---

53 Ottmar Ette: 'Faire éclater la problématique d'une littérature nationale: Entretien avec la romancière haïtienne Yanick Lahens à Berlin, le 24 mars 2002.' In: *Lendemains* 27 (105–106), p. 227.
54 Benítez Rojo: *La isla que se repite*, p. 414 and 243; *The Repeating Island*, p. 314, and 110–111.
55 'Human fuel for the burning.' Galeano: *Open Veins*, p. 59.

work to the establishment of the first 'Free territory of America' and Castro's socialist state.⁵⁶ Arenas's imaginary progressive prophet, however, can make sense of all this, even in the face of the festivals and parades that each of the powers-that-be stage:

> Dear...
> Behind all these public displays, behind all this marching around, the hymns, the unfurling of flags, the speeches, behind every official ceremony,
> lurks the intent of stimulating and raising your work efficient and
> intensifying your exploitation.
> It was Karl Marx who told me so, bursting into a laugh as he wheeled gracefully and set off at a trot behind the militarized children who brought up the rear guard.⁵⁷

The transtemporal space of the sugar plantations renders present to each other all these other manifestations of the camp in which humans are herded together, tortured, and exploited. This also includes the re-education camps of the Cuban Revolution to which *The brightest Star (Arturo, la estrella más brillante)* is the most convincing witness, both in terms of aesthetics and frictionality (that is, the spaces in-between diction and fiction):⁵⁸

> ... and Arturo thought, I'll bet if the others (the guards, he meant) decided to line up every one of them and have them shot by a firing squad, these prisoners would docilely hold out their hands to have them tied, walk docilely through the camp, halt when ordered to halt, and every one of them, with the inherent gullibility of household pets, would burst in silence, all of them, every single one of them, or all of them but him, because he was going to fight, he was going to rebel, he was going to testify to the horror, tell someone, lots of people, tell the world, or tell even just one person, as long as there was one person who had still an uncorrupted, incorruptible capacity to think, he would leave this reality with that one person ...⁵⁹

---

56 Reinaldo Arenas: *El Central: A Cuban Sugar Mill*. New York: Avon 1984, p. 86, 23, and 86.
57 Arenas: *El Central*, p. 12. 'Querido, detrás de todos estas fiestas públicas. Detrás de todo desfile, himnos, despliegue de banderas y elogios. Detrás de toda cennonia oficial, se esconde la intención de estimular tu coeficiente de productividad y de explotación. Esto me lo dijo Carlos Marx, haciendo un gracioso giro, soltando una carcajada y marchándose apresurado tras los fondillos de los niños-militares que integraban la retaguardia.' Reinaldo Arenas: *El Central*. Barcelona: Seix Barra 1981, p. 15.
58 For more on frictionality, see also Ottmar Ette: *Roland Barthes: Eine intellektuelle Biographie*. Frankfurt am Main: Suhrkamp 1998, p. 312.
59 Reinaldo Arenas: *'Old Rosa', and 'The brightest star': two novels*. New York: Grove/Atlantic, 1989, p. 72. 'Arturo pensaba que si en algún momento los jefes, los otros, hubiesen determinado que todos ellos debían ser fusilados, se hubiesen dejado, amarrar las manos tranquilamen-

The camp has become the *modèle reduit*, the *mise-en-abyme*, of an island with overlapping historically cumulative camp structures. No other island, no other place, than Cuba seems more suitable for showing such a transnational and transhistorical crosshatching of different camps. It was on Cuba where, at the beginning of Spanish colonial rule, the Indian population was exterminated through forced labor and de facto enslavement. It was also Cuba that, toward the end of the colonial period, witnessed the appearance of the first so-called concentration camps (campos de concentraciones) which predated even the notorious concentration camps that the British set up in South Africa.[60]

As 'exemplary place of modern biopolitics,'[61] the camp is closely linked with colonial wars and thus colonialism in general, a problematic that has received far too little attention. The long history of fingerprint technology to identify potential criminals and its historical refinements[62] shows that many practices first 'tested' in the colonies and other dependent territories were sooner or later brought home to the political and economic metropoles, albeit in modified forms. As Hannah Arendt pointed out in her meditations on power and violence, it is no coincidence that the era of imperialism was well aware of the 'boomerang effect' that the domination of other peoples had for Europe itself.[63] The philosopher of the elements and origins of totalitarianism took the brutal ac-

---

te, hubiesen caminado tranquilamente por el campo, se detendrían a la orden dada y todos, sin protestar, con la ingenuidad típica de los animales, hubiesen reventado en silencio, todos, todos, todos menos él, porque él se iba a rebelar, dando testimonios de todo el horror, comunicándole a alguien, a muchos, al mundo, o aunque fuese, a una sola persona que aún conservara incorruptible su capacidad de pensar, la realidad ...' Reinaldo Arenas: *Arturo, la estrella más brillante*. Barcelona: Montesinos 1984, p. 43.

60 See Giorgio Agamben: *Homo sacer: Sovereign Power and Bare Life*. Stanford CA: Stanford University Press 1998, p. 166.

61 Agamben: *Homo sacer*, p. 119.

62 For the establishment of fingerprinting in Great Britain circa 1900 as a criminological identification system as opposed to anthropometric methods, see Anne M. Joseph: 'Anthropometry, the Police Expert, and the Deptford Murders: The Contested Introduction of Fingerprinting for the Identification of Criminals in Late Victorian and Edwardian Britain'. In: Jane Caplan / John Torpey (eds.): *Documenting Individual Identity: the Development of State Practices in the Modern World*. Princeton/Oxford: Princeton University Press 2001, p. 164–183. Instructive is Joseph's observation concerning the transition from the anthropometric totality of a human body to an isolated or – apropos our theme – *insular* body part: 'Its adoption in late Victorian Britain signaled a changing conception of identity – from a frozen image in a photograph and a string of measurements of body parts to an image of patterned lines and ridges; from a construction that construed identity as emanating from the whole to a formulation of permanent identification from a part.' Joseph, 'Anthropometry,' p. 183.

63 See Hannah Arendt: *On Violence*. Boston, MA: Houghton Mifflin Harcourt 1970, p. 54.

tions of US police against rioting Berkeley students as a convincing example of this very 'boomerang phenomenon.'

If the camp can be considered the structural matrix of the island, the island in its entirety can be thought of as camp or prison. While such a semantic charge of the island can be found in the literatures of all Caribbean islands, it is notably frequent in Cuba, where searchlights visible from the coast signal the presence of a coast guard far busier protecting the land-water border from the island's own inhabitants than from any external enemy. Especially at the turn of the twenty-first century do we find more frequent literary portrayals of armed conflict at this contested boundary 'fence.' Jesús Díaz's *Tell me something about Cuba* (*Dime algo sobre Cuba*, 1998) is but one example.[64] The everyday presence of the 'prisoner situation' also appears with some frequency. Reinaldo Arenas's *Otra vez el mar / Once again, the Sea* (1982) and Zoé Valdés' *Café Nostalgía* (1997) show it in both brutal and subtle forms of surveillance. From the latter novel's deft alternation of inner and outer perspectives, of 'past' and 'present,' Cuba comes clearly into view as a prison island where spatial and also temporal barriers are crossed perpetually. Even in the visual arts do we encounter the image of the island as (prison) camp with relative frequency, for instance, in the paintings of Raúl de Zárate which obsessively depict the island as a camp complete with enclosures and border fences (see Figures 5 and 6).

---

[64] Jesús Díaz: *Dime algo sobre Cuba*. Madrid: Espasa Calpe 1998 [Available so far only in French and German translation. TN]

Fig. 5: Raúl de Zarate, *MECANICA NACIONAL* (2003), © Raúl de Zárate

Fig. 6: Raúl de Zárate, *no locomoción* (2004), © Raúl de Zárate

However one wishes to judge political developments in postrevolutionary Cuba, it is clear that the raft has become the theory metaphor for an island whose coastline is virtually endless from the perspective of both fractal mathematics and more traditional methods of measurement, and that, for all practical purposes, can never be absolutely 'secured.' As Iván de la Nuez put it, Cuba is the 'perpetual raft,' *La balsa perpetua*.[65] Well before the Cuban boat people began to appear in large numbers, Reinaldo Arenas had dreamed that the island could someday move off its territorial plinth and dock on to the coastline of other continents and countries. But even such imagined movements would not have, for Arenas, in any way changed or averted the course of the island's tragic history.[66]

In view of this long, painful, and complex relationship between island and camp, it should come as no surprise that a new chapter was added to the tale of this sinister symbiosis when, in the context of the so-called war on terror, the US government decided to use the Guantanamo Bay prison for those suspected of belonging either to the Taliban or other active terror networks. In his 2003 study of the state of exception as a paradigm of government during modernity, the Italian philosopher Giorgio Agamben analyses the legal, philosophical, and biopolitical dimensions of this development:

> The immediately biopolitical significance of the state of exception as the original structure in which law encompasses living beings by means of its own suspension emerges clearly in the 'military order' issued by the president of the United States on November 13, 2001, which authorized the 'indefinite detention' and trial by 'military commissions' (not to be confused with the military tribunals provided for by the law of war) of noncitizens suspected of involvement in terrorist activities.[67]

It is worthwhile not only to reflect on the omnipresence of the camp in the modern era and on the alarming intermittent states of exception connected with it, but also to think through the spatiotemporal specifics of the case of Guantanamo. Seven hundred people from forty countries were interned there for several years, having forfeited not only their civil rights but also their prisoner-of-war status and the protections of the Geneva Convention. They were isolated in individual wire cages of five square meters for an indefinite period in a camp at a

---

65 Iván de la Nuez: *La balsa perpetua: Soledad y conexiones de la cultura cubana*. Barcelona: Editorial Casiopea 1998 [Available so far only in German translation. TN]
66 See Arenas's revealing formulations in Ottmar Ette: 'Los colores de la libertad: Nueva York, 14 de enero de 1990'. In: Ottmar Ette (ed.): *La escritura de la memoria: Reinaldo Arenas – Textos, estudios y documentación*. Frankfurt am Main: Vervuert 1992, p. 88f.
67 Giorgio Agamben: *State of exception*. Chicago: University of Chicago Press 2005, p. 3.

military base that had originally been established on Cuba to supply US naval forces. The fact that this military base stemmed from the US intervention in the very colonial war during which the first *campos de concentraciones* were set up in Cuba is a particularly wry ruse of history.

The infamous prison camp known as Camp Delta is an island within an island on an island that belongs to the Caribbean island world but also, at the same time, part of the military network of the US armed forces. Prior to 2001, Guantanamo Bay had made international headlines as a reception camp and switchyard for, among others, Haitian boat people. But Camp Delta took on another aspect as an area unregulated by law, be it US, international, or Cuban law. It is well known that camp practices, which are impossible to distinguish from intricate methods of torture, have had a boomerang effect on civil rights and freedoms in the USA itself, and far beyond its borders. In the context of a 'world order' that has yet to be created, this effect remains an urgent topic for discussion.[68]

This legal no-man's-land is suggestive of a *mise-en-abyme* of the relationship between island and camp, a succession of self-similar relations that, paradoxically – if we are to believe Giorgio Agamben – represent a state of exception that is no accident in the factory of history but, instead, a paradigm. The legal isolation of this place of solitary confinement corresponds to an island situation that is spatially extraterritorial in relation to the continental USA. In Camp Delta, which was divided into four sections according to the prisoners' will to cooperate, the usual military law at Guantanamo is suspended. That it was necessary in this legal state of exception to create and construct a separate court building speaks to an almost inherent compulsion to territorialize even this legal no-man's-land through a 'normal' court building in which public defenders would be appointed by the Pentagon. Although the intense media interest in this prison in eastern Cuba may have profoundly contributed to a seeming architectural normalization, it has still failed to shift the trials to the continent. Islands are far more suitable for creating an area unregulated by law and for the efficient surveillance of prisoners, and not because of their infrastructural discontinuity.

No less disturbing is how this state of exception, ultimately only seemingly cut off from the mainland, is part of the camp paradigm that runs through Cuban history (and surely not through Cuban history alone): as a transtemporal fractal pattern that takes on the form of different historical constellations. Even

---

[68] See Tzvetan Todorov et al.: *The New World Disorder*. Cambridge, UK: Polity 2005.

the island as camp, as a microcosm of the I(s)land-world, belongs to a world of islands whose external relationality will be my final focus in this chapter.

Beyond Utopia: The fractal dynamics of the Caribbean

Much more could be said about the multi-relationality of the Caribbean island world and its relations to power, especially in view of internal power relations and their structural ties to (the uses of) violence. In this context, it would be useful to study the pirates, corsairs, and freebooters. In the island spaces they ruled (beyond territory in the narrower sense) such figures embodied the oscillating transitions from acratic to encratic structures,[69] from a being-in-power to a being-outside-of-power, for an astonishingly long period of time. It was perhaps the pirates and freebooters who most fully utilized the natural preconditions for developing their own island logic, itself conditioned by the 'mobile territoriality' of their ships. The island world they created oscillated strikingly between chaos and periodicity. Compared to this flexible system, the Spaniards' effort to connect the Caribbean with Europe's infrastructure, and the subsequent formation of what came to be known as the 'Black Atlantic,'[70] takes on the appearance of a hugely cumbersome machine built from countless military barracks, batteries, and bureaucracies, canals, churches, customs checkpoints, fortresses, highways, piers, soldiers, sailors, shipyards, warehouses, watchtowers, and weaponries.[71] This system brutally swept up the Caribbean during the accelerated globalization process of the first phase, when this island world was brought into ever more sustained contact with the most diverse regions of the world. No other region in the world was for such a long time at the mercy of external powers that devised biopolitics and adapted them to the natural and cultural conditions of this island world.

This does not mean that we must understand the Caribbean as a meta-archipelago that has, by definition, the benefit of having neither borders nor a center.[72] Early and sustained globalization in its various phases brought with it not only a countless networks but a proliferation of borders, which had an impact on economic and political spheres alike and led to that linguistic diversity of

---

69 For these terms within the (fragmentary) power theory of Roland Barthes, see Ette: *Roland Barthes*, p. 346–349.
70 See Paul Gilroy: *The Black Atlantic: Modernity and Double Consciousness*. London: Verso 1993.
71 See the list in Benítez Rojo: *Repeating Island*, p. 8–9.
72 Benítez Rojo: *Repeating Island*, p. 9.

today's Caribbean. It would be most apt to characterize this situation as a simultaneous lifting and multiplying of borders, a transareal, transcontinental, and translingual development that has been advancing no less rapidly in the cultural and literary realms. To wit, for some time now, Cuban literature has not 'only' been written in Spanish, nor Haitian literature in French or *français créole*. Cuban literature written in the USA, South America, South Africa, Spain, Germany or elsewhere avails itself of several languages in the same way that Haitian literature written in North America does.

There is much to be said for Antonio Benítez Rojo's claim 'that Caribbean literature is the most universal of all literatures.'[73] This does not, however, mean that *the* Caribbean literature – if indeed it existed in the singular – is, as it were, universally borderless, but that its borders have changed. In most cases, these borders have become more porous and, at the same time, as my above examples show, have proliferated. While the conventional (and trite) talk of the unity and diversity of the Caribbean and Caribbean literature is surely not wrong, it is only partly true. After all, the Caribbean and its literatures form a fundamentally complex system that consists of interactions, overlaps, and self-similarities which show the natural and cultural geometry of the Caribbean to be fractal. Alongside the 'Euclidean' discourse on unity and diversity should stand a fractal discourse and a theory informed by cultural studies which could do justice to the leaps, discontinuities, overlaps, and incoherencies of the Caribbean and its specific literary and cultural phenomena.

Isolation is only one part of the insularity that increasingly affects all Caribbean cultural, literary, and artistic developments. Insularity also refers to a multiply broken relationality within a space that is in no way homogenous but has an intense vectoral 'charge.' Labeling such a system 'fundamentally complex' ultimately means that an *isolated* view of the (national) literature of each individual island must take into account over-lapping transnational and transcultural networks, along with transcultural and translingual networks. Transdisciplinary approaches are required for such studies.

It seems to me that the aforementioned differentiation between overlapping internal and external relations is a good way to proceed. The references to the various regions of Africa, India, and China would stand for an external relationality, while the networks that develop, say, among the different ethnic groups in the Caribbean and in North and South America from a hemispheric perspective,

---

[73] Antonio Benítez Rojo: 'Three Words toward Creolization'. In: Kathleen M. Balutansky and Marie-Agnès Sourieau (eds): *Caribbean Creolization: Reflections on the cultural Dynamics of Language, Literature and Identity*. Miami: University Press of Florida 1998, p. 59.

describe the phenomenon of internal relationality. If one considers the distribution of African slaves within a Black Atlantic framework, the Caribbean island world has been the key node between external and internal relations since 1518. The hemispheric relevance, if not dominance, of this island world to the whole of the Americas remains undiminished, also with respect to music and literature, and even beyond. The Caribbean is an *area* that cannot be adequately grasped with the tools of traditional area studies.

As Ana Pizarro has emphasized in the introduction to her successful anthology, the Caribbean island world is always in motion and experiences continuous shake-ups as a result: 'If the cultures are no fixed formations but processes, then this insight proves largely plain when we approach the Caribbean. There, the elements in motion, the arrivals, hybridizations, overlaps, configurations in the process of structuration, de-structuration, and re-structuration, all sketch out a dynamic that announces at once splendor and turmoil.'[74] These constant and at the same time discontinuous movements find their way into intensely vectoral literatures that function as storehouses of accumulated knowledges-of-and-for-living. Together with rhythms and rhythmics, this wealth of movements is probably the most distinguishing feature of Caribbean literatures. To reduce all of this to specific aspects of a 'divergent' peripheral literature would mean to lapse into the old and discredited (if still observable) practice of purism that Derek Walcott castigated in his 1992 Nobel Prize speech:

> These purists look on such ceremonies like grammarians look at a dialect, as cities look on provinces and empires on their colonies. Memory that yearns to join the centre, a limb remembering the body from which it has been severed, like those bamboo thighs of the god. In other words, the way that the Caribbean is still looked at, illegitimate, rootless, mongrelized ... Fragments and echoes of real people, unoriginal and broken.[75]

It would be easy to find many examples that prove the vectoral characteristics of Caribbean literatures and their impressive ability time and again to provide *both* space *and* time for different cultural logics and directions. But the island world of the Caribbean is more than just a landscape of theory; it also renders visible theoretical practices often closely tied to literary writing. If one were to understand the Caribbean as a laboratory, as has been done at times, one should add that it is no longer a laboratory in which externally accumulated knowledge is translated into specific arrangements and subsequent explications, and has not

---

74 Ana Pizarro: *El archipiélago de fronteras externas: Culturas del Caribe hoy.* Santiago de Chile: Editorial de la Universidad de Santiago de Chile 2002, p. 27.
75 Walcott: 'The Antilles,' p. 67.

been that for some time now. Instead, the knowledge tested out in the laboratory setting of the Caribbean is knowledge that has been produced there. The Caribbean IslandWorlds produce and export not only sugar, fruit, and raw materials but also theories. The Caribbean has long been a space with a very high concentration of cultural and literary theoretical production. Theoretical concepts by Antonio Benítez Rojo, Aimé Césaire, Patrick Chamoiseau, Raphaël Confiant, René Depestre, Frantz Fanon, Roberto Fernández Retamar, Edouard Glissant, Stuart Hall, George Lamming, Iván de la Nuez, Gustavo Pérez Firmat, and Derek Walcott, among many others, have traveled well beyond the Caribbean sphere of influence for some time now; they have made the Caribbean a landscape of theory in a dual sense. Today, the Caribbean is one of the major exporters of cultural and literary theory, in addition to the many other (supposedly more 'typical') export products dictated by external markets. The ability and the necessity to think in and live according to different logics more or less at the same time has likely contributed to this situation.

Symptomatic of the formation of theory in the Caribbean is the fact that one can frequently observe the simultaneity of the non-simultaneous in this area as well, insofar as each of the various islands of theory generates a unique, to some extent independent field of reference, using discrete methodological and literary-historical points of reference. The concept of *créolité*, for instance, took hold in the francophone Caribbean half a century after the debates about *criollismo* in the hispanophone parts of the Caribbean. The difference is that *créolité* developed in a theoretical sphere that was unmistakably imprinted with poststructuralism and burgeoning postcolonial studies. Postcolonial scholars from the English-speaking work gratefully seized the problematic of creoleness and translated it into their own theoretical formulations. It is in this sense as well that the Caribbean exceeds the boundaries of its own sea and installs itself in a fractal geometry irreducible to simple causal relationships. Its shared foundation is, rather, a complex transcultural knowledge-for-living (together) based upon the experience of heterotopic plurality. The reason why the Caribbean offers such an exceptionally promising starting point for TransArea studies is not just its multi-relationality. For quite some time now, the Caribbean has not only been an object of study but also an inquiring subject. In the dialogue between Caribbean and extra-Caribbean theories, ideas emerge that throw a new light on cultural developments worldwide.

From the late-fifteenth to the second half of the twentieth century, Europeans have often turned the Caribbean into a projection screen for their utopian dreams. As we know, many of those utopias turned out to be nightmares. In Latin America, however, the power of the Caribbean islands to generate utopias has always had limits. Fernández de Lizardi's *The Itching Parrot* (*El Periquillo Sarniento*, 1816), which dates from a period of transition between colonial New Spain and postcolonial Mexico, was probably the first utopia created by a Hispanic-American author not to be set in the Caribbean. Instead, Lizardi displaced his utopia to the west, projecting it onto an island between Asia and America. From this island space, Lizardi could level a major social critique against a New Spain then ruled by viceroys. It would seem that, already by the beginning of the nineteenth century, the Caribbean could no longer serve as the site for utopias, if utopia were to be counternarratives. One hopes that today, the Caribbean, as an archipelago that vouches for the plurality of islands and, even more so, of IslandWorlds, has become an island world beyond utopia

4 Incubations

A National Literature without a fixed Abode? Fictions and Frictions in Twentieth-Century Cuban Literature

> 11. –*Boat*. We start at 11. We pass (4) Maisí and see the beacon. I on the bridge. At 7:30, darkness. Movement on board. The captain very moved. The boat is lowered down into the water. It pours as we pull away. We go off in the wrong direction. Different and confusing ideas among those in the boat. It continues to pour. We lose the rudder. We determine the direction. I row at the prow. Then Salas rows. Paquito Borrero and the General help at the stern. We strap on the revolvers. In the direction of the bay. The moon rises, red, below a cloud. We land on a rocky beach, *La Playita* (at the foot of *Cajobabo*). I am the last one in the boat and empty it. I jump. Incredible luck. We overturn the boat and the large water carafe. We drink málaga. High above rocks, through thorns and swamps. We hear noises and get ready, near a shack. Past a settlement, we reach a house. Near it, we sleep, on the ground.[1]

These are the dense words, illuminating events as though by lightning, that the Cuban poet, essayist, and revolutionary José Martí jotted down in his war diary to describe the improvised arrival of the row boat taking him, together with General Máximo Gómez and other followers, from the German freighter 'Nordstrand' to the coast of the Oriente Province in Cuba on April 11, 1895. The nocturnal arrival on Cuban soil put an end to the restlessness and drifting of exile which appear almost paradigmatically, as if in a final *mise-en-abyme*, on board of the ship exposed to waves and weather, before the red moon washes the night scene in her light and finally blurs the two poles that had dictated the course of Martí's life: 'I have two fatherlands: Cuba and the night.'[2] The landing,

---

[1] '11.–*bote*. Salimos a las 11. Pasamos (4) rozando a Maisí, y vemos la farola. Yo en el puente. A las 7 1/2, oscuridad. Movimiento a bordo. Capitán conmovido. Bajan el bote. Llueve grueso al arrancar. Rumbamos mal. Ideas diversas y revueltas en el bote. Más chubasco. El timón se pierde. Fijamos rumbo. Llevo el remo de proa. Salas rema seguido. Paquito Borrero y el General ayudan de popa. Nos ceñimos los revólveres. Rumbo al abra. La luna asoma, roja, bajo una nube. Arribamos a una playa de piedras, *La Playita* (al pie de *Cajobabo*). Me quedo en el bote el último vaciándolo. Salto. Dicha grande. Viramos el bote, y el garrafón de agua. Bebemos málaga. Arriba por piedras, espinas y cenagal. Oímos ruido, y preparamos, cerca de una talanquera. Ladeando un sitio, llegamos a una casa. Dormimos cerca, por el suelo.' José Martí, 'Diario de Cabo Haitiano a Dos Ríos.' In: José Martí: *Obras Completas*, vol. 19. Havana: Editorial de Ciencias Sociales 1975, p. 215.

[2] 'Dos patrias tengo yo: Cuba y la noche.' José Martí, 'Dos patrias.' In: José Martí: *Poesía completa*, vol. 1. Havana: Editorial Letras Cubanas, 1985, p. 127.

fortunate in every respect after the loss of the rudder, culminates in the leap of the self, immediately followed by a great feeling of joy: 'I jump. Incredible luck.'[3] Against all advice to continue to lead the revolution either from New York or Florida, the man who had long since become the mainspring and spiritual father of the war against colonial Spain – a war that would end in the political independence of his native island and that historians would remember as the *Guerra de Martí* – had, like Odysseus, returned to his home island after a restless exile. In Cuba Martí died a few weeks later, on May 19, 1895, in a skirmish with Spanish troops in Dos Ríos and found his final resting place.

The circle of a life of tireless rebellion against Spanish colonialism, and against a US neo-colonialism that Martí had diagnosed very early on, thus closed with the figure of a circle, with a return that, as the founder of the *Partido Revolucionario Cubano* had fully intended, imbued his life and his death with transhistorical significance. The scene of arrival ends with the conspiratorial community of the first-person plural, and the lexemes that shift the stresses of the last two sentences toward their ends are not coincidentally words that recur throughout Martí's poetry of exile: house (casa) and ground (suelo). Faraway Ithaca, the eastern part of Cuba with which Martí was unacquainted: a homecoming to an intimately familiar foreign place, described in the insistent, poetic language of a war diary that is perhaps the most intense expression of this political and literary life.

The thematic maps of the *Atlas histórico biográfico de José Martí*[4] give us an impressive image of the varied and restive movements in Martí's life, which, because it knew many places of residence, had no fixed abode. In a final gesture, the figure of the circle tries to invest the banishments, deportations, migrations, and travels across the Caribbean, Europe, South, Central, and North America with a sense of homecoming, a sense of fulfillment already prefigured in the joy of the self at the opening of the war diary. And yet, this leap of the self, like the figure of the circle itself, is deeply ambivalent in its hermeneutics: it is at once a leap into life and a dive into death. As through an immense compression, the precise observations not only of the revolutionary but also of the writer-poet flash in the few lines Martí devotes to the dramaturgy of April 11. Throughout the last of Martí's *Diarios*, these observations release a torrent of poetic images and a fascinating

---

[3] In his work, Martí aimed successfully at an effect after his death, an effort at the myth of the own life. A result is one of the most fascinating histories of reception not only in Latin America. See Ottmar Ette: *José Martí: Eine Geschichte seiner Rezeption*. Tübingen: Niemeyer 1991.
[4] See José Martí: *Atlas histórico biográfico José Martí*. Havana: Instituto Cubano de Geodesia y Cartografía, Centro de Estudios Martianos 1983.

series of dramatically heightened perceptions of himself and of others. With respect to poetic intensity, none of his many other texts can compare with this book of Martí's last days and his return to a foreign island world that fascinated the poet Martí. The open, paradigmatic Island World of exile, which most especially includes the ex-isle Manhattan from which Martí seeks to orchestrate Cuba's future independence, has become the closed I(s)land-world of the home island.

There may be no greater contrast to Martí's hermeneutic figure of the movement of an entire life than the movement of the Cuban poet, significant but still largely unknown, who died a few months later on the perimeter of the storm Martí had unleashed. Unlike the modernist writer turned national hero at Dos Ríos, Juana Borrero, namesake of Martí's fellow traveler, spent her life in Puentes Grandes close to Havana in the exhilarations of a late-Romantic atmosphere. Her idol and love of her life was the modernist Julián del Casal who died prematurely in 1893. Having grown up in a family of poets shaped by her poet-father, Esteban Borrero Echeverría, this highly talented and highly strung poet and painter who, differently though no less absolutely, wanted to transform her life into her own work of art, cast her spell over Carlos Pío Uhrbach, a modernist in Casal's mold. A relationship began, the heat of whose passion was rooted in the young woman's absolute claims to love and possession. For Borrero, who had firm roots in the family estate in Puentes Grandes, the island of Cuba, once also known as 'Juana,' was the only thinkable, the only livable, I(s)land-world.

A record of the fusion of love, life, and literature[5] so characteristic of Juana Borrero's writing has been preserved in a series of love letters that can be read as a chronicle of a death foretold. This record also marks the gender-conscious position of a young woman who desperately searched literature for models that would help her realize her own life in the male-dominated world of modernist poetry. But Juana Borrero, who had briefly met José Martí in his New York exile when she had accompanied her father to the USA during the preparations for conspiratorial activities, had to learn how painfully politics and the political intruded into her own life. First, her genial lover, from whom she, true to the figure of the 'sad virgin,' the 'Virgen triste,' in Casal's eponymous poem, always kept a physical distance, announced that he would actively participate in the war of independence. A little later she was told that her father, legitimately fearing reprisals and perse-

---

5 For details about this linguistic amalgamation, see Ottmar Ette: 'Die Fremdheit (in) der Mutterzunge. Emine Sevgi Özdamar, Gabriela Mistral, Juana Borrero und die Krise der Sprache in Formen des weiblichen Schreibens zwischen Spätmoderne und Postmoderne'. In: Reinhard Kacianka / Peter V. Zima (eds.): *Krise und Kritik der Sprache: Literatur zwischen Spätmoderne und Postmoderne*. Tübingen: A. Francke Verlag 2004, p. 251–268

cution, would move the entire family to the USA for their protection. Benjamin's Angel of History also entered Juana Borrero's life. Like him, she was expelled from paradise by a tempest that could not be contained.[6]

Juana resisted both plans with grim determination. In a long letter to Carlos Pío Uhrbach from January 11, 1896, written not in ink but in her own blood, she confronted him with the following choice: 'Your fatherland or *your Juana*: you choose' (Tu patria, o *tu Juana*: elige).[7] A mere week later, however, she had to depart, together with her family, for Key West in South Florida where her already precarious health would deteriorate rapidly. Six days before she died, on May 3, 1896, she dictated to her sister Elena what was probably the last letter to her lover from her forced exile: 'I am filled with horror and worry at the things that are happening there. For the sake of my recovery, I beseech you to steer clear of any danger.'[8] But not even this last wish was to be fulfilled: Carlos Pío Uhrbach died in the war of independence on December 24, 1897.

From the perspective of exile, Cuba, for Juana Borrero, had become the 'there' (*allá*) that José Martí wanted to change back into a 'here' at the end of his life. While Martí gained increasingly more control over his own movements throughout his life and sought to close the circle of his life with his return to Cuba, the young Juana Borrero never achieved such agency, her life coming to an end after a last forced leap across the Florida Straits in the halted movement of a hasty flight. In his verse drama *Abdala* from 1869, the sixteen-year old Martí had extolled the love for the fatherland over any other love, celebrating the death as *mártir* for the homeland in all its unmistakable tonal closeness to his own surname.[9] He had demanded an unequivocal decision between Spanish colonialism and Cuban independence in 'O Yara o Madrid.'[10] The eighteen-year old Juana

---

6 Walter Benjamin, 'On the Concept of History.' In: *Selected Writings*, vol. 4. Cambridge, MA: Harvard University Press 2003, p. 392. For the two figures of movement of the return of Odysseus and of the Angel of History, see chapter 2 in this book.
7 Juana Borrero: *Epistolario*, vol. II. Havana: Academia de Ciencias de Cuba 1967, p. 257.
8 'Estoy llena de horror y de inquietudes con las cosas que están pasando allá. Te ruego por mi curación que te pongas a cubierto de todo peligro.' Borrero: *Epistolario*, p. 367f.
9 'And if you die fighting, I grant you / the crown of the martyr for the fatherland!' (Y si mueres luchando, te concede / La corona del mártir de la patria!). See also the last lines: 'oh, how sweet it is to die, if ones dies / boldly fighting to protect the fatherland!' (Oh! qué dulce es morir, cuando se muere / Luchando audaz por defender la patria!). José Martí, 'Abdala. Escrito expresamente para la Patria.' In: José Martí: *Obras Completas*, vol. 18. Havana: Editorial de Ciencias Sociales 1975, p. 17 and 24.
10 José Martí, 'El Diablo Cojuelo.' In: José Martí: *Obras Completas*, vol. 1. Havana: Centro de Estudios Martianos 1983, p. 22.

Borrero, by contrast, saw herself as a martyr to her own love and demanded that her lover decide between her and his fatherland.

But contrasts notwithstanding, Martí and Borrero still share common ground, not only in their passionate death wish and therefore their living for death, but, above all, in the absolute nature of their respective claims to fashion their lives and their writing as unconditionally literary and in their ability to interweave their biographies, actions, and art so completely that it is impossible to separate them without significant semantic reduction. In the same way that the poetic and fictional elements, which the poems, lyrical landscape images, and narratives contain *in nuce*, are an unmistakably part even of the political discourse and the descriptive passages of Martí's diary, Borrero's correspondence includes the fragments of a lovers' discourse, albeit in compressed form. In her letters, we can recognize the origins of nuclei of poems, reflected upon in great detail, and even of whole poems, along with fictionalizations of her own life (glimpsed in her use of literary pseudonyms) whose tensions derives from the steady friction of fiction and fact. We find here a constellation of great importance especially for the twentieth century: the oscillation between fiction and diction, to use Gérard Genette's terms, creates a *frictionality*[11] that has proved particularly productive for Cuban literature. The patterns of spatial movement and the frictions between genres in the examples I have selected here emerge as emblematic of twentieth-century Cuban literature. Situated on the threshold of the Cuban Republic and its literature, José Martí's and Juana Borrero's lives, writings, and life-writings are not only indispensable embodiments of Cuban and Hispanic-American *modernismo*. They also prefigure a development I detail with the help of representative examples in the pages that follow. It is of utmost significance that José Martí's and Juana Borrero's writings represents the two major patterns of movement that my second chapter identifies as vital to the Literatures without a fixed Abode: (Odysseus's) return to a foreign home and the act of being blown away by the storm of progress which, in Benjamin's words, sweeps away everything and pushes the 'Angel of History …irresistibly into the future, to which his back is turned…'[12] At the dawn of the twentieth century, the century of dramatic migrations also and especially in Cuban history, Juana Borrero's and José Martí's respective texts embody, as if in

---

[11] For a discussion of this term, which could, albeit reductively, be described as a to and fro between fiction and non-fiction, see Ette: *Roland Barthes*, p. 308–312. I first applied this concept to Hispanic-American literatures in Ottmar Ette: "'Así habló Próspero': Nietzsche, Rodó y la modernidad filosófica de *Ariel*.' In: *Cuadernos Hispanoamericanos* 528 (1994), p. 48–62.

[12] Benjamin: 'On the concept,' p. 392.

a double helix, the motile patterns of a dialectic of homelessness without which the Literatures without a fixed Abode are unimaginable.

Place, nation, and language from the perspective of transareal motion

In his 1974 portrait of the Italian coastal town of Savona, Italo Calvino subtly draws attention to the need for multidimensional and, as it were, mobile, or *vectoral*, accounts of places and spaces:

> If one wants to describe a place, describe it completely, not as fleeting appearance but as part of a specific space that has a shape, a meaning, and a why, one has to depict it as crossed by the dimension of time, to represent everything that moves in this space, be it very rapidly or excruciatingly slowly: all elements that this space contains in its past, present, and future relations. A true description of a landscape thus includes the history of that landscape, the totality of all the facts that have gradually contributed to creating the shape before our eyes and the equilibrium between the forces that cohere and those that rupture, forces that manifest themselves at each moment.[13]

This passage may help us analyze a description of a certain landscape or space (the island of Cuba) with its related cultural phenomena (such as Cuban literature) less with regard to the surface appearance of a territory with rigid borders and local artistic phenomena than with a view to a hypothesized dynamics of movements. From this perspective, the island of Cuba appears as a place that, in the travelogues of so-called European discoverers, rose up from the sea of the histories of the Ciboney and Guanahacabibes and thus, as Fernando Ortiz once quipped, from Cuba's 'age of stone and wood' (edad de piedra y palo).[14] Cuba

---

13 'Se si vuole descrivere un luogo, descriverlo completamente, non come un'apparenza momentanea ma come una porzione di spazio che ha una forma, un senso e un perché, bisogna rappresentarlo attraversato dalla dimensione del tempo, bisogna rappresentare tutto ciò che in questo spazio si muove, d'un moto rapidissimo o con inesorabile lentezza: tutti gli elementi che questo spazio contiene o ha contenuto nelle sue relazioni passate, presenti e future. Cioè la vera descrizione d'un paesaggio finisce per contenere la storia di quel paesaggio, dell' insieme dei fatti che hanno lentamente contribuito a determinare la forma con cui esso si presenta ai nostri occhi, l'equilibrio che si manifesta in ogni suo momento tra le forze che lo tengono insieme e le forze che tendono a disgregarlo.' Italo Calvino: 'Savona: storia e natura.' In: Italo Calvino: *Saggi 1945–1985. A cura di Mario Barenghi*, vol. 2. Milan: Arnoldo Mondadori Editore 1995, p. 2390.
14 Fernando Ortiz: *Contrapunteo cubano*, p. 94. For the English version see *Cuban Counterpoint: Tobacco and Sugar*. New York: A. A. Knopf, 1947, p. 99.

emerged from the perspective of observers located on ships' decks; it originated in movement and *as* movement. As an important launching pad for the future colonization of other regions in the Americas; as a naval base for Spanish warships and trade fleets; and as a possible missile base in the superpowers' global poker game – the island's indisputable geostrategic importance continually transformed it into a space of dynamic movements whose scale was always global, from the first phase of accelerated globalization that began with Columbus to the current fourth phase. Cuba was a *global player* from the very start, even if the island began its career as a mere chip in the worldwide game of competing European powers.

Looking dispassionately at the emergence of Cuba's national literature during the nineteenth century, we quickly find that that literature, too, is the result of movement, for it did not originate in or from a single place. The foundational texts of the poet José María Heredia cannot be imagined outside of the tension between island and exile, colonial Cuba and independent Mexico, no more than Cirilo Villaverde's *Cecilia Valdés or El Angel Hill* (*Cecilia Valdés, o la loma del Angel*, 1882), a text that inscribed itself into the field of tensions between Cuba and the USA as the true foundational novel of Cuba's national literature and, at the same time, thanks to the history of its writing, as a bridge between the 1830s and 1870s. Even the great female poet of Spanish Romanticism, Gertrudis Gómez de Avellaneda, without whom neither Spanish nor Cuban literary history is imaginable, positioned her poems and narratives in a geopolitical web that was no less bipolar in relation to the Spanish motherland and the Cuban fatherland than Heredia's and Villaverde's works, except that Avellaneda did not write in exile. Her marvelously frictional autobiography provides striking evidence of this tension.[15]

As parts of a system of biographical and cultural coordinates within which Cuban national literature constituted itself decades before the island's political independence, nineteenth-century Mexico, the USA, and Spain, all of which enjoyed relations with France and England as well as with other regions of the American hemisphere, created the dynamic matrix that characterizing Cuban literature from its inception. From the beginning, the *spiritus rector* of this literature is a *spiritus vector*: it is a literature born out of and made up of movement.

How did Cuba's well-established national literature change and develop when the process of becoming a nation entered a new phase with the founding

---

[15] See Gertrudis Gómez de Avellaneda / Nina M. Scott: *Autobiografía y cartas*. Huelva: Diputación Provincial 1996. [For an English translation see *Sab and Autobiography*. Austin, TX: University of Texas Press 2003. TN]

of the nation-state and the institutional protections of political independence, an independence, however, that was very relative from the start, as is amply documented by the Platt Amendment and the recurring interventions of the hegemonic USA? It is hardly an exaggeration to define the first two republican decades of Cuban literature as a time characterized by an absence of the voices that had fallen silent at the end of the nineteenth century, the prolific output of many writers and intellectuals notwithstanding. The final decade of the nineteenth century witnessed not only the death of the aged Cirilo Villaverde in his New York exile, but also, even more importantly, the premature hush of such great, and far younger, authors such as José Martí, Julián del Casal, Juana Borrero, and Carlos Pío Uhrbach, even before the founding years of the Cuban republic as a result of the Spanish-Cuban-American war, in which the USA had purposefully intervened after long observation and preparation. Given the gaping hole that opened up at the beginning of the twentieth century as a result not of a lost generation but of one that had vanished, one could speak of a degree zero of Cuban literature, as long as one does not lose sight of the fact that the basic patterns of this literature – the (belated) dialogue between island and exile and the tradition of extra-Cuban relations for all cultural phenomena – persisted and continued to develop more rapidly, and in relative dependence on political trends. This is the reason why there was no real re-constitution of Cuban literature during the time of the republic's political constitution. Cuba's national literature had already enjoyed two heydays since, more than a hundred years ago, the foundations had painstakingly been laid for a Cuban nation that was always politically and economically unstable, that is, since the island had appeared on the political map. Both transareal and transcontinental in its orientation, Cuba's national literature not only predated the founding of the nation-state but was its indispensable precondition.

In the context of the more broadly internationalized Cuban literature that had emerged at least since the second phase of accelerated globalization, that is, since the beginning of the nineteenth century, the literary field during its early development in the nineteenth century can no longer be reduced to the rhythms and cycles of politics and of economics. Even though the hegemonic aspirations of the political arena had periodically strong repercussions for the literary field, they no longer went unchallenged even at times when the cultural policies of the Cuban state were speedily institutionalized. The presence and creativity of the parts of the literary field that existed outside Cuba were too strong for that to happen. Even during times when a uniform cultural policy, enforced by a host of institutions, tried to territorialize Cuban literature in significant ways, the 'extra-territorial' areas of Cuban literature succeeded in developing according to other logics. Regardless of all attempts at regulation, a relative degree of autonomy, even if cyclically threatened by politics, has always existed both within and without the island. Twentieth-century Cuban literature both before the 1959 revolution and afterwards is characterized by the dual logic of the play of *acá* and *allá*, here and there. This logic is ever-present, even if, at times, only in theory.

After the height of *modernismo* at the close of the nineteenth century, the first, still precarious flowering of Cuban literature in the twentieth century occurred only in the wake of the 1920s historical avant-gardes and the critical studies of worldwide vanguardist trends. Because of the problematic course of nation building during the first two decades of the Cuban republic, the emphasis was on essayistic writing and on a discussion of identity that grew rapidly in intensity because of the obvious political intrusions from without and also because of the budding 're-discovery' of José Martí, who was increasingly used to advance special political-ideological interests. In the thick web of periodicals (partly) influenced by avant-garde styles, a level of reflection emerged whose orientation was always pragmatic, always intent on possibilities for connecting literary-artistic with political-ideological avant-gardes. My following contemplations will show just how important a place frictional forms of writing and vectoral conditions occupied within Cuba's (national) literature which, from the outset, had a transareal and transcontinental disposition, and not only because of the biographies of its authors.

In his search for Cubanness, *cubanidad*, which haunted his entire generation, the writer and politician Juan Marinello, intimately familiar with Martí, emphasized just how difficult it was, already at the level of language, to draw the line between one's own and another's. He did this in a landmark essay from May 1932, written in the Presidio Modelo prison on the Isle of Pines, in which he reviewed Luis Felipe Rodríguez's collection *Marcos Antilla*: 'We exist thanks to an idiom that is ours while at the same time belonging to another' (Somos a través de un idioma que es nuestro siendo extranjero).[16] Even though Marinello may have defined the 'translational element' (elemento traductor) more narrowly in its significance for the Cuban condition than Gustavo Pérez Firmat would do more than fifty turbulent years later, Marinello still stressed the impossibility of attaining 'Cubanness' by retreating behind the barricades of what was presumably one 'own.' That one's 'own' was, in the end, inseparable from the 'other'

---

16 Juan Marinello: 'Americanismo y cubanismo literarios.' In: Juan Marinello: *Ensayos*. Havana: Editorial Arte y Literatura 1977, p. 48f.

even at the level of language[17] made inevitable, he argued, an almost paradoxical movement between 'the Cuban' and 'the Universal': 'To find a position on the difficult playing field of the universal, there is no other way than the one that leads us to our hidden cubanism which, as such, will create a vibration capable of reaching even the faraway spectator.'[18] Marinello does not imply a simple dialectic between the local and the global; even less is his an attempt at addressing only a distant reader. Rather, from the perspective of the prison in the specific situation of postcoloniality, in which this American writer would always remain a prisoner confined within the language of the former colonial master simply through his use of Spanish,[19] Marinello realized precisely the possibility for movement that would make the Hispanic-American reader of Cervantes's masterpiece not a second-rate interpreter of *Don Quixote* but a better reader in relation to a Spanish audience. For he was able to read from positions of proximity *and* distance at the same time. That reader was both intimately familiar with Spanish and simultaneously an observer from afar.[20]

Marinello's reflections, which foreshadow parts of Jorge Luis Borges's influential essay, 'The Argentine Writer and Tradition' (El escritor argentino y la tradición),[21] and show that the two share a Spanish point of reference (Miguel de Unamuno and his reading of *Don Quixote*), suggest a way for Hispanic-American, and especially Cuban, literature no longer to be torn between one's own and another's, but, rather, to be able to universalize the foreign inside one's own, and one's own within that which is alien. This possibility creates a new playing field for (Cuban) national literature in relation to world literature, which Borges would envision in even more subtle ways for Latin American literatures as a whole. Marinello already imagines not a movement reducible to a dialectic synthesis but a dynamic that remains open, a process, in short. Such a dynamic could be developed in the Cuba during the 1920, 1930s, and 1940s within a framework characterized by its recent postcolonial experience in relation to Spain and its contemporaneous neocolonial dependency on the USA. The desire

---

17 See Gustavo Pérez Firmat: *The Cuban Condition. Translation and Identity in Modern Cuban Literature*. Cambridge, UK: Cambridge University Press 2006. For the importance of translation in the context of my discussion, see especially chapter 5 above.
18 'Para lograr un puesto en la cancha difícil de lo universal no hay otra vía que la que nos lleve a nuestro cubanismo recóndito, que, por serlo, dará una vibración capaz de llegar al espectador lejano.' Marinello: 'Americanismo y cubanismo literarios,' p. 58.
19 Marinello: 'Americanismo y cubanismo literarios,' p. 48.
20 Marinello: 'Americanismo y cubanismo literarios,' p. 49.
21 Jorge Luis Borges: 'The Argentine Writer and Tradition.' In: *Odyssey* 1 (1961), p. 33–41; Jorge Luis Borges: 'El escritor argentino y la tradición.' In: *Sur* 232 (1955), p. 1–8.

for a stable nation translated into the insight that (recall Calvino) the place of this nation could be defined and described only through an endless movement on a transnational and transareal scale. Territory alone could, and should, not be a suitable playing field for such a process. Even Marinello's awareness of the postcolonial strangeness of one's own mother tongue already thwarts such a crude approach.

In 1940, the remarkable book *Cuban Counterpoint: Tobacco and Sugar* (*Contrapunteo cubano del Tabaco y el Azúcar*) by Cuban anthropologist and writer Fernando Ortiz inscribed itself into contrapuntal rhythms and dynamics that were well aware of their situatedness as a form of Writing-between-Worlds that had been, in a sense, pre-programmed in various and contradictory ways by the recourse to the Spanish language and its cultural traditions.

Migrants swept up in the hurricane of transculturation

No other twentieth-century Cuban author has molded Cuban thinking and writing, projections of the self and the other, more than the cultural theorist Fernando Ortiz who would soon be proclaimed the 'third discoverer' of Cuba (after Columbus and Alexander von Humboldt). Born in Havana in 1881 and raised on Menorca, he wrote and published his first work in Menorquin [a dialect of Catalán]. Familiar with island situations and transcontinental relations alike, Ortiz the scholar and essayist knew how to translate the mechanisms of exclusion that stemmed from his initially criminological interest in the black cultures of Cuba into an integrated projection of identity in the concept of a self-aware *cubanía*. He tirelessly disseminated this vision in numerous essays and books, and also with the help of many influential journals that he either founded or reanimated. Without Ortiz's writings, Afro-Cuban vanguardist narratives, such as Alejo Carpentier's *¡Ecué-Yamba-O!*, would no more have been possible than the experimental 'mulatto' sound poems in Nicolás Guillén's *Motivos de son* (Son motifs).

Much has been written about Ortiz's *Counterpoint* and its relation to the *Book of Good Love* (*Libro de Buen Amor*, 1343), one of the great texts of the European Middle Ages, and also to Bronislav Malinowski, probably the leading ethnologist of his time, who contributed a preface dated 'Yale, 1940' to the first edition of the *Contrapunteo*. Important for the kinds of questions I pose, however, is the fact that the text's double encoding, made explicit right from the start, due to its continuous oscillation between science and literature, between dictional and fictional forms of writing, shows the *Counterpoint* to be a highly frictional text.

To be sure, Fernando Ortiz's specific translational achievement is impressive, especially because of the writer's proclivity for neologisms that make his accomplishment more visible.[22] But the tension still present in the text today is a result of the friction of widely divergent forms of knowledge-for-living which Ortiz, through his transdisciplinary methodology, culled from various disciplinary fields of the Western sciences, from European literary history, and from non-Western representations and ways of storing knowledge. It may well have been Ortiz's early interest in the forms of everyday culture, particularly cooking, that led him to adopt the now familiar metaphor of the *ajiaco*, a stew of indigenous origins in which the different ingredients blend without melting into each other, without ever forming a 'finished' culinary unit.[23] His much-debated term *transculturación*, both impetus for and ingredient of his book, has as its thematic focus transgressive movements of varying transnational, transareal, and transcontinental kinds. The migratory movements of Antillean and continental Native Americans, Africans, Jews, Portuguese, British, French, North Americans, and Asians from all latitudes are centripetal from a Cuban perspective. Complementary centrifugal patterns of movement, perhaps best rendered through the transitory and transterritorial metaphor of migratory birds that never quite find a home, overlap with a 'hurricane of culture' (huracán de cultura)[24] powerfully and violently intensified by Europe.

There was no more important human factor in the evolution of Cuba than the first settlers' continuous, radical, and contrasting geographic transmigrations, economic and social; the perennial transitory nature of their objectives; and the unstable life they led in the country where they were in perpetual disharmony with the society from which they drew their living. Men, economies, cultures, and ambitions were all foreigners here, provisional, changing, 'birds of passage' hovering over the country, at its cost, against its wishes, and without its approval.[25] What took Europe a thousand years of cultural experience

---

22 See Pérez Firmat: *The Cuban Condition*, p. 16–33.
23 Ortiz's culinary interests are evident even from the first publication of the fourteen-year old Menorquin. See Fernando Ortiz: *Principi y prostes: Folleto de artículos de costumbres en dialecto menorquín*. Ciudadela, Menorca: Imprenta Fábregas 1895.
24 Ortiz: *Contrapunteo cubano*, p. 94; Ortiz: *Cuban Counterpoint*, p. 99.
25 Ortiz: *Cuban Counterpoint*, p. 101. 'No hubo factores más trascendentes para la cubanidad que esas continuas, radicales y contrastantes transmigraciones geográficas, económicas y sociales de los pobladores, que esa perenne transitoriedad de los propósitos y que esa vida siempre en desarraigo de la tierra habitada, siempre en desajuste con la sociedad sustentadora. Hombres, economías, culturas y anhelos todo aquí se sintió foráneo, provisional, cambiadizo,

occurred in Cuba in very few centuries as though in a time-lapse, an enormous acceleration that resulted in a 'change ...by leaps and bounds' (progreso a saltos y sobresaltos).[26] Walter Benjamin's tempest of progress has grown here into a hurricane of transculturation, and Cuba, viewed through the reticule of compressed and ever-accelerating globalization processes, appears as an island exposed to waves of water and migrants: a kind of in*cuba*tion of globalization whose quickening carries away everything and yet creates a culture of transculturation in the process – precisely *not* the non-culture of acculturation against which Ortiz deployed his term of *transculturación* in 1940, almost at the same time as Benjamin's 'About the Concept of History.' Here, we also see an Angel of History, one who, far away from Paradise, cannot close his wings against the onslaught of this Caribbean hurricane.

Many of the patterns of movements in Cuban history which Fernando Ortiz unearthed closely approximate the experiences of life and space we saw at the beginning of this chapter in José Martí's and Juana Borrero's writings. But the leaps and bounds, or 'shocks and aftershocks,' are characteristic of Cuban history and of the *Contrapunteo* itself, a text that excavates the phases of accelerated globalization in the Caribbean's world of islands with subtlety and humor. The structural frame of this frictional text already vexes at first glance: in a newer edition, the eponymous 'Contrapunteo' itself only takes up barely 90 pages, little more than a fifth of the book whose much longer second part, divided into 25 chapters with Roman numerals, has about 350 pages. Without being able to enter here into all the secret passageways of this textual pyramid with its two divergent signposts (that is, tables of contents), I want to point out that Fernando Ortiz's 1940 *Contrapunteo*, similar to Julio Cortázar's novel *Hopscotch* (*Rayuela*, 1963), invites at least two different ways of reading: a smooth, continual path from beginning to end *and* a reading in disjointed leaps and bounds, a bumpy ride reminiscent of the 'saltos y sobresaltos' in a text whose structure is not closed but open and rhizomatic. As in a hypertext, different textual planes, which are not necessarily connected on the metadiscursive level, can be combined into a moving text, a mobile of sorts, through different paths of reading. It is quite possible that Fernando Ortiz had in mind a different textual model, one that still belongs to modernity: Alexander von Humboldt's *Views of Nature* (*Ansichten der Natur*). Like the *Contrapunteo*, *Views* not only aspires to a 'combination of a literary with a purely scientific goal,' as Humboldt put it in his

---

'aves de paso' sobre el país, a su costa, a su contra y a su malgrado.' Ortiz: *Contrapunteo Cubano*, p. 95.
26 Ortiz: *Cuban Counterpoint*, p. 99; Ortiz: *Contrapunteo Cubano*, p. 94.

1849 'Preface to the second and third editions,' but also leaves ample room for additional textual modules to proliferate.[27] The scholarly-scientific notes grew from edition to edition until they finally took up five to ten times more room than the actual 'Views' themselves. Humboldt's notes also contained core narrative elements that threatened to become independent, another similarity with Ortiz's text.

Conversant with the work of both José Martí and Alexander von Humboldt to the point that he even published a Spanish version of the latter's *Political Essay on the Island of Cuba* (*Essai politique sur l'île de Cuba*),[28] Fernando Ortiz can, for my purposes, serve as a hinge. Not only would his *Contrapunteo* prove very influential in the areas of literature and science; at the same time, the text's style also showed, to aesthetic perfection, the transitions between historical avant-garde, post-avant-garde, and postmodernism which have become widely accepted in the Spanish-speaking world. As in the earlier and later cases of Jorge Luis Borges and Max Aub, a vanguardist 'inoculation' was necessary to protect these writers, who were intimately familiar with the historical avant-garde, from resorting to its patterns when they developed postmodern forms of writing.[29] The fact that both Borges's *Ficciones* and Aub's *Jusep Torres Campalans*[30] rehearsed the use of scientific-dictional writing may clarify that the *Contrapunteo*, published in the time intervening between these two texts, played an important constitutive role both textually and discursively (that is, with respect to literary-historical developments). The *Contrapunteo* combines discursive-descriptive forms of (re)presenting knowledge from the area of science with the more narrative shapes of knowledge from fiction and produces an idiosyncratic *science-friction* where knowledge (about and for life) is frictional and does not obey a single (binary) logic. In more ways than one, this *Cuban Counterpoint*, with its never-ending movements, situates itself within a Writing-between-Worlds that refers to the different phases of accelerated globalization, and the processes of transculturation connected with them, as much as it takes up resi-

---

27 Alexander von Humboldt: *Views of Nature*. Chicago: University of Chicago Press 2014, p. 27. 'Die Verbindung eines literarischen und eines rein scientifischen Zweckes.' Alexander von Humboldt: *Ansichten der Natur*. Nördlingen: Greno 1986, p. 9.
28 Alejandro de Humboldt: Ensayo político sobre l
a Isla de Cuba. Introducción por Fernando Ortiz. Havana: Cultural S. A. 1930.
29 To include the *Contrapunteo* in an amorphous idea of postmodernism seems to me too analytically imprecise; see Benítez Rojo: *Repeating Island*, p. 150–171.
30 See Ottmar Ette: *Literatur in Bewegung: Raum und Dynamik grenzüberschreitenden Schreibens in Europa und Amerika*. Weilerswist: Velbrück Wissenschaft 2001, p. 227–268 and 357–403.

dence in the oscillations between different fields and disciplines of knowledge production and in various literary genres and styles.

Flee(t)ing things in the vortex of the expressive American world

At the end of 'Romanticism and the American Fact' (El romanticismo y el hecho americano) the third and central talk in a series of five, delivered on January 22, 1957, Ortiz's famous contemporary José Lezama Lima combined two figures of movement that he saw as key to the 'American expression,' 'la expresión Americana':

> José Martí represents, in a great verbal Christmas, the fullness of the possible absence. In him culminate Fray Servando's dungeon, Simón Rodríguez's failure, and Francisco Miranda's death, but also the lightning flash of the seven intuitions in Chinese culture, which enables him to create and touch, through the metaphor of illumination, the vortex that destroys it; the mystery that does not stop the flight of the great losers and the oscillation between great destinies, and that he dissolves when he becomes one with the house that will be set on fire. We must situate his death within the Inca's Pachacámac, the invisible deity.[31]

Starting with Fray Servando Teresa de Mier's incarceration and the Mexican-Dominican friar's innumerable attempts at breaking out, Lezama uses the history of the struggle for Hispanic-American independence – for which Bolívar's teacher and counsellor Simón Rodríguez and Francisco Miranda also stand in – to construct a movement of historical acceleration culminating in the whirlpool that José Martí created and in which he and, as we have seen, many of his generation drowned. The path of the Americas in the nineteenth century does not therefore lead from the fixed place of the colonial prison (which Martí himself had to endure) to the equally fixed place of one's own independent home. Rather, it led, *pace* Ortiz and also Benjamin, into the eye of a twister destroying

---

[31] 'José Martí representa, en una gran navidad verbal, la plenitud de la ausencia posible. En él culmina el calabozo de Fray Servando, la frustración de Simón Rodríguez, la muerte de Francisco Miranda pero también el relámpago de las siete intuiciones de la cultura china, que le permite tocar, por la metáfora del conocimiento, y crear el remolino que lo destruye; el misterio que no fija la huida de los grandes perdedores y la oscilación entre dos grandes destinos, que él resuelve al unirse a la casa que va a ser incendiada. Su muerte tenemos que situarla dentro del Pachacámac incaico, del dios invisible.' José Lezama Lima, 'El romanticismo y el hecho americano.' José Lezama Lima: *La expresión americana*. Madrid: Alianza 1969, p. 116.

everything in its path. Returning briefly to my earlier claim that Martí belongs to the pattern of movement defined as coming home to a foreign land, I want to point out further that the author of *Our America* actually belongs to *both* patterns, combining the homecoming of Odysseus with the hurricane tearing at the wings of the Angel of History. In other words, Martí takes the dialectic of homelessness to the second power.

Compulsory immobility and extreme acceleration, but also flight, disappearance, and drowning, characterize a development Lezama sketches in polysemous words and that still promises fulfilment in the abundance of the cultures of America, Europe, and Asia he includes. Such fulfilment has transcultural and transcontinental significance. But neither a reterritorialization nor a steadying of flight and acceleration occur: the transhistorical movements overlap, even carry matters to another power, and they never come to rest, neither in the Cuban or Hispanic-American cultural contexts nor in Inca and Chinese cultures.

The flee(t)ing, that which never stands still, marks the verse of what was no doubt the leading group of Cuban poets in the twentieth century, brought together by the journal *Orígines* and the poetry and poetics of José Lezama Lima, a figure of mythical proportions even then. The opening poem of Lezama's 'Enemy rumors' (*Enemigo rumor*, 1941) reads: 'Ah, how you escape at the very moment / in which you just found your best definition.'[32] It is no coincidence that the 'the wind, the funny wind' (el viento, el viento gracioso) recurrently gusts above the 'discursive water' (agua discursiva) and the 'motionless landscape' (inmóvil paisaje) where flee(t)ing animals appear ('Antelopes, snakes with short, disappearing steps' [antílopes, serpientes de pasos breves, de pasos evaporados]); it blows to the dance of flee(t)ing images that may be defined but can never be held down and become static.[33] To put it in the words that he himself reserved for José Martí: José Lezama Lima's poetry is the lyric art of a 'fullness of possible absence.'

Where Lezama Lima in his Havana spoke of the 'birth of a Creole expression' (nacimento de la expresión criolla)[34] from the perspective of intellectual history, Antonio Benítez Rojo, in exile in the Northeast of the USA, moored his 'Creolization' (*criollización*) in the plantation, a structure that left its mark on the societies and economies of the entire Caribbean. It is as if the appearance of

---

32 'Ah, que tú escapes en el instante / en el que ya habías alcanzado tu definición mejor.' José Lezama Lima: *Poesía completa*. Havana: Editorial Letras Cubanas 1985, p. 23.
33 Lezama Lima: *Poesía completa*, p. 23.
34 The title of the fourth lecture at the *Centro de Altos Estudios* des *Instituto Nacional de Cultura* in the series mentioned above. See Lezama Lima: *La expresión americana*, p. 119–153.

the plantation initiated a chaotic, disordered, and frequently fragmented movement:

> There, as a child of the plantation, I am a mere *fragment*, or an idea that spins around my own *absence*, just as a drop of rain spins around the empty eye of the *hurricane* that set it going.... Creolization does not transform literature or music or language into a synthesis of anything that could be taken in essentialist terms, nor does it lead these expressions into a predictable state of creolization. Rather, creolization is a term with which we attempt to explain the *unstable* states that a Carribean cultural object presents over time. In other words, creolization is not merely a process (a word that implies forward movement) but a *discontinuous series of recurrences*, of happenings, whose sole law is change.[35] (Emphases added)

We can see that, time and again, similar lexemes not merely structure but dominate twentieth-century Cuban literature: 'hurricane' and 'absence;' 'fragment' and 'discontinuous movement;' 'instability' and 'emptiness.' Indeed, the unsteady movement, veering off course, as it were, in Martí's *Diary*, occurs in Cuban literature with great frequency. The aimless, restive drifting appears countless times even in Nicolás Guillén's Afro-Cuban verse which seems so different at first glance, with its indebtedness to sound-text relations and its adaptation of the popular musical form of the *son*. In his famous poem 'Walking' (Caminando) from the 1934 collection *West Indies, Ltd.*, the gerund of a verb of motion generates the rhythm. The poem opens with 'I walk aimlessly and walk, walk' (Voy sin rumbo caminando, / caminando).[36] Similarly, the figure of drifting dominates his subtly multifaceted 'Son for Antillean children' (Un son para niños antillanos) from the very start:

> On the sea of the Antilles
> floats a paper boat:
> flaots and floats the boat boat,
> rudderless.
>
> From Havana to Portobelo
> From Jamaica to Trinidad,

---

[35] Antonio Benítez Rojo: 'Three Words toward Creolization'. In: Kathleen M. Balutansky and Marie-Agnès Sourieau (eds.): *Caribbean Creolization: Reflections on the Cultural Dynamics of Language, Literature and Identity*. Miami: University Press of Florida 1998, p. 54–55.

[36] Nicolás Guillén: *El libro de los sones*. Havana: Editorial Letras Cubanas 1982, p. 70.

the boat boat floats and floats,
captainless.³⁷

One might add that there are also many examples of 'purposeful' movement and particularly returns to the home island in the literary work, and even more so in the biography, of Nicolás Guillén, whom the Cuban Revolution pronounced national poet. Guillén's life work surely aims at the implementation and thus also the territorialization of a thorough socioeconomic revolution, a goal for which he fought throughout his life. In this context, we may read his memoirs as an attempt at investing the movements of his life with a purpose materialized in the figure of the circle (island - exile - island). Yet, it is the unexpected movements – the many encounters in exile; the travels as representative of the revolution; and, finally, the countless well-travelled visitors he received in Cuba – that come to dominate his *Páginas vueltas* (1982). For an island, where most of his readers never undertook such worldwide travels, the sheer amount of goings and (home)comings (*vueltas*) Guillén describes in detail is remarkable.

Although known for his sedentary life, José Lezama Lima unfolded in his writing and thinking a global, transcultural network of dynamic relations. He spoke of the 'oscillation between two great destinies' that Martí resolved by connecting himself with the house that would be set on fire.³⁸ Irrespective of the complex symbolism of the 'burned house' (casa incendida) which plays with several cultural frames of reference, Lezama unmistakably addresses the oscillating movement that had already lefts its mark on the founding texts of Cuban national literature and that made it a Literature without a fixed Abode for which there had never been a shared home in Cuban history. No doubt, the driving spirit of Cuban literature is vectoral. It is a desire for reterritorialization, however, that, after its initial 'programming' in the nineteenth-century, never eschewed opposite, that is, deterritorializing, movements. These patterns of movement of the founding texts continues in Cuban literature to this day; they are stored in it and are often called upon in places where one would least expect them. This means that an entire national literature is based on an oscillation that is always oriented toward a center (the island of Cuba) without being able in the end to dwell in this center, which is always a precarious abode, at least so far. Expulsion and exile, migration and transculturation, diaspora and lack of a

---

37 'Por el Mar de las Antillas / anda un barco de papel: / anda y anda el barco barco, / sin timonel. // De La Habana a Portobelo, / de Jamaica a Trinidad, / anda y anda el barco barco, / sin capitán.' Guillén: *El libro de los sones*, p. 118.
38 'La oscilación entre dos grandes destinos.' Lezama Lima: *La expresión americana*, p. 116.

home are all inscribed in Cuban literature from the start. In this literature, the fleeting and the fleeing appear within the vortex of an American expression that Lezama Lima pinpointed unlike any other writer.

Especially in the case of Cuban literature, an analysis of movements and figures of movement is an apt cue for approaching more deeply-seated motives and emotions in the literary development of the twentieth century. Viewed from this perspective, Alejo Carpentier surely is no exception within Cuban literature. After all, topographic figures of movement that are hermeneutically decipherable are of fundamental importance in his novels and stories. Such figures permeate his entire oeuvre, from *¡Ecué-Yamba-O!* to 'The consecration of Spring' (*La consagración de la primavera*), from *The Kingdom of this World* (*El reino de este mundo*) to *Explosion in a Cathedral* (*El siglo de las luces*), from *The Chase* (*El acoso*) and *The Harp and the Shadow* (*El arpa y la sombre*) to stories such as 'The way of Santiago' (El Camino de Santiago), 'Journey to the Source' (Viaje a la semilla), and 'The Fugitives' (Los fugitivos).'[39] Carpentier even opened his approach to the 'City of the pillars' (*La Ciudad de las Columnas*), his homage to Cuba's capital, with an exemplary textual mobile: a lengthy quotation of the beautifully described entry into Havana harbor which Alexander von Humboldt reached after his journey to the Orinoco in December of 1800, an important date for the history of Cuban literature and science.[40] The city of the pillars turns out to be the city of incessant, transcontinental and transcultural, movements bound up in a multi-relationality that has its own poetry and (vectoral) poetics.

No other novel includes more intricate and compelling figures of movement between Old World and New World, and between North and South, than *The Lost Steps* (*Los pasos perdidos*, 1953).[41] The novel's basic pattern consists of frictional elements that oscillate between diction and fiction, such as autobiographical experiences, inserts, and revisions of dictional texts that Carpentier had originally planned to bring together in a separate book, the 'Book of the great savannah' (Libro de la Gran Sabana). Against the backdrop of this pattern emerge the different hermeneutical figures of movement, as if historically accumulated and artfully interwoven, together with their deliberate transgression.

---

39 See Alejo Carpentier: *War of Time*. New York: Knopf 1970.
40 Alejo Carpentier: *La Ciudad de las Columnas*. Havana: Editorial Letras Cubanas 1982, p. 9f. It is no coincidence that this voyage through the Cuban capital ends with a quotation from Baudelaire's *The Flowers of Evil* (*Les fleurs du mal*). Quotations, too, imply (intertextual) movements, as the multivalent Spanish word *cita* illustrates, so that quotations from travel texts can be read as doubled movements.
41 See Roberto González Echevarría: *Alejo Carpentier: The Pilgrim at Home*. Ithaca, N.Y.: Cornell University Press 1977.

Figures of movement from different historical eras disorient and redirect the quest motif so central to Western literature and the motif of flight, both of which demand deterritorializing movements and both of which drive the nameless first-person narrator. They connect the linear patterns of the medieval quest for the Holy Grail and the conquistadors' quest for El Dorado with the circular patterns of European travelers who returned from the Americas after their various discoveries and explorations. Faded in are also the pendulum movements that Pan-American and transatlantic air travel made possible after World War II, and that now apply to all jet-setting travelers 'between different worlds.' The overlap between journeys from widely divergent historical times, produced by intertextual markers, almost automatically generate the fourth dimension of (time)travel, a dimension already quite explicit in one of this novel's most important intertexts, Alexander von Humboldt's *Personal Narrative*.

The desire of Carpentier's musicologist-protagonist in *The Lost Steps* for a stable re-territorialization in another space, another time, and another culture, which he seeks to fulfil in his romance with Rosario – a relationship that translates conquistadors' dreams into projections of male sexuality – is, however, frustrated and destroyed by the mobility of the twentieth century. It is an airplane, the mode of transport that warps both time and space, which catapults the narrator-protagonist, believed lost in the interior, back into the utilitarian world of western civilization as if doing so were a matter of course. Even a second attempt to flee modernity proves pointless. The door to an earthly paradise, which Columbus had already assumed to be located in the watery world of the Orinoco, and to his beloved, a mestizo amalgamation of biblical Eve and Indian Goddess, remains locked forever. The failure of the 'Flight to Manoa,' as a German translator chose to render Carpentier's title, is final.

What succeeds, however, is the *expresión americana* of a *poeta doctus*, a learned novelist who understood well how to combine the intertextual fragments of a repressed western literature with cultural elements of African and American provenance and with expressions from the global(ized) media. The results are complex figures of movements that validate Juan Marinello's creolist claims to universality and prefigure an optimistic declaration penned not accidentally by a Cuban: 'that Caribbean literature is the most universal of all literatures.'[42]

---

42 Benítez Rojo: 'Three Words toward Creolization,' p. 59.

The inclusion and exclusion of territory and testimonial

Miguel Barnet's *Biography of a Runaway Slave* (*Biografía de un cimarrón*),[43] a text first published in 1966, combines the distinctly Cuban with the universal in a way completely different from what Marinello had imagined. This text was quickly translated into various languages, circulated worldwide, and became one of the key texts for understanding not only Cuban history but especially the breath-taking turn brought about by the victory of the Cuban Revolution in 1959.

Included in the Cuban canon only a few years after its first printing, the text was based on recordings of conversations between the ethnologist, poet, and storyteller Miguel Barnet and Esteban Montejo who, more than a hundred years old at the time of the recordings, shared with Fernando Ortiz's former student the stories of his life, especially from his time as a *cimarrón*, a runaway slave, during Spanish colonial rule. What resulted was a fascinating hybrid text substantiated by archival research, with which Barnet inaugurated the sub-genre of *novela-testimonio*, or testimonial novel, for which he himself had provided repeated theoretical underpinnings. In additional 'embodiments' of Cuban history that followed – *The Song of Rachel* (*La canción de Rachel*, 1969), *Gallego* (1981), and *A True Story* (*La vida real* (1986) – , Barnet developed, from a different perspective, the relationship between science and literature, between historical documentation and the novel, between diction and fiction, which had seen such great creativity and influence in the writings of Ferdinand Ortiz. Consistent with the concept and practice of the testimonial novel, *Biography of a Runaway Slave* is a profoundly frictional text[44] that has often been read dictionally (that is, as a 'document'), even though it contains, as the author himself has repeatedly stressed, literary-novelistic elements that infused the text with diverse, polysemous logics.

In the 1990s, the oft-emphasized 'complicity' (complicidad) and the 'collusion with the informant' (confabulación con el informante) became the subject

---

43 See Esteban Montejo / Miguel Barnet: *Biography of a Runaway Slave*. Willimantic, Conn.: Curbstone Press 1994 [For another English translation, see the differently titled *The Autobiography of a Runaway Slave*, by Esteban Montejo / Miguel Barnet (ed.): London: Bodley Head 1968. TN].

44 With respect to *Biografía de un cimarrón*, Antonio Vera-León also mentions friction; but he defines the term differently, that is, as 'friction between the subject of the transcription and the subjected of the transcribed narrative' (la fricción entre el sujeto de la transcripción y el sujeto de la narración transcrita). Antonio Vera-León: 'Hacer hablar: La transcripción testimonial'. In: *Revista de crítica literaria latinoamericana* XVIII (1992), p. 184.

of a groundbreaking discussion about the testimonial novel, which centered on *Biography of a Runaway Slave*.[45] The German historian Michael Zeuske has used meticulous archive research to show how much the Cuban writer 'corrected' Montejo's life-story of, especially through deliberate omissions.[46] It is especially telling that the *cimarrón*'s flight from slavery and from the colonial system of sugar production is reinterpreted by omitting the time of the republic – a difficult period in Montejo's life – and by foreshadowing Fidel Castro's revolution. As a result, Montejo's 'way' of life is refigured as a path that seems to lead linearly and logically from the rebellion against colonialism to the rebellion against neocolonialism and imperialism. Zeuske's historical research paints a rather different, more complex and contradictory picture that resists a figurative interpretation of Cuban history as much as it does the maroon's ideological stylization as transhistorical hero.

While Barnet's literary 'complicity' in abstracting Esteban Montejo into a rebel by eliding 'darker periods' in this 'biography of a runaway Negro slave' is obvious, it is also warranted by the frictional oscillation between novel and historical testimony. An innovative development of the markedly frictional pattern of Cuban literature which inaugurated the sub-genre of the testimonial novel, *Biography of a Runaway Slave* must be read within the historically unprecedented context of the Cuban Revolution. It is clearly not an accident that the text focuses of the story of a life that, as its title already announces, is significantly characterized by flight and chase and by a the lack of a fixed abode, even thought that life is, in the end, reterritorialized to some extent through the Cuban Revolution.

Reinaldo Arenas, whom Miguel Barnet had graciously interviewed after the publication of the former's first novel, presented an entirely different biography of a historical figure in *Hallucinations* (*El mundo alucinante*, 1969), a novel that also gained quick international acclaim in translation but was unwelcome in Cuba. Arenas's literary engagement with the figure of Fray Servando Teresa de Mier, to whose importance for Cuba Lezama Lima (whom Arenas admired) had

---

45 Abdeslam Azougarh: *Miguel Barnet: Rescate e invención de la memoria*. Geneva: Editions Slatkine 1996, p. 213.
46 See Michael Zeuske: 'The 'Cimarrón' in the Archives: A Re-Reading of Miguel Barnet's Biography of Esteban Montejo.' In: *New West Indian Guide / Nieuwe West-Indische Gids* LXXI.3–4 (1997), p. 265–279. The same issue includes a reply by Barnet entitled 'The untouchable Cimarrón' (281–289). See also Monica Walter: 'Testimonio y melodrama: En torno a un debate actual sobre 'Biografía de un cimarrón' y sus consecuencias posibles.' In: Janett Reinstädler and Ottmar Ette (eds.): *Todas las islas la isla: Nuevas y novísimas tendencias en la literatura y cultura de Cuba*. Frankfurt am Main: Vervuert/Iberoamericana, 2000, p. 25–38.

called attention, is by no means lacking in frictional elements. The central aim of this novel is not, however, to document the life story of one of the most interesting protagonists of the Hispanic American struggles for independence, a series of imprisonments and escape attempts across the Old and the New World that unfolds in Mier's memoirs. Rather, *Hallucinations* is the brilliant study of a life constantly persecuted and adrift, a biography that, at certain points, risks collapsing into the young Cuban novelist's own (auto)biography. A passage from the letter addressed to 'dear Servando', which prefaces this similarly hybrid text, reads: 'It was far more use to discover that you and I are the same person' (Lo más útil fue descubrir que tú y yo somos la misma persona).[47] A hallucinatory rebirth, a literary life cycle? Either way, this novel, which at once runs contrary to and mirrors Barnet's *Biografía de un cimmarón*, is one of the most important and stimulating Cuban frictions from the last century. At its center, once again, is an artistically doubled life without a fixed abode.

It is revealing that Reinaldo Arenas, in the different narrative and poetic cycles of his oeuvre, has examined an entire series of socioeconomic structures at the center of current and ongoing discussions. His volume of poetry, *El Central*, for instance, is a literary reckoning with the rapacious machine of Cuban sugar production, a transhistorical blend of that industry's colonial, neocolonial, and socialist-postcolonial manifestations. The 'sugar-centric' structures pervade all spheres of human society, collective and individual, due to the autocracy and totalitarianism that the sugarcane plantation (*el central*) produces. Arenas presents this centralization and the utter domination of life by a socioeconomic system that appears in all studies of the Caribbean as the defining pattern of the entire region, in harsh imagery, supplementing it with a literary analysis of the biopolitical effects of the camp, to use Agamben's term. *The Brightest Star (Arturo, la estrella más brillante)* from 1981 is an examination of the camps of the Military Units to Aid Production (Unidades Militares de Ayuda a la Producción, or UMAP), where undesired régime critics and homosexuals were to be 'reeducated.' In this novella, as in some of his other writings (see also chapter 3 above). Arenas views the camp not as an 'industrial accident,' an anomalous product of the Cuban Revolution, but as a deeply-seated expression of the authoritarian constitution of a society that also tried to exert its power on the (polysemous) 'naked life' (*zoé*) of the Cuban population.

---

47 Reinaldo Arenas: *Hallucinations: Being an Account of the Life and Adventures of Friar Servando Teresa de Mier*. London: Jonathan Cape 1971, p. 7. Reinaldo Arenas: *El mundo alucinante*. Barcelona: Montesinos 1981, p. 9.

No other Cuban author has represented the matrix of the camp, fed by the militaristic and monocultural traditions of nation-building in its various mutations and metamorphoses, with such resolute courage, fervor, and desperation, and directed our attention to the dimension of biopolitics and the biopolitical. In his highly frictional autobiography, *Before Night Falls: A Memoir* (*Antes que anochezca*, 1992), Arenas, who suffered from AIDS and committed suicide in New York in 1990, interweaves biographical with fictional elements in order to bring to light once more, obsessively and insistently, the mechanisms of exclusion and inclusion (along with the forms of humiliation related to those apparatuses) that he viewed as characteristic of state, family, and society in twentieth-century Cuba. He also deemed impossible all attempts at escaping the persecution and misery these mechanisms created in their wake. Written in exile in the USA, *Before Night Falls*, like *Hallucinations*, continues a tradition of frictional life-writing and also of a Writing-without-a-fixed-abode. The latter should be understood not just in a biographical or thematic sense but also, significantly, as structural within the longer history of Cuba literature as a national literature.[48]

We must not forget one thing in this context: that the Cuban Revolution, the most effective implementation of a modern project in Cuba, shaped the nation-state and its institutions in the areas of education, health, politics, science, and literature to an extent heretofore unknown. Connected with this were mechanisms of exclusion through inclusion (such as the camp) and of inclusion through exclusion (such as exile and migration) which, particularly in the 1970s, fortified the territorialization of ideas as those ideas became entrenched in the intellectual arena and the areas of science and scholarship. The following remark, which Juan Marinello, the first communist minister under Batista and later an influential intellectual of the Cuban Revolution, made in 1974 may stand in for countless similar utterances. Marinello bluntly confronted dissidents in the field of Martí studies with the remark that 'in today's Cuba there is no longer room for anti-Martí Martíans.'[49] This example shows that within the

---

48 It is not by coincidence that Arenas devotes *La loma del Angel* to what is surely the most famous novel of the Cuban nineteenth century, *Cecilia Valdés, o La Loma del Angel*, and its author Cirilo Villaverde. The latter began his novel in Cuba and completed it during his exile in New York City. [For the most recent translation of Villaverde's novel, see Cirilo Villaverde: *Cecilia Valdes or El Angel Hill*. Edited by Sibylle Fischer. Oxford: Oxford University Press, USA 2005. TN.]

49 '[L]os martianos antimartianos no tienen cabida en la Cuba de ahora.' Juan Marinello: 'Sobre la interpretación y el entendimiento de la obra de José Martí.' In: *Anuario del Centro de Estudios Martianos* 1 (1978), p. 9.

Revolution, which took its cues from the Socialist International, ideological boundaries were drawn in ways that left many intellectuals with only the choice among emigration, internal exile, or incarceration.

Such territorializations of power can also be found in Roberto Fernández Retamar's influential essay *Calibán* (1971), in which he shifts the balance within the Prospero-Ariel-Caliban triangle in favor of Caliban whom he invests with a new, Marxian meaning. *Calibán* shows this most clearly in the formula from Fidel Castro, which the text quotes approvingly: 'within the Revolution, everything; against the Revolution, noting' (dentro de la Revolucón, todo; contra la Revolución, nada). Written during the time of the Padilla affair and the open criticisms that many international intellectuals voiced in its wake of the cultural politics of the revolution, Retamar's essay turns vehemently against the 'counterrevolutionary platform' (plataforma contrarrevolucionaria) from Sartre to Severo Sarduy, from Carlos Fuentes to Mario Vargas Llosa.[50] The then-director of Casa de las Américas attempted to assemble the historical, political, and literary reference points of 'our authentic culture' which were to form a different, decolonized canon and horizon for future developments.[51] According to Retamar, Cuba's purpose was to be the home, and even more importantly, the launching pad for such revolutionary processes throughout Latin America and the Third World.

Retamar's discourse can be effortlessly traced back to José Martí's speech on the future liberation of Cuba which he envisioned to have consequences for the Antilles, the peoples of America, and the entire American continent.[52] In the context of the patterns of movements I have sketched here, it is easy to see that the Cuban Revolution, with all its consolidated territorialization, still preferred not to relinquish *de*territorializing movements that, after all, were valuable not only for increasing the export of Cuban cultural products, but also for 'exporting the Revolution.' There are reasons why Cuba, for decades, was one of the main exporters of theories and ideologies in the socio-political realm and the area of

---

50 Roberto Fernández Retamar: *Calibán y otros ensayos*. Havana: Editorial Arte y Literatura 1979, p. 74. For an English translation see *Caliban and Other Essays*. Minneapolis: University of Minnesota Press 1989, p. 36.

51 See Retamar: *Caliban*, p. 36–38; Retamar: *Calibán*, p. 76–79.

52 See, for instance, Martí's letter to Manuel Mercado, written just before his death in Dos Ríos: 'so that Cuban independence can, in time, prevent United States from expanding into the Caribbean and, with its added strength, pounce on our territories in the Americas' (impedir a tiempo con la independencia de Cuba que se extiendan por las Antillas los Estados Unidos y caigan, con esa fuerza más, sobre nuestras tierras de América). In Martí: *Obras Completas* (1975), vol. 4, p. 167.

art and literature. Cubans could feel the mechanism of Cuba's (cultural) politics that I have outlined here well beyond the island borders of the nation-state. The criticism Reinaldo Arenas voiced of the exclusion machineries at work in the Cuban exile community in Florida in *Before Night Falls*, and even more subtly in *The Doorman*, written from the liminal position of a concierge, illustrates that, due to a stronger desire for reterritorialization in exile, a deterritorialization of Cuba and Cubanness may very well reinforce, and extend, borders and mechanisms of exclusion, as was already the case in the nineteenth century. In many ways, Cuba's main island and its facing continental coastline are mirror images of each other.

Ostracism, open borders, and networks in Cuba's Literature without a fixed Abode

At the beginning of the 1990s and the collapse of de facto socialism throughout the Eastern bloc, the declaration of the so-called 'unusual period in times of peace' (período especial en tiempos de paz) signaled new developments in Cuba. In the 1990s, the 'island consciousness' (conciencia de isla) that essayist and cultural theoretician Jorge Mañach had missed and demanded in the 1940s,[53] and which had advanced since the early 1960s through the militarization of society and the unremitting US blockade, increasingly turned into an awareness of the existence of many different (Cuban) islands all over the world. The temporarily relaxed possibilities for international travel in Cuba at that time; the emergence of a Cuban network that was no longer centered in and controlled by Miami but spanned several continents; and the growing profile of a Cuban diaspora that had cleared its own spaces of movement beyond the traditional boundaries of exile – these factors, among others, produced a situation in the late twentieth century through which the different islands of the Cuban archipelago (Cubans in Cuba and Florida, Spain and Mexico, New York and Paris, even in East and West Germany) entered into a process of more intense communication.

As part of the Caribbean, one of the centers of internationally influential production (and export) of cultural theories, this Cuba of globalized Island-Worlds was no exception. Important impulses from Antonio Benítez Rojo, Gustavo Pérez Firmat, Roberto González Echevarría, and Iván de la Nuez, to name

---

53 See Jorge Mañach: *Historia y estilo*. Havana: Minerva 1944, p. 136, and Pérez Firmat: *The Cuban Condition*, p. 3.

but a few,⁵⁴ created a changed, more flexible image of a Cuban culture whose main orientation were no longer the binaries of the founding discourse of Cuban literature, binaries between island and exile, forced deterritorialization and desired reterritorialization. In their place appeared a much more complex reality that has transformed a translational into a multirelational logic and seems increasingly to detach itself from essentializing definitions of *the* Cuban. This does not, however, mean that 'old' logics and established mechanisms for inclusion and exclusion, complete with the border(s) they had created, disappeared.⁵⁵ The authoritarian mechanisms of exclusion and inclusion no doubt persist and often enough still demand their sacrifices. But they have lost their omnipotence and omnipresence. In the cultural mappings of the twenty-first century, Cuba has become an island of islands that, in the longer term, cannot be controlled from and ruled by a single center, not even from a dual (reflected and reflecting) center composed of Havana and Miami. What has evolved among the Cuban islands is not a 'literature without borders' but a national Literature without a fixed Abode, based on a tradition that reaches back into the nineteenth century.

As an example from the history of Cuban baseball may illustrate that an experience distant from national territory is not something entirely new in the sphere of 'the Cuban'. The Cuban Stars, one of the founding teams of the US Negro National League, were 'a homeless team that had neither a house nor a country' (un equipo *homeless*, sin casa ni patria); the term 'Cuban' referred neither to a home location nor to a territory. A utopian and, at the same time, atopic Cuba had long taken shape in the US imaginary: 'A detached, floating Cuba, a fugitive island of forbidden desires … the holy region of sin, of the liber-

---

54 Benítez Rojo: *The Repeating Island*; Pérez Firmat: *Life on the Hyphen: The Cuban-American Way*. Austin TX: University of Texas Press 1994; Roberto González Echevarría: *The Pride of Havana A History of Cuban Baseball*. New York: Oxford University Press 1999; and Iván de la Nuez: *La balsa perpetua: Soledad y conexiones de la cultura cubana*. Barcelona: Editorial Casiopea 1998.

55 In this respect, the unauthorized change of the title of my contribution to the Yale symposium 'Cuba: un siglo de literatura (1902–2002)' in the volume of conference papers is most unfortunate, since at issue, from my perspective, is precisely not a *literatura sin fronteras*, a 'literature without borders.'In the case of the literatures without a fixed abode, it would be more fitting to speak of a proliferation of different and differently drawn borders, but borders that have become permeable. See Ottmar Ette: 'Una literatura sin fronteras: ficciones y fricciones en la literatura cubana del siglo XX'. In: Anke Birkenmaier / Roberto González Echevarría (eds.): *Cuba: un siglo de literatura (1902 – 2002)*. Madrid: Editorial Colibrí 2004, p. 407–433.

ation of bodies, which had succumbed to the ritual violence of sports and sex.'[56] Today, the atopia of the Cuban (*lo cubano*), which developed in certain areas during the decades of a Cuban Republic dependent on the USA, has been replaced by a heterotopia that conceives of the Cuban neither as free-floating nor as only territorially fixed but as a highly complex and unstable relation. At the end of the twentieth century, that is, in the fourth phase of accelerated globalization, this relation encompassed almost all areas of Cuban culture. For quite some time now, this Cuba has not been limited to love and sports, rum and tobacco, entertainment or music but has expanded into the area of literature, even with some erotic connotations among international audiences. While, in the 1960s and 1970s, Cuban literature was read mainly in the context of the revolution, and not only in Europe, that situation has changed profoundly since the late 1990s. Antonio Benítez Rojo, whose studies significantly opened up the national borders of most research on Cuban literature in the direction of the Caribbean, could still assert, and not without a certain essentialist undertone, 'that Caribbean texts are fugitive by nature.'[57] Today, however, it is possible to say that Cuban literature is being written, read, and, especially over the past few years, awarded prizes in places all over the globe. That these days, writers and readers connect Cuban literature heterotopically with many different directions and with widely differing patterns of movements, does not, however, mean that the island, the revolution, and even more so, the nostalgia for it have completely faded into the background. The (memory of the) revolution has become a mandatory topic even in the literature of the worldwide Cuban diaspora. The dialectic I have observed between opening up borders and drawing new ones does not spell loss and repression, but signifies a multiplicity of perspectives, the creation of new meanings and logics that are linked with one another in fundamentally complex ways.[58] The distinct Cuban dimension of this literature, which is being written on many islands now, is not lost in the process, but results from an internal (Cuban) relationality, part of a network that functions within a transregional and transnational, as well as transareal and transcontinental spaces.

---

56 'Esa Cuba desasida y flotante, isla fugitiva de placeres prohibidos, ... la zona sagrada del pecado, de la liberación de los cuerpos, entregados a la violencia ritual del deporte y del sexo.' Roberto González Echevarría: 'Cuban.' In: *Encuentro de la Cultura Cubana* 15 (1999–2000), p. 109, 106.
57 Benítez Rojo: *The Repeating Island*, p. 25. 'Que los textos caribeños son fugitivos por naturaleza.' Benítez Rojo: *La isla que se repite* (Barcelona: Editorial Casiopea 1998), p. 41.
58 See Friedrich Cramer: *Chaos and Order: The Complex Structure of Living Systems*. Weinheim: VHC 1993, and chapter 3 above.

The concurrent vectorization of a Cuban literature understood in this way – a literature that is by no means only deterritorialized – combines with the frictionalization of very different forms of writing. Of special importance particularly in the area of cultural theory, as a continuation of sorts of the traditions of a José Martí and a Fernando Ortiz, is the oscillation between cultural studies theory and literary practice, between diction and fiction. *Encuentro de la cultura cubana*, a Cuban journal that has garnered significant attention in the last few years, exemplifies the connection of a transcultural *spiritus vector* that crosses cultural contexts with the frictionalization of literature and theory alike. Perhaps one of the most successful ventures of the late Jesús Díaz, a writer and intellectual who has greatly contributed to the exchanges among the different Cuban islands, this journal already in its title points not to a fixed abode, a *casa*, but, rather, to a meeting point, an *encuentro*. This encounter, as it were, is not about territorialization but about as many crossways and other points of contact as possible.

Such are the outlines of a playing field for a (national) Literature without a fixed Abode which has considerably extended and rendered more dynamic the coefficient of movement both within and beyond diasporic writing. This Literature without a fixed Abode is the reward for, but also the price of, an open relationality that, as a glance at Cuban literary history shows, has so often been threatened by authoritarianism and monoculture. The productiveness and worldwide status of Cuban literature today, extraordinary when one compared to the small size of the island's territory, are due entirely to this open relationality.

Let us consider all actual and conceivable differences, especially with regard to the mechanisms of exclusion and inclusion between what is written and, more importantly, published, on and off the island: precisely because Cuban literature has no fixed abode, one should not schematically divide it into island, exile, and diaspora. Such pigeonholing has long ceased to do this literature justice. The paths of the lives and the figures of movement of many of the Cuban authors I have mentioned challenge such reductive schemata, as do their texts, often written in a host of different places. At the same time, it might turn out that some of the meanings of the Cuban, which Roberto González Echevarría locates mainly in sports and sexuality, have, since the 1990s, become an international pattern of reception and a trademark of Cuban writing.

The novel *Café Nostalgia* (1997) by (*nomen est omen*) Zoé Valdés is a good example of this and other developments I have mentioned in this chapter. The text already signals its sensual dimension in its six chapter headings. The name of the protagonist Marcela connects with the sea, which has traditionally enabled the contact between the different islands, archipelagos, and land masses, and with the air, the heavenly biotope of the migrating birds that appear in Fernando Ortiz's fascinating textual mobile. Born in Havana in 1959, like Valdés herself, and therefore a child of the revolution, Marcela is the female counterpart of the protagonist of Marcel Proust's novelistic cycle *A la recherche du temps perdu* (variously translated as *Remembrance of Things Past* and *In Search of Lost Time*), whose structuring role in *Café Nostalgia* is quite deliberate. Marcela is constantly searching for a lost time and a lost island. Anonymous in the novel, where it is known only as 'That Island' (*Aquella Isla*), this island is left behind, suppressed, temporarily forgotten during other travels, simulated with the help of other islands, photographed during a brief return and then gladly left again, without, however, disappearing into the sea of memories. In this way, Valdés creates a heterotopia of a Literature without a fixed Abode, which has not lost its desire for reterritorialization – its national literary heritage – but which will never come to a centered standstill. Marcela is a parcel of land (*parcela*) on her home island, but also, at the same time, part of the other islands that constitute the Cuban archipelago worldwide.

At the end of this novel, neither the protagonist nor any of the other countless figures in this text, which markets (one might add, critically) the erotic as *very Cuban*, has the final word. For the final word is elegantly left to the phone answering machine, the quasi-testimonial recording device that can easily be frictionalized. During the course of the novel, this answering machine records the voices of innumerable 'migrant birds' (*aves de paso*). It becomes a seismograph of sorts, registering even the smallest changes; nothing is lost in its *camera obscura*. Into the long-delayed amorous encounter of the protagonist with Samuel intrudes the recorded voice of a Cuban friend, who gives up his life's work, his (static) book shop, in favor of a 'meeting place' (*encuentro*), 'a kind of salon,' in order to offset the agony of waiting with the dynamic of living, of transitory, joyous, and flee(t)ing movements.[59] In the literary capturing of this voice on the answering machine, we glimpse once again the testimonial and its frictions, even if only as a fading magnetic sound track. The many travels, with their ceaselessly varying figures of movement which give the entire text a breathless rhythm, pinpoint in the artefact of the answering machine the place and the function that perhaps best characterize Cuban literature more than a century after the great protagonists of *modernismo* fell silent. Cuban literature has become an echo chamber, a frictional sound box, and a reservoir of trans-

---

[59] Zoé Valdés: *Café Nostalgia: La turbulenta y hermosa corazonada de un abismo de que ne se podra volver.* Barcelona: Planeta 1997, p. 361.

cultural, transnational, and transcontinental movements whose relational dynamics are irreducible either to a single residence or a binary logic. Cuban literature indexes the odds and risks of a development that awaits all cultures as their histories move them beyond the nation-state. This is where their futures lie.

5 Translations

In Others' Words: Literary translation as Writing-between-Worlds

The literary translator as a pre-modern being

In our waning postmodern times, the translator still has what other cultural producers appear to have long lost: an original. Except in the special case of self-translation, the original is, for the translator, the Other per se, an Other whose words she has the task, or vocation, to carry over into that which is her own, that is, her own language. At least at first glance, the literary translator deals with a clearly defined interlocutor, with whose previous forms of artistic expression she must seek to engage fruitfully. Traditionally, this has made the translator a member of the group of all those, among them opera singers, concert pianists, actors, and conductors, whose performances are deemed secondary creations. The literary translator, however, distinguishes herself from them in that she does not bask in the limelight but languishes largely in obscurity. It is not a coincidence that the practice of literary translation evokes images of solitary deskwork, perhaps even at night, if the literary translator has a better paying day job. Financially, the literary translator is usually in a bad position. She makes barely a third of what her professionalized colleagues – technical translators and interpreters – can demand for their services. In fact, most literary translators do have so-called day jobs, if only because they give them access to the (relative) safety of employment benefits.

During the last few decades, the literary translator has become more of an object of public awareness. Since the 1960s, her name has gradually moved from a book's fourth page, where it appeared (if at all) in small script, into closer proximity to the author's name on the title page; it now often adorns the third page, in somewhat larger fonts. But this increased interest in translator and translation should not deceive anyone into thinking that the literary translator's image and professional reality have changed (that is, improved), quite regardless of all the prizes, fellowships, and awards that have been devoted to translation during the last decades. Should we, then, actively advise our students against entering the profession of literary translation?

A few years ago, one of the best-known translators in Germany, Curt Meyer-Clason, called literary translation a 'craft' about which there exists, and is not likely to exist, any consensus among the crafts(wo)men themselves. He added that translation is a 'profession with questionable income-producing potential and, at least in Germany, with low prestige-value.'[1] These are harsh words from a translator who has done so much to make Romance literatures and cultures accessible to German-speaking audiences and who, during the course of his own professional life, had himself experienced all the ups and downs of being reviewed and evaluated. Not even in 'the century of translation'[2] has the literary translator been promoted from her role as extra to that of a protagonist. She remains firmly ensconced in her marginal position as a '[part time] home worker in need of [social] protection.'[3] More pointedly, considering the different places writing has in today's field of literary production, one might say that the literary artist seems to write with her heart and soul, the literary scholar at times with her head, the reviewer usually from the hip, the polemicist, at times mislabeled a literary czar, with his gut, and the literary translator with her feet. Yet, it is the latter who follows in 'her' author's footsteps most closely and creatively.

---

[1] Curt Meyer-Clason: 'Vom Übersetzen.' In: Karin Graf (ed.): *Übersetzerwerkstatt 1990: Ein Brevier und Materialien für Übersetzer*. Berlin: Literarisches Colloquium Berlin 1991, p. 94.

[2] In 1993, books from 59 languages were translated in Germany. If one looks more closely at the number, however, one quickly notices that, in 1993, more than three of four translations were of English-language originals (69.4 %). With 6,843 titles, English as source language is far ahead the second rung, where we find French with 1,089 titles, followed by Italian (320 titles) and, Spanish with a total of 231 titles, after Russian and Dutch on place 6. If one takes the three major Romance languages as a single cultural area, the dominance of the English-speaking world is a bit easier to take. In 1994 the percentage of source texts in English was 71.4%, followed by French with 10.6%, Italian with 2.9%, Dutch with 2.5%, and Spanish with 2.2% (=220 titles). In 1995, English rose to 74% (French to 9.2%, Italian to 2.6%; Dutch down to 2.4%, with Spanish down to 1.9%, for a total of 198 titles). Eight years later, in 2003, and after reduction in translated books (9,854 titles in 1993, 10,206 in 1994, 10,565 in 1995, but 7,574 in 2003, a reduction by about one quarter), English as a source language of texts translated into German still dominated with 3,732 titles (or 49.3%), before French with 586 titles, Russian with 229 titles, and Italian with 211 titles, as well as Spanish with 137 titles (or 1.8%), after Swedish and Dutch. Other Romance languages, such as the world language Portuguese, were not considered in the statistic from 2004. If one were to ask about the ten most important source languages for German translations from 1994–2003, one finds that French held on to its second place throughout this period, right after English, while Italian had to cede the third place, which it had consistently occupied from 1993–2002, to Russian for the first time in 2003. Between 1994 and 2001, Spanish, which had been in fifth place after Dutch, rose to fourth place in 2002, only to fall to eighth place in 2003. Its highest rank among the overall German translations was 15.5% in 1992, with 10.6% in 2001 and 12.3% in 2003. See Börsenverein Deutscher Verleger-und Buchhändler-Verbände (ed.): *Buch und Buchhandel in Zahlen*. MVB Marketing- und Verlagsservice des Deutschen Buchhandels, GMBH, 1994 and 2004.

[3] Meyer-Clason: 'Vom Übersetzen,' p. 97.

There is no doubt that translation, to a degree heretofore unsuspected, characterized the end of the twentieth century as much as it does the beginning of the twenty-first. Translation processes intensify communication networks that, all undeniable asymmetries notwithstanding, are global in their reach. As the experiences and research of the past few decades shows, accelerated globalization, world-wide exchange, and cultural hybridization are not just words, mere clichés, but have already long become part of the daily experiences of a considerable part of humanity. Mass-cultural transnational information networks, transmissions of global reach, would simply be unimaginable without translation. What is being written today in London, Catania, or near Aracataca, Japanese or German readers may buy as soon as tomorrow. In some cases, as with not a few novels by the Cuban Miguel Barnet, (German) translations appear even before the Spanish original does. From this perspective, the literary translator appears like a small cog in the wheels of the worldwide networks of a highly profitable cultural industry, in which the literary authors themselves can be appointed to the position of superstars as readily as they can, *at the same time*, be demoted to that of mere impulse givers for complex transmedia marketing strategies. The authors themselves no longer lament such circumstances. Instead, they happily explore the creative potential of the venues either of the mass media or the high-culture industry, from audiobooks, [e-books], and movies to theater adaptations and opera performances. Umberto Eco, Michel Butor, Patrick Chamoiseau, and, first and foremost, Jorge Luis Borges, have become true masters of the form that perhaps best represents our era of different levels of network media: that of the carefully staged interview. Translation artists, however, do not typically bother with such easily consumable forms.

What happened to the translators of these literary stars? To say that that they are, as it were, lost in the fray or left behind would be both too cynical and too rash. These days, the practice of translation is culturally taken for granted to such a degree that its conscious perception requires what the Russian Formalists called deautomatization. Literary translation is so much a part of the network of our daily translation activities that we have to make an effort to recognize its fundamental and, at the same time, exceptional value.

Intralingual translation determines our daily lives. Whether, as is the case at universities in Germany's *Neue Bundesländer*, the 'new states' added to the Federal Republic through reunification, 'staff work' is known as 'home work,' or whether commissions turn our daily experiences into bureaucratic prose: all this is done by relying on a cultural skill that has been hammered into our heads since school, where we were systematically trained to repeat others' thoughts 'in our own words.'⁴ Any refusal to use these thoroughly rehearsed intra-lingual translation skills led, already in school, to the charge of 'copying' or plagiarism. The cultural technique of intralingual translation of the sort that Jakobson called 'rewording'⁵ has become so ingrained in our thinking that it is easy, after the 'linguistic turn' and the language philosophy of the turn of the century, to grasp the fundamental role such translation processes play in constituting subjectivity. We are beings made up of others' words.

Precisely because intralingual translation processes (which reside within the same language) as much as inter-semiotic translations, that is, 'translations' between different systems of signs within the semiotic thicket of our traffic signs, warning signs, billboards, Windows software programs, and so forth, have become basic cultural skills, such translations carry no special value for us. After all, all of us have learned the craft of these sorts of translations since early childhood.

Does it follow, then, that translation, as Meyer-Clason suggests, is 'merely' a craft? Fritz Nies, the initiator of the University of Düsseldorf's academic track in literary translation (a novelty within the academic landscape at least in German-speaking countries) would have had to have asked himself that question when he founded his program. But, unless he had wanted to pull the rug out from under a new program right from the start, his answer would have had to have been affirmative. Yet, when responding to the question of 'whether literary translation can be taught,' he conceded that gifted translators can no more be produced than genius conductors or actors.⁶ Nies's program has now a successful track-record of several years. But, in my view, it can only offer the apprentice literary translator as comprehensive a set of tools as possible: much, though by no means everything. There are good reasons why the literary translator is often compared to performing artists such as actors, pianists, and conductors: clearly, she is more than just a craftswoman.

---

4 See Friedrich A. Kittler: 'Autorschaft und Liebe.' In: Friedrich A. Kittler (ed.): *Austreibung des Geistes aus den Geisteswissenschaften: Programme des Poststrukturalismus*. Paderborn: Schöningh 1980, p. 142–73.

5 See Roman Jakobson: *On linguistic Aspects of Translation*. In: Stephen Rudy (ed.): *Roman Jakobson: Selected Writings. II. Word and Language*. The Hague: Mouton 1971, p. 260. Jakobson pointed out that all signs achieve meaning only through processes of translation (p. 261). In other words: comprehension is always to be understood as a process of translation.

6 Fritz Nies: 'Probieren statt studieren? Kurzpräsentation des Studiengangs.' In: Fritz Nies et al. (eds.): *Ist Literaturübersetzen lehrbar? Beiträge zur Eröffnung des Studiengangs Literaturübersetzen an der Universität Düsseldorf*. Tübingen: Narr 1989, p. 24.

If literary translation were a craft, then the hardest working students would also be the best translators. If it were a science, then their teachers would no doubt be the best translators. If one disregards the exception that proves the rule, one finds that neither the most erudite scholars nor the most devoted students are superior translators. Does this suggest that literary translators should be elevated to the status of writers and artists? No doubt, they are that, *too*, but only to the degree that they are also artisans and scholars. The most amazing poets are not the most talented translators – Wieland, George, or Rilke prove this rule.

Literary translation, then, is a creative activity *sui generis*. The place where it usually occurs is the desk, which resembles that of the artisan and the scholar, as well as that of the writer. The connection to the first may lie in the ready-to-use tools – encyclopedias, map collections, dictionaries – to the second in the more or less frequent excursions to the library, and to the third, finally, in the social obligations that even Marcel Proust could not avoid. The literary translator occupies a position that dates back to the time before the second half of the eighteenth century when two fundamental divisions emerged: on the one hand, the distinction between *artisan* and *artist* and, on the other, that between *science* and *letters*. Her profession may be more honorable, but that does not make today's literary translator an *honnête homme*, an 'honest man,' in the sense it had in seventeenth-century France.

The reader may follow my comments with growing worry. Not only did I start by exiling the translator from postmodernity, or so at least it would seem; now, I even refuse her entry into modernity. For the translator to belong to a system of knowledge that has not only pre-postmodern but also pre-modern traits may be exactly what accounts for the difficulty of her position within our globally connected societies, her increasingly professionalized status notwithstanding. The multi-media equipment on the translator's desk does not change this in any fundamental way. Is perhaps the odd 'skewing' of the pre-modern system of knowledge a secret reason behind the forced attempt to have computers replace the literary translator, and thus to have digital accumulations of data replace intercultural and transcultural hermeneutic experiences? If this were possible, it would indeed 'dispense' with a remnant of sociocultural pre-modernity. But we are far from that point. One might give a new twist to Werner Krauss's suggestive remark that the sole literal translation of the French eighteenth century was that of Voltaire, whose sole reason for translating Shakespeare's *Julius Caesar* was to prove 'that translation's loyalty would violate all the proprieties of French taste,' and that his would be the kind of translation 'that questioned the very principle of translation.'[7] All of today's translators are engaged in the effort at putting the lie to the claim of Voltaire, that 'last of the happy writers.'[8] Still, in spite of all her loyalty, today's literary translator does not enjoy a good reputation. Is she perhaps a sycophant, a flatterer? No, the exceptional translator is, rather, an excellent liar.

The literary translator as true liar

Historically, translators have generally been of ill repute: *traduttore, traditore* – a formulation that has been deeply embedded into our collective memory and which, as Roman Jakobson pointed out, not without a measure of sly humor, cannot itself be translated into other languages without significant loss.

In the relationship between 'Old' and 'New' Worlds, processes and problems of translation played a central role not just for those who traveled to the Americas. Hernán Cortés, for instance, cannot be trusted when, in his letters, or *Cartas de relación*, to Charles V., he 'carries across' Moctezuma's words. In fact, Cortés functions as a ventriloquist by putting into the mouth of the Other a justification of his very own plans and goals. Of even greater significance is the woman who was not only Cortés's lover but also the Spanish conqueror's interpreter and a strong supporter of his conquistadorial plans. For a long time, La Malinche became the (gendered) embodiment of the traitor of the New World's indigenous populations.[9] In this figure, whose key role countless images, among them the Florentine Codex, display, time and again, the image of the

---

[7] Werner Krauss: 'Das Problem der Übersetzung.' In: Werner Krauss (ed.): *Grundprobleme der Literaturwissenschaft: Zur Interpretation literarischer Werke*. Reinbek bei Hamburg: Rowohlt 1968, p. 137.
[8] Roland Barthes: 'Le dernier des écrivains hereux' (1958). In Roland Barthes: *Œuvres complètes*, vol. 1. Paris: Seuil 1993–1995, p. 1235–1240.
[9] For German studies of La Malinche and the complexities of her history, see, among others, Carmen Wurm: *Doña Marina, la Malinche: Eine historische Figur und ihre literarische Rezeption*. Frankfurt am Main: Vervuert 1996; Claudia Leitner: 'Zunge des Eroberers: Markenzeichen kultureller Alteritäten: La Malinche.' In: Eva Kimminich / Claudia Krülls-Hepermann (eds.): *Zunge und Zeichen*. Berlin: Peter Lang 1999, p. 41–70; also Barbara Dröscher / Carlos Rincón (eds.): *La Malinche: Übersetzung, Interkulturalität und Geschlecht*. Berlin: Verlag Walter Frey – Edition tranvía 2001.

translator as traitor assumes a peculiar concreteness.¹⁰ La Malinche's 'betrayal' was less of the translation than of those who were being translated, those whom she betrayed to the man with whom she slept. La Malinche is the interpretess, the *lengua*, the tongue in the ear of the conquistador Cortés who was as brutal as he was wily.

I will comment below in more detail on the relationship between translation and erotic desire. The traditional legend that has formed around the figure of La Malinche already shows that intercultural translation itself can be understood as a betrayal of one's own. La Malinche, in any case, seems to have provided Cortés with effective translations of what the natives perceived as his ill intentions. Without his *traduttrice traditrice*, the rationalistic, power-hungry Cortés would have had far greater difficulty recognizing his adversaries' culturally conditioned weaknesses and to conquer the Aztec empire in such a short time. Since the European conquest, interlingual and intercultural translation has been coded as betrayal in the Americas. Tzvetan Todorov concluded aptly that, in this context, understanding stood in the service of destruction.¹¹ This connection between understanding and destruction would be repeated in the history of the Americas with some frequency.

It is not difficult to find examples of translators who 'mastered' their original texts. One of those examples is that of J.S. Thrasher, the Anglo-American proslavery advocate, who successfully used his translation of Alexander von Humboldt's essay about Cuba, originally written in French, to turn the stout abolitionist into a proponent of the slave-trade and thus made Humboldt's writing serve his own interests in favor of the US South.¹² Even Camões's *Lusiads* (*Lusiades*) was not safe from distortions of this sort. Angered by Raynal's history of European expansion, the Scottish translator William Julius Mickle used his translation to turn the influential Portuguese poet into an apologist for (British)

---

10 It is only in recent years that this traitor betrayed by Cortés has become a positive figure particularly with respect to concepts of female and feminist identity. See Carmen Wurm: *Doña Marina*.
11 Tzvetan Todorov: *The Conquest of America: The Question of the Other*. New York: Harper Perennial 1992, p. 127.
12 See Alexander von Humboldt / John S. Thrasher: *The Island of Cuba, by Alexander Humboldt*. New York: Derby & Jackson 1856 [On Humboldt's reaction see Vera M. Kutzinski: 'Humboldt's Translator in the Context of Cuban History, by Fernando Ortiz.' In: Vera M. Kutzinski: *Alexander von Humboldt's Translantic Personae*. London: Routledge 2012, p. 93–110, TN].

colonialism.[13] Raynal himself, known for treating translation rather unscrupulously, was absorbed into the Spanish Enlightenment through translation and, at the same time, Hispanicized by it, even if sympathetically.[14] In all these cases, the 'betrayal of the original targets the reader, who is to be persuaded by the views not of the translation but of the translator. The voice of the translator replaces that of the Other, a process that one can indeed call an advanced form of written ventriloquism and which should be understood as an especially dangerous version of intercultural 'mediation.'

While there are countless examples of translations constructed to reflect the translator's own interests and biases and even used for propagandistic purposes, the fact that many more translations stand in the service of the original identifies intentional distortions as exceptions to the rule. Yet the uneasiness about translation remains. In my above examples, the translator becomes a forger who is less interested in Others' cultures and thoughts than in disseminating his own ideas under the banner of a prestigious foreign name; this, too, is an intentional playing with Others' words. The original becomes a mere pretext for one's own text. Betrayal, like forgery, is malicious deceit that aims for a certain effect on the reader through the misuse of a foreign author's name. Such abuses come to light as soon as one consults the original. In the case of Thrasher's translation, Humboldt even located them himself. But what about those forms of translational 'betrayal' that result neither from a clever translator's perfidy nor from an inept translator's good intentions?

Translating other cultural contexts is always tied to a sort of structural lie. The lie is all the greater the more separate the cultures the translation tries to connect. One might speak of an 'objective mendacity,' in Walter Benjamin's words, that neither translator nor translation can escape.[15] If one tries, for instance, to translate the religious ideas of pre-Columbian peoples into European languages suffused with Judeo-Christian discourses and concepts, one cannot help but bring into play entirely different contexts of religious meaning and experience. In each context, language provides the space within which thoughts and ideas can move and in which the translation itself can unfold. The

---

13 See Hugo Laitenberger: 'William Julius Mickle und seine Übersetzung der "Lusiaden."' In: Martine Guille and Reinhard Kiesler (eds.): *Romania una et diversa. Philologische Studien für Theodor Berchem zum 65. Geburtstag*. Tübingen: Narr 2000, p. 739–760.
14 See Manfred Tietz: 'L'Espagne et *l'Histoire des deux Indes* de l'abbé Raynal.' In: Hans-Jürgen Lüsebrink and Manfred Tietz (eds.): *Lectures de Raynal: L'Histoire de deux Indes en Europe et en Amérique au XVIIIe siècle*. Oxford: The Voltaire Foundation 1991, p. 99–130.
15 See Walter Benjamin: 'Notizen über 'Objective Verlogenheit' I.' In: Walter Benjamin: *Gesammelte Schriften*, vol. 6. Frankfurt am Main: Suhrkamp 1977–1985, p. 60–62.

term 'religious' alone introduces concepts and images to be translated into entirely different cultural environs complete with their different discursive horizons. This process is inevitable, for the significance of any sign comes about only through processes of intralingual translation that necessarily have to take recourse to concepts available to the reader or addressee. To be able to do justice to both original and reader, that is, to be equal to her task, the translator has to use a structural lie. If neither translator nor reader are aware of this fact, the structural lie, in its turn, (ab)uses the translation.

The structural lie is not a simple 'error' on the translator's part. For an error would spring from the translator's opinion, and opinions can be analyzed intersubjectively and, if necessary, be bracketed. An error is something in which a translator believes, something she deems, naively and wrongly, 'right' and 'true.' While error is a function of ignorance, a lie stems from an excess of knowledge that one does not, however, offer one's audience directly. It follows, then, that a good translator has to be a most persuasive liar.

The literary *traduttore* is thus neither a traitor, who consciously betrays what she translates, nor a forger who uses treachery to trick her audience; nor does she insists on her error and loses her mind because of it. Rather, the expert liar is a translator who is most intimately familiar with the sociocultural contexts of both source and target languages and who uses this dual knowledge to bridges the gap between both cultures, however provisionally and precariously. These bridges, however, belong to neither mainland. They constitute a separate area, which is a vectoral space of both transition and transitoriness. The good literary translator is fully aware of the ambiguity of intercultural translation processes. She knows that translations, in the contexts of their changing historical embeddedness, are as ephemeral and transitory as historically changing modes of reading with their always shifting horizons.[16] But if the translator is alert to the conditions of her actions and does not believe, naively, that she can disregard those conditions or contingencies (or stands above them), then she is able, from an intercultural or even transcultural perspective that oscillates between different cultural positions to make her source text speak in new ways. She can then not only recognize the structural lie at the basis of her (literary) practice but can actively bring it into play and make it fruitful for new insights. Italo Calvino's participation in the translations of his own texts points in this di-

---

16 This is also relevant to the relations between orality and writing which varies among cultures; see Karsten Garscha: 'Zum Phänomen der (fingierten) Mündlichkeit in der lateinamerikanischen Erzählliteratur.' In: Birgit Scharlau (ed.): *Bild-Wort-Schrift: Beiträge zur Lateinamerika-Sektion des Freiburger Romanistentages*. Tübingen: Narr 1989, p. 121–130.

rection and, at the same time, shows that the strongest loyalty to an original may consist in taking that original elsewhere in creative ways.

Most relevant to our inquiry is the fact that translations *illuminate* an original text from very different, intercultural and transcultural, perspectives and reveal layers of meaning that monolingual and monocultural modes of reading might easily miss. A literary-cultural industry that at once globalizes and is globalized in turn, and for which the name of the author still has a central classificatory and interpretive function, affords the *auctor* unique possibilities for semantic texturing. This texturing, in turn, can produce very particular forms of interaction and legitimation as part of the connection of author with translator and original with translation. The French translator of *The Castle of Crossed Destinies* (*Il castello dei destini incrociati*, 1973) agreed to sign his name to the translation, on which Calvino himself had worked, only under the condition that Calvino's name would appear on the title page as guarantor the original text and also the translation.[17] For an author to translate his own text is not only a form of self-interpretation but also a *réécriture*, a rewriting at an interlingual and *translingual* level that forever oscillates between different languages. Insisting on strict borders between writing and translating is inappropriate in such cases. Where, after all, would one draw the border between écriture and *traduction* in such a situation?

It is well to ask if the special case of self-translation can make any claims to changing our understanding of literary translation as a situation in which author and translator are not usually the same person. This extends to the question of readership, for the problematic situation I am sketching here requires, at least ideally, an active reader who recognizes the excess of knowledge that a successful translation proffers and knows how to use it. At times, however, even a bad or unsatisfactory translation, produced with the best of intentions, can reveal to the reader the structural lie and encourage, even force, him to perform his own interpretive and translational labor. A good example is the translation of Roland Barthes's *Le Degré zéro de l'écriture*, rendered in German as *Am Nullpunkt der Literatur* in 1959 and in English as *Writing Degree Zero* in 1964. The German translation is faithful not to the original but, rather, to the target lan-

---

[17] See Domenico D'Oria: 'Calvino traduit par Calvino.' In: *Lectures* (Bari) 4–5 (August 1980), p. 178. The title carries the addition 'Traduit de l'italien par Jean Thibaudeau et l'Auteur.' This confers upon the French text the author's stamp of approval, which makes it a continuation of *Il castello*. In this way, readers who engage in serious study of this Calvino novel, are forced to deal with the French version as well, since it throws new interlingual and translingual light on the purported original.

guage's context. The choice of this title is clearly due to an error on the part of the translator (or the publisher who tends to have significant input when it comes to book titles), since, for Barthes, the concept of *écriture* was, at that time, explicitly set off from the concept of *littérature*. Conversely, the phrase 'Nullpunkt der Literatur' (literature's ground zero) refers to debates about the so-called 'Literatur der Stunde Null' (literature of the zero hour), which were carried out with great vehemence in post-WWII Germany. This changed context brings into view a completely different reception climate and a completely different horizon of expectations with which the young Barthes's first book publication was met in Germany. And it was precisely this new, surprising light, which the author himself could not have planned or foreseen, that brought the French original into sharper, contrasting relief, showing the text in a sort of intercultural backlight through the detour via translation.

Does this not pose the danger of freezing an original in its monolingual meaning(s), of fixing it in its contrast to the translation and thus rendering it univocal? Not at all, just as long as we do not disregard the productive energy of either intentional or 'subversive' misreadings. Even if the German title is a case of an individual mistake, an obvious translation error, that error still shows that the original, in all its polysemy, can be inflected in different ways. Even in its seemingly static being-thus [So-sein], the original does not occupy the place of truth; rather, it contains *truths* and makes them available. With the help of the structural lie, the de- and re-contextualizations that are necessarily part of the translation process mercilessly draw out those truths as different inflections. They also, at the same time, can expose truths that would have remained unspoken and unopened without the translation. If one reads Roland Barthes's slender volume anew before the background of the German debates, it becomes clear that, at the level of literary history, it hides (or holds) within it a demand for a new beginning, which takes shape in the texts that the French theorist wrote later in life. Here, we see translation's proximity not just to reading in general but to a specific form of scholarly reading that brings out what had originally 'not been thought.'[18]

A good translation is neither treachery nor deceit but, paradoxically, a lie that brings to the surface other truths and Others' truths. It is a bridge that gives the reader who wanders between two worlds solid ground beneath his feet,

---

18 See Peter Utz: 'Transgressionen der Traduction: Robert Musils "Mann ohne Eigenschaften" und Philippe Jaccottets "L'Homme sans qualités."' In: Rainer Warning and Gerhard Neumann (eds.): *Transgressionen: Literatur als Ethnographie*. Freiburg im Breisgau: Rombach 2003, p. 151–172.

without, however, pretending to be dry land and, as such, territorializable. Such translation stands for a Writing-between-Worlds that can be assigned to neither shore. Translation's resides between cultures as well as between production and reception. Put differently, translation bridges both, short-circuiting them in the process. Much like sound literary scholarship, a good translation is necessarily self-referential in that it fulfills what the title page promises: that the author is in the company of a second guarantor and *auctor* who reveals herself as both reader and writer *at the same time*.

Unless it pursues primarily academic goals, literary translation, in contrast to literary scholarship, would do well to eschew footnotes and critical commentary. The translated text has to speak for itself; it has to explain itself and should not parade before the reader the knowledge of what has been 'added.' Translation's knowledge is discreet and sensual, that of literary scholarship sober and promotional. We encounter here anew translation's specific epistemic makeup. Translation proves once again a *both-and* configuration with paradoxical ties to a *neither-nor*. It is an oscillating figure of thought that defines the translator's professional position as author *and* copyist, and, at the same time, as neither.

The truths stored in the original text – and literature can be understood as a gigantic storehouse of all sorts of knowledge about life and survival – are opened up through structural lies for which (in contrast to individual error, forgery, or betrayal) there is no subject, no individual originator. The translational text can grasp in the words of the target language only that which is thinkable in it, or, at least, resides at the borders of what is thinkable. The structural lie represents the price that the translating culture must pay if it wants to expand its own possibilities for thought and thus its own philosophical, literary, and artistic forms of expression. In this sense, literary translation *targets* the target language without, however, becoming one with it; it tests new possibilities of national literature without, however, becoming itself (part of) a national literature by blending in with it completely. Does this make translated literature or literary translation a Literature without a fixed Abode? An initial response to this question is that literary translation is, at least, a practice of Writing-between-Worlds that can neither be fixed within nor absorbed into national literatures. From this perspective, the translator is a smuggler whose home is the borderland and whose only abode is movement. A good smuggler must be able to dissemble: she speaks the words of the Other otherwise, and she lies like crazy in re-creating the truths of the Other and in turning them into other truths. She is the true liar.

Literary translation as the work of the Other

The literary translator not only has an obligation to be precise and true in relation to the original; she is obligated to the original itself. In a certain way, the translator creates the author, the Other. The translator of Shakespeare continues to write the great poet's work (though not the text itself); in this sense, the translator is her author's creation. If there are literary scholars for whom – as Julian Barnes has commented somewhat rancorously[19] – a long dead author 'who must, one way or another, have paid a lot of [their] gas bills,' then there are also literary translators who receive from that author, to whom they feel a special obligation, a portion of his royalties from the beyond. In such cases and in this sense, presses and government offices are only trustees responsible for paying translators or scholars the amounts that an author has authorized. There is a reason why an author's rights extend to the translation, so that the suggestive 'edited by x and the author' could be applied to all good literary translations.

Translation is mediation. But we should not reduce it to the bipolarity of original and translation, of source and target languages. Translational mediation is not a one-way street from one language to another, from one culture to another, but has to be understood as a space onto itself, as a discrete place of writing that, in a paradoxical sense, writes into being interWorlds. When, at the end of Jorge Luis Borges's story 'Tlön, Uqbar, Orbis Tertius,' the world of Tlön crashes into 'reality,' the I-narrator retreats into the space of translation. Here is the final paragraph of this fantastically narrated text: 'Then English and French and mere Spanish will disappear from the globe. The world will be Tlön. I pay no attention to all and go on revising, in the still days at the Adrogué hotel, an uncertain Quevedian translation (which I do not intend to publish) of Browne's *Urn Burial.*'[20] Here, translation is a refuge, a sanctuary, a last possible retreat from a world that has come apart at the seams, from which the traditional world languages will soon be gone, a world in which everything is, asit were, tlöned. Why, then, bother to translate one moribund language (English) into another (Spanish)? If translation were mere mediation, to do so would be absurd. But if we read Borges's passage as a commitment to writing that continues in spite of external threats, then translation appears as writing in the midst of intensified inter-textual conditions. It is writing that seeks to set up an interWorld as an

---

19 See Julian Barnes: *Flaubert's parrot.* New York: Knopf 1985, p. 81.
20 Jorge Luis Borges: *Labyrinths: Selected Stories and Other Writings.* New York: New Directions 1964, p. 18.

anti-world, precisely because it cannot belong to a single language, even if it is that of the author. The source text and the model through which it is transformed and made one's own are both fixed, and only the place of the writing is made conspicuously transitory in the story through the autobiographical reference to a hotel. The hotel is a safe haven at times of crisis, but it is not a permanent residence. Here, the desire to write is strongest when writing is most confined.

This insight throws a clarifying light on Borges's 'Pierre Menard, Author of the Quixote,' a text that, as George Steiner has pointed out, is of great significance for translation theory.[21] In this story, the conditions of 'confinement' are even more intense because the result of Menard's writing, it seems, will be the already written great novel of Spanish literature, written by the Other in his words and already long in print. But why would one want to write Cervantes's *Quixote* once more? The outcome of the writing process is predetermined; it does not consist in achieving the greatest possible proximity to the source text but in becoming identical with it. In this way, the source text's difference can be freed from all its violence and raised to our awareness in a de-automatizing way. The narrator shows us how an identical textual passage – of all things, about the relationship of truth, history, and reality – can mean something entirely different in Cervantes's *Quixote* and in the new text that is identical to the 'original.' The quality of that difference becomes a function of changed contexts: 'History, the *mother* of truth: the idea is astounding. Menard, a contemporary of Henry James, does not define history as an inquiry into reality but as its origin. Historical truth, for him, is not what has happened; it is what we judge to have happened.'[22] This passage not only playfully questions a logocentric philosophy that depends on a single concept of truth; it also, at the same time, subverts the stasis of original and of the process of reading *fractally* by blending what is separated spatially and temporally in the same, the identical, text. Original and target appear as mutable categories (or destinations). Between them, a form of writing takes place that confines itself to the strictest borders, and that question the writer's subjectivity but not that of his writing. In this way, the *Quixote* begins to oscillate between the world of Cervantes's heroes and the world of Borges's Pierre Menard.

---

21 See George Steiner: *After Babel: Aspects of Language and Translation.* Oxford: Oxford University Press 1975, p. 70f. Steiner considered this story the most condensed prose text ever to have been written about the business of translation.
22 Borges: *Labyrinths*, p. 43.

To be sure, Pierre Menard is not a translator, a fact that George Steiner did perhaps not sufficiently consider. But from my perspective, Menards radicalizes the position of the first-person narrator who, at the end of 'Tlön, Uqbar, Orbis Tertius,' puts his trust into a kind of writing that is translation but not necessarily mediation. This is also why it does not need to be printed. As a rule, the literary translator concerned with mediation strives to publish her translation, even if this wish is not always granted. That mediation occurs only after publication should not deceive us about the prior writing process. There is hardly a form of writing that shies away more from the writer's individual, personal expression than literary translation. When she translates, as she usually does, different writers from different times, the translator's voice must not be audible in the same way, in the same tonality, in the case of different authors. She must be able to call upon a repertoire of different forms and facets of literary writing, of different literary styles, which makes her the literary industry's chameleon that must not show its own colors. At times, the translator even becomes an author who wears an invisibility cloak and thus does not make an appearance at all. In this, the literary translator resembles an actor who can leave her imprint on different roles without letting them all become the same. There are only two possibilities, then: either the translator has to surprise us constantly or she always plays the same role. Brilliant examples exist for both. Many translators' work always sounds the same, even when they take on texts from different centuries. They resemble the voices of certain performers of audio books who impose the same intonation and rhythm on vastly different texts.

The literary translator as creation of the Other oscillates not only between (at least) two different cultures and contexts but also, in her writing, between fiction and diction. Like a (bad) actor, who identifies too strongly with her role, she can add new elements to a source text, which, as experienced editors and publishers report, happens rather frequently.[23] Although it belongs to the realm of fiction, literary translation remains tied to the 'dictional;' it has to follows its lead and can be tested against it. Nonetheless, the history of literary translation includes enough instances both of translators' more frictional, and even fictional, writing and of the mode of re-poeticizing. The latter, where it is permissible for the translator-as-author to remove her invisibility cloak, has lost nothing of its higher prestige vis-à-vis literary translation. Still, literary translation as a fictional, dictional, or frictional mode of writing is always obligated to attend to

---

23 See Elisabeth Borchers: 'Übersetzer und Lektor.' In: Nies et al. (eds.): *Ist Literaturübersetzen lehrbar?*, p. 50f. This book includes several excellent examples of translations in which the translator's imagination has gone wild.

the dynamics of its own space between worlds, and this space has all the characteristics of a writing workshop, a laboratory of *écriture* as much as of *littérature*.

From the latter perspective, we can understand literary translation as an interlingual continuation of intralingual pastiche and thus as a literary form that exists, or is produced, under more intense intellectual and intercultural conditions. Similar to pastiche, a good translation has a certain (at times even ironic) distance to the original in that it also speaks of the original's other sides and sounds other notes. Neither error nor forgery but only lie and fiction can create that distance, which renders dynamic the relationship between the text to be translated and the actual translation. Precisely because translation wants to mediate between different cultures, it always has to remain in motion and must not blend into the target culture; it must transform the Other into a stranger who resides within the self. If translation does not succeed in this, then it does not contribute to innovative changes within its own culture.

I thus venture the following hypotheses: Philosophy is a discipline that works on the realm of what can be thought. Literature is the interactive storehouse of expressive forms that artistically play at the boundaries of what can be written. Literary translation, however, is a form of writing that explores and tests the limits of the thinkable and the writable through intercultural and transcultural dialogue. The translator's task is less that of a word artist, or even that of a juggler, than it is that of a person who, in writing, tests out the literary material of an Other whose creation she is. At times, she even pushes that material to a breaking point. Translation is thus the work of the Other on the self and indeed *within* the self; translation does not allow us to draw the borders between what is self and what is Other in any clear and reliable fashion. The translator, too, may say of herself, with Sartre: *Je est un autre* – I is another.

The literary translator as provocateur

To set up stable borders between poet and translator seems no more possible than to separate the translator from the scholar. In the last few years in particular, the relations between translation and other forms of knowledge production have multiplied and intensified. But translation as a form of scholarly writing is hardly limited to so-called translation studies. Although academically oriented translation studies have thus far predominated and have been defined almost exclusively as a form of applied linguistics, it is high time that translation studies also be understood and practiced, in a complementary sense, as applied *literary* scholarship.[24]

The insights of literary translators and translations contain an immense unused potential that is highly relevant to and valuable for literary studies. If literature is a gargantuan cumulative effort of working through, acquiring, and storing knowledge artistically, then the literature of translation is surely no less than that; at times, translation even does so in more powerful ways. Translation lends voice to complex textual and contextual, as well as cultural and intercultural, relationships. Translation per se is a form of knowledge production, although not in the way in which we commonly understand that phrase. It produces a kind of knowledge that, in more or less diffuse ways, forms the basis of translational practice. The precise relevance of this knowledge to literary scholarship has so far barely even been recognized.

The translator knows that her practice is not limited to a text that can be bound between two covers but extends to two different cultural contexts that are brought into relation in very direct, meaningful, and sensual ways. In this, translation is primarily an intricate hermeneutic process that itself can be hermeneutically decoded,[25] and which gives us valuable information not only about the source text but also about different contexts for textual production and reception. Translation is based on readers' prior understanding and simultaneously targets their future comprehension. Through its movement, it demarcates concrete conditions of, and possibilities for, intercultural and transcultural understanding. Translation offers valuable clues especially in situations where the contexts of either source or target cultures are eclipsed. On the one hand, we can, from the perspective of imagology, analyze a disregard for the cultural context that produced a given text in the first place in relation to stereotypes that exist in that context. On the other hand, an obvious neglect of a target language's context may grant insights into a culture's own intellectual history.

As is the case in the analysis of literary texts, translation does not yield such information directly but requires careful interpretation, including consideration of historical and sociological aspects as well as of intellectual history. To name only one example: the cuts that Alain-René Lesage made when he translated the

---

[24] See the speech Berthold Zilly gave when he accepted the Wieland-Preises; Berthold Zilly: 'Dankrede.' In: *Der Übersetzer* (Munich) 30.2 (April–June 1996), p. 3–5.
[25] In this sense, we cannot understand translation by questioning and bracketing the central position that interpretation occupies in the humanities. For such a 'non-hermeneutical' approach, see Hans-Ulrich Gumbrecht: *Production of Presence: What Meaning Cannot Convey*. Stanford CA: Stanford University Press 2004.

Spanish picaresque novel *Guzmán de Alfarache* by Mateo Alemán, which were related above all to 'excess morals' (moralités superflues), can only be understood against the background of the early French Enlightenment. Given the panorama of rigid Enlightenment positions that were then beginning to emerge, Alemán's didactic back and forth between *consejos* (advice) and *consejas* (fables or tales) would have seemed distracting. It is hardly surprising that Lesage would have combined his activities as a translator with writing his own picaresque novel, which allowed him to make the plot more dynamic by substituting 'philosophical' for 'didactic' commentary. Lesage's writing of *Gil Blas de Santillane* seems like the author's literary continuation of a translation that necessarily led from the interlingual to the intercultural realm. While *Gil Blas* retained the Spanish picaresque's first-person narrator, it also used that narrative perspective to depict the problems of contemporary France with even greater clarity. We should not forget here that shortenings and omissions in a translation are especially useful in shedding light on a target culture's horizons of understanding. They point to the gaps and, even more so, to the vacuums in the inter-cultural dialogue which leave their mark on a given translation, and which the translation, at the same time, tries to promote and accelerate.

With respect to literary scholarship, literary translation is and remains an irritating provocation. At universities, translation is usually excluded from courses. Since it presumably gets in the way of the students' direct contact with the original language in the original text, it is used clandestinely instead. Literary translation, therefore, not only confounds existing epistemological categories; it also offends in its role as mediator or meddler, as an activity that inserts itself between Self and Other, between one's own and other cultures. By doing so, with or without an invisibility cloak, translation appears to prevent the unmediated view of the Other, of the Other's culture. Only when we realize that this undisturbed, unmuddied, direct view is an illusion that occludes familiar filters and translation processes can we recognize the innovative potential that literary translation has for literary scholarship, both in research and in pedagogy.

Creating an awareness of translation's specific processes of intercultural and transcultural learning and interpretation can help us in crucial ways to reconstruct both the respective historical-cultural contexts and the views and practices that regulate the contact and possible relationships between different cultures at particular points in time. For instance, the fact that intense intercultural exchanges flourished between Italy and France during the Renaissance can be as significant as the absence of cultural translation in another context, such as the relations of German-speaking cultures with the (not only non-

European) fringes of regions where Romance languages are spoken. The role of the irritant that literary translation plays vis-à-vis literary scholarship cannot be 'remedied' through a form of translation studies that is exclusively linguistic in its orientation. Translation challenges literary studies by demanding a configuration of knowledge that can include and adequately account for literary translation. Literary scholarship that leans towards cultural studies can respond to this demand in unique ways.

The literary translator as matchmaker in the interWorlds

In his insightful study, Peter Zima has called attention to the fact that there are two basic positions in the history of translation theory. He argues persuasively that the notion that texts can be transferred to a target language 'without notable losses' can be dialectically related to the seemingly contrary claim that the very uniqueness of a work of art prevents it from being translated into a foreign medium.[26] The 'rationalistic idea of the equivalence of signs and the Romantic idea of untranslatability' should, according to Zima, 'be perceived as two sides of the same coin' which, although one can never see them both at the same time, always have to be thought of together.[27] Each side or position values signifier and signified, that is, content and formal expression, differently. I do not believe that they can be thought (of) together and grasped terminologically by differentiating between equivalence and analogy, as Judith Macheiner does rather constructively and convincingly, defining the former as the sameness of content and the latter as sameness of linguistic forms.[28] One of the problems that her distinction does not address has to do with translation's intercultural and transcultural dimensions: the question of how equivalence and analogy relate back to different historical, social, or artistic contexts within cultures' multi-polar magnetic fields.

We can only confront the discomfort with this perspective, derived as it is from Saussure's distinction between signifier and signified, by drawing across it

---

26 Peter V. Zima: 'Der unfassbare Rest: Die Theorie der Übersetzung zwischen Dekonstruktion und Semiotik.' In: Johann Strutz and Peter V. Zima (eds.): *Literarische Polyphonie: Übersetzung und Mehrsprachigkeit in der Literatur*. Tübingen: Narr 1996, p. 19.
27 Zima: 'Der unfassbare Rest,' p. 19.
28 See Judith Macheiner: *Übersetzen: Ein Vademecum*. Frankfurt am Main: Eichborn 1995, p. 22. For a critique of the concept of equivalence see, in addition to Zima, Mary Snell-Hornby: 'Übersetzen, Sprache, Kultur.' In: Mary Snell-Hornby (ed.): *Übersetzungswissenschaft – Eine Neuorientierung: Zur Integrierung von Theorie und Praxis*.Tübingen: Francke 1994, p. 9–29.

yet another distinction. Walter Benjamin's differentiation between 'objects of intention' and 'modes of intention' strikes me as an ideal response to this epistemological necessity.[29] By introducing this distinction, Benjamin confronted the fact that the object different languages intend can be the same, but that languages fundamentally differ in how they produce meaning.[30] For instance – and we can interpret Benjamin in this way – the German noun *Brot* (bread) is embedded in a cultural context, a history, and language uses that are completely different from that of the French *pain*.

Epistemologically, Benjamin's differentiation helps us perform a leap from linguistics (and also, for the most part, from traditionally oriented literary scholarship and comparative literature) to a form of literary scholarship that is more open to cultural studies.[31] There is no need, I believe, also to adopt Benjamin's quasi-theological Kabbalistic idea of mutually complementing languages (which Borges valued), a theory that, in the end, points in the direction of the lost totality of an Ur-language and of an untranslatable essential core. Nor is there any reason to agree with the premise of the fundamental untranslatability of unique linguistic creations because of the different cultural embedding of only seemingly equivalent terms such as *Brot* and *pain*. Rather, Benjamin makes us more acutely aware that translation does not occur directly and without mediation, in an airless vacuum, but that various culturally determined filters work to balance out the actual process of translation in relation both to source and target cultures. Optically speaking, we no longer focus on the result but on the prior intercultural and interlingual process of translation. This focus, however, destroys the illusion of immediacy. It is often experienced as distracting or troubling and can even have a painful effect on the viewer whom it separates from the 'original.' However we may wish to judge this situation, the object of our hermeneutic desire is removed from direct, immediate access.

In his *Maxims and Reflections*, Goethe shed light on the work of translation in both skeptical and humorous ways: 'Translators are like busy matchmakers: they sing the praises of some half veiled beauty, and extol her charms, and arouse an irresistible longing for the original.'[32] Through the figure of the

---

[29] Walter Benjamin: 'The Task of the Translator.' In: Walter Benjamin: *Illuminations: Essais and Reflections*. New York: Schocken Books 1999, p. 74.
[30] The problem of matching referentialities would also raise doubts.
[31] See Ottmar Ette: *ÜberLebenswissen: Die Aufgabe der Philologie*. Berlin: Kulturverlag Kadmos 2004.
[32] Johann Wolfgang von Goethe: *The Maxims and Reflections of Goethe*. New York: MacMillan and Company 1906, p. 156.

matchmaker, literary translation's erotic dimension comes into view. Our desire, if this is how we read Goethe, is for the beautiful woman, the original, and the translator's work makes us painfully aware that we have no direct access to her. All transparency is illusory; it gets tangled up in the veil. Instead of communicating directly with the beautiful woman, we communicate with the translator, who eloquently offers up the object of our desire. In place of unmediated, almost physical experience, we find verbal mediation: the matchmaker speaks to the desiring subjects in their own words in order, paradoxically, to *arouse* their desire for the original. The beginning, or origin, of translation is thus the desire for an Other to whom translation as matchmaking leads as if it were a bridge, at the same time that it obstructs any direct communication with the Other. This turns translation into a scandal and the translator into that scandal's representative. From such a traditional perspective, she is but a meddler, a tease, and a hindrance: she arouses desire without satisfying it.

But translation, as I have shown, is no substitute. Literary translation is not a search for equivalents. It is not a form of linguistic gymnastics but an attempt at taking the original elsewhere, at making it speak in other words within the context of a different culture or a different time. In this effort, we may find a ground for the observations of poet-translator Erich Fried who, in response to criticisms of his Shakespeare translations, quipped that a translation is never done.[33]

Even if one were skeptical of Walter Benjamin's apodictic remark that a literary, visual, or musical work of art is not directed at an audience,[34] one could confidently assert that the translator, in her task or role as 'busy matchmaker,' always addresses an audience. But in her text, the Other appears in two forms: as that which is (or those who are) desired *and* those who desire.

Literary translation is not just a way of speaking 'in other words;' it is a form of speaking *with* Others' words. In the matchmaker's communications, the Other is both author and reader. The translator speaks (or writes) in other words the words of an Other who – entirely in the sense of Baudelaire's opening poem in *The Flowers of Evil* (*Les Fleurs du Mal*), is also the author's 'Hypocrite reader, fellowman, – my twin!' (hypocrite lecteur, mon semblable, – mon frère!).[35] The

---

[33] See Erich Fried: 'Übersetzen oder nachdichten?' In: Nies et al. (eds.): *Ist Literaturübersetzen lehrbar?*, p. 36.
[34] 'For no poem is for the reader, no painting for the viewer, no symphony for the listener.' Benjamin: *Illuminations*, p. 69.
[35] Charles Baudelaire: *The Flowers of Evil*. Includes parallel French text. Oxford: Oxford UP 2008, p. 7.

literary translator doesn't just play with the words of a (perhaps long deceased) author but also with the words of a possible and potential reader. In this transtemporal sense, she is a central agent of Writing-between-Worlds. In this inter-World, translation works not only on and with other cultures' differences but also on and with the identity of one's own culture. As the translator's *semblable* and *frère*, the reader also speaks in the translation; he is present to the translation.

My discussion raises a number of philological and narratological problems that have rarely even been recognized as problems.[36] Literary translation's specific communication networks are far more intricate than they may appear. Until now, the figure of the translator, para-textually mentioned on the title page, had taken on a more concrete shape in afterwards, preambles, notes, and footnotes added on to the translation. The translation adds narratological dimensions to those already at play in the original, which the figure of the implied reader illustrates. If the presence of that figure can be analytically determined both in the original and in the translation, then there is also a second implied reader whom the translated text addresses. It is already in the choice of the target language that we can recognize this second implied reader as part of the conversation. It is the case, for instance, that certain expressions and formulations offers clues about whether the translator hails from a Swiss-German or an East-German cultural area, or is not a native speaker. Such selections can also make us aware of which implied reader the text primarily addresses. Consciously employed vernacular, such as the queer jargon of East Berlin[37] or the 'cool' vocabulary of the Freiburg scene, can invoke target audiences not present in the original well beyond stylistic choices. At times, the formal expansion of the narrator's function, as much as the presumably static experiential realm of the implied author, changes so fundamentally that it is as if a second communication network were added to the original one. To use Goethe's image, this second network veils the beautiful woman and, at the same time, unveils the matchmaker's skill in Writing-between-Worlds. In the case of a good translation, this does not diminish our desire but, instead, increases it, for the translation opens up dimensions of communication necessarily unknown to those who read 'only' the original but who can now perceive new facets of meaning. The skilled liter-

---

[36] See Berthold Zilly: 'O tradutor implícito: Considerações acerca da translingualidade de *Os Sertões*'. In: *Revista da Universidade de São Paulo* (São Paulo) 45 (2000), p. 85–105.

[37] About a successful translation of the lingo of Cuban homosexuals in the East Berlin scene, see the comments by Klaus Laabs: 'Traducir a Reinaldo Arenas.' In: *Apuntes Postmodernos / Postmodern Notes* (Miami) 4.1 (Fall 1995), p. 53–55.

ary translator shows us the beautiful woman (at least) in a double light: that of the source culture and that of the respective target culture. A comparative analysis, for instance, of West and East German translations could no doubt show just how different this light and its projections can be, beyond the different linguistic competencies of individual translators. Here, literary translation becomes the most creative form of active reception; it is an interpretive transformation and possession of aesthetic artifacts with fluid transitions to creative writing.

It is exciting and instructive to observe how the two communication networks I mention above blend with, and bleed into, one another in texts that participate in two or more languages and cultures, not only because of certain authors' biographies, are shot through with interminable processes of translation. Some examples of such *translingual* and transcultural texts from German-speaking contexts, which oscillate continually between different languages and cultures, are the writings of authors such as Emine Sevgi Özdamar, Yoko Tawada, and José A. Oliver.[38] Their texts' translingual characteristics show, in resounding aesthetic relief, that the proximity of literary translation's Writing-between-Worlds to the Writing-without-a-fixed-abode is by no means coincidental, and that any analysis of the Literatures without a fixed Abode must not neglect literary translation.

A certain assumption or chancing of alterity, even strangeness (not only in Benjamin's sense), is inevitable and even desirable in all translation processes, be they intercultural or transcultural, interlingual or translingual. Translation cannot do without it. In the same way that the translator speaks the Other's words, the Other's words speak her own text. As cultural mediator, the translator takes upon herself the responsibility for insuring that those words are neither those of the (historical) author alone nor those of the (targeted) reader. Her own text must create tension and mutual exchange between the two poles. As the Other's creation, the literary translator is a double agent who serves two masters. This is precisely what makes her position so enormously important, so difficult, and thus so rich in potential insights. Literary translation is artisanship, literary artistry, and philological interpretation all wrapped in one. It

---

38 The term 'translingual' as I apply it here differs fundamentally from Zilly's use (in 'O tradutor implícito') and Lydia Liu's in her *Translingual Practice. Literature, National Culture, and Translated Modernity – China, 1900–1937*. Standford, CA: Stanford University Press 1995. Both, in different ways, focus on translational processes at the level of the translator, not the author, processes that I, following Jakobson, regard as 'interlingual.' See also chapter 5 below.

opens up possibilities not only for linguistic but also for literary-critical analysis, especially when the latter is grounded in cultural semiotics.

In other words: the literary translator embodies the Other *within* us and demonstrates the power of twisted and unruly epistemological lines that run across, and at times afoul of, the usual borders of academic disciplines. In this sense, translations have genuinely transdisciplinary tendencies. The blueprint these lines trace is a mode of Writing-between-Worlds whose basic pattern is proportionally increased and intensified. Literary scholarship would do well to take careful note of these differently drawn, unruly borders and to take seriously the philological and literary challenges with which translation presents it. After all, what else can such *literary* scholarship do[39]? In the end, it, too, is an ingenious matchmaker who seeks to increase our pleasure of the text.

---

[39] See Ette: *ÜberLebenswissen*, p. 51–96.

6 Oscillations

Writing-Other(wise) between Worlds: About translingual writing in contemporary German-speaking Literature

'On Foreign Tongues': Writing-other(wise)

The writers who had fled to Mexico during the Spanish Civil War inspired Octavio Paz, in 'La paloma azul' (1959), to remark on the phenomenon of double expatriation that also existed in other parts of the world:

> They came to Mexico in 1939; and they have lived among us ever since. Are they Mexicans or Spaniards? This problem does not really interest me; I am content to know that they are writing in Spanish: language is a writer's only nationality. But our critics insist on continuing to treat them as foreigners; they ignore their names and their works in Mexican monographs and anthologies. Critics from Spain are even more arrogant and cutting in that they completely ignore the very existence of these writers. As a result, indisputable talents such as the poet Tomás Segovia and the critic Ramón Xirau live in a type of limbo, since they are doubly orphaned with regard to their country, doubly expatriated.[1]

Paz begins his reflections by emphasizing that the decisive factor is not a writer's national origin but his belonging to a language and thus to a linguistic group; after all, language, *la lengua*, is an author's 'only nationality.' Even before her escape from National Socialism, Hannah Arendt responded to the issue similarly when Karl Jaspers asked what Germany still meant to her: 'For me, Germany is the mother tongue; it is philosophy and poetry. For all that I can and must take responsibility.'[2] For the author of *The Origins of Totalitarianism* (1951), Germany was thus not a territory, a piece of real estate that would occupy a changeless place in the world; instead, it was something movable that would

---

1 'En 1939, casi niños llgaron a México; desde entonces viven entre nosotros ¿Son mexicanos o españoles? El problema me interesa poco; me basta con saber que escriben en español: la lengua es la única nacionalidad de un escritor. Pero nuestros críticos se obstinan en estudios y antologías mexicanos. Los de España, más soberbios y tajantes, ignoran hasta su existencia. Así, talentos tan claros como el poeta Tomás Segovia o el crítico Ramon Xirau viven en una especie de limbo, dos veces huérfanos de tierra, dos veces desterrados.' Octavio Paz: 'La paloma azul'. In: Manuel Durán (ed.): *Octavio Paz. Obras Completas*, vol. IV. México: Fondo de Cultura Económica 1994, p. 309.
2 Elisabeth Young-Bruehl: *Hannah Arendt: Leben, Werk und Zeit*. Frankfurt am Main: Fischer 2000, p. 161.

continue to evolve. Above all, Germany linked back to the mother tongue that anchored a familiar, collective, and cultural genealogy and community, almost as if it were rooted in the speaker's physical body itself. Hers was a Germany that one carries on one's tongue.

Revealing about Octavio Paz' remarks is also the fact that the exclusionary mechanisms within literary scholarship, bound up not in language but in territory and the nation-state, bring to light how extensive literary production can either be systematically disregarded or altogether silenced. Significantly, not just writers – such as the poet Tomás Segovia who fled to Mexico in 1940 and for whom writing in different exiles became the focal point and fulcrum of his lyrics – but also exiled literary scholars become victims of a territorializing and often at once totalitarian and exclusionary literary historiography. Other examples, as dazzling as they are depressing, are Ramón Xirau from the Spanish-speaking world and Erich Auerbach from a German-speaking context. Both literature and literary studies can (re)constitute and understand themselves as forms of writing without a fixed abode.[3]

For Octavio Paz and Hannah Arendt. a linguistic and literary community rooted in the *lengua materna* beyond any national borders and politically motivated exclusionary mechanisms was a comforting and productive thought. This idea was enormously important and circulated widely especially in the twentieth century, the century of migrations. In the last third of the past century, however, developments began to occur in the context of the fourth phase of accelerated globalization that were no longer associated just with literary greats such as Beckett, Conrad, and Nabokov but with broader spheres of writing whose different accents were increasingly hard to ignore. While the great exceptions did not become the rule, the rule itself grew brittle and structurally unsound. What happens when language, the tongue of this *lengua*, no longer follows maternal movements and sounds but appropriates new languages, foreign tongues?

Born in Tokyo in 1960, Yoko Tawada came to Germany on the Trans-Siberian railroad in 1979[4] and has since attempted multiple literary answers to this intriguing and complex question, for instance in her book *Überseezungen* (Translations, or tongues from abroad, or from across the waters) from 2002. In her story 'The ear witness' (Die Ohrenzeugin), a title that puns on the figure of the

---

3 See Ottmar Ette: *ÜberLebenswissen: Die Aufgabe der Philologie*. Berlin: Kulturverlag Kadmos 2004.
4 It is hardly an accident that the publisher's presentations of Yoko Tawada frequently mention the Trans-Siberian Railroad, which in Europe is connected above all with Blaise Cendrars's famous poem *Prose du Transsibérien et de la petite Jeanne de France* (1913).

eye witness much like the volume's title puns homophonically on the plural of the German noun for translation, *Übersetzungen*, Tawada writes:

> In Germany, most people would not assert that others must not write in the German language. But indirectly they keep letting one know that language has to be a possession. They say, for example, that one can never speak a foreign language as well as a mother tongue. One notices immediately that, for them, the most important thing is domination. I think that it is pointless to dominate a language. You either have a relationship with a language or you don't.
>   Others say that only in a mother tongue can one express one's feelings authentically, whereas in a foreign tongue one inevitably lies. It disturbs them in their quest for authentic feelings when they see their language on foreign tongues.
>   There are also people who claim that childhood is absent in a foreign tongue. Yet I found more childhood in the German language than anywhere else.[5]

These reflections on the part of Tawada's first-person narrator draw attention to other forms of exclusion that, as the author (who has published in both German and Japanese[6]) has her character explain, are as common in Japan as they are in Germany. In Germany, the basis for this exclusion is not territory, however nationalistically defined, to which the excluded either did not have access or had somehow lost access. Instead, exclusion has to do with acquiring a mobile cultural good – a particular language – in a way tantamount to stealing food out of someone's mouth, for this taking (over) is unprotected by way of a genealogy which the figure of the mother represents. A line of descent guaranteed by family ties authenticates and authorizes a linguistic community precisely by separating it from those who approach it as strangers and thus can own its language 'merely' as a foreign language. Through the authenticity that the mother tongue

---

5 'In Deutschland würden die meisten Menschen nicht behaupten, daß die deutsche Sprache von anderen nicht angetastet werden darf. Aber indirekt geben sie einem immer wieder zu verstehen, daß die Sprache ein Besitztum sein muß. Sie sagen zum Beispiel, daß man eine Fremdsprache nie so gut beherrschen könne wie die Muttersprache. Man bemerkt sofort, daß das Wichtigste für sie die Beherrschung ist. Meiner Meinung nach ist es überflüssig, eine Sprache zu beherrschen. Entweder hat man eine Beziehung zu ihr oder man hat keine. Andere sagen, nur in der Muttersprache könne man authentisch seine Gefühle ausdrücken, in einer Fremdsprache lüge man unwillkürlich. Sie fühlen sich bei ihrer Suche nach dem authentischen Gefühl gestört, wenn sie ihre Sprache auf fremden Zungen sehen. Es gibt auch Menschen, die behaupten, in einer Fremdsprache ist die Kindheit abwesend.' Yoko Tawada: *Überseezungen*. Tübingen: Konkursbuch Verlag Claudia Gehrke 2002, p. 109–110.
6 For her complete writings, see Albrecht Kloepfer / Miho Matsunaga: 'Yoko Tawada.' In: *Kritisches Lexikon zur deutschsprachigen Gegenwartsliteratur*, 64th supplement. Munich: Edition text + kritik 2000.

confers, as if it had been imbibed like mother's milk, a seemingly self-evident, 'natural' linguistic community can both authorize and deny access to authorship and a 'real feel' for the language. According to this line of thought, a national literature is an area open only to native speakers, who have been born into a (literary) language. This critical verdict, which frequently appears in book reviews in the guise of praise for some undefined 'exoticism,' resorts to the very last piece of property that those displaced and exiled during the Spanish Civil War and World War II believed still to have in their possession: the mother tongue.

Such mechanisms of exclusion have an afterlife even at times of an aggressive 'politics of integration' towards immigrants. Although 'one's own' language has long landed on 'foreign' tongues, and even though the new German immigration laws require that German, for many a guardian of the dominant culture, *be imposed* onto all aliens, drawing distinctions with the help of the mother tongue targets foreignness especially when the 'alien' wants to become 'familiar,' part of the national family, that is, when the 'immigrant' wants to claim 'German citizenship.' Translated into the realm of politics, one might distinguish an active from a passive right to choose one's language. While foreigners are of course free to choose a language as a foreign (or second) language, they cannot, according to native speakers' practices of linguistic dominance, ever qualify as authorized representatives of that language because their linguistic competence will always be inauthentic and unauthorized.[7] German literature as something that alien tongues may neither rule nor represent?

To be sure, the question of linguistic mastery is, first and foremost, a question about authorizing linguistic dominance and control and thus about socially legitimated authorship. As we read in Yoko Tawada's text, one can 'decide which foreign language one wants to learn,' but there is 'no choice with regard to one's mother tongue.'[8] Taking recourse to Gertrude Stein, the first-person female narrator reasons: 'the mother tongue makes a person; a person, in turn, can do something in a foreign tongue.'[9] In this way, the law of action, of doing

---

[7] There are parallels to the criticism that Derek Walcott's voiced in his Nobel speech (1992) about the idea that Caribbean literatures and cultures are 'inauthentic' and 'impure.' See also chapter 3 above.

[8] 'Man kann sich entscheiden, welche Fremdsprache man lernen will, während es bei der Muttersprache keine Wahl gibt.' Tawada: *Überseezungen*, p. 111.

[9] 'Die Muttersprache macht die Person, die Person hingegen kann in einer Fremdsprache etwas machen.' Tawada: *Überseezungen*, p. 111.

and changing (something), is expanded to include those who make a foreign language their own.

Is this a case of language theft or language abduction? Neither. Tawada's goal is no longer necessarily and primarily a perfect mastery of the target language, but, in the sense of doing-something-with-it, using that language in a deliberate attempt at lexical, orthographic, semantic, morphologic, and syntactic transformation.[10] This practice aims at belonging to a group (can we call it a community?) that is always created anew, part of which it is not to close one's eyes and ears to non-native speakers and their uses of German-language literature but to listen together to what foreign tongues do with a language that they have appropriated and thus long made their own.

These reflections apply of course also in reverse to authors who are native speakers of German but who use other languages and work with them as French, Spanish, or Japanese writers. To this day, traditional national-literary categories continue to obstruct the idea that literatures do not have a fixed abode, neither territorially nor linguistically. Yoko Tawada, who shuttles between German and Japanese and who has crosshatched both literatures in various ways, has translated this concept in the context of her own migration to Europe on the Trans-Siberian Railroad into the metaphors of the soul's movement:

> Even the Trans-Siberian Railroad travels faster than a soul can fly. During my first journey to Europe on the Trans-Siberian Railroad I lost my soul. When I returned by train, my soul was still heading for Europe. I could not catch it. When I returned to Europe once again, my soul was on its way to Japan. After that, I have flown back and forth so often that I no longer know where my soul is at any moment in time.[11]

Here, it is not just an author, and her literature, that is motion. Her soul, and her writing, has lost its fixed abode; they have become part of unstoppable figures of increasingly complex, inverse movements for which there is no longer a fixed point of reference in this web of differing velocities. But this loss is also a gain, a

---

10 In Gérard Genette's theory, the two opposite directions of movement stand for the pastiche's approaching a (textual) model or, rather, its transformation through parody; see Gérard Genette: *Palimpsestes: La littérature au second degré*. Paris: Seuil 1982.

11 'Sogar die transsibirische Eisenbahn fährt schneller als eine Seele fliegen kann. Ich habe bei meiner ersten Fahrt nach Europa mit der transsibirischen Eisenbahn meine Seele verloren. Als ich dann mit der Bahn wieder zurückfuhr, war meine Seele noch in Richtung Europa unterwegs. Ich konnte sie nicht fangen. Als ich erneut nach Europa fuhr, war sie auf dem Weg nach Japan. Danach bin ich so oft hin- und hergeflogen, daß ich überhaupt nicht mehr weiß, wo meine Seele gerade ist.' Yoko Tawada: 'Erzähler ohne Seelen.' In: Yoko Tawada: *Talisman: Literarische Essays*. Tübingen: Konkursbuch Verlag Claudia Gehrke 1996, p. 22.

driving force for (literary) production. What we have here are endless choreographies not only between different spaces and times, which in the above passage cannot be synchronized with the soul's movements, but also between Japanese and German, between a native tongue and another, foreign language, an oscillating that allows Tawada 'always to discover black holes in the linguistic web.' Above all, however: 'Out of these speechless holes arises literature.'[12]

The encounter with writing as movement between worlds and between languages opens a territorialized monolingual *écriture* that avails itself of only one (national) language to create new aesthetic practices which cannot be communicated in a single language. Key is to generate the dynamic, mobile-areas-between-linguistic-worlds, which Tawada's texts assiduously explore without pitching the mother tongue as 'natural' or 'one's own' against the foreign language as 'alien' and 'distant.' This is not a sketch of the conditions of writing in a 'no-man's-land'[13] but, rather, of the vital energy of a Writing-between-Worlds which, by the way, is far from being applicable exclusively to an individual experience. The Literatures without a fixed Abode have long infiltrated the spaces between national literatures and the literatures of the world which are not reducible to the sum of national literatures. Their importance will no doubt grow in the twenty-first century.

Yoko Tawada's texts put in practice a poetics that does not reside in the acquired foreign language as one would in a hotel room in which nothing may be

---

12 'Dadurch, dass ich in zwei Sprachen schreibe, entdecke ich ständig *schwarze Löcher im Gewebe der Sprachen*. Aus diesen schwarzen Löchern entsteht Literatur.' Yoko Tawada: 'Fragebogen'. In: *Deutschland*. Frankfurt am Main, August 1996, p. 54. See also Kloepfer/Matsunaga (eds.): *Kritisches Lexikon*, p. 2–3. When asked what she liked best about Germany, Tawada replied: 'The humanities at German universities. They constitute one of the few public spaces that are left where one can think for the sake of thinking and discuss for the sake of discussion. Tawada: 'Fragebogen,' p. 54.
13 This formulation can be found in Wim Wenders about Tawada's book *Talisman* on the Konkursbuch Verlag's homepage under 'Presseinformation Yoko Tawada' (see http://www.konkursbuch.com/html/net-fr-09/zu-talisman.html; accessed March 11, 2015): The book 'does not deal with 'Europe' versus 'Asia' or vice versa. It is a book from the no-man's-land where no word and no name and no sign has a meaning anymore, but where everything is questioned, where only perception, experience, and speaking itself counts. And then this little volume suddenly becomes something like a model of utopian narration and utopian travel.' [Es handelt nicht von 'Europa' versus 'Asien', oder umgekehrt. Es ist ein Buch aus dem Niemandsland, da, wo kein Wort und kein Name und kein Zeichen mehr etwas bedeutet, sondern wo alles in Frage gestellt ist, und wo nur das Empfinden, das Erfahren, das Sprechen selber zählt. Und dann wird dieser kleine Band plötzlich so etwas wie ein Modell von utopischem Erzählen und von utopischem Reisen.]

changed. Rather, they conceive of the foreign language as a linguistic space in endless transition. Linguistic space becomes a flexible space, from where one casts a quasi-ethnological glance at the world and its continuously reconfiguring of interWorlds.

The title that Emine Sevgi Özdamar selected for *Mother Tongue* (*Mutterzunge*, 1990)[14] sets an agenda no less than Yoko Tawada's choice of a title for *Überseezungen* does when it alerts us to a language's potential for change in the form of a homophonic pun. The foreign inflection is not a mandate but the launching pad for literary creativity. As in an echo chamber, other sounds and other words become audible behind and underneath familiar words. In a serious play of words, German is not only transgressed but programmatically transformed:

> In my language, 'tongue' means 'language.'
> A tongue has no bones: twist it in any direction and it will turn that way.
> I sat with my twisted tongue in this city, Berlin. A café for foreigners, with Arabs for customers, the stools too high, feet dangling. An old croissant sits wearily on the table. I give bakhshish right away, otherwise the waiter might feel ashamed. If only I knew when I lost my mother tongue ... I can remember sentences now, sentences she said in her mother tongue, except that when I imagine her voice, the sentences themselves sound in my ears like a foreign language I know well.[15]

From the very start, this text is shot through with a continuum of translations and 'tongues from abroad,' so that the translation process does not operate from a fixed point: thanks to the actual physical movements of the tongue without bones, without a 'hard core,' both mother tongue and foreign tongue undergo mutual transformations. Seemingly natural borders between foreign and native languages rupture and become permeable. The forever incomplete movement of adopting something foreign and in turn becoming estranged from what one thinks of as one's own, which characterizes both Özdamar's and Tawada's texts in extraordinary ways, is situated beyond what is a 'mere' intercultural relationship, in which one culture, from its assumed static solidity, would encounter another as alien. At issue is something else: transcultural movements that ceaselessly crisscross diverse cultures and languages, in an unfinishable *translation* or passage between different poles that are also continuously changing, precisely because they are part of an active web of metamorphosing translation processes. This is a literature whose tongue twists and turns.

---

14 See Emine Sevgi Özdamar: *Mutterzunge: Erzählungen*. Cologne: Kiepenheuer & Witsch 1998; and Emine Sevgi Özdamar: *Mother Tongue*. Toronto: Coach House Press 1994.
15 Özdamar: *Mother Tongue*, p. 9–10.

A single twist of the tongue suffices to initiate this process which is by no means just child's play but painful and accompanied by many losses and disarrays of speech. The tongue's eloquence, which may resemble acrobatics at first glance, requires room for a movement that re-creates itself time and again, as is illustrated in Yoko Tawada's *incipit*:

> When I wake up, my tongue is always a little swollen and much too big to move in my oral cavity. It blocks my breathing, I can feel the pressure on my lungs. How long this suffocating? I ask myself, and my tongue promptly shrinks. My tongue then reminds me of a used-up old sponge, stiff and dry, it slowly retreats into the esophagus, taking along my entire head.[16]

The 'swallowing up' of the head, followed by a metamorphosis and embodiment of the 'I' in/as the tongue – 'I was a tongue. That's how I left my house, naked, pink, and unbearably wet'[17] – begins the process of turning the I into language, pushing for the autobiographical 'I' while simultaneously undermining it:

> My entire body consisted of a tongue. So I did not get a job. Then I wrote an autobiography. The life story of a tongue. I present it to an audience... I cannot read the sentences, even though I wrote them. (How can I say 'I' so carelessly? Once the lines are written, they drift away from me and become another language, one that I can no longer understand).[18]

The I's life story has been infused with another language and the language of the Other,[19] which, as the rest of Tawada's story and, in fact, the entire volume illustrates, comprises all the figures and configurations of the 'I.' The self-writing of the I's autobiography takes on a life of its own during its transcultural

---

16 'Wenn ich aufwache, ist meine Zunge immer etwas geschwollen und viel zu groß, um sich in der Mundhöhle bewegen zu können. Sie versperrt mir den Atemweg, ich spüre einen Druck auf die Lungen. Wie lange noch dieses Ersticken? frage ich mich, und schon schrumpft sie. Meine Zunge erinnert mich dann an einen verbrauchten Schwamm, steif und trocken zieht sie sich langsam in die Speiseröhre zurück, dabei nimmt sie meinen ganzen Kopf mit.' Tawada, *Überseezungen*, p. 9. See also Yoko Tawada / Chantal Wright: *Portrait of a tongue: [an experimental translation]*. Ottawa, Ont.: University of Ottawa Press 2013.
17 'Ich war eine Zunge. Ich ging so aus dem Haus hinaus, nackt, rosa und unerträglich feucht.' Tawada, *Überseezungen*, p. 9.
18 'Meine ganze Person bestand aus einer einzigen Zunge. So bekam ich keine Arbeitsstelle. Dann schrieb ich eine Autobiographie. Die Lebensgeschichte einer Zunge. Ich trage sie dem Publikum vor ... Ich kann die Sätze nicht lesen, obwohl ich sie geschrieben habe. (Wie kann ich aber so leichtsinnig 'ich' sagen? Wenn die Zeilen einmal fertig sind, entfernen sie sich von mir und verwandeln sich in eine andere Sprache, die ich nicht mehr verstehen kann).' Yoko Tawada: *Überseezungen*, p. 10.
19 See chapter 5 above.

and transareal transit, which deprives writing of its power over the I in the same way that language cannot subjected to territorial rule and be colonized by a single place.

Where Yoko Tawada shows how the 'I' becomes foreign in an appropriated language, Emine Sevgi Özdamar illustrates the alienation from a mother tongue through a first-person narrator, a 'tongue whore' who always honors her grandmother for already having denounced the monogamy of languages and cultures.[20] In her first novel, *Life is a Caravanserai* (*Das Leben ist eine Karawanserei*, 1992), Özdamar's first-person narrator invents 'lies' based on reading *Robinson Crusoe* until her mother interrupts her laughingly and tells her: "There are seven kinds of whoring in the world.' I was a mouth whore, someone who whores with her tongue. OROSPU. I liked the word orospu.'[21]

As in Yoko Tawada's case, the opening mouth and the movable tongue become locations of the material body where different languages and cultures cross and become flexibly embodied.[22] Here speaking in foreign tongues, emigrated mother tongues, and immigrated tongues from abroad finds an actual place where words that have undergone multiple translations and tongue-crossings can assume material form.

Literature and writing aim at transferring knowledge, that is, knowledge-of-and-for living, in which the autobiographical does not orient itself toward the however constructed 'authenticity' of another culture and language. Instead, it derives credibility from the lie, from the tongue's volubility, which is always in the process of having to reclaim its ability to move in a space (that of the mouth). It follows that, here, literature is not at the service of an intercultural

---

20 See Emine Sevgi Özdamar: *Das Leben ist eine Karawanserei hat zwei Türen aus einer kam ich rein aus der anderen ging ich raus.* Cologne: Kiepenheuer & Witsch 1999, and *Life is a Caravanserai, Has Two Doors, I Came in One, I Went Out the Other*. London: Middlesex University Press 2000. In her first novel, Özdamar writes about the following about the narration's relationship with truth and lie: 'My mother said, "That's just a story, it didn't really happen." Grandmother said, "Why do you think it's just a story? It's true, my mother told it to me." Mother said, "Your mother was probably a tongue whore, just like you, Grandmother." Grandmother said, "The stars can speak to the stars, people cannot talk to other people."' Özdamar: *Life is a Caravanserai*, p. 199.
21 Özdamar: *Life is a Caravanserai*, p. 87.
22 Elizabeth Boa refers to the mouth and the tongue as the 'places of hybrid impurity in the mixing of languages' (see Elizabeth Boa: 'Sprachenverkehr: Hybrides Schreiben in Werken von Özdamar, Özakin und Demirkan.' In: Mary Howard (ed.): *Interkulturelle Konfigurationen: Zur deutschsprachigen Erzählliteratur von Autoren nichtdeutscher Herkunft*. Munich: iudicium, 1997), p. 115–138. See also Hansjörg Bay: 'Der verrückte Blick: Schreibweisen der Migration in Özdamars Karawanserei-Roman.' In: *Sprache und Literatur* 30.83 (1999), p. 44-45.

knowledge transfer in which 'one's own' and the 'foreign' encounter one another but remain separate. At stake for both Tawada and Özdamar is a transmission of knowledge in which the 'I' is always already a cultural other whose position cannot be fixed. In its perpetual linguistic crossings, the tongue is too fast for that: it is a mobile figure that has replaced the thoughtless and stubbornly monological 'I'.

In this way, the 'I' comes to stand for a multitude of words among words and languages among languages, for which the first-person singular is a projection screen and a space in which one can move. In Özdamar's *Mother Tongue*, Turkish and underneath it the (thanks to Atatürk's language politics) 'suppressed' Arabic can be heard again in manifold nuances.[23] Similarly, underneath the German 'I' in Yoko Tawada's *Überseezungen*, a number of possible Japanese meanings for 'I' come into view as well. The story 'An empty bottle' (Eine leere Flasche), for example, tells of the first-person female narrator's difficulties with this plethora of meanings, including notably her inability to place the I, only to emphasize in a second step that all those difficulties 'disappeared' after the move to Germany.

> An 'I' does not have to have a specific gender, age, status, history, attitude, personality. People can simply call themselves 'I.' This word consists only of what I say, or, more specifically, of the fact that I am speaking at all. The word points only to the speaker, without adding any further information about him. 'I' became my favorite word. I wanted to feel as light and empty as this word ... In Japanese there is also the word 'bin' [the first-person singular of the German verb *sein*, to be]; it sounds exactly the same and means 'a bottle.' When I start telling a story with the two words 'ich bin' [I am], a room opens up; the I is the movement of positioning the paint brush, and the bottle is empty.[24]

The paradox of the space that opens up through the I's journey to Europe rests on the idea that an 'emptying out' creates precisely the precondition for writing into the empty vessel of the word 'I' an absence, and simultaneously the possi-

---

23 See Kader Konuk: 'Das Leben ist eine Karawanserei: Heimat bei Emine Sevgi Özdamar.' In: Gisela Ecker (ed.): *Kein Land in Sicht. Heimat – weiblich?* Munich: Fink 1997, p. 146–147.
24 'Ein Ich muss kein bestimmtes Geschlecht haben, kein Alter, keinen Status, keine Geschichte, keine Haltung, keinen Charakter. Jeder kann sich einfach "ich" nennen. Dieses Wort besteht nur aus dem, was ich spreche, oder genauer gesagt aus der Tatsache, dass ich überhaupt spreche. Das Wort zeigt nur auf den Sprecher, ohne eine weitere Information über ihn hinzuzufügen. "Ich" wurde zu meinem Lieblingswort. So leicht und leer wie dieses Wort wollte ich mich fühlen ... Im Japanischen gibt es auch das Wort "bin" das klingt genau gleich und bedeutet "eine Flasche". Wenn ich mit den beiden Wörtern "ich bin" eine Geschichte zu erzählen beginne, öffnet sich ein Raum, das Ich ist ein Pinselansatz und die Flasche ist leer.' Tawada: *Überseezungen*, p. 56–57.

bility for different markings and meanings. This is much more than the mere conceptualization of an 'open,' fluctuating subject position. In the process of *one's own writing-other(wise)* the amalgamation of different languages intensifies the openness of the figure of the 'I,' created not interlingually but *translingually*, and, at the same time, draws attention to itself as a multiplicity. Writing one's own life otherwise and/or as other to oneself opens up a new, transcultural space for writing that moves between worlds and does not have a fixed abode.

'Words with bodies': taking-writing-elsewhere

In November 2004, when asked whether her flight from the military dictatorship in Turkey to Germany might also be interpreted as a flight into the German language, Emine Sevgi Özdamar replied with an unequivocal 'Yes':

> They always say that you lose your mother tongue abroad. I believe that one can also lose one's language at home. In bad times the language has dreadful experiences. During the period of the military coup, I felt that the Turkish words became sick. I felt that I had become very, very tired in my own language.[25]

Both in this passage, from an interview conducted on occasion of the being awarded the Kleist-Prize, and in her novels,[26] the Turkish-born writer who, like Tawada, has won numerous prizes, not only elucidates painful experiences with her own mother tongue, but also demonstrates that, in her writing, that mother tongue cannot be separated from her 'fatherland.' Özdamar's literary language creates a system of simultaneously *translingual* and *transcultural* communica-

---

25 'Man erzählt immer, daß man in der Fremde die Muttersprache verliert. Ich denke, man kann auch die Sprache im eigenen Land verlieren. In schlimmen Zeiten macht die Sprache eine schreckliche Erfahrung. Ich hatte das Gefühl, daß die türkischen Wörter während der Militärputschzeit krank wurden. Ich hatte das Gefühl, daß ich in meiner Sprache sehr, sehr müde geworden war.' Emine Sevgi Özdamar: 'Wir wohnen in einer weiten Hölle (interview with Nils Minkmar).' In: *Frankfurter Allgemeine Sonntagszeitung* (December 21, 2004), p. 23.
26 In *Seltsame Sterne starren zur Erde* (1976/77), for example, the first-person narrator, also unhappy with her Turkish mother tongue, wonders: 'How long does it take a word to become well again? They say that in foreign countries one loses one's mother tongue. Isn't it possible that one can lose one's mother tongue in one's own country?' [Wie *lange braucht* ein Wort, um wieder gesund zu werden? Man sagt, in fremden Ländern verliert man die Muttersprache. Kann man nicht auch in seinem eigenen Land die Muttersprache verlieren?] Emine Sevgi Özdamar: *Seltsame Sterne starren zur Erde: Wedding – Pankow 1976/77*. Cologne: Kiepenheuer & Witsch 2003, p. 23.

ting tubes. Her writing is not primarily concerned with the multicultural and multilingual side-by-sideness of different cultures and languages, nor with an intercultural and interlingual togetherness in which cultural and linguistic 'identities' enter into forms of communication that do produce any fundamental transformation of the 'oneself' (one's own). In the case of Özdamar (and all her female narrators as well), the trauma of a military putsch that triggered illness and troubled all aspects of life and communication resulted in the perpetual *queering* of different languages and cultures. What characterizes such translingual translation and writing processes is that they cannot be completed. Their most distinct feature is a movement that never reaches the point of immobility.

The double doors in the title of Özdamar's first novel – *Life is a Caravanserai has two doors, I came in one, I went out the other* – emphasize clearly that the author, born in Malatya in 1946, always constructs spaces as transitional, including temporal spaces such as life spans. They are transit rooms with more than one exit and more than one system of reference and communication. Even German, the language in which this novel is written, has acquired traces of the migration to Germany on which its protagonist embarks at the end of the book. One should also not forget that the entire novel is marked by incessant changes of place and by migrations, not to mention the constant diatopic and diastratic code-switching in Turkey itself. Vehicles for such place changes range from the soldiers' train on which the mother, pregnant with the female first-person narrator, travels deep into Anatolia, to 'train of whores' (Hurenzug) on which the now eighteen-year old travels to West-Berlin.[27] Intralingual[28] translation processes accompany the family's changes of place within Turkey, during which dialectical peculiarities of the Turkish languages are discussed time and again in the context of translocal and transregional migration. The narrator takes special notice of the foreign elements she finds in her 'own' mother tongue.

The narrator's transnational movements are already inscribed in the translocal and transregional migration within Turkey itself, in the same way that the intralingual translation processes always already point to later translingual developments. The time of narration often subtly blends in with the time narrated, as a result of which a choreography can unfold between the two doors in the novel's title. Two doors that are not so much the doors of a fixed and static room

---

27 Özdamar: *Das Leben ist eine Karawanserei*, p. 379; *Life is a Caravanserai*, p. 296.
28 For intralingual translation, see Roman Jakobson: 'On Linguistic Aspects of Translation'. In: Stephen Rudy (ed.): *Roman Jacobson: Selected Writings*, vol. II: *Word and Language*. The Hague: Mouton 1971, p. 260.

but doors on a train, of a life permanently on the move. The choreography may be understood as an autobiography without an autobiographical compact[29] and thus as a writing of one's own life that always connects the autobiographical features with the tongue whore's lies.

To equate the intratextual 'I' with the author outside the text would be as much of misunderstanding of this poetic text as it would be to overlook the host of associations and connections that exist between the two women and their life-journeys. The inscription of the 'I' outside the text into the 'empty vessel' of the 'I' in the text creates a friction[30] between diction and fiction, between nation and imagination. The movements through which prenatal and job-related migrations writes themselves into one another makes a life-in-motion accessible. *Life is a Caravanserei* is the product of a perpetual intertwining of different times and spaces, a process on which I elaborate below.

When she accepted the Adelbert von Chamisso Prize in 1999, Emine Sevgi Özdamar recounted, again, how she had come to the German language and how German had come to her. She explained that her delightful experiences with German words had enabled her to thaw out the 'Turkish words' she had 'put on ice.'[31] A travel metaphor borrowed from the Japanese helped her translate the liquefaction of the frozen words and the attempt not to arrest the movement she had initiated: 'A Japanese proverb says: Only traveling is beautiful – not arriving. Maybe it is the traveling that one loves about the foreign language. One makes many mistakes on the road, but one struggles with the language; one turns the words to the left and to the right, one works with the language, one discovers it.'[32] Özdamar shares the claim that she works with language and thus changes the initially foreign language itself through her traveling in it with the erstwhile translator Yoko Tawada, who perpetually ponders questions of translation in theory and in practice. But there are differences between them when it comes to the childhood of German words. Tawada's narrator protests against

---

29 With regard to this term, see the classical study by Philippe Lejeune: *Je est un autre: L'autobiographie de la littérature aux médias*. Paris: Seuil 1980.
30 For more on the term 'friction,' which is used repeatedly in this volume, see Ottmar Ette: *Roland Barthes: Eine intellektuelle Biographie*. Frankfurt am Main: Suhrkamp 1998.
31 '[M]eine türkischen Wörter, die ich ins Eis gelegt hatte.' Emine Sevgi Özdamar: 'Meine deutschen Wörter haben keine Kindheit: Eine Dankrede.' In: Emine Sevgi Özdamar: *Der Hof im Spiegel*. Cologne: Kiepenheuer und Witsch 2001, p. 130.
32 'Ein japanisches Sprichwort sagt: Nur die Reise ist schön – nicht das Ankommen. Vielleicht liebt man an einer fremden Sprache genau diese Reise. Man macht auf dieser Reise viele Fehler, aber man kämpft mit der Sprache, man dreht Wörter nach links und nach rechts, man arbeitet mit ihr, man entdeckt sie.' Özdamar: *Der Hof im Spiegel*, p. 131.

the idea that childhood is absent from a foreign language, emphasizing that she had 'nowhere found so much childhood as in the German language.'[33] Özdamar, by contrast, stressed the fact that 'my German words do not have a childhood, but my experience with German words is quite physical. For me, German words have bodies. I encountered them in the delightful German theater.'[34] For Özdamar, the staged body-words do not contain a childhood;[35] but thanks to their intensity and theatricality they open up the possibility for using them like costumes that may be left behind after the performance 'in the coatroom,' where one can find them again on the occasion of another enactment.[36] Are we to conclude, then, that literary language is nothing other than dressed-up 'theatrical magic'?

Özdamar's remarks do not at all mean that, for the I, the words do not have a history, that they are ready to wear off the rack and are easily exchangeable, if need be. Time and again, we find in Özdamar's prose interesting hints about the history of the German language, hints that, for a native German speaker, would not easily spring to mind. The narrator of the prose text 'Fahrrad auf dem Eis' (Bicycle on Ice), for example, notes that German, unlike other European languages that for centuries had served as colonial languages, made it difficult for foreigners to change it: 'in Germany the German language that foreigners speak has to make a long journey; it has to bend, be broken, and then stand up straight again.'[37]

This is exactly where we find the task of a German-language literature that is also, *at the same time*, a Literature without a fixed Abode. The purpose of writing-other(wise), a literary process based on endless translations and crossings, is to create new, unfamiliar ways into language, to discover language as a space of movement and performance in which very different staging and lighting are possible: to transform the 'tongue dance' (in Tawada's coinage) into a choreog-

---

33 'Aber ich fand nirgendwo so viel Kindheit wie in der deutschen Sprache.' Tawada: *Überseezungen*, p. 110.
34 'Meine deutschen Wörter haben keine Kindheit, aber meine Erfahrung mit deutschen Wörtern ist ganz körperlich. Die deutschen Wörter haben Körper für mich. Ich bin ihnen im wunderbaren deutschen Theater begegnet.' Özdamar: *Der Hof im Spiegel*, p. 131.
35 Azade Seyhan points to an earlier mention of this motif. See Azade Seyhan: 'Lost in Translation: Re-Membering the Mother Tongue in Emine Sevgi Özdamar's Das Leben ist eine Karawanserei.' In: *German Quarterly* 69 (1996), p. 421.
36 Özdamar: *Der Hof im Spiegel*, p. 132.
37 'Und in Deutschland musste die deutsche Sprache, die von Ausländern gesprochen wird einen langen Weg machen, sich biegen, gebrochen werden und wieder gradestehen.' Özdamar: *Der Hof im Spiegel*, p. 95.

raphy of body-words that, as costumes, are both present and latent in the performance, at once past, present, and future spectacle.[38] Authors such as Özdamar and Tawada take the German language elsewhere in a variety of ways. They do not resort to the language of former colonial masters (with which they would have been amply familiar since childhood), but learn these languages as part of a foreign country, an alien culture, ultimately to infuse them with very different cultural perspectives and take them in very different directions. But how and with the help of what procedures can such taking of a language elsewhere be achieved?

To begin with, this taking of a language elsewhere means to write oneself into an initially foreign language and, above all, to develop an understanding of its literary and literary-historical traditions. Emine Sevgi Özdamar's texts incorporate into their narratives citations, cross-references, reading experiences, and theater rehearsals in order to construct an intraliterary space that functions in a given text as if it were at once immanent library and source. Quotations from Nazim Hikmet or Orhan Veli, for instance, accompany the novel *Life is a Caravanserai* from the very start,[39] carefully weaving elements of Turkish history into descriptions of the protagonist's childhood and adolescence in the 1940s, 1950s, and 1960s, through which ingenuously to stage an 'opening' toward Western literary traditions. Mustafa Kemal Atatürk's proclaimed 'orientation towards the West' promoted the translation of 'all the classics' of Western literature into Turkish, which enables the young protagonist to play a minor role in Molière's *The Imaginary Invalid* (*Le malade imaginaire*) in Bursa.[40] With this role, literature begins to play a part in her life.

Already on the holy bridge of Bursa, the young girl solemnly vows one day to become an actress. In the following novel, *The Bridge of the Golden Horn*, set in the 1960s and early 1970s, the protagonist fulfills this promise to herself by attending the drama school in Istanbul and collaborating on staging the works of German playwrights, among others. Even in 'Strange stars stare at the Earth' (*Seltsame Sterne starren zur Erde*), which focuses on the years 1976 and 1977 in West and East Berlin, the young woman, who by then interns and assists Benno

---

[38] See Tawada: *Überseezungen*, p. 9.
[39] About the presence of Turkish literature, see Margrit Fröhlich: 'Reinventions of Turkey: Emine Sevgi Özdamar's *Life is a Caravanserai*.' In: Karen Jankowsky / Carla Love (eds.): *Other Germanies: Questioning Identity in Women's Literature and Art*. New York: State University of New York 1997, p. 58.
[40] See Özdamar: *Life is a Caravanserai*, p. 208. With respect to the choreography of cultures that is connected to this, see Ette: *ÜberLebenswissen*, p. 244–245.

Besson at the theater 'Volksbühne,' works once again on Molière who 'written, performed, unworried, omitted nothing.'[41] She reads Bulgakow's *The Life of Monsieur Molière* (1970) and remembers her beginnings on the Bursa stage.[42] Molière is here the personification of theater life as such.

It is no coincidence that at the center of the extensive German library in Özdamar's writings, littered as they are with allusions and references to, as well as quotations from, Heinrich Heine, Adalbert von Chamisso, Johann Wolfgang von Goethe, Else Lasker-Schüler, Kurt Weill, Peter Weiss, Heiner Müller and many others, resides a man of the theater: the poet Berthold Brecht. His name and life work leave their initial imprint on the first-person narrator when, during her time as a 'guest worker' in the West-Berlin factory Telefunkenwerk, she learns from the communist head of her Turkish women's residence hall that, in the daytime, he usually goes to the theater 'Berliner Ensemble' in East-Berlin to see Berthold Brecht's plays and to talk with Helene Weigel.[43] With the protagonist's own visit to the 'Berliner Ensemble,' Berthold Brecht's[44] theater theory and performance practice become just as important an element in her life's journey as the future commute between West and East Berlin, which had already been introduced in the stories in *Mother tongue* and then at the center of the novel *Seltsame Sterne starren zur Erde*, the last novel in the Istanbul-Berlin trilogy.[45]

That the poem by Else Lasker-Schüler,[46] introduced at the beginning of the novel and repeated as a leitmotiv throughout the trilogy, would supply the title

---

41 'Er hat geschrieben, gespielt, keine Angst bekommen, nichts ausgelassen.' Özdamar: *Seltsame Sterne*, p. 130.
42 See Özdamar, *Seltsame Sterne*, p. 129–130. While Molière is connected with the bridge in Bursa, the work at the drama school in Istanbul and also at the East-Berlin 'Volksbühne' is linked with the bridge of the Golden Horn and the bridge Spreebrücke, respectively. Both may be seen as places of transit, crossing, and transfer during the decisive phases in the protagonist's life and self-dramatization. When, on November 21, 1975, the day of the Spanish dictator Franco's death, she leaves Istanbul for Germany by train, she barely sees that the old bridge of the Golden Horn is being dismantled. See Emine Sevgi Özdamar: *The Bridge of the Golden Horn*. London: Serpent's Tail 2007, p. 256; Emine Sevgi Özdamar: *Die Brücke vom Goldenen Horn*. Cologne: Kiepenheuer & Witsch 1998, p. 330.
43 See Özdamar: *The Bridge of the Golden Horn*, p. 22.
44 The importance of Brecht's theater conception for Özdamar's writing has been pointed out by Bay: 'Der verrückte Blick,' p. 41.
45 The entire trilogy was published under the title *Sonne auf halbem Weg* in 2006. See Emine Sevgi Özdamar: *Sonne auf auf halbem Weg: Die Istanbul-Berlin Trilogie*. Cologne: Kiepenheuer & Witsch 2006.
46 The poem is 'Stars of Fate' / 'Sterne des Fatums' from the volume *Styx*, published in Berlin in 1902: 'Your eyes befor my life / Like nights, that long for the day, / And the humid dream lies

of the Berlin novel from 2003 may well be understood as a programmatic decision on the author's part. Where Berthold Brecht stands for the theatricality in Özdamar's writing – for her attentiveness to the materiality and substantiality of the stage props; the epic distance of the representational process; the intertwining of aesthetics with political action' and, last but not least, the alienating effects that emphasize the frictionality of Özdamar's writing time and again and undermine any potential identification – Else Lasker-Schüler, migrant, Jew, and woman, stands for that intense sense of being outside oneself that the chosen 'planetary' title of the novel signals: strange stars stare down upon the Earth. It is one of her temporary lovers who introduces the protagonist to the poetic qualities of Lasker-Schüler's language and to an insatiable longing for love in her lyrics.[47] In the explicit reference to Lasker-Schüler's poetry, the insight into the contribution that migratory writing makes to German-language literature overlaps with Özdamar's sensitivity to being at once inside and outside, a position that the writing of the great German and Jewish writer embodies as well.

An unquenchable longing for love also drives the young Turkish migrant, whose creator carries love (Turkish: Sevgi) in her name. Her great love, the Catalán Jordi, once asked her in the French Versailles in English what 'mon amour' meant in Turkish (resorting to the German word for Turkish). And the young woman, doubled in the mirror's reflection, told the mirror her name. Love in particular is not only a phenomenon of reflection, and the topical self-awareness that comes with it, but also a chain of translingual translations that are reflected back onto the I: '"What is *mon amour* in Türkisch?" She said to the mirror: "*Sevgilim.*"'[48]

It is impossible here to detail all the complex functions that the myriad intertextual references especially, but not exclusively, to German-language litera-

---

on top of them / Unfathomed. // Strange stars stare to the earth, / Ironcolored with trails of desire, / With burning arms, that are looking for love / And reach for the cool of the air. / Star in which the fate flows.' [Deine Augen harren vor meinem Leben / Wie Nächte, die sich nach Tagen sehnen, / Und der schwüle Trau liegt auf ihnen / Unbegründet. // Seltsame Sterne starren zur Erde, / Eisenfarb'ne mit Sehnsuchtsschweigen. / Mit brennenden Armen, die Liebe suchen / Und in die Kühle der Lüfte greifen. // Sterne in denen das Schicksal mündet]. Else Lasker-Schüler: *Sämtliche Gedichte*. Edited by Friedhelm Kemp. Munich: Kösel-Verlag 1966, p. 30. English translation quoted from Susanne Rinner: *The German Student Movement and the Literary Imagination*. New York: Berghahn Books 2013, p. 143.
47 See Özdamar: *Seltsame Sterne*, p. 58.
48 Özdamar: *Die Brücke vom Goldenen Horn*, p. 140. 'Der halbe Mann sagte im Spiegel: "Mon amour." Dann sagte er: "What is mon amour in Türkisch?" Sie sagte zum Spiegel: "Sevgilim."' Özdamar: *The Bridge of the Golden Horn*, p. 103.

ture serve in Özdamar's writing. But it is well to remember the author's intent, manifest in all her writings, to take German-language literature elsewhere so as to continue it and, as it were, take it further, particularly when it comes to experiences of exile, diaspora, and distant nearness in the writings of Heinrich Heine, Franz Kafka, Berthold Brecht, Else Lasker-Schüler, and Peter Weiss. German-language literature has become a projection screen of desire, in which the loving I can translingually reflect itself as it passes through different linguistic worlds. As the serene narrator of the next novel in the trilogy is well aware, love is most closely related to writing, to literary work. Who can know 'how much emotional training' Brecht had undergone with all his lovers: 'Maybe it was all material for his plays and books.'[49] German-language literature does indeed offer many mirrors.

With the desire to take German-language literature elsewhere also connects the resolve to shape such writing as linguistic and cultural displacement and, moreover, as a vectorization of *any and all* spatial references. Özdamar's spatial constructs always rely on a heterotopia of voices that speak from different places, whose steady and at the same time unstable movements do not produce any stationary loci between the worlds.

Writing oneself into German-language literature is thus a process of taking that literature elsewhere that can be observed on a variety of different levels. The translation's perpetual transfers in transnational and transcultural spaces, with their numerous inroads into supposedly stable grammatical, lexical, morphological, semantic, or syntactic structures, result in a sensitization not simply to words among words, but also, as I will show in the following section, to places among places. As a continual bouncing from one place to another, displacement and heterotopias create a Literature without a fixed Abode which, as a concept that is positioned crossways, does not entirely fit categories such as 'national literature,' 'migration literature,' or 'world literature.' A Literature without a fixed Abode does of course contribute to a national literature; as the example of Cuban literature in chapter 4 illustrates, it can even shape a national literature in fundamental ways. Precisely because it *both* highlights *and* crosses borders between nation-states and national literatures, a Literature without a fixed Abode sets in motion the often static concept of migration literature, whose sole significance no longer lies in the fact of migration. A Literature without a fixed Abode also problematizes homogenizing concepts of world literature

---

49 'Brecht hatte auch viele Geliebte, aber die Arbeit hat er nie aufgegeben. Wer weiß, wieviel Gefühlstraining er gemacht hat. Vielleicht war alles Material für seine Stücke und Bücher.' Özdamar: *Seltsame Sterne*, p. 132.

by always rendering visible new borderlines that can, admittedly, be traversed in many ways. In writing that continues a given (national) literature by taking it *elsewhere*, quite literally to other places, places and space do not disappear but multiply and become more dynamic – they shift. How, then, does this process of dislodgment be represented in literature, and how does it connect with the problematics of writing-other(wise)?

'Through these same streets': Writing-in-and-out-of-languages

During the day I went to the drama school on the European side, then to the Cinemathèque, then to the 'Captain' restaurant, and then I came back to the Asian side of Istanbul to my parents' house as if to a hotel. I slept in Asia and when the bird Memish began to sing in the morning sailed to Europe again.[50]

These few lines, which close the first chapter of Emine Sevgi Özdamar's *The Bridge of the Golden Horn*, encapsulate the protagonist's choreography after her return from Berlin to Istanbul where, in the second half of the 1960s she had started a three-year program to become an actress. For this experienced traveler, the Istanbul apartment in which her parents finally settled at the end of their many migrations in search of work, is a hotel, a transitional space that cannot be a fixed abode. In this respect, she is unlike her family. While the Asian part of Istanbul serves her as a sort of 'safe haven' (as would be the case at the time of political prosecution during the military dictatorship), her parents set the house rules for the 'hotel,' even if their daughter, during her brief radically-left activist period, sells off all of her parents' furniture without checking with them first.

A nearly twenty-minute boat ride between Istanbul's Asian and European parts opens and closes a daily routine that takes place in the European part of the metropolis on both sides of the bridge of the Golden Horn.[51] What shapes

---

50 Özdamar: *The Bridge of the Golden Horn*, p. 169. 'Tagsüber ging ich zur europäischen Seite zur Schauspielschule, dann zur Cinemathek, dann zum Restaurant 'Kapitän', und dann kam ich zurück zur asiatischen Seite von Istanbul zu meinem Elternhaus wie in ein Hotel. Ich schlief in Asien und fuhr, wenn der Vogel Memisch am Morgen zu singen anfing, wieder nach Europa.' Özdamar: *Die Brücke vom Goldenen Horn*, p. 221.
51 For the history of the two bridges between both European parts of Istanbul and their positioning in a personal city map, see Emine Sevgi Özdamar: 'Mein Istanbul'. In: *Der Hof im Spiegel*, p. 67–76. First published in: *Die Weltwoche* (August 6, 1998). In this text, the 'theatricality' of this bridge-construction becomes apparent in the staging of difference: 'The bridge was like a stage: Jews, Turks, Greeks, Arabs, Albanians, Armenians, Europeans, Persians, Circassians,

this quotidian routine is, on the one hand, the professional training of a prospective actress for whom Brecht's theater has become an important focal point and her personal development on the other. She gradually turns into a self-confident intellectual within male-dominated leftist circles where she also receives an intense sentimental education. The second chapter in part two of the novel continues these spatial considerations: 'At that time, in 1967, there was no bridge yet between Asia and Europe. The sea separated the two sides, and when I had water between my parents and myself, I felt free.... The Asian and the European side in Istanbul were two different countries.'[52] The constant shuttling between these two 'countries' becomes a habitual exercise that enables the first-person narrator to write her professional, intellectual, and sexual Bildungsroman[53] far away from parental control, whenever necessary. It would, after all, be easy enough to claim that one had missed the last boat to Asia. At a first glance, the separateness of Asia and Europe seems fundamental and no doubt offers the protagonist some protection. But it is also, at the same time, an everyday experience she shares with thousands of commuters on the boats. The steamboats connect Istanbul's two sides in the life of the only twenty-year-old woman like a shuttle, and they weave the texts as a fabric of continuous trans-lational passages that do not settle down in the 'in-between.' Instead, the space between the continents and the city's neighborhoods becomes a space in which one can move, a space filled with a ceaseless spatiotemporal back and forth that renders visible how the Writing-between-Worlds works and translates it into a cityscape of theory.

It is astonishing how precisely and at the same time subtly Özdamar, a few years later, transfers the model of the city of Istanbul she introduces in *The Bridge of the Golden Horn* to mid-1970s Berlin. In *Seltsame Sterne*, the partitio-

---

women, men, horses, donkeys, cows, chicken, camels all crossed the bridge' (Die Brücke wurde wie eine Bühne: Juden, Türken, Griechen, Araber, Albaner, Armenier, Europäer, Perser, Tscherkessen, Frauen, Männer, Pferde, Esel, Kühe, Hühner, Kamele, alle liefen über diese Brücke). Özdamar: *Der Hof im Spiegel*, p. 71.

52 Özdamar: *The Bridge of the Golden Horn*, p. 171. 'Zwischen Asien und Europa gab es damals, 1967, noch keine Brücke. Das Meer trennte die beiden Seiten, und wenn ich das Wasser zwischen meinen Eltern und mir hatte, fühlte ich mich frei ... Die asiatische und die europäische Seite in Istanbul waren zwei verschiedene Länder.' Özdamar: *Die Brücke vom Goldenen Horn*, p. 222.

53 Irmgard Ackermann calls *Die Brücke vom Goldenen Horn* an 'Entwicklungsroman', a 'coming-of-age novel'. See Irmgard Ackermann: 'Emine Sevgi Özdamar.' In: *Kritisches Lexikon zur deutschsprachigen Gegenwartsliteratur. 62th supplement*. Munich: Edition text + kritik 1999, p. 5.

ned city that continues to break apart into different sectors is also split up into two parts – the Eastern Bloc and the Western Bloc – that, just like Asia and Europe, represent at first glance two irreconcilably different 'countries' that face each other across the armed fortifications of hostile ideologies. The Berlin wall now replaces the straits of the Bosporus whose boats have become the commuter trains that also take twenty minutes to carry the young Turkish woman, with her tourist visa but without a fixed abode, from the graffiti-covered western side of the wall across to the other side. Until she receives a three-month visa from officials in the capital of the German Democratic Republic (GDR), the actress who, after her release from pretrial detention in Turkey can no longer practice her profession in her home country, lives rent free in a West-Berlin flat-sharing community that also comes with 'family ties' – a situation clearly reminiscent of her parents' 'hotel' in Istanbul. Just as in Istanbul, the protagonist finds herself in a structure she cannot change – even though no one controls her and she is quickly accepted into the emphatically anti-bourgeois group with whom she shares the apartment to the point of joining a lusty, and lustful, splash in the bathtub.

Despite all her important experiences in this community in the West-Berlin neighborhood of Wedding, which she portrays affectionately and wittily, albeit not without a touch of sarcasm, she finds her actual fulfillment in East Berlin where she can dive into 'her' Brechtian theater world and where, after having obtained her East-Berlin visa, she moves in with a young woman into a new setting that she describes with as much love for detail. The 'tongue whore's' Robinson Crusoe has returned to his divided island of Berlin and transforms the city into a stage with a set that is at once German-German and East-West. This island is also a landscape of theory that makes palpable Emine Sevgi Özdamar's poetics.

Once again, the two parts of the city that belong to different 'countries' and 'blocs' are clearly set apart at first sight. Yet, unlike in Istanbul, communications – between East and West just as previously between Asia and Europe – come about not only through telephone calls and occasional eye contact but are also intensified and knit together more closely through the daily commuter train rides. Separated from her husband after a marriage in Istanbul, the protagonist shuttles between different apartments and occasional lovers who appear and disappear, all the while remaining without a fixed abode. Like in the leitmotiv in Else Lasker-Schüler's poem that provides the novel's title, she is '*searching for love with burning arms.*'⁵⁴ For this young woman, Berlin is, in many ways, the city of desire.

Within the Berlin city limits, one encounters an almost contact-less *multicultural* side-by-sidedness along with a broad range of *intercultural* relations, that is, reciprocal contacts among linguistic, cultural, or also socio-political groups. During her first year with Telefunken in West Berlin, the young Turkish woman does not make it far beyond learning newspaper headlines by heart, a multilingual side-by-sideness of languages that allows for so little contact that it might be called 'speechless.' Eventually, a language course near Lake Constance, as a result of which she can at least utter a clear 'excuse me, can I say something,'⁵⁵ allows her in her second period of life in Berlin to take a job as an interpreter for Siemens in which she lingually communicates between Germans and Turks.⁵⁶ Translations – private and professional, oral and written – play an important role in her later life, for instance, when she translates the notes of Brecht student Benno Besson for her jailed actor friends in Turkey, so that they can stage the venerated master's work.

Superimposed upon such a practice of interlingual and intercultural translation (that is, translation between two languages and cultures neither of which relinquish their respective 'standing ground') are *transcultural* experiences that may be understood as a prehistory of one's own writing, a writing already shaped by transcultural and translingual processes. The migrant's apologetic question in the intercultural conversation gradually yields to the conviction, based on her transcultural experiences, that she no longer has to bite her tongue but really has her say in German. The former 'messenger' (Botin)⁵⁷ between groups that constitute two separate linguistic (and also social, cultural, and political) communities increasingly comes into her own through a language that flows from perpetual *crossings*, or hybridizations. In this way, a room of one's own in which to think, speak, and write opens up beyond interlingual translation.

---

54 See Özdamar: *Seltsame Sterne*, p. 9. In this poem by Else Lasker-Schüler, the longing for love and the search for one's self are once again inseparable.
55 Özdamar: *The Bridge of the Golden Horn*, p. 79. 'Entschuldigung, kann ich was sagen.' Özdamar: *Die Brücke vom Goldenen Horn*, p. 108.
56 See Özdamar: *The Bridge of the Golden Horn*, p. 81–82.
57 See Özdamar: *The Bridge of the Golden Horn*, p. 85, and *Die Brücke vom Goldenen Horn*, p. 117. The metaphor of the female 'messenger' for the complex procedures of translation that set space, time, and culture in motion also appears in Yoko Tawada's story 'Die Botin' in Tawada: *Überseezungen*, p. 44–50.

If one examines the structures of space and movement in Emine Sevgi Özdamar's writings more closely, one finds that the same thing that occurs at the level of the word happens at the level of place: other places appear beneath and behind places on the textual surface, just as other words become visible and audible. Istanbul, for example, forever appears in Berlin, not exactly as a 'Little Istanbul,' but because the movements in Berlin recall and repeat earlier movements in the other city. Important here is that, in Özdamar's writing, all processes of comprehension and development acquire not only spatial dimensions but *vectoral* directionality as well. Each movement in her texts is already an accumulation of, and storehouse for, prior movements, much as in Yoko Tawada's 'A story in/of layers' (Eine Scheibengeschichte), the spine 'stores all the postures that one has assumed throughout one's life.'[58] That is, a specific movement in the present still contains traces of the directions of past movements, so that vectoral patterns can be understood as movements that consist of many dynamic forces from the past. Today's movements comprise yesterday's and also anticipate tomorrow's.

In this sense, the poetic prophesy of the husband whom the narrator leaves behind in a forest house on the Asian side of Istanbul, comes to pass. He sends the following lines along with his wife, who appears to be leaving Istanbul behind:

> You will not discover new countries, nor other seas.
> The city will follow you. Through these same streets you will
> Stroll, age in these same neighborhoods.[59]

It is hardly surprising, then, that the house in the forest, which is visible from Istanbul's European side, has its counterpart in Berlin. Shortly after the protagonist dreams about the Istanbul house, in which she spent blissful months with her husband, a colleague from the East Berlin camera crew and his wife invite her to their 'remote forest cabin.' There, she tries desperately to calm herself

---

[58] 'Mag sein, dass CDs in einer anderen Sprache nichts mit den Bandscheiben zu tun haben, aber wenn wir Englisch sprechen, haben wir Disketten in der Wirbelsäule. Darin sind alle Körperhaltungen gespeichert, die man im Leben eingenommen hat.' Tawada: *Überseezungen*, p. 116.

[59] 'Du wirst keine neuen Länder entdecken, keine anderen Meere. Die Stadt wird dir folgen. Du wirst durch dieselben Straßen streifen, in denselben Vierteln alt werden.' Özdamar: *Seltsame Sterne*, p. 56. As Özdamar herself notes, these lines are an excerpt from a poem by Constantine Cavafy. See also Transit above.

with the thought that she 'is in a different forest' now.[60] In cinematic terms, this is one of countless crossfadings through which Istanbul appears in Berlin on all levels and in all senses. Even when a water pipe bursts in the East-Berlin street Unter den Linden, the protagonist is reminded of a linden tree next to the Istanbul forest house, a memory that sets in motion an associative chain reaction through which this first-person narrator, as is her wont, links literature – a Turkish poet-friend – with love: 'Tonight a pipe purportedly burst in the street Unter den Linden. The street was flooded. There were fire trucks and police cars everywhere below the linden trees. There was also a linden tree next to the forest house in Istanbul. A poet-friend often sat under it, his hair covered with blossoms. In Turkey they say that the fragrance of linden tree blossoms drives young girls mad.'[61] Even though the protagonist has difficulty thinking about both parts of Berlin as one, the border between West and East Berlin soon appears to her as 'a great sea' (ein grosses Meer) just as in Istanbul, and just as in Istanbul, it invites her to cross over.[62] Not only the 'morning mood' but also the 'smell' in the East Berlin streets instantly brings to her mind the Turkish metropolis: 'a smell of coal and exhaust fumes, just as in Istanbul.'[63] Even when watching a US film with Rod Taylor, she is reminded that this was one of her 'childhood films from Istanbul;'[64] the images, noises, and smells from the city on the Bosporus overcome her instantly and unwittingly. Almost any object or sensation can trigger a cross-fading between Berlin and Istanbul and create a 'bridge Unter den Linden' in East Berlin. This is not just a function of the superposition of *The Brige of the Golden Horn* and *Seltsame Sterne starren zur Erde*. The one city is always present underneath the other; it follows the migrant with its specific intertwining of space with movement, and of love with literature.

---

60 '"Du bist jetzt in einem anderen Wald," dachte ich, "du wirst nie zu dem alten zurückkehren."' Özdamar: *Seltsame Sterne*, p. 113; see also p. 28.
61 'Heute abend soll Unter den Linden ein Rohr geplatzt sein. Die Straße war überschwemmt. Überall standen Feuerwehrautos und Polizeiautos unter den Linden. Auch am Waldhaus in Istanbul gab es einen Lindenbaum. Darunter saß oft ein Dichterfreund, seine Haare waren voller Blüten. In der Türkei sagt man, daß der Geruch der Lindenblüten junge Mädchen verrückt macht.' Özdamar: *Seltsame Sterne*, p. 95–96.
62 Özdamar: *Seltsame Sterne*, p. 18.
63 'Die Morgenstimmung und der Geruch in den Straßen von Ostberlin erinnerten mich daran, wie meine Großmutter jeden Morgen den Ofen heizte … Ich atmete die Luft tief ein, ein Geruch von Kohle und Autoabgasen wie in Istanbul.' Özdamar: *Seltsame Sterne*, p. 81.
64 'Im Fernsehen sahen wir uns noch einen amerikanischen Film mit Rod Taylor an, einer meiner Kindheitsfilme aus Istanbul.' Özdamar: *Seltsame Sterne*, p. 123.

The process of ceaselessly writing both cities and their partitions into one another, which occurs as a result of the protagonist's travel movements, also repeats itself in the superimposition of the structures of living arrangements. Already in the residence hall for Turkish women in Berlin, which during the first stay in Berlin is deliberately written-otherwise as 'Frauenwonaym' (a homophonic version of the properly spelled 'Frauenwohnheim'[65]), we can detect spatial structures with which the protagonist becomes familiar during her second stay in the city on the river Spree. The living arrangements in these dormitories, with their clear classifications and sexual as well as gender-specific boundaries, find their parodic, and paradoxical, equivalent flat-sharing community of the Wedding neighborhood in West Berlin. There, as in the women's dorm, the new arrival not only washes the dishes right from the start but is also emphatically told that any (sexual) relations with other residents is strictly off-limits. In all the novels, communal living arrangements create their own world, a transitional space of sorts that may temporarily become a phalanstery. It is only when a friend tries to leave the Turkish women's dorm that the narrator notices that Berlin 'This Berlin had not existed for us yet. We had our hossel [Wonaym], and the hossel [Wonaym] was not Berlin. Berlin began only when we left the hossel [Wonaym].'[66]

The ungrammatical writing-other(wise) of the proper German word for dorm, 'Wohnheim,' as 'Wonaym' literally shows up the drawing of limits and the impoverished exchanges that exist in a multicultural context. Even in the flat-sharing communities, internal communication often overlays the perception of the city, as the conversations with flat mates, along with noises from other floors, always draw attention and drown out other perceptions. We have here the soundscape of communal life. As in the story 'The courtyard in the mirror' ('Der Hof im Spiegel') that is set in Düsseldorf, noises from alteration shops and sewing machines, even from the brothels in that house, pervade the Wedding commune's flat. Of chief importance are not only visual but also acoustic sensations: languages, screams, and everyday noises. What eventually puts an appropriate end to this example of communal living are not the voices and nois-

---

[65] The spelling can be found already in the title of the first chapter in the first part of Özdamar, *Die Brücke vom Goldenen Horn*, p. 11 [But not so in the English version, where the title has been translated as 'The Long Corridors of the Women Workers' Hostel.' Özdamar: *The Bridge of the Golden Horn*, p. 3. TN]
[66] Özdamar: *The Bridge of the Golden Horn*, p. 44. 'Dieses Berlin hatte es für uns bis jetzt nicht gegeben. Wir hatten unser Wonaym, und dieses Wonaym war nicht Berlin. Berlin begann erst, wenn man aus dem Wonaym herausging.' Özdamar: *Die Brücke vom Goldenen Horn*, p. 63.

es from the brothel that travel through the heating pipes to the bed of the occasional lover, but the noisily staged orgasms of new flat mates.

No less than the West-Berlin collective, the smaller-scale and, in some respects more 'bourgeois,' living arrangements in East Berlin pose questions about the possibilities for living together that are already familiar from the time in an Istanbul 'commune.' The 'film commune' that the protagonist joins in Istanbul in an attempt to distance herself from her family's lives, anticipates the flat-sharing commune in Wedding. Both have phalanstery-like characteristics that combine living with work:

> During the day the boys went out into the streets and with an eight-millimetre camera filmed people they thought were being exploited. Then they developed the film in a darkroom, hung it on a clothes line in the big room and dried it with my hairdryer. The sewing machines of the Turkish Greeks worked below, the whores' beds worked above, and the hairdryer worked in the film commune.[67]

The West-Berlin commune cannot be understood without the Istanbul film commune, just like the West-Berlin student protests against the Shah's visit and Benno Ohnesorg's death cannot be grasped without the events in Paris in May 1968, the Turkish student groups in West Berlin and Paris, and the student revolts in Istanbul (that already hint at their later bloody suppression). Words beneath words; places beneath places; movements beneath movements; forms of living beneath forms of living; events beneath events: *Life is a Caravanserei*, *The Bridge of the Golden Horn*, and 'Strange stars stare down at the Earth' tell the story of a life largely chronologically, incorporating glimpses of relevant historical contexts that range from Turkey's contradictory modernization through Atatürk and the experiences of the generation of '68 to the late forms of the Cold War, the leftist terrorism in West Germany in the 1970s known as the 'German Autumn,' and the Fall of the Berlin Wall. It becomes clear that, in addition to these syntagmatic elements, what determines the processes of comprehension in the novel itself are above all the paradigmatic structures that endlessly super-

---

[67] Özdamar: *The Bridge of the Golden Horn*, p. 237. 'Die Jungs gingen tagsüber auf die Straßen und filmten Menschen, von denen sie dachten, daß sie ausgebeutet werden, mit einer 8-mm-Kamera. Dann entwickelten sie den Film in einer Dunkelkammer, hängten ihn im großen Zimmer auf eine Wäscheleine und trockneten ihn mit einem Haartrockner. Unten arbeiteten die Nähmaschinen der türkischen Griechen, oben arbeiteten die Hurenbetten und in der Filmkommune arbeitete der Haartrockner.' Özdamar: *Die Brücke vom Goldenen Horn*, p. 305. The ever-present motif of sewing and the sewing machine connects directly with the mother figure, and simultaneously with the motif of injury, as, for example, at the beginning of the story 'Der Hof im Spiegel'. In: Özdamar: *Der Hof im Spiegel*, p. 11–12.

impose themselves upon one another. The crossfading technique of writing languages and cultures into one another illustrates that Istanbul's European part, which encompasses both sides of the bridge of the Golden Horn, cannot be thought without the Asian part any more than West Berlin can be understood without East Berlin, Berlin without Istanbul, and Germany without Turkey.

This is not an intercultural communication but a transcultural crosshatching, a choreography of movements that crisscross diverse cultures, in which euphoria can by no means be understood just as lust but is frequently filled with tension and pain. We can see here fractal, multiply refracted and, at the same time, 'insular' patterns and structures that are key in the Literatures without a fixed Abode. The vectorization of all references, which I have already mentioned several times, occurs not in a continuous but in a discontinuous, frequently fractured post-Euclidian space (see especially chapter 3 above). The omnipresence of the mirror-motif in Özdamar's novels – after all, the mirror also becomes the place where all the dead from different times and spaces congregate[68] and thus a frame for all stories – accentuates processes of reflection, refraction, and crossfading more noticeably. Remarkably, the alternate reciprocal mirroring of Istanbul in Berlin and Berlin in Istanbul thus de-essentializes cultural difference rather undramatically, almost as if it were an afterthought. I will discuss the repeatedly refracted movement of crossfadings and translations more thoroughly in the final section of this chapter.

'At least twenty passports': Writing-between-Worlds

Just as the family's migrations within Turkey's national space in *Life is a Caravanserei* anticipate the first-person narrator's transnational migration in *The Bridge of the Golden Horn* and *Seltsame Sterne starren zur Erde*, the ship's moving between Asia and Europe prepares the path for the daily border crossing between West and East Berlin, between the Western Allies and the states of the Warsaw Pact. Just as the 'soldier's train' through Anatolia anticipates the 'train of whores' and all the other trains that will carry the protagonist from Turkey to Germany, the spatial movements between the young women's apartments in the West-Berlin Wedding and the East-Berlin Pankow neighborhood already signal how commonplace a practice it has become to crisscross the Wall, that hypervisible symbol of the border between two antagonistic powers that once seemed

---

68 Özdamar: 'Der Hof im Spiegel,' p. 24: 'All the dead live in this mirror' ('Alle Toten wohnen in diesem Spiegel').

to be cemented for all eternity.⁶⁹ Of course, writing Istanbul and Berlin, East and West, Orient and Occident into one another does not start from a fixed place, not even from a localizable interstitial space such as Homi Bhabha's 'third space.' Instead, it springs from the manifold (and perpetually oscillating) movements that interweave seeming opposites without, however, neutralizing or homogenizing them. Writing-between-Worlds does not create a sealed-off room of its own but opens up new transcultural, translingual, and transareal spaces in the process of traveling.

In Emine Sevgi Özdamar's writings, which not only emigrated into German-language literature but also take this literature *elsewhere*, migrations move to center stage. In the case of Turkey and Germany, these migrations have a transnational dimension, in the case of Asia and Europe a transcontinental one. At the same time, the author, who now lives in Berlin, placed two national and two *urban* spaces at the center of a trilogy whose setting is the very fulcrum of West-East history, a position between two continents and power blocs that repeats itself in the novels' topography and organization.

Of particular interest in this context are translocal movements, in which transnational and transcontinental relations may be focused as in a concave mirror. While, to the German reader, the Berlin Wall personified, in an almost paradigmatic manner, the massiveness and impermeability of a border replete with border controls and a death zone, the increasingly casual, daily border traffic 'within' a Germany that separated East from West, socialism from capitalism, and the troops of the Warsaw Pact from those of the NATO, disclose at once the arbitrariness of national borders, the futility of securing them, and also the possibility for overcoming them.

The cross-border commuter with her Turkish passport, a West-Berlin residence permit, and an East-Berlin visa, who soon becomes a familiar presence to the border guards, stubbornly violates the borders as she shuttles back and forth between both Germanies, both Berlins, and their very different languages. In Istanbul, during her transfers between the Asian and the European sides, she could already observe how the sharply drawn borders were increasingly reflected among the readers of newspapers with different political orientations and alliances: 'At the newspaper kiosks the left-wing, fascist and religious newspapers hung next to one another, all in Turkish, but it was as if there were three foreign languages. On the ship everyone opened their left-wing, fascist or reli-

---

69 As regards the undermining seemingly well-established borders, see Fröhlich: 'Reinventions of Turkey,' p. 70.

gious newspapers, and one didn't see any faces anymore.'⁷⁰ The de-individualized readers of these conflicting newspapers talk only among themselves. They practice their important words only among themselves; they sit apart from one another, ride on different buses, throw the others' newspapers into the sea, and soon 'two political groups fought each other with rolled-up newspapers.'⁷¹ Translation processes between hostile 'foreign languages' no longer take place. Words become weapons; verbal communication degenerates into more and more violent confrontations; bloody hostilities ensue; leftist demonstrators are persecuted, hunted down, and murdered. Armed leftist groups are founded. Just like Trotsky, Lenin, or Stalin, like Mao, Castro, or Ché Guevara, they 'dressed up' and invented ever 'new languages.'⁷² The protagonist buys 'all these periodicals' and '[sits] in the toilet for a long time to learn these new languages.'⁷³ The mother tongue increasingly disintegrates into foreign tongues that have to be acquired studiously in the ensuing Babel.

In Berlin, the language acquisition within a language, with its traces of intralingual translation, opens a view onto the linguistically marked border between East and West. Its initial manifestation at the border crossing Friedrichstrasse is a pile of discarded Western newspapers. They may not be carried to the Eastern part of the city and remain at the border, which is thus also a linguistic border. The newspapers with their headlines represent belonging much like passports do, granting access at some borders while making admission more difficult at others. Time and again, Özdamar fades in the history of such acts of border demarcation, while simultaneously revealing their absurdity especially when it comes to nation-states. These sorts of belonging eclipse human faces and destinies in the same way that the newspaper headlines efface their readers. Özdamar succinctly observes in an interview: 'National pride gives me hives. It's really sufficient to say I was born here or there. Nothing more. In fact, you should have at least twenty passports, because you never know which countries will become enemies next. Or maybe a world passport. Or none at all.'⁷⁴ That it is a writer born in Turkey who discovers entirely new sides not only

---

70 Özdamar: *The Bridge of the Golden Horn*, p. 230. 'An den Zeitungskiosken hingen die linken, faschistischen und religiösen Zeitungen nebeneinander, alle in türkisch, aber es war wie drei Fremdsprachen. Im Schiff öffneten alle ihre linken, faschistischen oder religiösen Zeitungen, und man sah keine Gesichter mehr.' Özdamar: *Die Brücke vom Goldenen Horn*, p. 295–296.
71 Özdamar: *The Bridge of the Golden Horn*, p. 230.
72 Özdamar: *The Bridge of the Golden Horn*, p. 230.
73 Özdamar: *The Bridge of the Golden Horn*, p. 231.
74 'Von Nationalstolz kriege ich Allergien. Es reicht doch zu sagen, ich bin da oder dort geboren. Mehr nicht. Überhaupt, man müsste mindestens zwanzig Pässe haben, man weiß ja nicht,

to Berlin but also to the German-German problem and who presents them in persuasive literary forms, strikes me as especially noteworthy because migratory knowledge and migratory language can vectorize forms of 'belonging' that once seemed the static attributes of a state and as such quite unmovable. From a translingual perspective that traverses different languages, not only the 'foreign languages' within Turkish but also those that have developed within German, are in dire need of translation. Merely to translate from East to West, and West to East, is not enough.

The vectorization of geographical, topographical, and linguistic movements does not aim at patterns of movement that are abstractions of history but at patterns that take in and store historical phenomena and practices. From a dynamic perspective that continually moves among several languages, Emine Sevgi Özdamar writes European history otherwise, such that Europe, which has always been in motion, has to be understood *as movement*.[75] In Özdamar's work, Istanbul and Berlin become remarkable literary reflectors of a translational vectorization that show how boundaries of all sorts are drawn, and, above all, how they are often both crossed and crossed out. How better to understand languages than through translation? And better to grasp borders than through continual crossovers, traversals, and travel?

Translingual translation, transcultural writing-other(wise), and *translocal writing languages elsewhere* are thus vitally important aspects of the writing-into-one-another of languages and literatures with the aim to break up and set in motion the hardened surfaces that exist in the realms of politics and national literature. Such writing allows for a Writing-between-Worlds that functions spatially and temporally, and that does not retreat into interstices or niches – even those of a migration or migrant literature – but, rather, uses the spaces between our worlds for varied and unexpected movements, temporal shifts, and knowledge transfer. To translate a Literature without a fixed Abode that resides between worlds would thus be the attempt to carry a writing-other(wise) and writing-elsewhere into national-literary spaces. Those spaces have not disappeared, nor will they; but they are in the midst of a profound transformation. Understood as passage through and with the words of the other (see chapter 5 above),

---

welches Land sich als nächstes mit welchem verfeindet. Oder einen Weltpass. Oder keinen.' Özdamar: 'Wir wohnen in einer weiten Hölle,' p. 23.

75 See Klaus J. Bade: *Migration in European history: The making of Europe.* Oxford: Blackwell 2003. See also Ottmar Ette: 'Europa als Bewegung: Zur literarischen Konstruktion eines Faszinosum'. In: Dieter Holtmann / Peter Riemer (eds.): *Europa. Einheit und Vielfalt: Eine interdisziplinäre Betrachtung.* Münster: LIT Verlag 2001, p. 15–44.

translation would then not only be irreplaceable but also indispensable for the survival of societies that do not wish to sacrifice their long histories of exchanges to theories of a clash of cultures motivated by power politics. Cultural differences certainly do not disappear in Özdamar's texts; but they are de-essentialized and thus become habitable, experienceable, and livable, in the sense of producing and storing knowledge of and for living.

It is not only on the level of the story of a single life and its specific knowledge of and for living but also in their linguistic constructedness that Emine Sevgi Özdamar's texts pave the way the way for *trans*lingual processes of translation that, given the existence and reinforcements of national-literary borders, should no longer have to ask apologetically if they may say something.[76] Literatures without a fixed Abode are, after all, no longer the exception, even if national-literary histories continue to ignore them.

As was already evident at the outset of this chapter, for writers whose work may be counted as part of the Literatures without a fixed Abode, the tongue is the physical embodiment of trans*lingual* movements. It is no coincidence, then, that the Chicana writer Gloria Anzaldúa, whose work crosses borders in multiple ways and senses, places the (female) tongue at the very beginning of 'How to Tame a Wild Tongue,' a chapter in *Borderlands / La Frontera* (1987). In this chapter, a male dentist grows increasingly impatient in his efforts to anesthetize the female protagonist's tongue:

> 'We're going to control your tongue,' the dentist says, pulling out all the metal from my mouth. Silver bits plop and tinkle into the basin. My mouth is a motherlode....
> 'We're going to have to do something about your tongue,' I hear the anger rising in his voice. My tongue keeps pushing out the wads of cotton, pushing back the drills, the long thin needles. 'I've never seen anything as strong or as stubborn,' he says. And I think, how do you tame a wild tongue, train it to be quiet, how do you bridle and saddle it? How do you make it lie down?[77]

While the English-speaking dentist in Anzaldúa's popular book represents the rather ineffective attempt on the part of a hegemonic language to dominate the Hispanic mother tongue, Yoko Tawada similarly creates one of those transcultural and translingual tongues that stand for a writing anchored in the physical

---

76 See Özdamar: *The Bridge of the Golden Horn*, p. 79.
77 Gloria Anzaldúa: *Borderlands / La Frontera: The New Mestiza*. San Francisco: Aunt Lute Books 1987, p. 53. For the literary authentication strategies of Chicana women writers, see the wonderful monograph by Anja Bandau: *Strategien der Autorisierung: Projektionen der Chicana bei Gloria Anzaldúa und Cherrie Moraga*. Hildesheim: Olms 2004.

body and that oscillates between diverse languages and cultures. Her 'Tongue dance,' whose protagonist consists of 'a single tongue,' also, not coincidentally, features a dentist who hates tongues 'because they disturb him during the treatment.'[78] Tawada's 'The Woman with two shells' (Die Zweischalige) even stages a tongue surgery that should make it possible to speak without any injuries. After the doctor has shackled the tongue to an 'operation table' the size of a palm, he injects 'an anesthetic in the middle of the tongue,' so that the narrator's tongue cringes but can no longer 'roll back to the depths of [her] throat.'[79] Tawada's *Überseezungen* are also in need of treatment for numerous painful speech disorders,[80] but in the end they cannot be silenced, just like the tongues in Gloria Anzaldúa's and Emine Sevgi Özdamar's texts which embody a *translingual* writing characterized by translation processes that cannot be brought to a close. A literature that speaks with and in many tongues.

In Özdamar's texts, purportedly firm borders make possible the protagonist's quickly oscillating movements in Istanbul and Berlin. It may not be too daring to connect this translocal structure with the space that the twisting and turning of the tongue creates in the clearly defined oral cavity. This, however, does not mean that such literature melts on the tongue, but that it is acutely conscious of its often painful movements. In a recontextualization of the opening of *Mother Tongue*, which I cited earlier, Emine Sevgi Özdamar stresses the following point in her aforementioned acceptance speech: 'They say that the tongue does not have any bones. I twisted my tongue into German and suddenly I was happy – there, in the theater, where the tragedies touch you and at the same time promise you a utopia.'[81] The promised happiness of the utopia is not limited to the clearly circumscribed space of a theater stage but, rather – like

---

[78] 'Mein ehemaliger Zahnarzt hasste Zungen, weil sie ihn bei der Behandlung stören.' Tawada: *Überseezungen*, p. 10–11.

[79] 'Der Arzt fesselt meine Zunge an einen Operationstisch, der so groß ist wie seine Handfläche, und spritzt in die Mitte der Zunge ein Betäubungsmittel. Sie zuckt zusammen, will sich in die Tiefe meiner Kehle zurückrollen, aber zum Glück kann sie sich nicht bewegen.' Tawada: *Überseezungen*, p. 41.

[80] About literary speech disorders, see Ottmar Ette: 'Die Fremdheit (in) der Mutterzunge: Emine Sevgi Özdamar, Gabriela Mistral, Juana Borrero und die Krise der Sprache in Formen des weiblichen Schreibens zwischen Spätmoderne und Postmoderne.' In: Reinhard Kacianka / Peter V. Zima (eds.): *Krise und Kritik der Sprache: Literatur zwischen Spätmoderne und Postmoderne*. Tübingen: Francke 2004, p. 251–268.

[81] 'Ich drehte meine Zunge ins Deutsche, und plötzlich war ich glücklich. Dort am *Theater*, wo die tragischen Stoffe einen berühren und zugleich eine Utopie versprechen.' Emine Sevgi Özdamar: 'Meine deutschen Wörter.' In: Özdamar: *Der Hof im Spiegel*, p. 129.

imaginary bridge Unter den Linden in Berlin – proves to be the promise of a tangible atopia in language that cannot be tied back to any specific place. In Emine Sevgi Özdamar and Yoko Tawada, the twist(ing) of the tongue into German, into the foreign language, suggest another translation (or 'Überseezunge,' that is, overseas tongue) for my initial quotation from Octavio Paz, which had probably not occurred to the Mexican poet. In this translation, *la lengua* would not be the (mother-)tongue but the tongue that can also move in other, foreign languages. A writer's only belonging (nacionalidad) would thus be his or her own tongue, regardless of whether that tongue follows the sounds and movements of a mother tongue or those of another, acquired language. This fading – even if not vanishing – of the difference between 'mother tongue' and 'foreign language' has to do with the tongue's volubility and the translingual writing-between-different-tongues that characterizes the Literatures without fixed Abode. Its productive oscillations, its creative crossings, make it possible today that literature's ancient promise of happiness be redeemed elsewhere and otherwise.

7 Confrontations

The Transareal Worlds of the ArabAmericas: Chronicle of a Clash Foretold

ArabAmerican Greetings from a Camp in the Caribbean

> Dear Mother,
> I am writing to you from the seaside resort of Guantanamo Bay in Cuba. After winning first prize in the competition, I was whisked to this nice resort with all expenses paid. I did not have to spend a penny. I and Jamil [Al Banna] are in very good health. Everybody is very nice. The neighbors are very well behaved. The food is first class, plenty of sun and pebbles, no sand I'm afraid. Give my salaam to everybody and my special salaam to Wahab. I wish him the very best with his life, religion and business. I hope to see you soon if you want. Your son, Bisher.
> P.S. Please renew my motorbike insurance policy.[1]

The carefully considered words Bisher al-Rawi puts in this letter to his mother encapsulate his situation as a long-term prisoner in the US Camp Delta, Guantanamo Bay, near the Cuban city of Guantánamo. Is this a fiction or a very real nightmare? Surely it is both, and this unresolvable entanglement is both intentional and staged. The words are from act two of a play by South African writer Gillian Slovo, who lives in the UK, and the British journalist and scholar Victoria Brittain. It was produced for the stage in 2004 by Nicolas Kent and Sacha Wares in London and New York.[2] In ways that are at times subtle, at others sensationalistic agitprop, *Guantanamo* denounces the fate of the incarcerated, the torture-like treatment of those denizens of a *univers concentrationnaire* set up on the US base in the Cuban province of Oriente, with flagrant disregard for international legal standards as part of the 'war on terror' campaign of a government whose official policy was to promote human rights across the world. The play's plot claims to have been taken from reality, or, in the words on the title page of the

---

[1] Victoria Brittain / Gillian Slovo: *Guantanamo: 'Honor Bound to Defend Freedom,'* taken from *spoken evidence.* London: Oberon Books 2004, p. 30. I thank Peter Hulme for alerting me to this play's existence.

[2] The world premiere was held at the Tricycle Theatre in London on May 20, 2004. Five of the British Guantánamo prisoners who were either mentioned or actual characters in the play were not released until late February 2004. In preparation for the play, interviews and conversations with them were conducted in late March and early April 2004 (see Brittain/Slovo: *Guantanamo*, p. 3–4).

printed edition: *taken from spoken evidence*. The audience thus has every right to expect a truthful portrayal. In keeping with this expectation, five British Guantanamo prisoners are joined by British Foreign Minister Jack Straw and U.S. Defense Secretary Donald Rumsfeld, among others, who are present in the form of quotations from them. Fiction *and* documentation: The greetings from a camp in the Caribbean are directed at theater audiences and readers; they concern us and touch us.

The words of UK resident Bisher al-Rawi play ironically, even sarcastically, with the common Western perception of the Caribbean as a vacation paradise under palm trees, where tourists who want for nothing. This reality can indeed be observed just a few kilometers away from Camp Delta. But the radical break that separates the camp on the military base from the no less island-like hotel facilities, where the very same nature is meant to serve an entirely different role and function, may remind us that Cuba is an island of islands and thus a highly complex (meta) island-world. The largest of the Antilles is an archipelago and also a fractal world of islands; these manifestation face each other with such pointed contrast that they might as well belong to different worlds entirely. And they do. The Guantanamo Bay military base has its origins in the age of US troops' intervention in Cuba's colonial war of liberation against Spain, which, thanks to superior military technology, brought the USA a quick victory, dominion over broad sectors of the Caribbean, and expansion into the Latin American region. At the same time, Spain, the first colonial power to have set up concentration camps (*campos de concentraciones*) for its enemies for the first time in history during the war José Martí unleashed in 1895. was banished from the Americas once and for all.[3] The location for Camp Delta was indeed well chosen.

Concentration camps, then, are not completely foreign to Cuba; prior to Camp Delta, however, they had been used only for residents of the island itself. Nothing except for their shared place on Cuba, seems to connect the anti-terror camp with the resorts about which the camp inmate writes his family. And yet, each of these self-enclosed I(s)land-worlds, situated in a Cuba that itself has broken down into many smaller insular structures, share in a common development of which Bisher al-Rawi makes us subtly aware. They are part of a globalization process that began on these very islands, the Antilles, with their so-called discovery by Christopher Columbus, alias Cristóbal Colón. The four phases of accelerated globalization have left particularly deep imprints on Cuban history and geography. The developments at the end of the fifteenth and in the first

---

[3] See Giorgio Agamben: *Remnants of Auschwitz: The Witness and the Archive*. New York: Zone Books 2002, p. 175.

half of the sixteenth century; in the second half of the eighteenth century; in the last third of the nineteenth century; and in the final third of the twentieth and incipient twenty-first century were felt in this region with far greater intensity than anywhere else on earth. Evidence of this intensity abounds, from the existence of the military base and the tourism industry at the beginning of the twentieth century, initially US-dominated, to the installations and facilities for presumed terrorists and vacationing tourists at the dawn of the twenty-first century.

Tourists, like terrorists, reach Cuba by airplane – one of the parallels drawn in the above citation – the very means of transport that controls people's transatlantic movements, alongside with the Internet, in the networked age. At a time when the US economic embargo against Cuba was still fully intact, making it difficult for US citizens to visit the island, it was highly illogical that Guantanamo Bay would have been the preferred destination for US transport planes dropping their cargo of purported terrorists on the Caribbean island. Unlike the tourists' charter flights, however, the US military transport planes took off from Afghanistan and Iraq. In this way, they were connected with the transatlantic migrations of the third phase of accelerated globalization during the final third of the nineteenth and the beginning of the twentieth century, which brought many Arab migrants first to the Caribbean and, from there, to other parts of the Americas. Although Bisher al-Rawi may be unaware of this, the lines he writes to his worried family, always threatened by censorship, inscribe themselves in a history of ArabAmerican relations and, moreover, in a history of ArabAmerican writing that has always been a writing-between-worlds in more ways than one.

The *friction* in these lines from the pen of the Muslim Camp Delta inmate, oscillating between nightmare and fiction, consists in the very fact that they remember this complex history of voluntary and compulsory migrations and transatlantic transfers in a compressed and dramatic manner. The forgotten history of the ArabAmericas is just as multifaceted as it is fascinating. Literature in particular has in store for us the knowledge of and for living and survival that developed over the course of that history in the very space where two heterogeneous cultural areas intersect.

Towards an ArabAmerican library

In the contexts of the notion of the *Clash of Civilizations*, so effectively popularized after the publication of Samuel P. Huntington's book in 1996, and the 'war on terror' that George W. Bush's administration propagandized as a counterstrike to September 11, 2001, it is surely no accident that, at the time, several

Hispanic American and Arab governments would also commemorate the multifarious past and present connections between their countries. On May 10 and 11, 2005, representatives of South American and Arab states met at the invitation of the Brazilian president in Brazil's capital, where they laid out the shared goal of 'strengthening biregional relations, increasing cooperation and establishing a partnership to pursue development, justice and international peace' in a joint 'Brasilia Declaration.'[4] The specified goal was to propose an actual 'construction of a world where tolerance and inclusiveness prevail,' a 'reorganization of world politics in the twenty-first century' under the auspices of multilateralism and designed as an alternative to the self-fulfilling prophecy of the 'clash of cultures.' Clearly directed against all forms of unilateralism, the accord of this first summit meeting of the countries of Hispanic America with 22 member states of the Arab League addressed issues as varied as the founding of a Palestinian state alongside Israel and within the borders of 1967, the Iraq war, and the US sanctions against Syria. Even the question of the Falkland Islands, the spread of atomic weapons, and the containment of the drug trade made it onto the agenda in the final declaration of the summit, to which US representatives were not admitted even as observers.

The heads of government paid special attention to cooperation in the area of culture, recognizing from the very outset the 'positive role of South American citizens of Arab origin in the advancement of biregional relations.'[5] These words re-illuminate an old story: the history of Arab immigration which, for a long time, had hardly been a topic of public discourse, and the peaceful coexistence with Arab immigrants across the whole spectrum of Hispanic American countries. Emphasizing the importance of a population group that linked both areas historically and culturally amounted at least to an attempt to leave behind static, bilateral idea and begin to introduce a dynamic, transareal dimension into Arab-Hispanic American relations. What stands out, in addition to the agreement on mutual cultural dialogue and exchange and the creation of research institutions and programs designed to foster biregional cooperation, is the joint declaration of intent to enlist specialists to establish a 'South American-Arab Library' and to make available translations of works deemed important by each

---

4 Cumbre América del Sur and Países Arabes. *Brasilia Declaration* (1, 'Preamble'); quoted from the website of the Brazilian foreign ministry Embassy of Saudi Arabia at http://www.saudiembassy.net/_Preview/archive/2005/statements/page18.aspx. I thank Günther Maihold for pointing this out to me.
5 *Brasilia Declaration*, Paragraph 3.1.

culture.⁶ Driven by processes of migration, the shared history of Arab and South American (or, better, Latin American) countries, was recognized at the highest political level, as was the need to pursue forward-looking joint cultural projects such as an Arab-Latin American library. In this way, the migrants' routes led to a new politics whose goal was to improve pathways of knowledge that had been built long ago but had rarely entered the stage of conscious reflection. Without underestimating other aspects of the 'Declaration of Brasilia,' such as planned economic, financial and social cooperation, and also collaboration on technology and information in all areas of sustainable economics, new biregional, or more comprehensively transareal expansions of horizons appeared, above all, in the cultural sphere. The promise of such developments was to advance relations between these two regions of the world in a South-South context independent of Europe and the USA.

To be sure, disagreements among the Latin American countries and the absence of many Arab heads of state overshadowed the summit meeting, and the economic and trade policy goals that the Brazilian government in particular had projected onto this summit were not realized, or only indirectly. The founding of a joint committee of Mercosur and the Gulf Cooperation Council with the goal of a free-trade agreement may be regarded with as much skepticism as many other ambitious declarations of the summit.⁷ Moreover, one might argue that the political positions in the final declaration, whose criticisms of US politics with regard to the Near and Middle East could not be missed, were decidedly in the interest of the Arab countries. Categorizing the summit as a mere 'Arab Summit' does not, however, do justice to the long-term importance of this meeting for the political and also, above all, the cultural sphere.⁸ This is not to mention the fact that the Latin American countries, under the stern gaze of the USA, gained more latitude in their foreign policy relations. It was the first time that a declaration was formulated not on a binational level but on a level that concerned the areas of the Latin American and Arab countries in their entirety, emphasizing the need for supporting 'cultural identities' and a mutual dialog about cultural aspects of coexistence.⁹ Even the hoped-for cooperation in the realm of audiovisu-

---

6 *Brasilia Declaration*, Paragraph 3.5. According to paragraph 3.7, a seminar of specialists for the founding of such a library in Aleppo, Syria, was to be conducted in October 2005 [There is no evidence that this seminar ever occurred. TN].
7 See the critical comments from the Konrad Adenauer Foundation in Wilhelm Hofmeister: 'Ein Gipfel der falschen Erwartungen und des falschen Zungenschlages: Das 1. Gipfeltreffen Südamerika–Arabische Liga.' In: *Focus Brasilien* 4 (2005), p. 1–7.
8 Hofmeister: 'Ein Gipfel der falschen Erwartungen,' p. 6.
9 *Brasilia Declaration*, Paragraph 3.3.

al and other communications media, as well as in education, including the university sector, points to an effort to assign an important and meaningful function to culture in the strengthening of South-South relations in the context of ArabAmerican tensions, specifically to the 'diversity of the cultural heritage of their countries.'[10] One would expect this rapprochement to have opened up new paths of knowledge that also, once again, raised awareness of the intercultural and transcultural experiences of Latin Americans of Arab extraction, which, even though they had fallen into oblivion in public discourse, had more of a presence in literature. Even if one understands the project of a 'Latin American-Arab Library' primarily as a biregional attempt to establish a canon of the literatures of Latin America and the Arab world through their respective major representatives, one can still glimpse the possible emergence of a transareal and transcultural dimension above and beyond the biregional and intercultural one. This would mean that instead of, or in addition to, a static adding up of 'great works' that appear significant in each cultural space, there would be a dynamic understanding of cultural mobility which could entwine the two cultural spaces more firmly. Focusing our attention on the movements that connect and interweave the two areas, my following remarks explore an ArabAmerican Library that is at once *transareal* (instead of only biregional) and *transcultural* (not just intercultural).

Patterns of arrival and motion in an ArabAmerican turnstile

The 2000 novel *La caída de los puntos cardinales* (The loss of the cardinal points) by the Colombian author Luis Fayad would occupy an important place in such a transareal ArabAmerican Library. We witness toward the end of the novel's first part the arrival of a group of Arab immigrants on the Caribbean coast of Colombia at the beginning of the twentieth century:

> Yanira wore a white blouse with embroidered borders and a high neckline and a long skirt no different from that skirts that women who they would later see in the village. What distinguished here was her cloth bag which was shot through with colored threads and in which she stored her hand luggage. Dahmar had on a white silk shirt and European-cut pants of classy fabric which he had bought during their stopover in Marseille. His fellow countrymen wanted to disembark together on the gangway, all the way at the end; when then set foot on land, they were made to form a group. The customs officer declared cheerily that the foreigners, among them the Turks, had to take a few step away from the others.

---

10 *Brasilia Declaration*, Paragraph 3.11.

Dahmar translated this order for his countrymen, and the youngest of them, about eighteen, felt ill-treated.
–Turks? he said to himself and turned to Dahmar. Tell him who we are.
–Here we are Turks, Dhamar replied.
From the letters that they had received while still in Lebanon, they knew that this is what they called them here because they carried passports from the Turkish authorities.
–I think that my father was thrown in jail because of the Turks, said the one who felt ill-treated, and now they call me a Turk.[11]

In travel literature, the place of arrival is always highly charged; during the course of arrival, layers of meaning entangle and central patterns of meaning surface. The scene of arrival that Luis Fayad unfolds here with such mastery inaugurates a play of similarities and differences that relates the group of immigrants from Lebanon to the local population even before the former leave the ship. Clothing plays a key role in this play of dissimilarities, in which Dahmar, with his European attire purchased en route in Marseille, occupies an intermediary position between Arab and Latin American worlds. Apparel is significant in this passage not only because it functions as a mark or symbol of identity, but also because the textile trade becomes a considerable economic pillar for many of the immigrants as the novel progresses, just as it did in the social reality of Colombia.

When Dahmar translates for the immigrants who cannot yet speak Spanish the command that all 'foreigners – including 'Turks' – remain separate from the other passengers, he takes on a mediating role for the second time, one that in-

---

[11] 'Yanira llevaba una blusa blanca con bordados cerrada en el cuello y una falda larga que no se distinguía de las faldas de las mujeres que vieron luego en el lugar. Se distinguía por el bolso de tela tramado con hilos de colores que le servía de equipaje de mano. Dahmar iba con una camisa blanca de seda y un pantalón de tela fina de corte europeo adquiridos a su paso por Marsella. Sus paisanos quisieron bajar juntos por la pasarela y de todas maneras al final, cuando tocaron tierra, los hicieron formarse en grupo. El agente de aduanas anunció con tono alegre que los extranjeros debían apartarse unos pasos, entre ellos los turcos. Dahmar les tradujo la orden a sus paisanos y el más joven, de unos dieciocho años, se sintió maltratado.
—¿Turcos?—se preguntó y se dirigió a Dahmar—. Dile quiénes somos.
—Aquí somos turcos—, dijo Dahmar.
Por las cartas que llegaban al Líbano sabían que en este lado les daban ese nombre por cargar el pasaporte de las autoridades turcas.
—Pensar que mi padre estuvo preso por culpa de los turcos —dijo el que se sentía maltratado—, y ahora me llaman turco.' Luis Fayad: La caída de los puntos cardinales. Bogotá: Editorial Planeta Colombiana 2000, p. 84 [This novel has not been translated into another European language. TN]

volves translation in many senses. This interlingual action at the very moment that the passage from the Old World to the New has been completed is revealing insofar as the Colombian authorities not only redefines the Lebanese immigrants but also assign them a new identity. For the Colombians, they have become Turks, even though their families suffered under Turkish rule in the Ottoman Empire. Ironically, their flight from the Turks in the Old World results in their being identified as Turks in the New World. The translator, however, came prepared for this quid pro quo, since other Lebanese emigrants' letters had already reported in detail about the game of misrecognzing their political and cultural identities. The passage (trans-lation) to a new world comes with the imposition of a 'foreign' identity, which some perceive as injurious: setting foot in the country of immigration transforms the Turks' opponents into Turks themselves almost overnight.[12] Migrating from the Arab to the Latin American world – and with it a sequence of deterritorialization and reterritorialization – changes attributions of identities fundamentally, thanks to a radical recontextualization that recodes and sets in motion linguistic and conceptual, political and cultural positions.

The refugees who have just fled Lebanon, a country, as we will see below, plagued by civil wars, know that civil strife also looms in Colombia; yet upon their arrival, they do not find any indications of acts of war of any kind. Those conflicts, an officer explains to them, are taking place faraway in the country's interior.[13] Upon their very arrival, then, the immigrants encounter intimations of all of those violent conflicts in which some of them become ensnarled later on. The young Hassana and others also soon familiarize themselves with fruits and products, as well as with linguistic expressions and the quotidian characteristics of the Colombian Caribbean coast. On their trip to nearby Barranquilla, the Arab migrants discuss the trees and the many birds whose song awakens them in the morning.[14] It is the discovery of the New World as a world new to them, and with which they attempt to become gradually familiar.

The novel's carefully contoured plot shows how the Lebanese become 'turcos' and these fake Turks and their children slowly become Colombians of Arab descent who initially secure their survival and in the end, thanks to their hard work, build their own lives, with all its cares and worries, in a country convul-

---

12 The Scottish traveler Cunningham regarded this naming of the Arab population ot the Caribbean coast he visited as cruel; see Jorge García Usta: 'Arabes en Macondo.' In: *Deslinde* 21 (1997), p. 127.
13 Fayad: *La caída*, p. 84.
14 Fayad: *La caída*, p. 91–92.

sed by acts of violence. The Latin American country becomes a second home for all of them. At the end of the novel, we are told the following about Yanira, whom we have met as Dahmar's young wife in the arrival scene: 'Yanira remained pensive. She remembered how, when her first son was born, she had felt that she finally had something of here, and now that Dahmar was buried near her house, she could be nowhere else. Muhamed replied that he had felt the same during the course of the past year.'[15] In the triangle of her feelings and experiences between her first child's birth and her first husband's death, and the impending fulfillment of a second love, there is no other place for this woman from another country who lives in her own house: Lebanon is both preserved and canceled out in Colombia. In Yanira's house, the experience of birth, death, and love suspends the contrasts not only between spaces but also between temporalities, as the lyrically sensual ending of the novel shows in her dis-robing:

> Yanira folded back the corner of the sheet and the cover and started to undress. The lamp spread its light across the entire night. Silence spread and mingled with the air. There was nothing that needed to be said, to call out one's names or to celebrate being together. They had the sensation that they had never hurried anything to be in this moment; nor had it come to them too late.[16]

Even though I cannot pursue here all the twists and turns of migratory origin in Fayad's novel, I want to highlight two other aspects important for my line of inquiry. For one, it is no coincidence that this migration from a country in the Arab world torn apart by civil war to a country in the American hemisphere similarly torn apart would lead across the Caribbean, for centuries the hub for the slave trade and also for a multitude of large-scale migrations and displacements. The wave of migration from Arab countries – especially from Syria, Palestine and Lebanon – which began in the second half of the nineteenth century and reached its peak at the turn of the twentieth, follows the old transatlantic routes that channeled the ever-asymmetrical 'exchange' between the continents of the Old World and the different regions of the 'new' continent. The Caribbean coast of Colombia is but one part of a complex circumCaribbean and hemisphe-

---

15 'Yanira se había quedado pensativa. Recordaba que al nacer su primer hijo sintió que por fin tenía algo de aquí y ahora con Dahmar enterrado cerca de su casa ya no podía ser de otro lugar. Muhamed repuso que en ese último año había sentido lo mismo.' Fayad: *La caída*, p. 321.
16 'Yanira deshizo una punta de la colcha y una de la manta y empezó a desvestirse. La iluminación de la lámpara continuó toda la noche. El silencio se regó tejido en el aire. No hubo nada que decirse, ni para llamarse por sus nombres, ni para celebrar el encuentro. Fluyó la sensación de que si nunca se adelantaron para estar en ese momento, tampoco llegaron tarde a él.' Fayad: *La caída*, p. 322.

ric matrix of relations that connects very varied spaces – natural, sociopolitical, economic, and cultural. In this fractal, vectorial space riven by discontinuities of all kinds, translocal and transregional, transnational and transareal relations are mediated and literally translated into other logics. This novel by an author who was born in Santa Fé de Bogotá in 1945 and has lived in Barcelona, Paris, Stockholm and Berlin, among other places, since the 1970s, illustrates these relations and translations memorably. As the novel's title already announces, the cardinal points of orientation in Luis Fayad's work fall victim to such unsteady and yet powerful movements and eventually dissolve. The novel turns initially delocalized and subsequently translocalized knowledge, based on an oscillation between the places of reference in the Old and the New Worlds, into the fulcrum of a literature that can be characterized as a writing without a fixed abode. Time and again, the *puntos cardinales* of this Colombian writer level out within a constantly shifting magnetic field.

La caída de los puntos cardinales creates an intricate intertextual network that is of interest here insofar as it regards the texts of another Colombian author whom we may also associate with the Caribbean. Muhamed, the character from Fayad's novel mentioned above, had fought for several years as a soldier among the insurgent troops who ultimately capitulated to the government army. Once again, the events of that civil war, only the most recent in a long series of civil wars, parade in front of his (and our) eyes in rapid succession:

> During the battle he had saved the life of fellow soldier and was himself saved by someone else; had to flee from a fortified place; hid and returned to the front; was present at the very moment when they wanted to shoot and did not shoot Colonel Aureliano Buendía; participated in the taking of villages; guarded prisoners and was trusted sentry in the barracks. After the defeat, he did not flee and made it to Ibrahim's house.[17]

Not only for Colombian readers does the mention of the name Aureliano Buendía call to mind Gabriel García Márquez's *A Hundred Years of Solitude* (*Cien años de soledad*, 1967), the Colombian Nobelist's magnum opus. Although Buendía's family history is at the center of this novel, many allusions to Arab immigration in the Caribbean coastal area of Colombia cryptically pervade it at the same

---

[17] 'En la lucha salvó de la muerte a un compañero y fue salvado él mismo por otro, tuvo que huir de una plaza, se escondió y volvió al frente, presenció el momento en que iban a fusilar al coronel Aureliano Buendía y no lo fusilaron, estuvo presente en la toma de pueblos, cuidó prisioneros y fue centinela de confianza en los cuarteles. Al ser derrotado no se orientó en la fuga y fue a dar a la casa de Ibrahim.' Fayad: *La caída*, p. 136.

time.[18] The Arab migrants had to be part of this Latin American microcosm; after all, they contributed decisively to the progress of this part of Colombia and left their mark on its economic, social, and cultural development.

The relationship to another novel by Luis Fayad's compatriot also comes to mind, one whose protagonist hails from a family of Arab immigrants and in which – as in *La caída de los puntos cardinales* – Aureliano Buendía is also mentioned only once: *Chronicle of a Death Foretold* (*Crónica de una muerte anunciada*).[19] Not only the *intra*textual relationship between García Márquez's own novels becomes evident here, but also the *inter*textual affiliation between Luis Fayad's ArabAmerican migrant novel and *Chronicle of a Death Foretold*. First published in 1981, this text that has long since become a classic of Latin American literature and, as my following remarks will show, also deserves to be included in a transareal ArabAmerican Library for several reasons.

Chronicle of a clash of cultures foretold?

There is no question about Gabriel García Márquez's familiarity with the ways of life and the knowledge for and about living of the descendants of Arab migrants on the Caribbean coast. Already in his childhood and youth did he keep company with many families of Arab extraction and later cultivated these contacts in his professional and private life. Given the historical development of Colombia and the writer's personal life, it is hardly surprising that there are 'Arabs in Macondo,' especially since García Márquez' married Mercedes Barcha, the daughter of an Egyptian engineer brought to the country by General Rafael Reyes to implement certain projects.[20] García Márquez thus frequently concerned himself with the characteristics of the immigrants, chiefly from the Near and Middle East, from Syria, Palestine, and Lebanon. They also traveled to other regions of the Caribbean and Central America, such as Cuba, Haiti, the Dominican Repub-

---

[18] See García Usta: 'Arabes en Macondo.'
[19] For this single direct reference to Aureliano Buendía, see Gabriel García Márquez: *Crónica de una muerte anunciada*. Barcelona: Editorial Bruguera 1981, p. 55. There, Bayardo San Román's father, General Petronio San Román, is introduced as the hero of the nineteenth–century civil wars, 'one of the major glories of the Conservative regime for having put Colonel Aureliano Buendía to flight in the disaster of Tucurinca.' Gabriel García Márquez: *Chronicle of a Death Foretold*. New York: Knopf – Vintage 2003, p. 33.
[20] See García Usta: 'Arabes en Macondo,' p. 137. References to relationships between Garcia Márquez and the Arab families Mattar, Janne, Kusse, and Cassij during his time in Sucre are also included.

lic, and Trinidad, even Costa Rica and Honduras, and many settled in Colombia, especially along the Río Magdalena and the Caribbean coast, the main settings for García Márquez's novels. As a result, Arab immigrant groups are as significant a part of the living population in these regions as they are in Gabriel García Márquez's narratives.

What the Near and Middle Easterners found in Colombia in the 1880s was an economically and socially backward periphery that forced upon them hard living conditions while also offering opportunities for social advancement. The strongest economic pillar of the immigrant groups that entered the country in several waves until the mid-twentieth century was trade of the sort that we find in the 'Street of Turks' (Calle de los Turcos) in García Márquez's Macondo. While, in *Chronicle of a Death Foretold*, García Márquez shifted the first Arab migrants' arrival to the initial years of the twentieth century, presumably for narrative reasons, the way in which he portrays the socioeconomic and cultural embeddedness of the population groups of Arab extraction carefully reflects the historical realities in Colombia. Incidentally, the waves of immigrants from Arab countries to Colombia ran dry shortly after the middle of the last century, when most of those migrants traveled to the USA and Canada instead.

The circumstances surrounding the appearance of *Chronicle of a Death Foretold* have been amply discussed. In 1981 Gabriel García Márquez dramatically broke his years of silence as a writer with this short five-part novel. He had maintained that silence of protest for the entire duration of the US-supported dictatorship of Augusto Pinochet who had come to power in Chile through a bloody coup on another September 11, that of 1973. Due to the carefully prepared international marketing strategy for the book, which involved a collaboration among four different publishing houses, the first print run totaled one and a half million copies worldwide. Promoting the novel's distinctive 'Latin Americanness' under the label of magical realism (realismo mágico) ensured that its reception would focus on certain aspects: the central plot line of the murder in response to violated family honor;[21] the blood wedding of a Latin American (Colombian) family tragedy invested with evangelical significance via the New Testament;[22] the importance of elements specific to the genres of criminal and de-

---

[21] See Stanislav Zimic: 'Pundonor calderoniano en Hispanoamérica (con ilustración en 'Crónica de una muerte anunciada' de García Márquez).' In: *Acta Neophilologica* XXXIV.1–2 (2001), p. 87–103.
[22] See Rubén Pelayo: 'Chronicle of a Death Foretold' (1981). In: Rubén Pelayo (ed.): *Gabriel García Márquez: A Critical Companion*. Westport, Conn.: Greenwood Press 2001, p. 111–113.

tective novels;[23] and the ways in which the complex structural arrangement of this narrative contributes to its suspense.[24] In these readings of *Chronicle*, the layers of meaning related to the text's ArabAmerican dimension, on which I elaborate below, were largely eclipsed.

The novel's central narrative filament, which García Márquez creates by opening the story *in medias res* and developing it piece by piece through an elaborate sequence of prolepses and analepses, revolves around the fact that the filthy-rich newcomer Bayardo San Román wants to take Angela Vicario as his bride. He forces her to marry him, arranges a lavish wedding to which the entire town is invited, and then returns the bride to her family on the wedding night because she is presumably no longer a virgin. On the morning of her 'rejection,' the apostolically named brothers Pedro and Pablo avenge this family disgrace, by now common knowledge in the town, with the blood of the man whom Angela Vicario names as the supposed perpetrator: Santiago Nasar. The ArabAmerican element – that is, the complex relations between Arab and American worlds – plays a key role in this novel which, thanks to the bundling of its narrative threads, cannot hide its penchant for portraying the 'unheard-of event.' Although this element pervades the entire text and plays a pivotal role, it has received at best minimal attention in academic scholarship. When acknowledged at all, passing references to certain characters' Arab roots have typically been deemed quite sufficient. After all, the enigmatic structure of this *Chronicle of a Death Foretold* seems to be associated mainly with the (no doubt also important) thematic areas I mention above.

Yet, already the first sentence, one of the most famous incipits not only in Latin American literature, includes several references that point to ArabAmerican meanings: 'On the day they were going to kill him, Santiago Nasar got up at five-thirty in the morning to wait for the boat the bishop was coming on.'[25] The very name of the protagonist, whose murder is at the center of the novel's plot and temporal structure, refers to an ArabAmerican isotopy insofar as the two components of his name are of Spanish, that is, Western-Christian, *and* Arab

---

23 See Hubert Pöppel: 'Elementos del género policíaco en la obra de Gabriel García Márquez'. In: *Estudios de Literatura Colombiana* 4 (1999), p. 23–46.

24 For a detailed narratological and intermedial analysis of the novel and its translation into film, see Sabine Schlicker's *Verfilmtes Erzählen Narratologisch-komparative Untersuchung zu 'El beso de la mujer araña' (Manuel Puig / Héctor Babenco) und 'Crónica de una muerte anunciada' (Gabriel García Márquez / Francesco Rosi)*. Frankfurt am Main: Vervuert 1997, p. 280–373.

25 García Márquez: *Chronicle*, p. 3; 'El día en que lo iban a matar, Santiago Nasar se levantó a las 5.30 de la mañana para esperar el buque en que llegaba el obispo.' García Márquez: *Crónica*, p. 9.

provenance. The spelling of the last name draws attention to the fact that the Arab name has been Hispanicized and adapted to the writing habits of Spanish-speaking countries. At the same time, the wait for the expected arrival of the bishop, who, accompanied by his 'Spaniards,' will bless the harbor and the city from the river boat but, contrary to the hopes of the city's residents, will not actually set foot there, points to the distinctly Catholic religious affiliation of the protagonist who is presumably from a Christian Arab family. This affiliation resonates with the especially high percentage of Christian migrants from the Near and Middle East, while at the same time indicating the pressure the local population placed on the migrants to adapt, which certainly played a role in this ostensible profession of the Catholic faith. Luis Fayad had by no means forgotten these components in his successful fashioning of his own arrival scene, in which he has his border official, who knows the answers to expect from the Arab immigrants, ask dourly, 'What is your religion? I know very well that you will tell me that you are Christians even though that is untrue.'[26] The religious distrust that the local population has of the new arrivals of Arab (that is, 'Turkish') extraction forces the latter into an exaggerated practice of Catholicism.

Interspersed with the individual strands of the story are enduring elements that amalgamate into this novel's deceptively simple narrative structure the history of immigration not only of the family but of Arab groups more broadly. The publicly proclaimed murder that the Vicario brothers commit, killing Santiago Nasar because their sister Angela holds him responsible for her lost virginity, tears open again ethno-cultural lines of conflict that we can identity in the characters' everyday lives only through precise detective work. The unprompted reactions to the bloody deed offer an important hint at these concealed, if by no means invisible, conflict zones and group memberships. Even after the wedding party is over, Pedro and Pablo Vicario continue to celebrate lightheartedly and fraternally not only with the narrator but also with Santiago Nasar. But when, after murdering Nasar, they are pursued by a 'group of roused-up Arabs' (grupo de árabes enardecidos), they duck as quickly as possible into a church.[27] Even in the almost lovingly prepared jail in their hometown, in which at first they feel 'safe from the Arabs' (a salvo de los árabes), Pablo Vicario still fears that his incessantly urinating brother Pedro might have been poisoned by the Turks' evil tricks (vainas de los turcos).[28] Fearing attacks, Colonel Aponte, the town's

---

26 '¿Qué religión tienen ustedes? Ya sé que me van a decir que son cristianos aunque no sea verdad.' Fayad: *La caída*, p. 86.
27 García Márquez: *Crónica*, p. 79; *Chronicle*, p. 48.
28 García Márquez: *Crónica*, p. 127 and 129; *Chronicle*, p. 79–80.

mayor, temporarily harbors the brothers in his own home, until the investigating magistrate transfers them to the prison in neighboring Riohacha.[29] The widespread fear of violent retaliations by the 'Turks' is a clear indication of existing multicultural fault lines and fissures.

Instilled with the knowledge of local life, the homodiegetic narrator knows just as well as the town mayor does that the twin brothers' fear (*terror*) of attacks parallels the perception on the street, that is, by the general population who continues to fear 'revenge by the Arabs' (una represalia de los árabes).[30] The townspeople are less concerned about poison than about the possibility that the Arabs might drench prison and prisoners with gasoline at night and set them ablaze. What indications are there for this? Are these the contours of a 'clash of cultures'? The narrator attempts to mollify and calm his readers:

The Arabs comprised a community of peaceful immigrants who had settled at the beginning of the century in Caribbean towns, even in the poorest and most remote, and there remained, selling colored cloth and bazaar trinkets. They were clannish, hard-working, and Catholic. They married among themselves, imported their wheat, raised lambs in their yards, and grew oregano and eggplants, and playing cards was their only driving passion. The older ones continued speaking the rustic Arabic they had brought from their homeland, and they maintained it intact in the family down to the second generation, but those of the third, with the exception of Santiago Nasar, listened to their parents in Arabic and answered them in Spanish. So it was inconceivable that they would suddenly abandon their pastoral spirit to avenge a death for which we all could have been to blame.[31]

The history of Arab immigration in the Caribbean region, sketched here in a few lines, projects the image of a minority with close linguistic, onomastic, cultural, economic, and matrimonial bonds. Their cultural orientation and socio-

---

29 See García Márquez: *Crónica*, p. 129; *Chronicle*, p. 80.

30 García Márquez: *Crónica*, p. 130; *Chronicle*, p. 81.

31 García Márquez: *Chronicle*, 81. 'Los árabes constituían una comunidad de inmigrantes pacíficos que se establecieron a principios del siglo en los pueblos del Caribe, aun en los más remotos y pobres, y allí se quedaron vendiendo trapos de colores y baratijas de feria. Eran unidos, laboriosos y católicos. Se casaban entre ellos, importaban su trigo, criaban corderos en los patios y cultivaban el orégano y la berenjena, y su única pasión tormentosa eran los juegos de barajas. Los mayores siguieron hablando el árabe rural que trajeron de su tierra, y lo conservaron intacto en familia hasta la segunda generación, pero los de la tercera, con la excepción de Santiago Nasar, les oían a sus padres en árabe y les contestaban en castellano. De modo que no era concebible que fueran a alterar de pronto su espíritu pastoral para vengar una muerte cuyos culpables podíamos ser todos.' García Márquez: *Crónica*, p. 130.

economic integration do not, in the eyes of the narrator, make it seem likely that they, as a group, would take revenge for the murder of one of their own, an act for which, the narrator admits, not only the Vicario brothers but ultimately all of the town's residents are responsible in a certain sense, or at least share responsibility. Even the suspicious fears of the seasoned Colonel Aponte, that a bloody culture war might be about to erupt in his little town, are allayed once and for all when he visits each of the Arab families in town and is able to establish that they are mourning rather than harboring any plans for revenge.[32] What's more, even those who had pursued the murderers right after the bloody deed, carried out in the midst of people who had witnessed the murder without doing anything to prevent it, dispute that they had ever intended to take the murderers' lives. The hundred-year-old Suseme Abdala even sends the Vicario brothers a special medicinal tea to help allay Pedro Vicario's suffering. The Arab, or better, ArabAmerican community takes pains to send out signs of reconciliation and to return to a peaceful coexistence, as if nothing had ever disturbed this peace. In García Márquez's Caribbean microcosm, the danger of a 'clash of civilizations' that the residents of non-Arab extraction fear is thus dispelled, at least on the side of the *turcos*. In the events surrounding Santiago Nasar's murder, 'the Arabs,' or 'Turks,' may well be portrayed as a potentially dangerous group and kept under surveillance by the government; but they obviously present no threat to peaceful coexistence.

The Arab immigrants are of course but one part of the heterogeneous population: *Chronicle of a Death Foretold* also includes references to Spaniards, Catalonians, freebooters, other groups of European immigrants, and, above all, former slaves who had been stolen from Africa. Just a few hours before his death, Santiago Nasar shows the narrator and the Vicario brothers at the newlyweds' house a flickering light near Cartagena de Indias, supposedly marking the place in the Caribbean Sea where a slave ship from Senegal sank long ago and where the unredeemed souls of the slaves appear to this day.[33] A centuries-old migratory hub with all its horrors and its wealth, the Caribbean is omnipresent.

The ethno-cultural heterogeneity of the population on the Caribbean coast, and not only Colombia's, is a part of the Caribbean universe. At the same time, however, it is clear in this novel that the Arab immigrant families, even in the third generation, are still recognizable as an independent group and are perceived as such 'from the outside.' It is thus worth looking more closely at the literary representations of these Colombians of Arab extraction. Is Santiago Nasar's

---

32 See García Márquez: *Crónica*, p. 131; *Chronicle*, p. 82.
33 See García Márquez: *Crónica*, p. 108; *Chronicle*, p. 67.

belonging to this group, as most research so far has assumed, really of only marginal importance?

Lines of conflict in the ArabAmerican context: Clash of genders and clash of cultures?

Within an immigrant society – and there is no question that Colombia was an immigrant society during the second half of the nineteenth century and the first half of the twentieth – Arab immigrants constitute but one migrant group, albeit a visible one, in the Caribbean. Their marriage practice in particular shows a distinctly *multi*cultural pattern of behavior within a parallel social sphere which confirms the 'coexistence' of different (ethno)-cultural groups and anchors its own future in an ArabAmerican genealogy. Santiago Nasar, too, follows the rules of the game which this group observes for the most part. After having been initiated into the arts of carnal love by the seductive brothel owner in his youth, he always keeps an eye out for sexual dalliances with other women, just as his father did with girls of inferior social status such as Victoria Guzmán. When it comes to his own marriage, however, only a girl of Arab extraction will do. He therefore unconditionally accepts the contract his parents made years ago with the parents of his future – and by no means beloved – wife Flora Miguel.[34] One cannot overlook here the predominant patriarchal traits that remain unchallenged within the ArabAmerican community. They even regulate the way men behave toward each other. The male community members' escapades are blithely tolerated. Nahir Miguel, the father of the bride and uncontested ruler in his home, is the first to sense the danger threatening his future son-in-law. He offers Santiago Nasar in Arabic either to hide him in his house or to arm him with his rifle so that he is not defenseless before the Vicario brothers. In contrast to his daughter, the seemingly imperious man who wraps himself in his 'Bedouin caftan' (chilaba de beduino) in his home but not on the street, never once calls into question the contracted marriage of the ethnically Arab couple.[35] The patriarchal dominance constitutes a largely stable, secure, and insular sphere that defines the rules of marriage to which the women must submit, even if doing so leaves Flora Miguel, after Santiago Nasar's murder, desperate enough to throw

---

34 See García Márquez: *Crónica*, p. 178; *Chronicle*, p. 111.
35 See García Márquez: *Crónica*, p. 181; *Chronicle*, p. 13.

herself at a 'lieutenant of the border patrol' (teniente de fronteras) who later has her working for him as a prostitute.[36]

Santiago's father, Ibrahim Nasar, also embodies the patriarchal type in his family. As the narrator recounts, Ibrahim had come to the village with the last Arabs at the end of the civil war[37] and rebuilt the warehouse on the main square, which had fallen into disuse because large ships could no longer put in at an inland river port choked with sand. He was able to use to his advantage the fundamental economic changes implied here, establishing a cattle hacienda and ascending to the town's ruling class. Within just a few years his societal integration appears successful. The Nasars are respected in the ArabAmerican community and in the structure of the town as a whole, enjoying power and influence. Next to Bayardo San Román, who had arrived a few months before his wedding with Angela Vicario for unknown reasons, Santiago is considered the indisputably best match in town. Does this not amount to a t story of perfect social integration?

To his son, with whom he is very close, Ibrahim Nasar speaks Arabic; when Santiago's mother is present, they switch to Spanish so that she is not excluded.[38] Santiago feels drawn to both parents, but his phenotype is clearly 'branded' as Arabic: the slim, pale man who has just turned twenty-one possesses 'his father's Arab eyelids and curly hair.'[39] Several Orientalisms, always patrilineal with reference to the father, are scattered throughout the text as if they were markers of identity. It is, after all, his father who teaches Santiago how to handle firearms, to hunt with falcons, to love horses, and instils in him bravery and caution: 'From his father he learned at a very early age the manipulation of firearms, his love for horses, and the mastery of high-flying birds of prey, but from him he also learned the goods arts of valor and prudence.'[40] Given the example of his father, it is no surprise that Victoria Guzmán wants to spare her daughter Divina Flor the fate she once suffered at the hands of Ibrahim Nasar: to be used as a sexual object, then demoted to domestic servant while another takes on the position of official (although unloved) wife. When Santiago Nasar reaches for her beautiful daughter on the morning of his death, as he always does as if out

---

36 See García Márquez: *Crónica*, p. 156; *Chronicle*, p. 97.
37 See García Márquez: *Crónica*, p. 21; *Chronicle*, p. 11.
38 See García Márquez: *Crónica*, p. 16; *Chronicle*, p. 7.
39 García Márquez: *Chronicle*, p. 7. '[L]os párpados árabes y los cabellos rizados de su padre.' *Crónica*, p. 15.
40 García Márquez: *Chronicle*, p. 7. '[D]e su padre aprendió desde muy niño el dominio de las armas de fuego, el amor por los caballos y la maestranza de las aves de presas altas, pero de él aprendió también las buenas artes del valor y la prudencia.' *Crónica*, p. 16.

of habit, Victoria, long since aware that Angela Vicario's brothers are lying in wait for Santiago with their knives, threatens the 'white one' (*blanco*) with a sharp kitchen knife.[41] She uses this knife to cut open a hare whose entrails she throws to the dogs a short while later. Santiago Nasar will collapse in this very same kitchen, with his belly cut open and intestines oozing out, only few hours after that. This *mise-en-abyme* of the entire plot makes clear that there is a direct connection between Santiago Nasar's violent death and the presence of his deceased Arab father, both in his physical appearance and in the sexual relations the latter practiced. It would appear that the gender relations in this tragedy, whose seeming inevitability is a function of the hierarchical relations between men and women, constitute an intermediary plane where the lines of cultural conflict burst open and imperil peaceful coexistence.

First, it is important to note that multicultural coexistence does not obtain on the plane of gender relations. At the very latest, Santiago Nasar's designation as 'blanco' draws our attention to the fact that this is not marriage behavior characteristic of the ArabAmerican community. Instead, we are confronted with gender-specific patterns of behavior and ways of life which Santiago Nasar, through his machismo, shares with the overwhelming majority of the male population in Colombia, where he was born. In his 'whiteness' also resonates social differentiation, that is, his belonging to a white aristocratic class and caste of leaders. While Santiago Nasar's cultural background may be more complex than that of the village's other residents, he is nevertheless ensnared in the world of patriarchal values he shares with Bayardo San Román, the Vicario brothers, and the narrator. His patriarchal father's Arab-American influence cuts across the macho behavior patterns shared by the entire population of this small town on the Caribbean coast of Colombia. The overwhelming majority of the townsfolk cover up Santiago Nasar's murder, announced countless times and not prevented countless times, which takes place execution-style in the main square in front of everyone and in broad daylight[42] in a subversion or parody of the lock-

---

41 García Márquez: *Chronicle*, p. 9. Victoria's daughter knows that, very soon—if only temporarily—she is destined for Santiago Nasar's bed: 'she knew that she was destined for Santiago Nasar's furtive bed.' *Chronicle*, p. 10. '[S]se sabía destinada a la cama furtiva de Santiago Nasar.' *Crónica*, p. 19.

42 See the application of this concept to Leonardo Sciascia's novel *The Day of the Owl* (*Il giorno della civetta*), where the murder takes place not in some hidden place, but, like in *Chronicle of a Death Foretold* right at the beginning of the text on the main square and in the morning light, in Albrecht Buschmann: *Die Macht und ihr Preis: Detektorisches Erzählen bei Leonardo Sciascia und Manuel Vázquez Montalbán*. Würzburg: Königshausen & Neumann 2005, p. 57. Despite all

ed-room puzzle.⁴³ At the level of gender relations, Santiago Nasar, by crossing different (gender) cultures, participates *transculturally* in the situation that turns Bayardo San Román, Santiago Nasar, and the Vicario twins into the protagonists of a tragedy in which they are at once perpetrators and victims. The son of an Arab migrant and a Spanish-speaking mother, Santiago Nasar does not represent a detachable alterity but an Other *within* his own self which cannot be ascribed either to self or to other, nor even to a space between them. Even if he himself remains unaware of it even to the moment of his death, he embodies an interWorld that has no spatial location; rather, it is constituted by movements between different poles which can be ascertained but not arrested. Such movements also pose the need to modify the concept of strangeness that one of Elias Khoury's narrators uses when he comments on Santiago Nasar's death: 'He [Santiago] experienced the strangeness at the instant of death, in that solitude which led him into spheres whose existence he had not thought possible.'⁴⁴ In the play between identity and difference, between Latin American and Arab worlds, Santiago Nasar stands for the complicated entanglements and interconnectedness within the ArabAmerican, in whose interWorlds foreignness and familiarity fuse.

The men's gender-specific enmeshments mirror, in reverse hierarchy, the situation of the women who play their own culturally contingent role within the gender struggles in *Chronicle of a Death Foretold*. The youngest daughter of a family living in humble circumstances, Angela Vicario is representative of this mirroring reversal.⁴⁵ Her father, Poncio Vicario, loses his sight while working as 'poor man's goldsmith' (orfebre de pobres),⁴⁶ and the resulting precariousness of the family's economic situation is what makes it possible for Bayardo San Román to use his money quite literally to 'buy' the bride he happens to see one day and immediately desires. The bride's upbringing, the responsibility of her mother, Purísima del Carmen, is always divided along gender lines and includes

---

diegetic and plot-specific differences, the parallels between the novels of Sciascia and García Márquez are obvious.

43 Prudencia Cotes, the fiancée of one of the two murders later deposes that she never would have married Pablo Vicario had he not acted as he did to save the family honor; as it was, she waited patiently for three years until Santiago Nasar's murderer was released before tying the knot. See García Márquez: *Crónica*, p. 102; *Chronicle*, p. 63.

44 Elias Khoury: *Der geheimnisvolle Brief*. Munich: C.H. Beck 2000, p. 45 [No English-langue translation available as yet. TN]

45 In the sociocultural and gender-specific sense, the Vicario family, in keeping with its name, would be a family of vicars, of 'representatives.'

46 See García Márquez: *Crónica*, p. 50; *Chronicle*, p. 30.

the strict sexual surveillance of the daughters to preserve the family honor: 'The brothers were brought up to be men. The girls had been reared to be married.'[47] No wonder, then, that the narrator's mother firmly believes that these women will make their husbands happy; they were, after all, 'raised to suffer' from the day they were born.[48] Angela's marriage to Bayardo is thus based on a double hierarchy that takes into account gender relations and socioeconomic situation. The bride's plays no role in this, for 'love can be learned too.'[49]

Nothing in the novel reasonably suggests that Santiago Nasar is actually responsible for Angela's lost virginity. The maternal supervision of the girl outside the home was flawless; nor could the investigating magistrate on the case find any indications in Santiago's life. The narrator himself alleges that Santiago was much too 'haughty' even to notice the girl, and. more importantly, makes us aware that they belonged to 'two completely different worlds' (dos mundos divergentes).[50] This remark of course raises the question as to which of the different worlds are at issue here. Neither the residents of the town nor academic scholars have tired of proposing the most widely diverging theories about Angela's lost virginity. Might the narrator himself be responsible, so that his spinning of the detective yarn would ultimately amount to nothing but a perfect deception to divert any suspicion from himself?[51] Why, then, to counter this argument, should he refer to the difference of the worlds of Angela and Santiago? If he were indeed the perpetrator, it would be in his interest to exonerate himself and cast a negative light on Santiago. One might also consider that much in the context of the obvious patriarchal gender domination speaks for the fact that Angela might have become the victim of sexual coercion or rape within the family itself, especially since her father Poncio's blindness, with regard to Oedipus, suggests at least a proximity to the violation of the incest taboo in mythical and literary history.[52] Yet Angela Vicario, too, is both victim and perpetrator. No

---

47 García Márquez: *Chronicle*, p. 31. 'Los hermanos fueron criados para ser hombres. Ellas habían sido educadas para casarse.' *Crónica*, p. 51.
48 García Márquez: *Crónica*, p. 52; *Chronicle*, p. 31.
49 García Márquez: *Chronicle*, p. 35. 'También el amor se aprende.' *Crónica*, p. 56.
50 García Márquez: *Crónica*, p. 144; *Chronicle*, p. 89–90.
51 This reading appears to be indebted to an idea by Angel Rama; see Armando Silva: 'Encuadre y punto de vista: Saber y goce en *Crónica de una muerte anunciada*'. In: Universidad Nacional de Colombia and the Instituto Caro y Cuervo (ed.): *XX Congreso nacional de Literatura, Lingüística y Semiótica. Memorias. 'Cien años de Soledad,' treinta años después*. Bogotá: Universidad Nacional de Colombia 1998, p. 23.
52 What also speaks for this is Angela's comment on the death of her father shortly after Santiago Nasar's murder: 'His moral pain carried him off' (Se lo llevó la pena moral).' García Már-

sooner has she identified Santiago Nasar as the guilty party that her brothers, pig butchers by profession, grab their knives. Why does Angela name Ibrahim Nasar's son? Perhaps because, so the speculation in the novel goes, she could not count on her brothers to attack a rich man who possesses great wealth? Do Angela and Santiago belong to two different worlds in this economic sense? Do not the 'two completely different worlds' also carry cultural inflections? When, at the end of the second of five chapters, or acts, of this tragedy, her brother Pedro interrogates Angela, who has been abused by her furious mother, her answer comes astonishingly quickly:

> She only took the time necesary to say the name. She looked for it in the shadows, she found it at first sight among the many, many easily confused names from this world and the other, and she nailed it to the wall with her well-aimed dart, a butterfly with no will whose sentence has always been written.
> 'Santiago Nasar,' she said.[53]

Although the death sentence for Santiago Nasar is as quick as it is unexpected, it was already written, had always been a certainty. Is it the ruse of the unconscious or of fate – as the investigating magistrate believes[54] – or perhaps of a kismet that humans cannot be direct but only interpret in keeping with divine will? Either way, Angela's answer materializes with the same suddenness and directness as her brothers' fears that the Arabs might poison them and the residents' worries that the Arabs might roast the Vicario brothers alive. No less abrupt is the reaction of Yamil Shaium, the Arab shopkeeper who laughs about an Arabic pun with Santiago Nasar just a few moments before the latter's death, in grabbing his big-game rifle to chase after the two murderers, supported by other, albeit unarmed Arabs. Pedro and Pablo Vicario seek refuge in the sanctuary

---

quez: *Crónica*, p. 83; *Chronicle*, p. 133. See especially Elena Rahona / Stephanie Sieburth: 'Keeping Crime Unsolved: Characters' and Critics' Responses to Incest in García Márquez' *Crónica de una muerte anunciada.*' In: *Revista de Estudios Hispánicos* 30 (1996), p. 433–459. Also Pöppel: 'Elementos,' p. 36; and Silva: 'Encuadre,' p. 21.

53 García Márquez: *Chronicle*, p. 47. 'Ella se demoró apenas el tiempo necesario para decir el nombre. Lo buscó en las tinieblas, lo encontró a primera vista entre los tantos y tantos nombres confundibles de este mundo y del otro, y lo dejó clavado en la pared con su dardo certero, como a una mariposa sin albedrío cuya sentencia estaba escrita desde siempre. —Santiago Nasar —dijo.' *Crónica*, p. 78.

54 See García Márquez: *Crónica*, p. 180; *Chronicle*, p. 113. There, the investigating magistrate notes with red ink: 'Fatality makes us invisible' (La fatalidad nos hace invisibles). Names and persons appear as out of nowhere and suddenly become invisible again, as if they were obeying a predetermined fate.

of the church, retracing the diagonal track of death that a revolver bullet carved into the town's geometry years ago when a shot inadvertently fired from Ibrahim Nasar's pistol crossed the main square on which his son would to be stabbed to death and reduced to rubble a life-sized statue of a saint on the high altar of the Catholic Church on the opposite side.[55] Just seconds before the two brothers' lethal attack, a bystander calls out to the unarmed Santiago Nasar that the 'Turk' should take a different path.[56] Immediately before his death, then, the son of Arab immigrants turns from 'blanco' back to 'turco,' from white landed proprietor to Oriental migrant. As if in response, Santiago Nasar appears more handsome than ever in the face of death, with his 'Saracen face with its dashing ringlets.'[57] The public execution and death in front of everybody changes Santiago, oft-admired for his almost magical talent for disguising himself, into a Saracen, an Arab.[58]

In the fraction of a second, it seems, sociocultural demarcation lines are activated, along with their associated mechanisms of exclusion and inclusion; nothing much has changed even in the third generation, despite the Arab migrants' attempts to adapt to the local population. No matter that Ibrahim Nasar ostentatiously baptizes his cattle ranch 'The Divine Face' (*Divino Rostro*),[59] and no matter how much Santiago Nasar is able to donate to the bishop, whose ring he wants to kiss: in the eyes of those who do not have roots in the Near and Middle East, the group of 'Arabs,' like their migrant ancestors before them, always remain 'Turks.' Even if these 'Arabs' have no intention of committing the atrocities of which they are believed capable, hidden underneath the seemingly smooth surface of coexistence are nevertheless fault lines of conflict between the Spanish speakers and the speakers of Spanish *and* Arabic, rifts that can break open at any time. It is worth recalling here that the apostle Santiago, the 'true James' of all pilgrim legends on a still Arab-influenced Iberian peninsula,

---

55 García Márquez: *Chronicle*, p. 6; *Crónica*, 13.The narrator adds that Santiago Nasar would remember this lesson for the rest of his life; from then on he always kept his weapons separate from his ammunition.
56 García Márquez: *Crónica*, p. 184; *Chronicle*, p. 115.
57 García Márquez: *Chronicle*, p. 120. '[R]ostro de sarraceno con los rizos alborotados.' *Crónica*, p. 192.
58 García Márquez: *Crónica*, p. 106; *Chronicle*, p. 65.
59 Despite the narrator's protestations to the contrary, this name might also be read as an indication that Divina Flor, Victoria Guzmán's daughter, is also Ibrahim Nasar's child. Then, of course, a connection between Santiago and her would be an unwitting violation of the incest taboo.

was the patron saint of the Spaniards in the *reconquista*'s fight against the Saracens.

From the middle of the novel onward, Orientalisms, that is, textual elements attributable to a specifically 'Arabic' isotopy, proliferate in unexpected places. Two examples will suffice. First, the investigating magistrate discovers that one of the pig butchers' two murder weapons a kind of 'miniature scimitar' (alfanje en miniatura).[60] When the narrator attempts to forget the horror by visiting the brothel's Madame María Alejandrina Cervantes after Santiago Nasar's funeral, he finds the high-class prostitute absorbed in the work of mourning: as always when she is grieving, she stuffs herself with unimaginable amounts of food, sitting in front of her 'Babylonic platter' (platón babilónico) completely naked, 'squatting like a Turkish houri' [a la turca] on her queenly bed.'[61] It is as if the woman with the great erotic aura, who had held the youthful Santiago Nasar so spellbound that his father once had to banish him to the hacienda for a time, is becoming-Oriental. She is so 'Orientalized' that she has to halt her attempts as a professional 'beast of love' (bestia de amor) to abduct the love-hungry narrator to the land of ingenious sex acts when she still detects on her lover the dreadful stink of the Santiago Nasar's body, cruelly cut open and quickly decaying.[62]

Let us not forget that the perspective of the narrator, to whom the stench of his dead friend's decay still clings, is not an 'objective' position. While his mother, Luisa Santiaga, is Santiago Nasar's godmother and the person after whom he was named, the narrator himself is clearly not one of the 'Turks.' Between the time of the story and the time when he tells it, however, he marries into an Arab-American family, reporting to us outright that, in the middle of Bayardo and Angela's turbulent wedding party, he proposed to Mercedes Barcha, fresh out of primary school and not yet of age. That his later wife would remind him of this proposal fourteen years later is a sly autobiographical flash that at once frictionalizes the position of the text-internal narrator with that of the text-external, real author, Gabriel García Márquez. As an only seemingly unimportant biographical snippet, the fade-in of the real author's wife flags his position as a Colombian of non-Arab descent who married a Colombian from an Arab immigrant family. Although it may appear idle at first glance, the question of how this *Chro-*

---

[60] García Márquez: *Chronicle*, p. 58–59. The narrator explains that no German knives could be imported at the time because of the war. *Crónica*, p. 95.
[61] García Márque: *Chronicle*, p. 77; *Crónica*, p. 124.
[62] García Márquez: *Crónica*, p. 125; *Chronicle*, p. 78.

nicle of a Death Foretold might have turned out, had it been presented to us by an 'Arab' narrator is still compelling.

Santiago Nasar's murder from a Lebanese perspective

The Lebanese writer Elias Khoury, born in Beirut in 1948 to a Greek Orthodox family, offers a host of possible answers to this question. His 1994 novel, 'The Mysterious Letter' (Arabic: *Majma' al-asrar*), a title that would literally translate as 'A collection of secrets,'[63] refers explicitly to García Márquez's *Chronicle of a Death Foretold* on multiple occasions, shrewdly drawing attention to the observer's altered position in relation to the characters of the Colombian intertext. Comprised of several self-contained short stories told by different narrators and intricately woven together into a whole, Khoury's narrative does in fact formulate a number of possible literary answers, or at least different techniques of narrating from an Arab perspective. The transareal shift in perspective, which leaves the Latin American cultural area, is signaled in several ways. For instance, Santiago Nasar's description in *Chronicle* as a slim, pale young man with 'Arabic eyebrows' and 'his father's curly hair' is cited verbatim and associated with the appearance of a certain Ibrahim Nasar in Beirut, whose lover Norma describes him for her girlfriends from school. Norma, however, as we find out, 'did not speak of 'Arabic eyebrows,' because she was Arab herself.'[64] In this way, the internal Arab perspective not only of the unhappy lover but also of the entire novel with the various positions of its narrators is labeled quite clearly. 'The Mysterious Letter,' then, contains a message for García Márquez – and for his readers.

What is the relationship between 'The Mysterious Letter' and *Chronicle of a Death Foretold*? Elias Khoury's novel, too, starts with a puzzle: In Beirut, the greengrocer Ibrahim Nasar is found dead in his bed, while his lover, discovered half-naked in a closet, screams and cries that she is lost, for the man who had

---

63 [There is as yet no translation of this novel into any European languages. TN] See the fine survey by Friederike Pannewick: 'Elias Khoury.' In: Heinz Ludwig Arnold (ed.): *Kritisches Lexikon zur fremdsprachigen Gegenwartsliteratur*. Munich: edition text+kritik 2001. See also the detailed interview with Elias Khoury in Sonja Mejcher: *Geschichten über Geschichten: Erinnerung im Romanwerk von Ilyas Huri*. Wiesbaden: Reichert Verlag 2001, p. 125–153, and Stefan G. Meyer: 'The patchwork novel: Elias Khoury.' In: Stefan G. Meyer (ed.): *The Experimental Arabic Novel: Postcolonial Literary Modernism in the Levant*. New York SUNY Press 2001, p. 129–140.
64 Khoury: *Der geheimnisvolle Brief*, p. 37 [All page references are to the German translation of this novel. TN]

promised her matrimony and had deflowered her could now no longer marry her and save her from destitution. The text, which plays with elements of a detective novel just as García Márquez's *Chronicle* does, features the shared surname, to which I will return below, and an overall mystery plot, in addition to a series of crossings that, at first glance, concern connections between murder and love, lost virginity, and gender relations dominated by patriarchy. Because Khoury weaves the intertextual threads between the two, short novels of similar length skillfully and tightly, it is no surprise that *The Mysterious Letter* also poses the central questions of *Chronicle of a Death Foretold*:

> Everyone knew that Santiago was to be slaughtered this morning. Why didn't anyone warn him? Perhaps because they did not believe it, as they maintained. Or did they let him walk into a certain death because he was an Arab? Why was the immigrant Lebanese, who spoke Arabic although his mother had not mastered this language, allowed to die in this brutal manner? ...Because he was a stranger? Does foreignness mean death?[65]

The already mentioned shift in perspective becomes apparent in the way in which these questions are formulated. They first ask about a possible relationship between the murder and the victim's Arab, or Lebanese, origins, while at the same moving foreignness – certainly the main issue in all of Khoury's work – to a central positon. As a 'stranger in a strange land,' Santiago Nasar not only went into raptures over the local cockscomb soup but also, like his father, preferred to eat cooked yogurt and to drink tequila as arak liquor.[66] A strategy of writing takes form here: Elias Khoury's novel picks up on the Arab elements of the Latin American text, intensifies them, and develops them further from a transareal perspective. Reading and writing, that is, the reading of a foreign text and the writing of one's own novel, go hand in hand here. The Lebanese author claims that he discovered for himself very early on that reading is a way of writing, and writing a way of reading.[67]

With his fine literary sensibilities, Elias Khoury tried to pick up the threads of the Arab (or Oriental) elements I discuss above and weave these into a dense network of relations that links the two novels. Each of the partial stories, introduced with the opening formula 'The story started like this,'[68] sheds a different light on the enigmatic plot of the novel itself, and often also on that of the 'foreign' novel. In this way, the 'collection of secrets' that the Arabic title announc-

---

65 Khoury: *Der geheimnisvolle Brief*, p. 37.
66 Khoury: *Der geheimnisvolle Brief*, p. 38.
67 Elias Khoury in Mejcher: *Geschichten über Geschichten*, p. 131.
68 Khoury: *Der geheimnisvolle Brief*, p. 5.

es does in fact emerge. The mysteries inter-illuminate each other. It is no coincidence that the violence committed against Santiago Nasar in *Chronicle of a Death Foretold* reminds one of the narrators of the reports of Santiago's father Ibrahim Nasar, who spoke 'about the violence and the bloodbaths in the distant village with an unpronounceable name.'[69] The link thus created at the novel's start further unfolds in one of the complexly interwoven partial stories at the end.

Many long years ago, when Ibrahim Nasar was only ten years old, a letter had voiced the death of a distant relative in Colombia, dealing a blow to all emigration plans of the relatives still remaining in Lebanon, including Ibrahim himself. Evidently, this letter, which Ibrahim was never to see, instilled the fear in everyone that they might be persecuted as Arabs in Colombia and cruelly slaughtered just as Santiago Nasar was. Disappointed by life, Ibrahim years later tracks his own family history, hoping to find not only the oft-invoked gold treasure, but also the no less legendary letter from distant Colombia:

> Besides, he believed he would come upon that mysterious letter with the news of Santiago Nasar's death, about which the Colombian author Gabriel García Márquez was later to write, as if he were depicting the murder of Abd al-Djalil on the square in Ain Kisrin during the horrible bloodbath of 1860. As if he were depicting how Abd al-Djalil Nasar reeled under the blows of the short scimitars for an entire hour, how he tried to pick up his guts, which spilled out on to the ground, collapsed on top of them and died.[70]

Here, additional relationships between the two novels become apparent. The mysterious letter that relayed the news of Nasar's death to Lebanon *corresponds* with a no-less-mysterious document in *Chronicle of a Death Foretold*, where an unknown man, whose identity never could be ascertained, stuck under the door of Santiago Nasar's house an envelope with a written warning. This letter contained detailed information about the impending murder, the reasons the perpetrators gave, the murderers themselves, and the planned location of the crime.[71] Like all the other inhabitants of the house, Santiago had simply overlooked the envelope lying on the ground, which was not found until after his murder. These two mysterious letters, each of which announces Santiago Nasar's death in the respective novels, merge two massacres that are temporally and spatially quite separate, such that the description of one slaughter can serve very well to depict the other. Through this merging, settings in the mid-

---

69 Khoury: *Der geheimnisvolle Brief*, p. 37.
70 Khoury: *Der geheimnisvolle Brief*, p. 195.
71 García Márquez: *Crónica*, p. 26; *Chronicle*, p. 14.

nineteenth and the mid-twentieth centuries, together with a village in Lebanon and a small town on the Caribbean coast of Colombia, become transtemporally and translocally congruent. The Lebanese author also does not neglect to 'anticipate' temporally the 'Arab' murder weapon the Colombian author brings into play in the form of the scimitars that the murderers in Lebanon use to commit their ghastly butchery. Behind one slaughter, another becomes visible as a kind of backdrop, whose bloodstain runs through history and through the stories. This concertinaing allows us to glimpse centuries of migration history, in which the hope for a stable, certain residence is time and again drowned in blood.

The intertextuality Elias Khoury creates can be characterized spatially as a transareal relation on a transcontinental scale. With respect to both locations – which are overlaid by even more locations of migration as the novel continues – this intertextuality is also translocal and rural.[72] In other words, the Lebanese author hooks his text into a Colombian author's highly successful novel, through which the Colombian interpretation opens up in both translocal and transareal directions. This also has repercussions for the how we understand García Márquez's text. At stake here is more than just the writing of a successive and preceding family history. Rather, Elias Khoury picks up on the elements of migration history in such a ingenious way that a transtemporal and transareal network of relations emerges in the translocal context. This network cuts diagonally across different time-frames and spaces, not only making Colombia and Lebanon appear as countries distant from one another, but also, in a vectoral sense, shifting the focus to the many complex *movements* between the two countries. Lebanon and Colombia are not simply the clearly distinct countries of origin and destination in a typical emigration history; due to a multitude of directly and indirectly networked communications, their relation is one of intimate exchanges. What happens in one country also affects the other.

The structural homologies illumined in this manner concern the omnipresence of violence, of slaughters and bloodbaths, of wars and civil wars, of flight and emigration, and of social, economic, and gender dependencies. In the context of their *areas*, moreover, both countries are linked through their colonial histories either with European hegemonic powers or the Ottoman Empire and the regional powers that ruled after its collapse, and they are marked by these asymmetrical relations. Cultural differences notwithstanding, the theme of lost

---

72 Elias Khoury establishes an analogous translocal, urban relation between the city planning reconstruction program in Beirut and the intensive construction activity in Berlin; see the Lebanese author's statements in Stefanie Borgmann: 'Städte sind wie Geschichten.' In: *Die Zeit* 45 (November 1, 1996), p. 80.

virginity the novels share also refers to the male-dominated gender relations that play a major role in the plot of both narratives. The transcontinental and transareal relation between the Middle East and the Caribbean emphasizes here the equivalent ways in which the potential for structural conflict manifests itself, especially in gender-specific and religio-cultural contexts. There are good reason, then, to speak of an ArabAmerican mesh of relations that makes any restriction to a purely national approach seem inadequate.

Yet, the central question, the riddle that runs through both novels, remains: How could the bloodbath happen in the first place? One of Elias Khoury's narrators notes that the village of Ain Kisrin had initially been unaffected by the massacres spreading in the Lebanon Mountains.[73] Everyone in the village continued on with everyday life, as if the altercations that had been erupting since 1858 and their horrific excesses simply did not exist. On February 12, 1860, however, the Abu Amer family was wiped out at the edge of the village. Immediately, 'the village divided itself into two families,' the Abu Amers and the Nasars, Druses and Catholics who had lived together well and peacefully until that time. Even though there had been 'no real reason' for hostilities[74] the knowledge-for-living-together that had stabilized relations for a long time despite the bloody battles between the Maronite church and Druse feudal rule surrounding the village, imploded within a short time. Unproven allegations that a priest from the Nasar family had been responsible for the massacre were enough for the men to slaughter each other with knives and send the village up in flames.

Places, times and cultural contexts will change, and unproven charges will continue to have devastating effects. The story of a man from the Nasar family who ran for miles with a knife in his back before collapsing and dying on the outskirts of Beirut foreshadows Santiago Nasar's final journey, as he is sliced open and brutally stabbed to death in his Colombian village. Stories, places, and temporalities overlap in this highly vectorized text: one bloodbath always predicts the next one. Memories 'rise to the surface as if oozing from an old, unhealed wound.'[75] And thus the Nasar family is not the only one to think about flight and emigration: 'Grandmother wanted to emigrate; everyone dreamed of emigrating; and the ships sailing for Marseille were crowded with people from the Western Bekaa Valley, from Zahle, and from the mountains.'[76]

---

73 Khoury: *Der geheimnisvolle Brief*, p. 159.
74 Khoury: *Der geheimnisvolle Brief*, p. 160.
75 Khoury: *Der geheimnisvolle Brief*, p. 161.
76 Khoury: *Der geheimnisvolle Brief*, p. 162.

Nasar's journey to Latin America via Marseille is thus in the offing. It is the same journey on which many Lebanese had had to embark since the devastating civil war of 1858–60 and about which a young Elias Khoury once wrote a study at the École Pratique des Hautes Études in Paris under the tutelage of Alain Touraine.[77] Although the colonial, or historical, constellations varied, it seemed as if the series of civil wars in Lebanon would never end: all the way to the self-destructive civil war that began in 1975 and left the country to hemorrhage for decades. Elias Khoury himself had participated in this war as a militant combatant and recorded his horrifying experiences in the novel *The Little Mountain*, first published in 1977 and translated into English in 1989.[78] No doubt, there is a structural connection between the experience of the Colombian *violencia* in Gabriel García Márquez's work and the battles of the Lebanese civil war in Elias Khoury's. Both novels are chronicles of foretold violence; both pose the urgent question of what caused such violence to erupt and be tolerated in these respective settings.

Already as a student of sociology back in Paris, young Khoury had to take note of the fact that the descendants of the victims and survivors had filed away into 'the book of oblivion' the horrors of the massacres that had started in 1858.[79] This would explain his efforts to transform the plight of historiography into the virtue of the novel, and to unearth through literary means the history and stories that had been neglected for so long. After taking up arms for the Palestinian resistance after the Arab defeat by Israel in 1967,[80] the young man learned his lesson from the bloody conflicts during the course of his own life and became a militant, uncompromising representative of, and advocate for, literature and its importance for (not only Arab) societies. To defend literature militantly does not mean to using literature as a vehicle for militant purposes and messages that are alien to it. Khoury's commitment to literature derives from the insight that literature and life cannot be separated and that ideology has no

---

77 See the interview with Elias Khoury in Mejcher: *Geschichten über Geschichten*, p. 131.
78 On the importance of this novel in the context of contemporary Arab literature, see Edward Said's foreword in Elias Khoury: *Little Mountain*. Manchester: Carcanet Press Limited 1989.
79 Khoury: *Der geheimnisvolle Brief*, p. 159.
80 See Khoury's interview with Mejcher in her *Geschichten über Geschichten*, p. 129: 'When I entered university, the June war of 1967 broke out. It changed my life.' In very similar terms, the Palestinian literary and cultural theorist Edward Said summarized the experience of this generation; he, too, spoke of the Israeli defeat of Arab troops as a turning point in his life. See also Edward W. Said: 'No Reconciliation Allowed.' In: André Aciman (ed.): *Letters of Transit: Reflections on Exile, Identity, Language, and Loss*. New York: The New Press 1999, p. 101.

place in literature.[81] From this flows a writing project that has learned the lesson of history and militantly promotes a knowledge-for-living that uses the openness of literature to make and keep history – and one's own stories – radically open.

The (hi)stories that literature unfolds create and comprise their own ploys. It is quite possible, then, that the Catholic priest Abdallah Nasar, whom some blamed for the massacre in Ain Kisrin, would be the one to become the ancestor of the Colombian Nasars. We are told that he had fled to Beirut, from there to Marseille and finally on to Colombia, where he founded 'the family's emigrated branch.'[82] A religious fanatic and provocateur as progenitor? Were his entanglements ever revealed, or did they become part of the book of oblivion? But how can one break the cycle of violence and halt the bloody return of repression through forgetting and suppression?

Already a century later, if we are to believe Elias Khoury's narrators, the mysterious letter with the news of Santiago Nasar's slaughter in Colombia will recall this almost forgotten, repressed Lebanese (pre)history and shatter all travel plans of the family of Ibrahim Nasar, the future greengrocer. In the end, it becomes clear that the family patriarch, Jakob Nasar, has not entirely forgotten the bloodbath of Ain Kisrin and has a ready explanation for the brutal events: the curse of Abd al-Djalil, who, as we have seen, collapsed under the blows of the scimitars, still haunts the family.[83]

Four times one hundred years of foreignness

To be sure, the history of the family – and thus the history of the atrocities – goes back even further. Ibrahim Nasar, whose murder opens the volume, knows it only vaguely from hearsay. What is known, however, is that the family was originally named Atwi and only received the sobriquet Nasar in Ain Kisrin. According to the stories, the family, which presumably originated in Izra' in Hauran had emigrated to Kana in southern Lebanon long ago, in stages over a period of two hundred years. The last to emigrate, near the end of the eighteenth century, were the members of the branch that was to receive the name Nasar, and the reason for this – how could it be otherwise? – was a murder, only this

---

81 Khoury quoted in Mejcher: *Geschichten über Geschichten*, p. 134.
82 Khoury: *Der geheimnisvolle Brief*, p. 159.
83 Khoury: *Der geheimnisvolle Brief*, p. 163.

time 'the emigrant was not the perpetrator but the victim.'[84] Bedouins from the Golan Heights had attacked the family and killed three brothers. In far-off Kana, such an act had already compelled the Atwis, emigrants since the late sixteenth century, to convert to Islam to prevent further attacks. Without tracing all the details of a history that the novel presented as fragments, one can still see that the migration from Lebanon to Colombia is merely a new stage in a centuries-long succession of murders and emigrations, each producing further massacres and waves of refugees. The younger generation in Elias Khoury's novel may no longer try to flee to Colombia, Venezuela, or Mexico but instead to Canada, since the Canadian authorities issued immigration visas for Lebanese Christians after the most recent Lebanese civil war.[85] The changed destination for emigrants, no longer to the South, but to the North of the American continent, is but a sign of the modified (and historically traceable) factors that pull Arab-American refugees while the push-factors remain the same. Movements upon movements, migrations upon migrations – and always the danger that the coexistence established with so much effort may drown in a bloodbath that, in turn, either triggers new migrations or thwarts them elsewhere. Elias Khoury links here the endless succession of ever-new migrations with the leitmotif of foreignness and being-foreign that pervades all of his texts. It is not difficult to recognize that 'it does not require any emigration or expulsion from paradise to be foreign.' It is indeed very much possible that a person might be 'a stranger in his own house and among his own neighbors.'[86]

In 1993, a year before 'The Mysterious Letter' was published, Elias Khoury had already developed this leitmotif in multi-faceted poetic form in his novel *The Kingdom of Strangers* (first English edition in 1996). It sounds like a mixture of intra- and intertextual references for Khoury to pursue the topic of foreignness from Gabriel García Márquez's Santiago Nasar in Colombia, via Albert Camus's figure of the stranger in Algeria (Meursault in *The Stranger* [*L'étranger*]) and his own novel's characters in Lebanon all the way back to Adam, the original father, who was not only 'the first foreigner,' but also 'the first Arab poet' and 'the first human' – similar to Camus's *The First Man* (*Le premier homme*).[87] He spoke the first language, 'the language of Paradise and of Hell,' followed by 'the curse that ripped language apart in the Tower of Babel,' much like the

---

84 Khoury: *Der geheimnisvolle Brief*, p. 25.
85 See Khoury: *Der geheimnisvolle Brief*, p. 15, 209 and 214.
86 Khoury: *Der geheimnisvolle Brief*, p. 54.
87 Khoury: *Der geheimnisvolle Brief*, p. 42. Gallimard in Paris issued this book from Albert Camus's estate in the same year as 'The Mysterious Letter.'

country torn apart by the Lebanese civil war in 1860 was transformed 'into the Tower of Babel.'[88] From this time on, people face each other as strangers; they no longer speak the same language and are unable to find a way out of the Babylonian confusion of languages.

Not only does Khoury expertly muster scattered references to the literatures of the twentieth century, Ancient Arab poetry, and stories from *The Arabian Nights*, but also to the tradition of world books. Those include of course the Bible and the Quran, in whose stories and figures the characters of Elias Khoury, the writer between cultures, are mirrored time and again. In *The Kingdom of Strangers*, the question 'What am I writing?' prompts not just a timid response that reflects the insecurity of both narrator and narrative ('I don't know. I feel the words decaying and dissolving');[89] it prompts a vision of Christ at the Dead See:

> Yet I see him today, in 1991, at the close of a barbaric century, which started with a massacre and ended with a crime. I see him, lonely, dead, crucified. He is walking on the water.
> The only one who is a foreigner.
> A stranger in the realm of strangers, which he, or so the white Cherkessian believed, wanted to found.[90]

Widad, the 'Cherkessian,' sees Jesus Christ as the epitome of a stranger in which her own image, her own fate, is reflected. That the white Cherkessian is not a Cherkessian at all, as the Lebanese world around her and she herself believe, but rather a woman kidnapped as a young girl from her native village in Azerbaijan, enslaved, and finally sold to Lebanon by way of Alexandria, may explain why Widad begins to sing 'The Stranger' with such fervor during religious services.[91] In the kingdom of strangers, everyone – victim and perpetrator alike – is a stranger in relation to everyone else: having been stirred up and tossed about in countless migrations without any real origin and without a real future; time and again having been forced painstakingly to create life knowledge that works as a knowledge-for-living together peacefully, at least for a time. Often enough, however, an unforeseen coincidence is enough to set off the kind of

---

88 Khoury: *Der geheimnisvolle Brief*, p. 42 and 160.
89 Elias Khoury: *The Kingdom of Strangers: A novel*. Fayetteville: University of Arkansas Press 1996, p. 39.
90 Khoury: *The Kingdom of Strangers*, p. 39.
91 Khoury: *The Kingdom of Strangers*, p. 43, 40.

chain reaction that has so cruelly characterized the twentieth and twenty-first centuries.

Stolen from her native village, Widad spends her entire life making herself understood in a foreign language, until, at the end of her life, she loses the mastery of this foreign language along with her memory: a Babylonian confusion of languages *in nuce*. This devoted, self-sacrificing, and yet unfathomable character – one of the most beautiful, most lovingly shaped female characters in the Lebanese author's fictions – had long since been transformed into 'a history of silence.'[92] What does this history of silence have to do with the history of writing? When the first-person narrator tells Widad's story to Salman Rushdie in London in 1988, the latter advises him to turn it into a novel. The narrator, however, confesses his fear, the fear of 'being pushed to the edge or devoured by the story,' even of 'becoming part of the story without knowing how it will proceed and turn out.'[93] For the narrator, Rushdie himself is the best example that such anxiety is warranted, since Rushdie, back then before the publication of his *Satanic Verses* (1988), had not sensed that writing was to become 'his undoing.' All the greater the risk for an author who emigrates to London at the age of sixteen, writes his novels not in his native Urdu but in English, and ultimately, like Widad, forgets the foreign language he had learned in his old age, so that in the end he will not even be able to read his own books![94]

Too horrifying not to be true, this story clearly gets under the skin of the narrator, whom we cannot simply equate with Elias Khoury. Incorporating Salman Rushdie into *The Kingdom of Strangers* introduces a frictional dimension, an oscillation between the fiction internal to the text and the reality external to it, which is also, at the same time, a metafiction that reflects upon the fiction of the novel. What is contemplated in these passages, however, is not only the fiction but also the friction, so that one might speak of a *metafrictional* dimension. Salman Rushdie embodies the writer who literally abandoned his fatherland *and* his mother tongue, and who stands for the kind of writing without a fixed abode that scares the first-person narrator. The example of the writer without a fixed abode illustrates with an excess of clarity that tales can devour those who tell them and thus commit literary cannibalism on their creators: 'I remember saying to Rushdie that his choice would make him a potential hero of one of his novels someday. I had no idea that a life of suffering was in store for him, more

---

92 Khoury: *The Kingdom of Strangers*, p. 98.
93 Khoury: *The Kingdom of Strangers*, p. 98.
94 Khoury: *The Kingdom of Strangers*, p. 99.

terrible than any a hero had ever lived through.'[95] The warning to the writer is all too clear: think twice about what you write, for you may have to live through it. Literature and life cannot be separated, are so intimately related to each other that they induce anxieties that literature – as it does in Jorge Luis Borges's *Tlön, Uqbar, Orbis Tertius* – could force its way into one's life and change it.[96] The metafictional and metafrictional passages in Khoury's *The Kingdom of Strangers* also include reflections about 'the contemporary literature of the Third World,' which Western eyes all too readily dismiss as 'unreliable.'[97] But how, the first-person narrator asks adamantly in view of his narrated time and narrated situation in Lebanon, can we 'combine and link together [the scattered stories] in a country in which all connections have been annihilated?'[98] There are good reasons why Edward Said emphasized that writing novels in societies as torn apart as those of Palestine or Lebanon is something very risky and highly problematic.[99] In fact, Lebanese literature offers a particularly resonant demonstration of how categories such as national literature and world literature lose relevance because they do not take in more than descriptive elements.[100]

The polyglottism and worldwide dispersal of such a Literature without a fixed Abode – for which Cuban literature is perhaps the best example in the New World (see chapter 4 above) – does precisely not mean that it therefore loses explanatory power, credibility, and 'authenticity.' Still, from the perspective of such a transcultural and transareal Lebanese literature, the question of truth is posed even more keenly, as it does not intend to relegate its own hurtful history either to the 'book of oblivion' or surrender it to the interests of certain ideologies.[101] But how, Khoury's narrators ask time and again with often agonizing persistence, can one counter the danger of seeming untrustworthy? How

---

95 Khoury: *The Kingdom of Strangers*, p. 105.
96 For how this text by the Argentinian writer fits within frictionality, see Ottmar Ette: *Literatur in Bewegung. Raum und Dynamik grenzüberschreitenden Schreibens in Europa und Amerika*. Weilerswist: Velbrück Wissenschaft, 2001, p. 227–268. Elias Khoury made a quite concrete and unpleasant experience when a story written by someone else forced its way into his own life in France in October 2001, just a few weeks after September 11; see Elias Khoury: 'Wie der Westen Arabar produziert: Erfahrungen eines libanesischen Schriftstellers mit der französischen Polizei – und drei Gründe, nicht zu reisen.' In: *Die Zeit* 47 (November 15, 2001), p. 46.
97 Khoury: *The Kingdom of Strangers*, p. 104.
98 Khoury: *The Kingdom of Strangers*, p. 105.
99 Edward W. Said: 'Foreword'. In: Khoury: *Little Mountain*, p. xiv.
100 See Andreas Pflitsch: 'Literatur, grenzenlos: Aspekte transnationalen Schreibens.' In: Christian Szyska / Friederike Pannewick (eds.): *Crossings and Passages in Genre and Culture*. Wiesbaden: Reichert Verlag 2003, p. 87–120
101 Khoury: *Der geheimnisvolle Brief*, p. 159.

can one find the truth and represent it in a literarily convincing manner? In today's 'age of documentation,' documentation for this age can surely not be the answer to such a question.[102] As the narrator knows, Latin American authors draw their 'legends of the present from oral tradition,' a method that of Elias Khoury's narratives employ.[103] In response to his lover Maria's question of what truth is, the first-person narrator finds, already in the first part of *The Kingdom of Strangers*, an answer characteristic of Khoury's subtle humor and also disconcerting, but only at first glance: 'The conjunction of two lies.'[104] Writing, and not only Khoury's figures of the writer know, 'means lying.'[105] It follows, then, that the meeting of two written stories, such as *Chronicle of a Death Foretold* and 'The Mysterious Letter,' represents the literary conjunction of two lies. But this encounter, as we now know, drives the truth out into the open.

But which truth? Thanks to Elias Khoury's story, Gabriel García Márquez's Santiago Nasar can look back on a history not only of one hundred years of solitude, but of four hundred years of rootlessness, emigration, and violence, the foretelling of his death effectively moves hundreds of years back into the past, where it can already be read between the lines of oral histories that attempt to remember a family history as a history of migration. As we know, the history of the Colombian Santiago Nasar is based on a true story that García Márquez transformed into his own narrative three decades later. For his part, Elias Khoury turns García Márquez's narrative into a story that tells of human foreignness through a string of murders and migrations which seems hopeless and neverending. Humans appears as prisoners of their own foreignness, as a strangers among strangers who can attack, slaughter, and devour each other at any time. But is there really no escape from the spiral of expulsion and emigration, violence and counter-violence?

ArabAmerican Writing-between-Worlds

Being-strange and human foreignness are, as I have shown, of vital importance to Elias Khoury's novels. The clearly accentuated transhistorical continuity of the cyclical time structure so frequently present in his works does not, however, not fall into the ahistorical construct of an ontology of strangeness in the king-

---

102 Khoury: *Der geheimnisvolle Brief*, p. 159.
103 Khoury: *The Kingdom of Strangers*, p. 122.
104 Khoury: *The Kingdom of Strangers*, p. 37.
105 Khoury: *The Kingdom of Strangers*, p. 66.

dom of strangers, detached from time and space. Another look at the double(d) network of specifically ArabAmerican relations, which García Márquez deftly interweaves and Elias Khoury takes logically further, will show that even the connection between massacre and migration is by no means an inevitable given.

It makes sense to begin with the observation that the news of young Santiago Nasar's murder, located at the seam, as it were, of *Chronicle of a Death Foretold* and 'The Mysterious Letter,' does not prompt any migrations. While the perpetrators' family is urged to leave the place of the murder, the town's residents of Arab extraction seeks not to jeopardize their coexistence with the other Colombian residents through acts of vengeance. Instead, the representatives of the grieving Arab community emphasize that this community renounces violence, and they attempt to secure future coexistence with a gesture of good will by sending medicinal herbs to Santiago's murderers. They do everything to avoid a collision of cultures.

In Elias Khoury's novel, the news of the death of a grandson of Lebanese immigrants similarly results in the revocation of all emigration plans, since the members of the branch of the family that has remained in Lebanon interpret the collectively committed murder as the sign of a collision in the sense of a 'clash of civilizations.' While the Arab migrant families that have taken up residence in Colombia have drawn lessons from their history and their own family's stories (which can be read as the series of massacres and migrations), the Nasars in Lebanon are aware of the same family history and no longer believe that they will be able to escape that history through emigration. They remain prisoners of a history that forever seems to repeat itself. It is clearly no accident that the time period at the center of the novel, which begins with multiple references to the founding of the state of Lebanon in 1943 – and thus with the promise of a new chapter of postcolonial history – ends with the year 1976 amid a new round of violence and counter-violence, bloodshed and revenge, massacre and counter-terror. As the narrator tells us, the death – or murder – of the greengrocer Ibrahim Nasar in 1976 saves him from having to live through yet another bloodbath that would take place in Ain Kisrin and the surrounding villages in 1983.[106]

For Elias Khoury, who was working on *The Little Mountain* and fighting in the civil war in 1976, the year in which his later hero, Ibrahim Nasar, dies, the exit from the spiral of violence began on January 20, 1976. On that date, Palestinian freedom fighters massacred the Christian residents of a small town south of Beirut in what was clearly intended as an act of revenge for the atrocities the

---

106 Khoury: *Der geheimnisvolle Brief*, p. 169.

Christian militias had committed against the residents of Palestinian refugee camps a few days earlier. Elias Khoury saw this terrifying experience as the actual cause for his 'exit' from the ideologically motivated 'logic' of the civil war: 'It was the crucial moment when I discovered that our ideology did not protect us from behaving in a savage, fascist way. What is the meaning of all our discourse and all our ideology if we kill children, women and men because they are Christians or Muslims or whatever?'[107] To Khoury, who grew up in a Beirut borough with a majority Christian population and came from a Greek Orthodox family, and who had taken up the Arab cause at an early age, had joined the Palestinian resistance in Jordan and received military training in a PLO camp in Syria, the scenario of mutual killing based on different religious affiliations could no longer be justified as a 'just cause' or a 'just war.' From this point onward, the Lebanese author unfurled the hopelessness of such a murderous and suicidal cycle not only in his own life, but also in his literary work.

'The Mysterious Letter' not only outlines the centuries-long entanglement of the Nasar family as both offenders and victims in a history of murder and migration. It also inscribes the knowledge-for-living-and-surviving-together that this history produced for the family members who migrated to the New World. In terms of literary theory, his novel can be understood as an allograph, that is, a 'foreign' author's continuation and taking-elsewhere of *Chronicle of a Death Foretold*, a form whose spatial-temporal extension of the narration into the nineteenth century and to the Middle East effects a transareally-grounded re-semanticization of the reference text. As a result, Santiago Nasar appears no longer only from the Colombian perspective of a Latin American author, but also, at the same time, in the writing of an Arab novelist within the Lebanese tradition. In this way, the two novels begin to blend together into a shared story and history.

In this meeting of the two fictions, or lies, lies the *true* significance of this ArabAmerican experiment. Literature becomes the place of movement where the allographic continuation and taking-elsewhere of a reference text becomes a mutual embedding of the stories and histories of different cultures. This transcultural embedding, in turn, creates a *Writing-between-Worlds* that cannot be adequately understood either from a national-literary perspective or as world literature. At issue here are not static literary territories, but vectoral forms and strategies of writing within the possibilities of transareal patterns of movement. One might describe the merging of the two novels in the same way as Yoko Ta-

---

107 Khoury's interview in Mejcher: *Geschichten über Geschichten*, p. 133.

wada used the example of Paul Celan to explain the encounter of an original with its translation. In the case of optimal translatability, this encounter is always already present in the 'original,' in the text that comes first chronologically, rather than produced as part of the process of translation.[108] It is in precisely this manner that García Márquez's *Chronicle of a Death Foretold* has always included its ArabAmerican continuation. The truth of both novels lies in the fact that in each, the interWorld of the respective other, 'foreign,' text has always resided within its 'own' textual body.

The transareal intertextuality Elias Khoury envisions thus brings to our minds a Writing-between-Worlds that cannot necessarily be counted as writing-without-a-fixed-abode, even if the Lebanese author has, for years, regularly commuted between the Middle East, Europe and the USA. What this kind of intertextuality certainly requires is a high degree of familiarity with different cultural and religious contexts that ought not to be just blended but deeply embedded within each other. Transculturally crosshatching Eastern and Western, Christian and Muslim, Arab and American cultural perspectives thus illuminates new configurations of meaning within García Márquez's complexly structured world of the characters who surround Santiago Nasar.

The interplay between *Chronicle of a Death Foretold* and 'The Mysterious Letter' clarifies how a transareal scholarship interested not in fixed spaces and territories but in movements and mobile entanglements can produce a new relationality that neither limits itself to local or national viewpoints nor dissolves its object of study into generalized global contexts. The intertextually generated oscillation between different logics reveals a history of multiple migrations behind the character of Santiago Nasar and the members of his Arab, or better, Arab-American, community. This migration history shapes a specific knowledge-of-and-for- living marked by the history of the Middle East. The family's migration to Colombia radically delocalizes this knowledge, as the above excerpt from Luis Fayad's novel also shows. At the same time, however, this delocalized knowledge creates not multicultural but intercultural and transcultural areas of application and playing fields.

Still, the transformation of delocalized into translocalized knowledge that continuously translates into one another the experiences of country of origin and country of destination and generates self-similar fractal patterns of transcultural practice in the sense of a *mise-en-abyme*, by no means excludes the possibility that certain events in the country of immigration might foster an

---

108 Yoko Tawada: 'Das Tor des Übersetzers oder Celan liest Japanisch.' In: Yoko Tawada: *Talisman*. Tübingen: Konkursbuchverlag Claudia Gehrke 1996, p. 129.

antagonistic logic of cultural collision[109] or a 'clash of civilizations.' In a discreet, but by no means concealed manner, *Chronicle of a Death Foretold* demonstrates how an element that belongs equally to the patriarchal gender orders of both Hispanic and Arab traditions – the problem of 'lost' virginity – can evoke seemingly hidden strains of cultural confrontation and render them contagious. The fact that Santiago Nasar is unable to recognize these fault lines that are hardly invisible in their explosive danger and would ultimately extinguish his own life, can surely be interpreted as a warning that the societal integration of migrants should never be seen as finished, not even in the third generation. One should not understand cultural heterogeneity exclusively as a cultural treasure but also as a potential conflict ready to erupt at a moment's notice. At the same time, however, it becomes clear how much potential for knowledge exists in a literature that may be called ArabAmerican in the fullest sense of the term. Where the Colombian author turns us into the only seemingly detached spectators of a foretold execution, whose reasons would not hold up to scrutiny even beyond the Caribbean coast of Colombia, the Lebanese writer presents us with an incessant succession of violent acts from which to distil the mechanisms of a society's self-destruction that we can observe not just in Lebanon.

Edward Said attested to Elias Khoury's 'profoundly postmodern literary career,' rather an oversimplification from today's perspective. It is worth mentioning, however, that among the many publicist activities for which Khoury was responsible during his decade as editor of a leading publishing house in Beirut, were Arabic translations of a host of 'great postmodern Third World classics.'[110] Not least among them were writings by Latin American authors Miguel Ángel Asturias, Carlos Fuentes, and of course Gabriel García Márquez.[111] No wonder: the writers of the Latin American 'boom' have enjoyed steady popularity in Arab countries for some time now. Recalling the 'Declaration of Brasilia,' one might say that, by translating and disseminating Spanish-language texts in the Arab-speaking world, Khoury actively contributed to creating a 'Latin American-Arab Library' *avant la lettre*.

With 'The Mysterious Letter,' Khoury moved from his previous *intercultural* project into the realm where he created in his own writing an 'Arab-Latin Amer-

---

109 On this term and its historical manifestations, see Urs Bitterli: *Die 'Wilden' und die 'Zivilisierten': Grundzüge einer Geistes- und Kulturgeschichte der europäisch-überseeischen Begegnung*. Munich: Deutscher Taschenbuch Verlag 1982, p. 130–160.
110 Said: 'Foreword,' p. xvii.
111 At least this had been the original plans. García Márquez was later published by another press.

ican Library' with clear *transcultural* traits. Understood in this way, such an 'ArabAmerican Library,' which would include Elias Khoury and Luis Fayad's texts along with Gabriel García Márquez's *Chronicle of a Death Foretold*, inaugurates a new dimension of an ArabAmerican Writing-between-Worlds. This writing is important not only for uncovering a history believed to have been forgotten but for suggesting future possibilities far beyond the political visions of the summit of Brasilia. Because of being bound up in life, the knowledge-for-living that this literature/library stores and keeps available is especially crucial for our survival in an atmosphere characterized more than ever by the notion of a 'clash of civilizations.' For one, we should be aware 'that only through telling stories does the past become extant.' For another, we must not forget the inescapable truth of which *The Kingdom of Strangers* reminds us: to be able to tell a story, one must survive it.[112] It is in this physical and narratological sense that literature is always already knowledge-of-and-for-survival.

---

[112] Khoury: *The Kingdom of Strangers*, p. 36: 'Faisal did not tell any more stories, for he did not survive the next one.'

8 In(tro)spections

Voyages into the realm of the dead: Border experiences of a literature 'after' migration

The children of migration

> Because they had all left, like thousands, tens of thousands, hundreds of thousands, who every day departed from all the countries on all the continents, who left alone or with their family, and they took the bus or the train, the boat, or maybe theiy took the plane, in the most unfathomable situations, between two railway cars, on a landing gear, crowded together on floating boards that took on the name and the appearance of a ship the easier to seduce them, until a captain collected the money for the passage, for which they had saved up for so many years through their hard work and sacrifices, and either left them to their fate in the middle of the ocean – for it would have never occurred to him to deliver them to dry land – or else drowned with them. Because they had left like all those who left to escape war and persecution, hunger, misery, poverty, or sheer tedium, believing that they would find a better life somewhere else, more to the west, more to the north, believing that there was a flickering light on the horizon which pointed the way, and they had set out on foot, had undertaken the journey, had crossed cyclones and dry land, time even, one day to arrive – those who really arrived – at the land of which they had dreamt.[1]

In this highly rhythmical passage, to which sound is vital, the narrator of Cécile Wajsbrot's novel *Mémorial* sketches the image of a migratory planet, of migration as omnipresent. Everywhere, we meet people who, in an effort to save their skins or search for a better life, for better living conditions, gave up their earlier abodes and set out. It does not matter whether these migratory movements use

---

[1] 'Car ils étaient partis comme des milliers, des dizaines, des centaines de milliers qui partaient tous les jours de tous les pays sur tous les continents, qui partaient seuls ou en famille, et ils prenaient le car ou le train, le bateau, ou ils prenaient l'avion, dans les situations les plus incroyables, entre deux wagons, dans le train d'atterrissage, entassés sur des planches flottantes qui prenaient le nom et l'aspect de bateaux pour mieux les séduire jusqu'à ce qu'un capitaine recueille l'argent du passage économisé depuis tant d'années, à force de travail et de privations, et les largue quelque part en pleine mer – n'ayant jamais eu l'intention de les faire accoster – ou sombre avec eux. Car ils étaient partis comme tous ceux qui partaient, pour fuire des guerres ou des persécutions, la famine, la misère, la pauvreté ou seulement l'insatisfaction, croyant trouver ailleurs, plus à l'ouest, plus au nord, une vie meilleure, croyant apercevoir à l'horizon une lueur tremblante qui guidait leur chemin et ils avaient marché, voyagé, traversé les tempêtes et les terres, et traversé le temps, pour arriver un jour – ceux qui arrivaient – au pays dont ils avaient rêvé.' Cécile Wajsbrot: *Mémorial*. Paris: Zulma 2005, p. 14f.

either railroad tracks or roads, either airplanes or boats, or whether they lead from east to west or from south to north. The destination of this departure, this exodus, is always an arrival at a place that promises the better future so ardently desired. For this future, one is willing to risk and use everything one managed to save in the past and under difficult conditions. People smugglers, however questionable they may be, become the potential midwives of the dreamt-of new life.[2]

The persecuted and the ousted, the refugees and the rootless, whom we can find everywhere, project their hopes onto the horizon of the suddenly expanded foreign space and of their own lives, thereby creating a motile figure of the hasty flight, the rushed departure from the original space, in which future assumes spatial dimensions as an arrival at another place. This motile figure of a crooked, broken line from east to west, from south to north, extends transgenerationally – beyond one's own life – to the children of the uprooted and displaced persons, for whom the 'new place,' there Here and not the There, is to become a homeland. Opportunities for a better life await. Ensuring one's own survival is the prerequisite for later generations' happier life.

The first-person narrator-protagonist in Cécile Wajsbrot *Mémorial* (2005) belongs to this second generation, those children of migration on whom all of the refugees' hopes concentrate:

> And then we arrived, we, their children, and no sooner did we enter the world than we bore their hopes, because we would achieve the things that they had not been able to achieve, and they had the idea that they had left because of us, because they knew that during the course of their own lives, they would not have the time to catch up, they could settle, but they could not anchor themselves, grow roots, which we should do and right from the start, we were burdened with their lives, with their disappointments and at the same time their illusions, and we became carriers of desires that were not our own. But the wound they wanted to ignore, the scar they liked to forget, the name they never uttered: We heard it in the heart of their silence, as it pounded against the walls of our rooms, surrounded us with echoes from another world, from another time, and while they wanted and imagined us to be fully from here [*ici*], we were from there [*là-bas*] before we had ever been there, and even if we were never to go there, from there or from another place, and they lost this unequal battle from the beginning – a desperate struggle – against circumstances – and so did we.
> The wind blew.
> – What are you looking for there?
> – An earthquake.

---

[2] See Eva Horn et al. (eds.): *Grenzverletzer: Von Schmugglern, Spionen und anderen subversiven Gestalten*. Berlin: Kulturverlag Kadmos 2002.

– Because we left.
– Don't turn around.³

These few lines from the beginning of the first of three parts in *Mémorial* provide the basic structure of a text that is utterly captivating from the very start because of its polyvocality, a text that the cover and the book jacket, if not the title page, identify as a novel. We immediately notice in the narrative a sharp separation between 'them' and 'us,' between the third-person plural and the first. For the outset, two generations with very different life experiences stand opposed. After all, the children of migration do not share either the figure of movement of the flight, the departure, the act of leaving behind everything that their parents did, nor the desired 'rooting' at the destination of their migration. The second generation grows up knowing that 'something is not right.'⁴ The children of migration are not completely absorbed in the Here but carry within them the village that once was their parents' and their ancestors' unquestioned Here of a home however defined. Something unmentionable is ever-present. The old flight routes and migrations are stored transgenerationally and constitute a vectoral (family) memory at the very point in time when the parents want their children to live exclusively in the new Here. But this Here is different: Here is another place (Ici est un autre).

It is no wonder, then, that, at some point in her life, the principal first-person narrator – there are other, additional narrators in the story – decides to take off and, throwing all caution to the winds, embarks on a search for the family's

---

3 'C'est alors que nous venions, nous, leurs enfants, et que dès la naissance, nous portions leurs espoirs car nous accomplirions les choses qu'ils n'avaient pas pu faire et leur venait l'idée qu'ils étaient partis pour nous, car ils savaient qu'en une vie, ils n'auraient pas le temps de rattraper, ils pouvaient s'installer mais ils ne pouvaient pas s'ancrer, s'enraciner, cela, c'était à nous de le faire et dès le commencement, nous étions lestés de leur vie, de leurs désillusions en même temps que de leurs illusions, et porteurs de désirs qui n'étaient pas les nôtres. Mais la blessure qu'ils voulaient ignorer, cette cicatrice qu'ils oubliaient volontiers, ce nom qu'ils ne prononçaient jamais, nous l'entendions au cœur de leur silence se répercuter contre les murs de nos chambres, nous encerclant d'échos venus d'un autre monde, d'un autre temps, et tandis qu'eux nous voulaient – nous croyaient – pleinement d'ici, nous étions de là-bas avant d'y être allés, quand bien même nous n'irions jamais, de là-bas ou d'ailleurs, et d'emblée ils perdaient ce combat inégal – combat désespéré – contre les circonstances – et nous avec eux. / Le vent soufflait. / – Que cherches-tu là-bas ? / – Un tremblement de terre. / – Car nous avons quitté. / – Ne vous retournez pas.' Wajsbrot: *Mémorial*, p. 15–16.
4 Wajsbrot: *Mémorial*, p. 25.

origin and thus her own origin as well. The children of migration move in a spatiotemporal field of coordinates into which their ancestors' spatial, temporal, and mobile structures extend and produce multiply broken fractal patterns that always leads us (and them) to suspect other journeys beneath their own journeys. In this way, the protagonist embodies a complexly ramified figure of movement in which the Here has not become a 'natural' residence but demands a There that, in spite of all the silence of the parents' generation – and precisely because of it – has always been there and has always been marked as such.

The overlaps and overhangs of the various transgenerational temporal planes, characterized as they are by multiple ruptures, might explain why the narrator's figure of movement – and that of her generation, as is implicit in the first-person plural – cannot be a simple return in the sense of either a re-entrance or a harmless visit to a home that has long been distant, perhaps even quaint. At stake is a profound engagement with the present circumstances of one's life on a migratory planet marked by persecution, displacement, and extermination. At stake is also a world after Shoa.

In the echo chamber of voices without a fixed abode

The second passage I cite above at some length represents a failed intergenerational contract. Although it becomes the surface onto which the first generation of migrants projects its wishes and yearnings, the second generation does not internalize these projections, does not own them as images of selfhood and blueprints for their lives. It is the secrecy about the secretiveness, the prodding of the repressed, that prohibits the children of migration from being unquestioningly a part of their native land, of a Here without a There. The parents' silence echoes from the walls of the children's rooms. It points beyond the space of a settled life to the motile space of a quest that keeps the voices of the past, the There in the Here, present in the present moment. A stereophony, a polyphony of simultaneity, commences, fanned by questions that the I has to confront: 'What are you looking for there'?

In *Mémorial*, Cécile Wajsbrot takes up where her short book *Beaune-la-Rolande* (2004) leaves off, especially with the play between voices and voyages, *voix* and *voies*, through which the native Parisian imagined her belated figuration of the (French) concentration camp (see the last section of chapter 2). It was in France that the echo effect of the homophones *voies* and *voix* answered the question of what remains of Auschwitz today with a references to the omnipresence of Auschwitz.⁵ The extermination camp in Poland is always already present in the French transit camp of Beaune-la-Rolande; the camp structures are permanently layered. As they said in Beaune-la-Rolande: 'Auschwitz is not in Poland; it is a place that has no location; it is everywhere and nowhere.'⁶

Mémorial takes further the omnipresent dispersed traces from *Beaune-la-Rolande* and translates them in aesthetically convincing ways into a novel broken up in so many ways that it remains forever fragile. While Wajsbrot considerably lessens the autobiographical aspects of her novel, she does not entirely eschew the frictional oscillation between the fictional world of the novel and its autobiographical priming. Much more important, however, than the search for autobiographical elements in the text is the recognition that *Mémorial* is less about a place for commemoration than it is about the art of memory nourished by movement because it comes from movement. The whole text consists of myriad layered movements, even if its initial figure of movement, the snowy owl (harfang des neiges), is at first portrayed as a motionless bird of prey in the frozen circumpolar regions of the northern hemisphere. The italicized chapters inserted between each narrative section of the novel's three parts tell of this white bird – it is as if it were the counterpart of the black raven Jacobo from Max Aub's 'Raven manuscript' (*Manuscrito cuervo*; see section 3 in chapter 2 above) – and break through the novel's structure in a mainly discursive way that at once refract the narrative flow and oddly reflect on it. But unlike Jacobo, who believes that his observations on a concentration camp in Southern France give him access to the concentrated human condition,⁷ the *harfang des neiges* bluntly turns its back on humanity: Its attention is on the spaces of cold and ice in which humans cannot dwell permanently; nor can they rule them. Even if the owl may appear motionless to the casual observer, the bird is still associated with movement and migration from the very start of the novel. It is one of the '*migratory birds*' (*oiseaux migrateurs*) always gliding soundlessly above the wasteland of the tundra and the ice in '*silent white flight*' (*vol silencieux et blanc*).⁸ Impressive about the solitary bird of prey, which looks for prey and patrols the horizons of a place unsuitable for human settlement, is not only the

---

5 See Giorgio Agamben: *Remnants of Auschwitz: The Witness and the Archive. Homo sacer III.* New York: Zone Books 1999.
6 'Auschwitz ne se trouve pas en Pologne, c'est un lieu indéfinissable qui est partout et nulle part.' Cécile Wajsbrot: *Beaune-la-Rolande*. Paris: Zulma 2004, p. 55.
7 See chapter 7 in Ottmar Ette: *ÜberLebenswissen: Die Aufgabe der Philologie*. Berlin: Kulturverlag Kadmos 2004.
8 Wajsbrot: *Mémorial*, p. 7.

'harmony of its movements,' but also the complete whiteness of its feathery coat, its penetrating, almost piercing eyes, and its utter soundlessness, its 'silence' within a void bereft of humans. Like the raven Jacobo, the snowy owl literally enables a birds-eye view on the human condition. The beating of its wings can be felt throughout *Mémorial*.

That the silence in the bitter cold introduces the isotopy of secretiveness and hushing in connection with frostiness and iciness creates a tight connection with *Beaune-la-Rolande*. In that novel, following the ideas of Rabelais, it is perhaps the noblest task of literature to 'thaw' the frozen voices of the past, to transport them to the living presence, and to make them audible again. The snowy owl with its penetrating gaze, then, stands for the presence of those regions of frozenness that elude human access and do not permit survival: for that 'odd and obscure atmosphere in which noting could be created and nothing could survive – a layer of ice of unusual thickness.'[9] As a being without a fixed abode, the *harfang des neiges* –and in this it approximates literature – dares to go farther than humans who are settled or desire being settled typically go. It circulates in those regions in which human words are frozen and from which they need to be dug out, 'thawed', snatched from the past and made available.

The presence of past voices creates a key structural element in a novel that is a virtual echo chamber: the past is brought into the present and resonates there. These omnipresent, almost otherworldly voices are of very different kinds and often contradict each other; they query the I and its actions from various perspectives. Every single movement and deliberation that the I makes are subject to commentary, discussion, and challenge. For the protagonist, this child of migration who, contrary to all of her parents' hopes, appears to have neither roots in France (although she does in the French language) nor a fixed abode, the voices of the past become obsessively audible below the silence, and they do so in transgenerational and transtemporal ways. Past and present are inseparably, though not evenly, linked, indeed wedged into one another. Reminiscent at times of a prose poem, Cécile Wajsbrot's text memorably sounds this multiplied colloquy, this silenced polylogue, from the point of view of a narrator who is a child of migration and also, as we will see below, a child of Auschwitz.

---

9 '[U]ne atmosphère étrange et indistincte où rien ne pouvait ni se former ni survivre – une couche de glace d'un épaisseur inhabituelle.' Wajsbrot: *Mémorial*, p. 12.

In the vectoral memory chamber of precursors and descendants

The I travels from the very outset of the novel. Waiting on the platform for a train that will arrive not half an hour late, as is first announced, but an entire day late signals the imminent journey's unique temporality. Rumors circulate that hostilities between two countries might have broken out, and that the borders might have been closed; vaguely, vestiges of the history of two countries separated by a border river and long-standing enmity begin to appear. The great History, however, the history of hot and cold wars, remains in the background: Other sources of conflict demand the full attention of the protagonist who hopes to be able to cross the border to Poland as soon as possible. The cold on the train platform in a country somewhere between France and Poland prepares for the approximation of another world from whose entry the I has actually been barred: the world from which the surviving part of the family had fled to France decades ago. Within the family, this world had been hushed up for a long time, and it does not come as a surprise that the progressive illness that has been spreading in the parents' generation is likely Alzheimer's.[10] The narrator, however, wants to know, wants access to the memory of her family which transcends her individual life. The journey thus leads not only across a political border, a border between systems, and a linguistic border. The journey back to Kielce in central Poland is also a return to the family's origins covered with the frozenness of the word as if with a thick sheet of ice. What is the price of this foray into a distant, frozen past?

It is clear from the start of the novel that the protagonist's return is neither motivated by mere curiosity nor a final return to a family's country of origin. In *Mémorial*, the motile figure of return is associated with death. Unfathomably for the narrator, those members of the family who had survived the Shoah and returned to Kielce became victims of another pogrom.[11] What remains of Auschwitz? Once again, it was the allegation of ritual murder that became the occasion for persecuting Jews. The bodies were simply thrown into the river; after the genocide, people put up steles at the cemetery, together with a monument, a 'memorial' to commemorate the massacre and to serve as admonition.[12] At the places of remembrance, a culture of commemoration in love with monuments, contained, dead. The cemetery has long been orphaned.

---

10 See Wajsbrot: *Mémorial*, p. 17, 54, 87, and 153.
11 See Wajsbrot: *Mémorial*, p. 56f.
12 Wajsbrot: *Mémorial*, p. 133.

Not only going back but just looking back can be fatal. We find several references to the myth of Orpheus and Eurydice and the lessons of their story: 'not to turn around, not to look back, deliberately to become blind to the past, in order to advance, to continue on – to be able to live.'[13] The I searches for this ability to live, this knowledge-for-living – and yet, it turns around, facing death without fear. Suddenly, the view opens onto a landscape fertile with ancient myth. The river turns into the River Styx, a name deliberately linked with the snowy owl via the natural-scientific label *stryx* (Greek for owl).[14] A border experience begins to come into view at the very river that separates the living from the dead. Does the *harfang des neiges*, whose name appears to come from Old Swedish, keep watch over the realm of the dead? And is the protagonist not a transgressor who does not respect the impenetrable border between the living and the dead? Is not her own life at risk when she is caught in the maze of the river of death in Kielce, so unremarkable now that she can barely make out in it the 'dreadful image of an aquatic minotaur demanding his due'?[15]

Looking back, yes, but not going back. The hermeneutical figure of an I-in-motion, a self that always feels the There in the Here and also senses the Here left behind in the There that has now become the Here, may be understood as the swinging of a pendulum, a movement that creates a vectoral space for life and for memory to live and survive. *Ici* and *là-bas* are defined spatially and temporally. Right from the start, the transnational and transareal journey, which, as in *Beaune-la-Rolande*, connects landscapes with very similar features,[16] carries with it a transtemporal dimension in which different temporalities intersect and cross-sect continuously. The crossing of different temporalities that transcend one's own individual lifetime works to harness the I transgenerationally to a genealogy that is made present anew time and again and which constitutes the I in the process of looking back onto a century of horrors. The There becomes audible in the Here, the past in the present, the you in the we. Thus begins a play of layerings and infiltrations which pervades and vectorizes every single reflection and experience beyond a mere return that might end in death.

But why go through all that? In her efforts to trace an 'origin' (origine), a line of descent, so that she can live in the future, the first-person narrator wres-

---

[13] '[N]e pas se retourner, ne pas regarder en arrière, se rendre volontairement aveugle au passé pour pouvoir avancer, continuer – pouvoir vivre.' Wajsbrot: *Mémorial*, p. 45.
[14] Wajsbrot: *Mémorial*, p. 67.
[15] '[L]'image effrayante d'un minotaure aquatique réclamant son dû.' Wajsbrot: *Mémorial*, p. 128.
[16] Wajsbrot: *Beaune-la-Rolande*, p. 41.

tles with an explanation for the feeling 'that my country was not altogether my country, but the country to which I will go (where I would go, if this train ever arrives) is not mine either.'[17] The traveler, it seems, risks becoming a prisoner of her own labyrinth;[18] she is pulled into the whirlpool of her own return, a return to the realm of the dead. The forces that pull her into the river are strong, and one can feel in them the movements that have turned the river into a river of the dead. War and dread, waves of refugees and deportations, are still present. But the knowledge that the I's journey is more than just 'a return delayed by several decades' protects her.[19] Many other, historically accumulated movements overlap with(in) the I's travels, movements that this progeny connects choreographically with her ancestors and their time, but also with her own lifetime. Already in the first three parts of the novel, we begin to glimpse the outlines of a vectoral memory space that the medium of literature shields against disease, against any form of memory loss.

The I searches for a path between the Scylla of return to the purported origin and the Charybdis of the motto with which migrants typically inculcate their children in their new home: '*In the future, you will do it better than we.*'[20] What follows is the same dialectic of homelessness that transformed Odysseus's voyage into a return to a strange land (see chapter 2 above). In dialogue with the voices that speak to her from nowhere, the first-person narrator realizes that returning is impossible: 'One did not return, one never returns, I said to myself on the train platform where night fell, what one left behind has changed, even if there were no great transformations, solely because time has passed or one has changed oneself, which really amounts to the same thing.'[21] Is it that Odysseus, unlike Benjamin's Angel of History, has a chance for a happy homecoming, especially because his journey is not, strictly speaking, a return?

---

17 '[Q]ue mon pays n'était pas tout à fait mon pays mais celui où j'allais (où j'irais, si ce train arrivait) n'était pas non plus le mien.' Wajsbrot: *Mémorial*, p. 13.
18 Wajsbrot: *Mémorial*, p. 13.
19 Wajsbrot: *Mémorial*, p. 16.
20 '[T]u feras mieux que nous.' Wajsbrot: *Mémorial*, p. 18.
21 'On ne revient pas, on ne revient jamais, me disais-je sur le quai où la nuit tombait, ce qu'on a quitté a changé, même s'il n'y a pas eu de grandes transformations, par le simple passage du temps, ou on a changé soi, ce qui revient au même.' Wajsbrot: *Mémorial*, p. 59.

The children of Auschwitz

Journeys often promise happiness. The protagonist's trip to Poland is by no means the first journey to a foreign country by a woman who ultimately does not feel that she truly belong anywhere. Early on, the neither-nor of belonging neither to the country of origin nor to the country of destination leads the French-born narrator to work as a foreign correspondent (a term that carries multiple meanings here) far away from Europe in a southern capital in the shadow of active volcanoes, where she is waiting for an earthquake. Writing in the French language that her immigrant parents never managed to master fully opens up for her a mobile space that allows her to live far away from the field of tensions between the country of origin and the country of destination in her parents' migration. At the same time, this distance also enables her to look at her own world from the outside. Even language becomes a deterritorialized medium that reflects the familiar within the foreign, and the foreign within the familiar. Distance seems to heal the wounds of the past.

This extraterritoriality, however, proves to be an 'alienated' existence in a time whose hours have already elapsed: a life subject to recall. The transcontinental correspondence of a correspondent without a fixed abode does not grant access to that region of silence over which the snowy owl, a migratory bird that equally crosses space *and* time, seems to keep vigil.[22] It is only the train trip to Poland, to Kielce, that directly and mercilessly confronts the narrator, who has fled from Europe to a hot climate, with this 'universe of ice' (univers de glace), a region that, for her, is uninhabitable and off-limits.[23] It is a region that requires persistent inspection and introspection.

At the beginning of this process, there is an explosion. When, in the second part of the novel, the narrator learns from a fellow-passenger on the train that this woman lives in the small industrial town of Auschwitz, she is unable to pronounce the name of the Polish town of Oswiecim. The name Auschwitz detonates like a bomb, and not only in the narrator's ears. Right after this explosion of words, there is a climatic change: 'the word hurled cold' (le mot jeta un froid) into the train compartment.[24] The word Auschwitz has the effect of transporting the two women, who converse in French, the language of the migrant child, 'into other spaces and other times,' more than the train they ride.[25] An already

---

22 See Wajsbrot: *Mémorial*, p. 67.
23 Wajsbrot: *Mémorial*, p. 25.
24 Wajsbrot: *Mémorial*, p. 71; see also p. 73.
25 Wajsbrot: *Mémorial*, p. 72.

positioned memory space begins to surface; it neither denies nor needs the place of memory in its concrete topographical localization. Important are only the vectoral signs of movements at once long past and also (in the) present: the lines of movement of those who were able to save themselves by fleeing to a foreign country, and of those who, like many of the narrator's relatives, were deported to the extermination camp of Auschwitz. It was hardly an accident that the Nazis chose a railway hub as the location of this extermination camp. It is also no accident that Cécile Wajsbrot, in whose writings rail cars of varying sorts are the principal means of transport, places this conversation on board of a moving train, whose movement resounds with the forebears' deportations and migrations.

The conversation on the train recalls the sharp-edged ruptures and borderlines of a splintered family genealogy which run through the names of Auschwitz and Kielce, infused as they are with an experience of terror. Similarly recollected are also the voice of those who have been silenced, voices that now shine light on the history of extermination and displacement from their different angles. They incessantly confront the narrator with this history and thus also with the border that separates the living, the survivors, from the dead whose lives were snuffed out. Once made to explode, the name Auschwitz reverberates endlessly in the echo chamber of the family's history. How does one repress that which does not stop exerting pressure in so many different voices?

The presence of the placeless, but not wordless voices clarifies that the narrator is both a child of migration and a child of Auschwitz. At the same time, however, she is clearly separate from the generation of her parents, for whom survival was all that mattered:

> –Those who live to see everything strive to survive and know what they have to do. Their victory is to have survived.
> –The other ones do not know it. They are born and are at a loss, because they carry the burden of an unspeakable event.[26]

If, for the generation of those who fled in time, mere survival qualifies as victory, what might be the victory of later generations, of those who experienced the 'mercy of a belated birth'? The protagonist can escape neither in space (the flight to a 'New World' far away from Europe) nor in time (the flight towards the future, into repressing and forgetting the past). She is all too aware of the perils

---

26 '–Ceux qui vivent pendant sont tendus vers la survie et savent ce qu'ils ont à faire. Leur victoire sera d'avoir survécu. –Les autres ne savent pas. Ils viennent au monde, désemparés, car il pèse sur eux un événement dont on ne parle pas.' Wajsbrot: *Mémorial*, p. 87.

of forever being a prisoner of the past: condemned to remember, eternally to remember, as if the past in all its forms were the only time with which I could do something.'[27] It falls to her and her generation to translate the first generation's survival knowledge into the second generation's knowledge-for-living. She has to escape the reduction to only one temporal plane and recreate the connection of past, present, and future. Above all, she has to become aware of her own life as a life (and a script) without a fixed abode. This is the wisdom that the snowy owl, '*a solitary creature that circles above bare, ice-covered plains,*' represents in its special ability to orient itself and move beyond the typical human geometry and its compass needles.[28]

The first person narrator seeks to rekindle her life – 'provided that life does not consist in a search for an answer to a single question'[29] – with the help of a knowledge-for-living in which the various spaces and times are better interwoven than before thanks to new transections and new pathsways, so that she might evade being held captive by the past and the ice-cold storage of life. Her train trip serves the purpose of helping her live in the present, today, without having to relinquish glancing back at the past, which, as Orpheus and the fate of Eurydice show, can be life-threatening. A comparison with *Beaune-la-Rolande* allows us to realize the vital, indeed life-saving, role literature might play in helping us 'to get from being frozen to thawing.'[30] It is literature that creates communications, connections between different spaces and temporalities within a geometry that does not exclude as amorphous and thus irrelevant that which is discontinuous, broken, rent, and fragmented.

The image of the island appears repeatedly in *Mémorial*. Suffering is represented as 'an island to which access is barred,'[31] an island one is forever trying to leave. When she is alone in her hotel room, the protagonist compares herself to someone 'shipwrecked on a desert island,'[32] even though this island is surrounded not by the sea but by a river, the river of Kielce. But there are far too many voices on this island. In the protagonist's isolation and insulation, these

---

[27] '[C]ondamnée à la mémoire, l'éternel souvenir, comme si le seul temps que je savais utiliser était le passé sous toutes ses formes.' Wajsbrot: *Mémorial*, p. 107.
[28] *'[U]n être solitaire qui tournoie au-dessus d'étendues désolées et glacées.'* Wajsbrot: *Mémorial*, p. 95. The emblematic connection of the owl with wisdom, which we know from antiquity, is mentioned explicitly.
[29] '[À] supposer que la vie ne soit pas la recherche d'une réponse à l'unique question.' Wajsbrot: *Mémorial*, p. 115.
[30] 'C'est la littérature qui nous fait passer du gel au dégel.' Wajsbrot: *Beaune-la-Rolande*, p. 52.
[31] '[U]ne île dont les abords sont interdits.' Wajsbrot: *Mémorial*, p. 104.
[32] '[N]aufragé échoué sur son île déserte.' Wajsbrot: *Mémorial*, p. 128.

voices take up more and more space, as the text shows with its growing number of insertions. To re-open this isolated I(s)land-world towards the multi-relationality of a world of islands, an archipelago, requires considerable effort. The past seems to dominate everything with its voices, even suppressing the protagonist's feeling of hunger: 'It is the past, I said to myself, the past which feeds and stuffs me; it leaves no room for what is yet to come, for the future – what can I still live for?'[33] At least at this point, it becomes clear that the supremacy of the past has turned into a question of survival for the protagonist: the realm of the dead intrudes more and more into that of the living. And death lurks. For the narrator who, alone in her hotel room, falls prey to the monsters of the past, the return to Kielce could have fatal consequences. What, after all, remains there to be lived for when the past puts the present in cold storage? Nowhere on the horizon is there a Promised Land.

Here *and* there

The experiences of the first generation of refugees demonstrate the extent to which survival can take the place of life and push it aside. One of the voices from the past confirms this: 'Yes, if one survives, there is nothing left of living.'[34] Just like the refugees and exiles of the first generation, the protagonist errs in search of her own life, and just like them, she does not know where to go: 'Where to now?' (Où aller?).[35] Continuing to live in this shattered time (*temps éclaté*)[36] is very close to a life in the realm of death. Yet, even in this region endangered by death, the I still looks for a new way, her own path, that promises freedom. The French '*trouver sa voie*'[37] stands at once for finding a way and finding one's own voice (*voix* echoes in the French lexeme *voie*). Among all the voices from the past, which already appear to sound from within the protagonist herself,[38] she searches for a voice of her own which houses the voices of the others, the dead, at the same time. But only literature is equal to this task, a

---

33 '[C]'est le passé, me disais-je, le passé que me nourrit et m'encombre, qui ne laisse pas place à la suite, l'avenir – que puis-je vivre encore ?' Wajsbrot: *Mémorial*, p. 129.
34 'Oui, quand on survit, il ne reste plus rien à vivre.' Wajsbrot: *Mémorial*, p. 147.
35 Wajsbrot: *Mémorial*, p. 152.
36 Wajsbrot: *Mémorial*, p. 153.
37 Wajsbrot: *Mémorial*, p. 159.
38 'Il n'y avait pas d'entre-deux possible, c'était ici ou là-bas – ici et là-bas pouvaient changer de place, s'inverser mais il fallait partir ou rester.' Wajsbrot: *Mémorial*, p. 97.

literature that consciously evolves polyphony and mobility without being committed to a *single* place, not even a place of memory.

In the last section of the novel's third and final part, the protagonist is faced with a seemingly unambiguous alternative: 'There was not possible in-between; it is either here or there –here and there could change places, invert themselves, but it was still either leaving or staying.'[39] Here *or* there? An interstitial location, a place in-between, does not seem to exist. And yet, an interWorld comes into existence to the extent that the poles can be reversed, so that and the There is always already stored in the Here, just as the voices from the past are always already contained in the voices of the present.

The journey to the realm of the dead, and thus the scrutiny of the realm of the past, would not be complete without the protagonist having searched for and visited the house in Kielce in which the family's history is concentrated. Approaching this (presumed) house, however, is experienced as entering a 'forbidden zone' (zone interdite),[40] as an illegal border crossing; it is as if the house were a minefield. Here, *nothing* is the way it used to be, the voices inside tell her. It is impossible to return to some sort of home. Other people with their own stories and histories, their own memories, have been living here for a long time now. *Ici est un autre* – Here is elsewhere.

Guided by the image of the train tracks that vanish in the distance, the protagonist seems to decide quickly between the Here that has becomes a There, and the There that has become a Here.[41] The first-person narrator retrieves her suitcase, leaves her hotel room, rushes to Kielce train station, and, only a few lines down, finds herself back in Paris, a city that she, like someone who has just awoken from a hundred-year sleep, hardly recognizes anymore. In a place presumably her own, she now has a 'feeling of strangeness' (sentiment d'étrangeté) and the impression that she has not returned home.[42] Returning to Paris by the very same routes that her parents took as refugees is, once again, a return to a foreign country, and, even more so, to the uncanny.[43] The protagonist's own apartment now seems as foreign as a hotel room. The novel expertly accentuates what is uncanny (unheimlich) about the return to a foreign land through the presence of the already familiar foreign voices. Suddenly, the river

---

39 Wajsbrot: *Mémorial*, p. 165.
40 Wajsbrot: *Mémorial*, p. 165f.
41 Wajsbrot: *Mémorial*, p. 158.
42 Wajsbrot: *Mémorial*, p. 170.
43 See Sigmund Freud: *The Uncanny*. London: Penguin Books 2003. https://books.google.com/books?id=QQdBlDBUFywC.

and the cemetery of Kielce are present in Paris. The return trip to Paris, which the text completely omits, is not a real homecoming, because the uncanny has taken up residence in the supposedly familiar home; it is not possible close one's eyes to it, to keep it a secret. The neither-nor of not-belonging has turned into the *both-and-also*, in which different, overlapping and mutually permeating, temporal and spatial planes co-exist in the present: this is the interWorld that Cécile Wajsbrot's *Mémorial* creates in a disheartening fashion. The contrast between Here and There has evaporated in an oscillating interworld that has repositioned itself from an external topography to the protagonist's interior. At the end of the novel, all outside movements come to a halt; the melt into the universe of voices that no longer know a fixed abode. *Mémorial* ends with the falling asleep of an exhausted and worn-out protagonist. At this point, it is difficult to tell the difference between falling asleep and dying because of her intimate familiarity with the voices of the dead:

> I will stretch out next to them, stay inside their universe, where there is no struggle, where nothing happens, in a world without stakes, without a past that suffocates one, without a future that makes one afraid, a uniform, eternal world – I will stretch out next to them, just as I have dreamt from time to time, and then close my eyes, fall asleep.[44]

A world without origins and without a future? The ambiguous openness of this ending leaves unanswered the question of whether dissolving the borders between the realm of the dead and that of the living is a dream or a nightmare. The transtemporal, transcultural, and transspatial co-presence of temporalities and spaces leads to a region that is weary of life, a place that has no more promises in store, except for a communion with the dead. Either way, the narrator in the end remains caught in an interWorld between the living and the dead, in the here *and* there of a history of migration that is one of many on this migratory planet. *Mémorial* shows in a striking way that life 'after' migration is still life under the spell of migration.

This also, and especially, applies to writing 'after' migration. For it, there is also no return to a *degré zero* of movement, however it may be configured. Everything is stored in literature's multiply refracted fractal field of vectors. The end of the novel arrests the protagonist's movements, but not the movement of a literature that watches the frozen regions hostile to life with the penetrating eyes

---

[44] 'Je vais m'étendre à côté d'eux, rester dans leur univers sans lutte où rien n'arrive, un monde sans enjeu, sans passé qui écrase, sans avenir qui fait peur, un monde uniforme, éternel – je vais m'étendre à côté d'eux comme j'en rêvais parfois, et puis fermer les yeux, m'endormir.' Wajsbrot: *Mémorial*, p. 174.

of a snowy owl, and that crosses temporalities and spaces especially where they are inaccessible to humans. What are the possibilities of a literature that derives its knowledge from the continuous crossing of the minefield of the past? What can it do?

In Cécile Wajsbrot's text, literature itself becomes a memorial to what has been silenced and repressed for a long time, and not only in the very concrete sense of the murder of Jews after the murder of Jews. Where Max Aub's black raven Jacobo, in the *Manuscrito Cuervo*, regarded the whole world as a concentration camp, Wajsbrot's nameless white owl roams a frozen world 'without a future and without a past,' a space in which no human civilization has left permanent traces.[45] Where Jacobo's gaze monitors a camp in which, according to him, the whole (human) world is concentrated, *'the concentration of spirit'* (*la concentration de l'élan*) finds its expression in the flight of the snowy owl.[46] Jacobo leaves behind a manuscript, the snowy owl only the choreography of its flights. The wisdom of Cécile Wajsbrot's white raven avoids humans who conquer, rule, and possess territories. It focuses instead on its movements and circles a universe in which the children of migration (and the children auf Auschwitz) live both in the Here and the There, in the Then and the Now *at the same time*. For this, they do not need a fixed abode.

A literature of liminality

Like Cécile Wajsbrot, who was born in Paris in 1954, Sherko Fatah, born in the former East Berlin in 1964, is a child of migration. The son of a German mother and a father from the Kurdish part of Iraq – or the Iraqi part of Kurdistan – grew up in the capital of the GDR until his family moved to West Berlin via Vienna. Fatah stayed in touch with Iraq, not only during his childhood in (East) Berlin when he spent longer periods of time his paternal home country, but also while he was a student of philosophy and art history in then-West Berlin. As an article Fatah wrote for the *Frankfurter Allgemeine Zeitung* testifies, he has managed to keep up this relationship to this day. The telephone conversations prior to the

---

45 'Il plane au-dessus d'étendues désolées, l'été va venir et il a regagné son domaine – son royaume – un lieu sans avenir ni passé où n'existe nulle trace, nul vestige d'aucune civilisation, une terre que ne fut jamais occupée, toujours trop loin du pouvoir central.' Wajsbrot: *Mémorial*, p. 163.
46 Wajsbrot: *Mémorial*, p. 163.

second Iraq war, which this article mentions, clearly convey the familiar distance that characterizes Sherko Fatah's relations to (northern) Iraq.[47]

All differences notwithstanding, the parallels between Sherko Fatah and Cécile Wajsbrot can by no means be reduced to the biographeme of belonging to a 'second' generation. More important is that both the French and the German author connect in their writing national literatures with another, more broadly transnational and transareal, space and thus narratively widen the field of vision of their respective national literatures. Karl-Markus Gauss writes the following about Sherko Fatah and his first novel, 'In the Borderlands' (*Im Grenzland*)[48]:

> He has a story to tell for which there are hardly any comparisons in German literature, and he tells it in a way that we know here only through translations. That German literature is now being written by authors who are called Sherko Fatah and who, as Germans, dip into the fund of family traditions that connect them with distant regions of the world, means unquestionably that German literature is being enriched. This writing bring to German literature new topics, foreign tonalities, unfamiliar perspectives, in short: the world.[49]

'In the Borderlands' was published in 2001 and won both the 'aspekte' literary award for best first prose narrative written in German and the German Critics' Circle Award that same year.[50] While one should be careful, as I have pointed out repeatedly, not to pigeonhole authors within the presumed foreignness of so-called faraway regions of the world, this early review of Fatah's novel shows just how much the writer's 'foreign' sounding name, the *nom de plume*, already inscribes this difference paratextually. This, incidentally, is another parallel that links Sherko Fatah and Cécile Wajsbrot.

The phenomenon of 'foreignness' is of course not limited to the realm of the paratextual or to the novel's narrative, that is, the setting of the plot in a distant

---

47 See Sherko Fatah: 'Warum bleibt mein Onkel in Bagdad? Stimmungen in der Republik der Angst: Das große Hoffen auf Saddams Sturz.' In: *Frankfurter Allgemeine Zeitung* (Frankfurt am Main) 41 (February 18, 2003), p. 33.
48 [No English translation of this novel is available to date. All page numbers are to the German paperback edition: Sherko Fatah: *Im Grenzland*. Berlin: btb-Verlag 2003. The first edition was published in 2001 by Jung & Jung in Salzburg, Austria. TN]
49 Karl-Markus Gauss: 'Fremde Welt, so nah: Der kurdisch-deutsche Autor Sherko Fatah schreibt seinen ersten Roman.' In: *Die Zeit* (Hamburg) 13 (2001).
50 [In March 2015, the Robert Bosch Foundation honored Fatah with the Adalbert-von-Chamisso Prize. Although this prize was for Fatah's entire body of work, his most recent novel, *Der letzte Ort* (The last place) received special mention. TN]

country which, for its German audience, is literally located 'in wild Kurdistan.'[51] The author himself wisely called attention to this problem in a very specific way:

> I live in Germany and wrote this book in German. The landscape I portray is thus not my home. My father comes from the northern part of Iraq. Childhood memories, later travel experiences, and, when it comes to events during the war, stories by relatives helped improve my touristic gaze. Still, as narrator, I wanted to keep my distance, that is, to refrain from pretending a closeness that is not my main interest in this novel, even though it is based on facts. Many other books are surely better suited, I think, to cover the ever-present great demand for folklore. By contrast, to lend expression to a perhaps universal foreignness is a completely different project. I want to put it plainly: Even the sympathetic reader will probably find it difficult to find his way into this foreign world (which I have allowed to remain foreign). But if that same reader also found it hard to leave that world, I would have succeeded in reaching in my goal.[52]

Sherko Fatah walks on the edge by refusing to be located and folklorized in the foreign while, at the same time, creating a foreignness in the text, and thus in the reader, which cannot be located anywhere but which is universal. Fatah's writing is about the creation of a foreignness that inheres within the text itself and makes it into a foreign world that casts its spell on the audience. This world is located beyond any more or less decorative 'foreign' scenery, beyond the characters' geographical placement.

It is worth pointing out that landscape does play a fundamental role in the plot and for the poetics of the novel. Although, during the course of the novel,

---

51 [*Durchs wilde Kurdistan* (1892) is the title of a novel by Karl May (1842–1912), popular German author of adventure novels set in 'exotic' countries. TN].
52 'Ich lebe in Deutschland und habe dieses Buch in deutscher Sprache geschrieben. Die von mir dargestellte Landschaft ist also nicht meine Heimat. Mein Vater stammt aus dem nördlichen Teil des Irak. Zur Verbesserung meines touristischen Blicks trugen Kindheitserinnerungen, spätere Reiseerlebnisse und, was die Kriegsgeschehnisse betrifft, Erzählungen von Familienmitgliedern bei. Dennoch galt es für mich, als Erzähler Distanz zu wahren, das heißt keine Nähe vorzugaukeln, welche in diesem Roman, auch wenn er in vielem auf Tatsachen beruht, nicht im Zentrum des Interesses steht. Um den gewiß immer großen Bedarf an Folklore zu decken, sind, wie ich meine, viele Bücher besser geeignet. Eine vielleicht universale Fremdheit zum Ausdruck zu bringen, ist demgegenüber ein ganz anderes Projekt. Ich will es einfach sagen: Es wird wohl selbst dem geneigten Leser nicht ganz leicht fallen, in diese fremde und fremd belassene Welt hineinzufinden, fände er aber ebenso schwer heraus, hätte ich mein Ziel erreicht.' Sherko Fatah: 'Sherko Fatah über sein Buch,' <www.lyrikwelt.de/gedichte/fatahg1.-htm> (accessed 07.06.2015).

region is only mentioned in passing and rarely identified nationally,[53] many markings situate the novel's s plot exclusively in the triangle where Iran, Iraq, and Turkey meet. This does not, however, mean that we only need to locate the titular 'borderlands' on a map and that the novel is limited to one region that can be territorialized. As in Cécile Wajsbrot's novels, the journey to the borderlands is a journey to the realm of the dead, to a minefield. As in *Mémorial*, a destructive war is not far off in Fatah's novel, and it casts its shadows over the events. Reduced to a minimum of plot action and presented in constant overlays and time warps, the events in both novels unfold within an environment hostile to humans. Wajsbrot's and Fatah's text both focus on liminal experiences set in a landscape of death. The dark river that seems motionless to the protagonist who has to cross it each time he enters the mine-infested borderlands, has aspects of the river of the dead, the River Styx.[54] Each step the solitary border crosser takes could be his last. Like Cécile Wajsbrot, Sherko Fatah leads his readers into a minefield, which signifies not one specific locale but an existential situation that threatens human lives. 'In the borderlands' does not conjure up a spiritual landscape but engages us in a slow, groping exploration of the human condition.

As in *Mémorial*, war has created immense minefields everywhere, and quite literally in Fatah's novel. Buried just below the surface are tons of explosives ready to kill those who dare to enter the forbidden borderlands. The very space that, during the Ottoman Empire, was an area of flourishing trade and cultural exchanges among Istanbul, Baghdad, and Teheran, has now turned into a zone of extreme isolation, policed by border guards, soldiers, and secret services. There are, of course, always holes even in such tight border security. Anyone who wants to move around in this region must possess very specific expert knowledge.

We can detect here another parallel between the two texts I analyze in this chapter. Fatah's protagonist is like the narrator in Cécile Wajsbrot's *Mémorial* in that he has embraced the self-appointed task to cross regions marked by a past war, regions that are uninhabitable, virtually nameless, and unmentionable. Where the French author places at the center of her novel a child of migration searching for the traces of her family's and her community's history, 'In the borderlands' features a smuggler who tries to secure his family's income by trans-

---

53 This paratextual positioning already occurs on the back cover of the paperback edition: Sherko Fatah: *Im Grenzland* (Berlin 2003). For a clear national assignation, see Fatah: *Im Grenzland*, p. 30.
54 Fatah: *Im Grenzland*, p. 79.

porting illegal luxury goods across a border that has become practically impassable. Both protagonists, who remain nameless, seek to survive. For this reason, the smuggler, having bought a detailed map of the minefields installed by the military from a former soldier, spends many years acquiring precise knowledge of the strictly guarded and secured borderlands. He is, therefore, able to orient himself exactly in the field on his continuous trips across the border, using only the routes and pathways he knows to move in mined territory. When he carefully digs up the mines one by one on his way out to create a passage that no one else can use, he always buries them again upon his return to make the paths he uses unusable to others. It comes as no surprise, then, that he refuses to share his knowledge with a United Nations mine-clearing commando.[55] The fact that the borderland is full of mines forms, after all, the basis of his livelihood without which he would hardly be able to feed his wife and three children. Ironically, he has to have an interest in the state's maintaining the very borders he constantly crosses and in the very existence of those mines he repeatedly digs up and re-buries. As a smuggler, he needs the artificial border he himself disrespects because he depends on it for his income.

Suffering not only from the war and its continuing consequences but also from a near-perfect surveillance by a violent and repressive system, the people of the (Iraqi-Kurdish) borderlands have long fallen into poverty. Because of an embargo, whose historical model is likely the UN embargo, the goods that are so badly needed, such as medications, cannot enter the country. This is an opportunity for the protagonist, for it is only in this way that he, as a smuggler, can rise to an important figure with access to the circles of influential traders. The people order from him alcoholic beverages from Turkey, foreign cigarettes, medication, baby food, and especially electronics, such as laptops and VCRs. This is dangerous business, but it burgeons. Because of his alliances with local elites who live off the illegal and the remaining legal trade, and also because of his (not always entirely voluntary) cooperation with representatives of the state's 'internal security' who control him from within the 'Red House,'[56] the smuggler, once a simple black market dealer who used to earn his living in city, becomes a border violator who is anything but a subversive dissident, even a Robin Hood of the poor. The border violator's ambivalence is more typical of him:

In the same way that each violation of the law creates an awareness of the law, each illegal border crossing increases the knowledge of gaps and weaknesses in surveillance and control. In his violent or imaginative, wily or unscrupu-

---

55 Fatah: *Im Grenzland*, p. 61–63.
56 Fatah: *Im Grenzland*, p. 70.

lous seeking out and taking advantage of the weak spots of border regimes, the border violator, despite himself, is a competent and innovative security advisor when it comes to border safety. Trespass, then, not only leads to perforation but also accomplishes a more and more seamless securing of borders.[57]

The Turkish border officials on one side usually allow the smuggler, for a small fee (a road toll of sorts), to pass the border with his illegal goods, and the Iraqi secret service on the other side tacitly tolerate his activities. Clearly, the damage his activities do to the state economy is fairly insignificant compared to the potential benefits that his constant 'explorations' in the border region might bring the Iraqi state. The protagonist thus does not hesitate to collaborate with the secret police and the border patrol for as long as doing so also serves his own purpose. An example here is the search for his son, as we will see below.

Through his illegally crossing of the nation-states' borders (in their function as barriers to trade), a smuggler, even 'unwillingly and often unconsciously,' becomes a practitioner of a potentially 'borderless flow of capital and goods,' indeed a 'globalizer par excellence.'[58] There are good reasons, then, why the narrator in Sherko Fatah's 'In the borderlands' works intensely against any idealizing, romanticizing, or folklorizing of the figure of the smuggler and thus resists any all-too willing identification with him on the part of the reader. Fatah's smuggler is, of course, a cunning, sly character whose existence is threatened and who fights to survive in a repressive world hostile to humans. But all the courage he musters for his risky trips across the border notwithstanding, Fatah's smuggler is not cut from the cloth of great heroes.

Yet we have to be careful. As a lone transgressor and trespasser, the smuggler is not so unlike the writer, a maverick who, like the smuggler, always needs to find his own path in largely unexplored territory, and who makes a living from disrespecting all sorts of ideological, linguistic, and genre-specific, and aesthetic boundaries. Their very existence is what makes (licit and illicit) crossings possible in the first place. The writer, too, moves across territory below whose surface explosives are buried, and words that, just like the name 'Auschwitz' in *Mémorial,* might blow up like bombs. Of course, a writer can make the smuggler a reflection of himself. For these reasons, it is worth considering 'In the borderlands' from the perspective of literature as contraband: for the writer can see himself as a resident of a borderland, of an interWorld, whose trails and secret pathways he knows intimately.

---

[57] Eva Horn et al. (eds.): *Grenzverletzer: Von Schmugglern, Spionen und anderen subversiven Gestalten.* Berlin: Kulturverlag Kadmos 2002, p. 9f.
[58] Bettina Paul et al.: 'Der Schmuggler'. In: Horn et al. (eds.): *Grenzverletzer,* p. 108.

Survival stories from a no-man's-land

While the smuggler in Sherko Fatah's novel has a family and owns a house, he is constantly on the move, except for short breaks on either side of the borders. He moves in an interWorld populated by border patrols, militias, scattered guerrilla fighters, and occasional robber bands. Through this world run his own secret pathways that connect the villages on both sides of the border as though they were islands. The result of state borders and politically motivated attempts at segregation, the artificial difference between the islands accounts for the tensions between shadow economy and an economy characterized by constant shortages, between international supply and national demand, which produce and reward the smuggler's border-crossing oscillations. Between the islands separated by uninhabitable territory, even minimal relations develop only with great difficulty, and these relations are subject to strenuous surveillance and, at best, connivance on the part of the state.

Not only goods come from outside. From beyond the border also hails the smuggler's nephew, a guest who appears in the very first sentence of the first of a total of twelve chapters:

> When the visiting guest heard about the death, the smuggler had already been gone for days. The man had headed out without knowing about the death of his son, now officially confirmed. Before that, however, he had left the rest of his family, his wife and the two adolescent children. As if he sensed something about the future, the smuggler had begun to burn his bridges behind him.[59]

This opening, plotted from the point of view of the end of the story, 'gives away' at least part of the outcome of the events told in the novel. We learn what the smuggler is only be able to surmise much later in the text: that his oldest son, barely thirteen, who had had contact with Islamists in a Quran school,[60] has been murdered by 'internal security' forces. This boy's completely meaningless death throws into relief a dictatorship more than willing to use violence in its ruthless fight against any sort of opposition, even religiously motivated opposition. And none of the other powers in the three-state region have any scruples

---

[59] 'Als der zugereiste Gast von dem Trauerfall hörte, war der Schmuggler schon seit Tagen unterwegs. Ohne vom nunmehr offiziell bestätigten Tod seines Sohnes zu wissen, hatte sich der Mann auf den Weg gemacht. Vorher jedoch verließ er den Rest seiner Familie, seine Frau und die beiden halbwüchsigen Kinder. Als ahnte er etwas vom Bevorstehenden, hatte der Schmuggler begonnen, die Brücken hinter sich abzubrechen.' Fatah: *Im Grenzland*, p. 5.
[60] See Fatah: *Im Grenzland*, p. 83–85.

either when it comes to violence. All of the father's attempts to use his connections to free his son – even if those are entirely dependent on the good will of the state – have therefore failed: the interrogations by secret service officials; the trip to the capital; and the countless bribes the father paid for months to be able to track his disappeared son. With his wife seems resigned to the situation, the smuggler burns his bridges. The man's previously restless movements untie him finally from his family, from his own village, perhaps even from his own country.

Right from the start, the visitor from abroad misses him. Much points in the direction that the nephew will advance to the position of the story's real narrator. With a conceit that Gustave Flaubert already employed in *Madame Bovary*, Sherko Fatah gives his narrator a cameo in the first few lines of the text, the better to make him disappear. The guest, the nephew who, although he is part of the family, sees the house of mourning from the outside, is at a distance from the events. This same distance seems to allow the German-speaking author to cover the text with the experience of foreignness as if it were a universal mantle. Fatah's contrivance is a literary strategy that has certain consequences. The fact that this extraterritorial narrator, who is also a homodiegetic narrator (as part of his local family's community of mourners), can 'come and go' without effecting even the slightest change,[61] inaugurates a game whose points of reference we may well identify as the Flaubertian categories of impassibility (*impassibilité*), impersonality (*impersonnalité*), and impartiality (*impartialité*). The distance between the guest and the smuggler is present right from the start. Because of that distance, the uncanny cannot assume the airs of the familiar and the close, the homely and the domestic.[62] Not only the smuggler, but also the nephew himself is a traveler who, from a distance of 'a few thousand kilometers by plane and with overland communal taxis across the mountains,'[63] has come from far beyond the border, only to disappear again in the same way, perhaps to the Germany about which the Turkish border soldiers and torturers talk.[64] Not only does the nephew speak German; the entire horizon of his knowledge is 'oriented' towards the (reader from a) German-speaking world.

---

61 Fatah: *Im Grenzland*, p. 6.
62 Consequently, the home, whenever it is mentioned, appears in a dreary light: 'in these dark rooms one was not a guest but really, in a miserable and frightening way, at home' (in diesen dunklen Räumen war man nicht Gast, sondern eigentlich, in einem trostlosen und erschreckenden Sinne, zu Hause). Fatah: *Im Grenzland*, p. 7.
63 '[E]in paar tausend Kilometern per Flugzeug und mit geländegängigem Sammeltaxi durchs Gebirge.' Fatah: *Im Grenzland*, p. 11.
64 Fatah: *Im Grenzland*, p. 162.

What does the nephew want in this border town in northern Iraq? We learn little about his motives, not much more than the fact that he is looking for 'clues about the life, the past, and perhaps even the future' of the smuggler.[65] Is he a sociologist or an ethnologist, a storyteller perhaps? Beginning with the second chapter, his mobile perspective suffuses the portrayals of the unsteady world of his uncle who, in the nephew's eyes, is not just a resident of the small town but a 'peculiar denizen of the borderlands' (ein sonderbarer Bewohner des Grenzlandes): 'he was a messenger from the now almost impassable land around the city, from there, where only the farmers, who had no choice, lived.[66] No doubt, the smuggler is an emissary not a farmer. Not coincidentally, the beginning of a conversation between nephew and uncle mentions a farmer who had gone to his fields and was killed by an exploding mine. Only a 'large, roasted leg' (grosses, geröstetes Bein) remained of him. The smuggler stresses that 'precisely the part of him with which he touched the mine was left over.'[67] Even if the smuggler is afraid that this might happen to him, it does not. His knowledge is survival knowledge, the art not to die in an environment hostile to humans – in a realm of the dead, of those killed senselessly, among them his oldest son, the 'little buck' (Böckchen).

Only those who survive, who have survived, can tell stories. The others become stories and history. As distant and strange uncle and nephew may seem to each other, both are positioned on the side of the storytellers from the outset. One smuggles himself into the story, the other traffics in stories: signs of life and signs of survival, for which literature takes responsibility – a literature that has something to tell but that does not have a fixed abode. Smuggler and guest, uncle and nephew, narratee and narrator belong to two different generations. Keeping in mind *Mémorial*, they are distant from each other and yet belong together.

The life in northern Iraq of which the novel gives us glimpses resembles life in a sequestered I(s)land-world. There are no more watch makers in the border town, only boys that assemble 'new' watches from the discarded pieces of old ones. Here, life consists of the remains of the past. It is only when the nephew realizes 'how pared down life was here' that he begins to feel 'truly foreign'

---

[65] 'Hinweise auf das Leben, die Vergangenheit, vielleicht sogar die Zukunft.' Fatah: *Im Grenzland*, p. 126.
[66] 'Er war ein Bote aus dem fast unbetretbar gewordenen Land um die Stadt, von dort, wo nur die Bauern, die keine Wahl hatten, lebten.' Fatah: *Im Grenzland*, p. 9–10.
[67] 'Genau der Teil von ihm war übriggeblieben, mit dem er die Panzermine berührt hat.' Fatah: *Im Grenzland*, p. 9.

(wirklich fremd).⁶⁸ If not for the smuggler, the border town would long have become 'an island of the previous day' (Insel des vorigen Tages), an enclosed world in which anything 'new' can only be a combination of old shards. The past rules a present whose instruments of suppression tolerate no future. The randomly rigged watches show this. As in Cécile Wajsbrot's *Mémorial*, the past has commenced its rule over the present and at best permits the smuggling in of tiny glimpses of the future.

The immense difficulty of 'clearly distinguishing the inside from the outside,' on which the narrator remarks, makes us notice that the representation of the external world, the mountainous landscape, is always a representation of the inner world, so that all readings that focus on the mountain ridges are also readings of character traits. The outside can easily smuggle in something from the inside, under the radar, so to speak, of the 'gentle' reader. Below the spatial movements lie intellectual and emotional movements; below the impertinence toward state borders is the trespass of other border relations, all in the unrelenting struggle to survive. The stories of Beno, a shady secret service man, who relates, among other things, how he survived an attack by a technologically far more advanced army in the first Iraq war,⁶⁹ are also survival stories. The narrative layers them across the smuggler's stories and accumulates what the survivors know about survival: knowledge of life, and knowledge that life has of itself, are prerequisites for survival. Beno's stories smuggle an always encoded secret message that the listener has to decipher, a message that contains instructions for survival. Storytelling keeps appearing as a survival strategy, as when the smuggler, during his trips across the border, knows just how important it is to keep up the conversation with the border soldiers. In order to survive, one has to know how to smuggle the inside into the outside.

Unsurprisingly, this is precisely what creates a closeness between the smuggler and the secret agent. Beno knows, too, that the desert is 'not a landscape but a state of continuous transformation.'⁷⁰ The smuggler has a similar view of the borderlands in their 'planned-unplanned blockage of this potential living space.'⁷¹ He knows that this no man's land between Iraq, Iran, and Turkey is not, all perceptions to the contrary, a motionless landscape but, rather, a

---

68 '[W]ie reduziert das Leben hier war.' Fatah: *Im Grenzland*, p. 15.
69 'Inneres und Äußeres klar zu unterscheiden.' Fatah: *Im Grenzland*, p. 38ff.
70 '[K]eine Landschaft, sondern ein Zustand aus ständigem Wechseln.' Fatah: *Im Grenzland*, p. 38.
71 '[P]lanvoll-planlosen Sperrung dieses möglichen Lebensraumes.' Fatah: *Im Grenzland*, p. 60.

'state of continuous transformation' produced by the ceaseless sedimentation of external and internal movements: a mobile border condition of the world, and also of the I which is left to its own devices and just wants to 'get through.'

Much in this compellingly narrated novel is less a question of arriving than of getting through. Consequently, the smuggler experiences 'homecoming' (Heimkommen) as an 'entrance into an utterly different realm of his life,' as entry into a 'populated space in which the rules were also those of others,' It is a 'female space' (weiblicher Raum) covered with 'something like constant, quiet activity' (etwas wie ständige, leise Betriebsamkeit) but in which there was 'still an unbending border' (eine unnachgiebige Grenze).[72] This is clearly not the center of the man's life. His real living space is the blocked and yet passable transit space of the no man's land in which he follows his own paths and rules. And this no-man's-land is universally borderless and vectorized. In fact, this path does not just lead across the borderlands. It is everywhere, wherever he went.'[73]

The contraband (of) literature

Military and secret agents try to tap the smuggler's knowledge about the borderlands and use it better to control the no-man's-land. The smuggler cooperates, since he knows all too well by this point in the novel that his son has been arrested, together with Iranians who are preparing for a coup in the neighboring Iraq. Flying across the borderlands in a helicopter, the smuggler show the Iraqi officers and soldiers details that only he knows, including 'his own' path across the minefields. The military men quickly decide that they know everything, and the chopper veers off:

> The smuggler took a last look at his path which he would probably never again see in this way. It seemed small and unimportant, and yet he had never before had a stronger certainty than he did in this moment, the certainty that the path belonged only to him in the quietude of his solitary marches and with all its horrors.[74]

---

72 '[D]en Eintritt in einen völlig anderen Bereich seines Lebens'; 'bevölkerten Raum, in dem auch die Regeln der anderen herrschten.' Fatah: *Im Grenzland*, p. 98.
73 'Im Grunde führt dieser Pfad nicht nur durch das Grenzland. Er war überall, wohin er auch ging.' Fatah: *Im Grenzland*, p. 100.
74 'Der Schmuggler warf einen letzten Blick hinaus auf seinen Pfad, den er wohl nie wieder so zu sehen bekommen würde. Klein und unbedeutend erschien er, und doch hatte er nie stärker als in diesem Moment die Gewissheit, dass er ihm allein gehörte in der Ruhe seiner einsamen Märsche und mit all seinen Schrecken.' Fatah: *Im Grenzland*, p. 117.

The helicopter needs only a few seconds to travel the distance for which the smuggler needs hours on the ground. The view from above, the bird's eye view, uncovers the path, but at the same time obscures the experience of using it. The smuggler's trail is accessible only to the eye's distant view, not to the close-up view that only walking it – or better, the act of groping, crawling, finding the mines and digging them up of them – makes possible. The point here is that there is no goal, no arrival; this space, the borderlands, is but a pretext for the process of crossing it, for processes of reading and writing in the minefield:

> The smuggler always became aware of the seriousness of the situation after the digging up, when he could make out the letters that were precise about where the soccer ball should hit the upper disk and push it down. Whatever they meant, these signs had no decorative purpose. They were sitting on the small, greenish-brown surface as if they were remnants of an age-old inscription in an inaccessible place, not meant to be read, covered with soil, destined to disappear in the explosion, in the wound and in the pain, and to communicate their message in this way. They were like a frozen countdown before the detonation.
> The smuggler held his head close to the ground and crawled slowly on his knees. What he, protected by the rim of his straw hat, saw in front of him was a clearly-defined, but now even narrower path. The small stones that himself had put down as secret blazes guided him, but only centimeter by centimeter, for he had to find the exact location in his memory. When he had found it, he stopped immediately. He pulled a piece of paper out of his coat pocket and compared the schematic drawing with the ground in front of him. The position of the stones were the same on both paths, on the drawing and on the actual one. He folded the paper and put it away.[75]

---

[75] 'Immer nach dem Ausgraben kam dem Schmuggler der Ernst der Lage wieder zu Bewußtsein, wenn er die Schriftzeichen erkennen konnte, die genau da verliefen, wo der Fußballen die obere Scheibe treffen und niederdrücken sollte. Diese Zeichen, was immer sie anzeigten, hatten nichts Zierendes. Sie lagen in der kleinen, grünbraunen Fläche wie nicht zum Lesen vorgesehene Reste einer uralten Inschrift an unzugänglichem Ort, bedeckt von Erde, dazu bestimmt, in der Explosion, in der Wunde und im Schmerz zu verschwinden und so ihre Botschaft zu überbringen. Sie waren wie ein erstarrter Countdown vor der Detonation. Der Schmuggler hielt den Kopf dicht über der Erde und rutschte auf den Knien voran. Was er, beschirmt von der Strohhutkrempe, vor sich sah, war ein festumrissener, aber nun nochmals extrem verengter Pfad. Die kleinen Steine, die er selbst als geheime Markierung ausgelegt hatte, leiteten ihn, aber nur zentimeterweise, denn er mußte die genaue Lage in seiner Erinnerung finden. Wenn er sie hatte, verharrte er sofort. Er holte seinen Zettel aus der Manteltasche und verglich die Schemazeichnung mit dem Boden vor sich. Die Positionen der Steine stimmten auf beiden Pfaden, dem gezeichneten und dem wirklichen, überein. Er faltete das Papier zusammen und steckte es wieder fort.' Fatah: *Im Grenzland*, p. 101f.

This immense slowness of advancing on the path on which this man, loaded down with contraband, would crawl back stands in a vivid contrast to the speed with which the soldiers fly across the borderlands in their helicopters. The smuggler cannot afford to scan the signs only superficially, to fly across then, as it were. Reading the letters on the mine, on the ground, and on the drawing, is supplemented by the marks and notes that the smuggler writes both on the ground and on paper. These processes of writing and reading take place against the background of the threat of a possible detonation that could bring a sudden end to everything. Why did the smuggler not stay in the city? He is not interested in the visits with his sister, who lives on the other, the Turkish, side of the border with her husband, in whose house the smuggler stores his contraband, and with whom he joins in his feverish, incestuous nightly phantasies.[76] Nor is he interested in the contents, the ever-changing objects of his smuggling, which he carries across the border for his customers. At the center of his life is the path, *his* path, the decoding of the signs and the very act of smuggling itself – a careful, gentle fumbling under the spell of death, a sudden explosion that he himself has caused.

When, during his search for his son who has been caught in the fangs of 'internal security,' the smuggler begins to dig up the past and to understand the mechanisms of surveillance, Beno shows him the limits inside the 'Red House': 'Here, there is no past, at least not for people like you. No past and also no future. For you, there is only the present – everything else is a restricted area.'[77] Death threatens the smuggler at the slightest deviation from this present, from his path across the minefield. This is why his sister advises him not to search for his son, 'not to follow the tracks' (nicht den Spuren folgen) but to wait: more he could not do.[78] But the smuggler follows his own inner rules; he cannot wait, he cannot be still. In doing so, he also uncovers contact mines. When he visits a secret service prison in the city, he bribes officials, and he speaks with prisoners. Faced with the increasingly likely death of his son, for which he feels partly guilty for having left the 'little buck' in the school of the Islamists, the smuggler, much like his nephew, searches for 'clues about life, the past, perhaps even the

---

76 See Fatah: *Im Grenzland*, p. 174–176.
77 'Es gibt hier keine Vergangenheit, jedenfalls nicht für solche wie dich. Keine Vergangenheit und auch keine Zukunft. Für dich gibt es nur die Gegenwart – alles andere ist Sperrgebiet.' Fatah: *Im Grenzland*, p. 146.
78 Fatah: *Im Grenzland*, p. 149.

future.'[79] All this he shapes into stories, as his sister observes: 'His talking got away from him; it unrolled like a heavy bale to become a long, long panel of fabric. Unmoving and with an almost dreamy look, she listened to him as if he were one of the storytellers in the market.'[80] The material weave of text and the orality of stories that are told because the teller has survived them point to another one of the smuggler's paths, the one he creates with language: the trail of a length of fabric, of a text that winds its way through the borderlands of literature, that studies (or inspects) these borderlands and sneaks information out of this forbidden area. Acts of inspection and introspection occur simultaneously. The smuggler knows well that 'to ferret out and take advantage of these breaches and crannies was his business and now also his passion.'[81] The smuggler not only trades in alcoholic beverages and computers; he also smuggles stories from the realm of the dead, where his son, as he begins to suspect, also dwells, stories that bear witness to survival and that help one keep on living.

Like the story of the smuggler, these are stories told by someone unsettled. There are reasons why the smuggler despises 'the belief that one can possess land…. one could fence it in, litter it with mines or cultivate it but not possess it.'[82] This is the nomad's contempt for everything sedentary, a disparagement of everything that perceives space but not movement, refuses to believe that movement exists. *His* possession, *his* 'property,' however, is the path that 'existed in his head and nowhere else.'[83] Does his son, whom he neglects because of his smuggling trips, really fall 'victim' to this path, as Beno suggests in the novel's final sentence? We know only from the beginning of the text that the smuggler does not return to his family and that he cuts the last of his remaining ties. This is also where the story about the smuggler breaks off. What becomes of the uncle, what of the nephew? Has one become a storyteller and the other just a part of history? What matters for the children of migration – among whom we would presumably have to count the nephew – is neither the arrival nor even the homecoming. Writing 'after' migration still means writing under the aegis of mi-

---

[79] 'Hinweise auf das Leben, die Vergangenheit, vielleicht sogar die Zukunft.' Fatah: *Im Grenzland*, p. 126.
[80] 'Sein Reden löste sich von ihm, es entrollte sich wie ein schwerer Ballen zu einer langen, langen Stoffbahn. Sie lauschte ihm regungslos und mit beinahe träumerischem Blick, als wäre er einer der Geschichtenerzähler auf den Märkten.' Fatah: *Im Grenzland*, p. 148f.
[81] 'Diese Lücken, diese Schlupfgänge zu finden und zu nutzen, das war sein Geschäft und inzwischen wohl auch seine Leidenschaft.' Fatah: *Im Grenzland*, p. 152f.
[82] '[D]en Glauben daran, Land besitzen zu können;' 'seiner Meinung [nach] konnte man es einzäunen, verminen oder bepflanzen, aber nicht besitzen.' Fatah: *Im Grenzland*, p. 130–131.
[83] 'Er existierte in seinem Kopf und nirgends sonst.' Fatah: *Im Grenzland*, p. 186.

gration. Below the movements, there are other movements; below the words, other words and places are stored, words that might go off, explode, at any moment. Inspection easily becomes introspection that explores minefields. A Literature without a fixed Abode is tasked with getting through these minefields with its vital contraband: providing the knowledge that this path exacts its sacrifices but also, at the same time, enables life and survival that take their cues from the continual crossing of the (concept of the) national, from the restless trespass of border spaces in transareal and transcultural, translingual and transtemporal senses.

'Hope the voyage is a long one'

In a short text that oscillates between essay, poem, and autobiographical narrative, José F.A. Oliver, born to Andalusian parents in the Kinzigtal Valley in the Black Forest in 1961 and thus also a child of migration, reflects on growing up in a strangely familiar native land. Under the title 'wortaus, wortein' (wordout, wordin), an existential (language) situation unfolds in Oliver's sketch, published in 2005, in a rapid sequence of images. Continual change between German and Spanish, Alemannic German and Andalusian characterizes this (language) situation. The traditions of all these languages, and their different guises, come together – how could it be otherwise? – in a house:

> There was a house that was two houses. Two houses that made flesh of two cultures. A house and two floors, two languages. Open windows and doors, porthole into a journey that had long arrived in the multiple. The Alemannic dialect of the first floor, the Andalusian of the second. In between steps without grammatical gender. Blueprint for a play for meanings: the word's body and the word's soul. Just a few steps separated and united the female moon and the male moon: la luna, the moon.[84] One feminine, the other masculine. Or was it the other way around?[85]

---

84 [Moon is masculine in German and feminine in Spanish. TN].
85 'Da war ein Haus, das zwei Häuser war. Zwei Häuser, die zwei Kulturen verleibten. Ein Haus und zwei Stockwerke, zwei Sprachen. Offene Fenster und Türen, Luken in ein Reisen, das längst im Mehrfachen angekommen war. Der alemannische Dialekt des ersten Stockes, das Andalusische des zweiten. Dazwischen Treppenstufen ohne grammatikalisches Geschlecht. Entwurf ins Spiel um die Bedeutungen: Wortes Körper und Wortes Seele. Ein paar Treppenstufen nur, die trennten und verbanden Mondin & Mond: la luna, der Mond. Weiblich die eine, männlich die andere. Oder war es umgekehrt?' José F.A. Oliver: 'wortaus, wortein.' In: Karl-Heinz Meier-Braun / Reinhold Weber (eds.): *Kulturelle Vielfalt: Baden-Württemberg als Einwanderungsland.* Stuttgart: W. Kohlhammer 2005, p. 306. Also José F.A. Oliver: 'wortaus, wortein.' In:

The division of the house, a riff on the doubleness of the I and his other, offers space for border crossings as a virtually homely-unhomely practice of everyday life. We can add to Arthur Rimbaud's famous *Je est un autre* (I is an other) a no less fundamental *Ici est un autre* (here is an other).[86]

A space for movement and a borderland, the steps of the stairs suggest that the house does not stand for closeness to the soil, for settledness, and for territoriality but is constructed from linguistic movements that are by no means free of conflict: 'Let loose on a language that smelled of soil, made one forget the dead, and that – I only realized this much later – actually rejected us. Had to. German and yet not german. Spanish and yet not spanish. In motion: I. In-between: cognizance.'[87] No surprise, then, when, in the interWorld outlined here, the house, whose biographical version actually stands in *Haus*ach in the Black Forest (something deliberately omitted from the text), is tied to movement, to all forms of transit: Hausach, after all, is located near the Black Forest train and associated with long train journeys to the parents' Andalusian homeland. At the same time, the 'Haus' in Hausach is also related to the image of migration, the father's arrival in the cold, snowy abroad,[88] and to the journey in the text, in the poem itself:

> sometimes a single poem can explain the world
> at times, it is enough simply to open the text that lies in front of one to a random page and to rest with it for a short while. Perhaps even to stay in this or that line of a stanza for the duration of a thought or an emotion, to watch a word go or to lend one's senses to an unexpected image, in order to travel on in language afterwards. As in a train that one still always re-boards at some point, without a definite destination in mind. A train that one deboards somewhere with equal certainty, when one thinks one has arrived.[89]

Mein andalusisches Schwarzwalddorf: Essays. Frankfurt am Main: Suhrkamp 2007, p. 17–31. On Oliver, see also Ette: *ÜberLebenswissen*, chapter 8.
86 On Rimbaud, see Philippe Lejeune: *Je est un autre: L'autobiographie de la littérature aux médias*. Paris: Seuil 1980.
87 'Losgelassen auf eine Sprache, die nach Erde roch, Tote vergessen machte und die uns – das wurde mir erst viel später klar – eigentlich ablehnte. Ablehnen musste. Deutsch und doch nicht deutsch. Spanisch und doch nicht spanisch. In Bewegung: Ich. Dazwischen: Bewusstes.' Oliver: 'wortaus, wortein,' p. 310.
88 Oliver: 'wortaus, wortein,' p. 306 [See also 'Hausach' in Oliver: *Mein andalusisches Schwarzwalddorf*, p. 9–16. TN]
89 'manchmal kann ein einzelnes Gedicht die Welt erklären / bisweilen genügt es, den Text, der vor einem liegt, an einer unerwarteten Stelle einfach nur aufzuschlagen und in ihm für eine kurze Zeit innerzuhalten. Vielleicht gar für die Verweildauer eines Gedankens oder einer Gefühlsregung in dieser oder jener Verszeile einzukehren, einem Wort nachzublicken oder einem

Already in the polyvocal and multilingual act of opening the book, of lowering one's gaze and letting it sink down, this poem about the polyvocality and multilingualism of a house (of languages, not of language) which 'explain[s] the world,' is itself a movement that pauses briefly.[90] In the act of reading, this movement then becomes a train whose tracks lead 'everywhere' (überallhin), while always storing the movements of the father, the ancestors, and prior travelers in its schedule and its routes. *One train can disguise another.*

The same applies to journeys and to images. In the (book) journeys of the children of migration, the dead and their travels, their displacements and emigrations, their secret escape routes are always (made) present. They are journeys into the realm of the dead, inspections that become introspections: texts and literatures that ferret out the unhomely in the homely, the homeless in the home, always following the tracks.

When, in 2004, José F.A. Oliver spent the month of May in Cairo under the auspices of a Goethe-Institute program on 'German Authors in Arabic Cities,' he made an excursion to Alexandria, today El Iskandariya, This excursion turned into a journey into the realm of the dead for him. More specifically, into the realm of a renowned dead writer, Constantine P. Cavafy, aka Konstantinos Kavafis. The result of Oliver's visit to the museumized residence of this poet, who became the founder of the modern Greek lyric without ever having spent much time in Greece, was a poem that was included in Oliver's Cario diary under the entry May 17, 2004. A year later, it was published with a few minor revisions as 'Kavafis. El Iskandariya' in Oliver's book of poems titled 'Finnish provisions for the winter' (*finnischer wintervorrat*):

> coptic icons. Above the ledge
> their shrine & 1 long ago in greek amphoras
> the silver rust trace of a mirror
> in the study across the way. In the oval
> Mohamed's eye
> gaze: 1 gut
> ted car below the window / '1 red
> skeleton' / in the Rue Lepsius [then-
> word]. It is being painted
> in the Sharm-El-Sheik Street

---

unverhofften Bild die Sinne zu leihen, um anschließend in Sprache weiterzureisen. Wie in einem Zug, in den man irgendwann doch immer wieder einsteigt, ohne ein bestimmtes Ziel vor Augen. Ein Zug, den man dann irgendwo ebenso bestimmt wieder verlässt, wenn man glaubt, angekommen zu sein.' Oliver: 'wortaus, wortein,' p. 305.

90 Oliver: 'wortaus, wortein,' p. 305.

when he explained to me
what a *hamil* is & the slippers
of the women at prayer. Kavafis spoke
of the House of the Soul of
House of the body & of
that of the flesh
& growing into the mirror
the open roofs of the houses / night-
widened & at the retreat of the day
the oranges piled up into a turban. His bed
room as if unabandoned. I put on the poet's prayer shoes
& den odor of unsung lovers[91]

koptische ikonen. Über dem brett
ihr schrein & 1 verzeiten in griechischen amphoren
die silberrostspur eines spiegels
im Arbeitszimmer gegenüber. Im oval
Mohameds augen
blick: 1 aus
gehöhltes auto unterm fenster / ‚1 tot
skelett' / in der Rue Lepsius [damals-
wort]. Es wird lackiert
in der Sharm-El-Sheik-Strasse
als er mir erklärte
was ein *hamil* sei & die pantinen
der frauen beim beten. Kavafis sprach
vom Haus der Seele vom
Haus der Körpers & von
dem des Fleisches
& wuchsen in den spiegel
die offenen dächer der häuser / nacht
Geweitet & im rückzug des tages
Die zum turban aufgetürmen apfelsinen. Sein schlaf
zimmer wie unverlassen. Ich zog die gebetsschuhe des dichters an
& den geruch der unbesungenen liebhaber[92]

In these verses, dedicated to a paternal poet, the journey into the realm of the dead becomes a process of making present a voice through which the Greek's translated phrases rise up from below the words of the German-language poet.

---

[91] [Oliver's poems are impossible to render in another language. My attempt at translating them into English is largely literal. I thus find it necessary to include the German as a guide. TN]

[92] José F.A. Oliver: 'Kavafis: El Iskandariya.' In: José F.A. Oliver: *Finnischer Wintervorrat: Gedichte*. Frankfurt am Main: Suhrkamp 2005, p. 62.

In the path from the bedroom to the study and back again, which the poem mirrors twice, there is no arrival but a meeting, no return but a route lengthened through oscillation. The lyric instant, the flash of an eye, soars above the roofs of the city. In this moment, the gaze across the bay of Alexandria flashes one last time, along with the maturing wisdom of which Constantine Cavafy writes in his poem 'Ithaka (1911):[93]

> As you set out for Ithaka,
> Hope the voyage is a long one,
> Full of adventure, full of discovery,
> ....
> Hope the voyage is a long one.
> May there be many a summer morning when,
> With what pleasure, what joy,
> you come into harbors seen for the first time;
> may you stop at Phoenician trading stations
> To buy fine things.
> Mother of pearl and coral, amber and ebony,
> sensual perfume of every kind –
> as many sensual perfumes as you can;
> and may you visit many Egyptian cities
> to gather stores of knowledge from their scholars.
> ....
> Ithaka gave you a marvelous journey.
> Without her you would not have set out.
> She has nothing left to give you now.
>
> And if you find her poor, Ithaca won't have fooled you.
> Wise as you will have become, so full of experience,
> You will have understood by then what these Ithakas mean. [94]

---

[93] See Marguerite Yourcenar: 'Konstantinos Kavafis: Eine Einführung'. In: Robert Elsie (ed.): *Konstantinos Kavafis: Das Gesamtwerk; griechisch und deutsch*. Zurich: Ammann 1997, p. 5–49 [See also Robert Charles Evans: *A Critical Introduction to C.P. Cavafy*. Chapel Hill, NC: University of North Carolina Press 1988; and G. Jusdanis: *The Poetics of Cavafy: Textuality, Eroticism, History*. Princeton, NJ: Princeton University Press 2014. TN]

[94] Constantine P. Cavafy: *Collected Poems*. Princeton, NJ: Princeton University Press 1992, p. 36–37.

9 Configurations

Literature as Knowledge-for-Living, Literary Scholarship as Science-for-Living

From the Garden of Knowledge

Friedrich Nietzsche's 'On the Uses and Disadvantages of History for Life' (1874) has probably been the most influential of his four 'Untimely Observations.' With a nod to Goethe, Nietzsche writes in his preface that he hates everything that merely instructs without invigorating. He adds:

> We need history, certainly, but we need it for reasons different from those for which the idler in the garden of knowledge needs it, even though he may look nobly down on our rough and charmless needs and requirements. We need it, that is to say, for the sake of life and action, not to turn comfortably away from life and action, let alone for the purpose of extenuating the self-seeking life and the base and cowardly action. We want to serve history only to the extent that history serves life: for it is possible to value the study of history to such a degree that life becomes stunted and degenerate–a phenomenon we are now forced to acknowledge, painful though this may be, in the face of certain striking symptoms of our age.[1]

Nietzsche's unfashionable reflections on 'symptoms' of his times have had both a troubling and a vitalizing effect on how we think about history as it relates to life. In this chapter, as throughout this book, the central question for me is one that Nietzsche himself addresses even more directly in *The Gay Science* (1882): How do history and knowledge production relate to individual and collective life? How can we get beyond what Nietzsche derides as 'the repulsive spectacle of a blind rage for collecting, of a restless raking together of everything that has ever existed' and 'the dust of bibliographical minutiae'?[2]

Nietzsche's observations may have an even more astonishing and invigorating effect if we apply them to literary scholarship, asking what uses the study of literature has for life. What would literary criticism – and critical theory – look like if we asked about their meaning for life? What possibilities might they offer if they did not just remain within the confines of a 'garden of knowledge,' the

---

[1] Friedrich Nietzsche: 'On the Uses and Disadvantages of History for Life.' In: Friedrich Nietzsche: *Untimely Meditations*. Cambridge, MA: Cambridge University Press 1997, p. 59.
[2] Friedrich Nietzsche: *The Gay Science*. New York: Dover Philosophical Classics 2006, p. 75.

primary setting for academic literary scholarship? How might one think about the relationship between this relatively autonomous professional *hortus* and life, whose broader meaning appears oddly to be excluded from the philological 'garden of knowledge'?

First, one should ask whether such questions are even legitimate. Why should literary scholarship concern itself with life or, at least, with literature's relation to life? In our western democracies during the second half of the twentieth century, have we not taken long enough to fight for the relative autonomy of the field of literature, the *champ littéraire*, as well as for the intellectual field, the *champ intellectuel*,[3] in a process that will never quite be complete? There is also the worry that a closer relationship between the humanities and life could cover over the entelechy of literary and theoretical knowledge production with a lie that might destroy our historically grown insights into the complex internal logic of this 'garden of knowledge.'

The purpose of my observations, which, I hope, are untimely in a positive way,[4] is not to minimize or limit the degree of complexity that characterizes our understanding of literary production, critical theory, and literary-scholarly reflection. In no way do I want to misunderstand literature as a mere reflection of society in a vulgar-Marxist or positivist sense. Such theories of reflection reduce intertextuality to a mere positivistic analysis of sources, recklessly eclipsing, among other things, cultural differences and crossovers in literary writing. At the same time, any inquiry into the uses of literary scholarship, including theory, cannot but raise questions about specific historical, cultural, and socio-economic contexts, not to mention academic politics and educational policies. The latter have changed quite fundamentally of late and not at all in beneficial ways for literary scholars.

Scholarship on literatures and languages – what used to be called 'philology' and still is in many quarters outside of the USA – has long lost its momentum in public intellectual discourse. This marginalization occurs precisely at a point in history when we need the humanities to help solve one of the most urgent problems of the twenty-first century: how radically different cultures might

---

3 Pierre Bourdieu's study of academia continues to be readable and relevant. See Bourdieu: *Homo academicus*. Standford, CA: Stanford University Press 1984; and Joseph Jurt: *Das literarische Feld: Das Konzept Pierre Bourdieus in Theorie und Praxis*. Darmstadt: Wissenschaftliche Buchgesellschaft 1995.

4 As Nietzsche observed toward the end of his preface to 'On the Uses': 'I do not know what meaning classical studies could have for our time if they were not untimely – that is to say, acting counter to our time and thereby by acting on our times and, let us hope, for the benefit of a time to come.' Nietzsche: 'On the Uses,' p. 60.

live together in mutual respect for their differences. I need not discuss here the multitude of reasons why the humanities – and literary scholarship above all else – have lost the public's appreciation to such a large degree, while at the same time statistical evidence shows incontrovertibly that humanistic study continues to attract young people. How can we secure the existence of these disciplines and assure their future survival? We need to re-orient the humanities in this changed environment and to ask anew the question that Goethe posed in a different historical context: tell me, what is life to you?[5]

When one examines the development of the humanities, especially during the second half of the past century, one notices that the term 'life' has almost entirely disappeared from methodological and ideological debates. While this does not automatically entail a loss of these debates' relevance for life, it does mean that a space for reflection has been lost to the humanities. Other academic fields have increasingly occupied this space and its potential for creating meaning and for connecting meaning with action. Through the term 'life sciences,' a constellation of bio-technological disciplines has appropriated the term 'life' in a very effective, deceptively self-evident ways, increasingly robbing the humanities of any authority to produce knowledge about life. This narrowing of *bios*, a broadly conceived understanding of life that includes specifically cultural dimensions, to a bio- and natural-scientific concept is dangerous for the life of a society and for its cultural and intellectual development. Can humanists change this course?

For the humanities to survive in our present and future societies, it is vital that they conceive of themselves as *sciences for living*. Literary scholars can take the lead by capitalizing on their discipline's critical function to develop an open concept of life and of knowledge *about* and *for* living, systematically interrogating the 'uses and disadvantages' literary scholarship has for life. Such knowledge must 'serve life' in that it has to be grounded in dialogue and theory rather than in ideology.[6] This trajectory might prevent literary scholarship, along with the rest of the humanities, from comfortably settling down in a Nietzschean garden of knowledge increasingly walled off both from the concept and the practice of life. The reorientation toward the idea of life that I advocate here cannot be a superficial, short-lived tactic. Rather, it ought to be a systematic

---

5 Extensive volumes give proof of the fact that the bio-sciences take up this question time and again, in a way that is both PR-effective and thorough. See Detlev Ganten et al. (eds.): *Leben, Natur, Wissenschaft: Alles was man wissen muss*. Frankfurt am Main: Eichborn 2003.
6 Nietzsche: 'On the Uses,' p. 59. For a differentiation of theory and ideology, see Peter V. Zima: *Ideologie und Theorie: Eine Diskurskritik*. Tübingen: Francke 1989.

and concerted effort to think through the obligations that the *sciences humaines*, the human sciences, have to our societies and to begin to realize their immense potential for improving how people live with each other. Any academic discipline that does not make its knowledge available to the society in which it exists shirks its responsibility toward that society and, in the end, has largely itself to blame for being pushed aside.

Should the humanities confront the natural sciences? No. Rather than attacking the semantic reductionism of the biosciences' concept of 'life,' humanists need to initiate a serious dialogue with them. This dialogue has to include literary and cultural knowledge, thus making possible a more complete understanding of life and of the humanities as part of the sciences for living. Doing so would break down the imaginary border between Charles Percy Snow's 'two cultures,' whose hypothetical existence many still take for granted on the discursive level and, even more so, on the level of academic politics and policies. We need to create a contrastive *and* complementary web of knowledge and comprehensive 'scientific' systems that include humanists as equal partners. In the end, literary criticism and theory will likely survive only if they formulate strategies and approaches that would include them fully in a non-reductive conception of the sciences for living.

Life, the 'Life Sciences,' and the Sciences for Living

In his groundbreaking study *The Order of Things* (1966), Michel Foucault analyzes the fundamental transformations that occurred in the field of natural history between 1775 and 1795. The French archeologist of science concluded that 'the general principles of taxonomy – the same principles that had determined the systems of Tournefort and Linnaeus and the method of Adanson – preserve[d] the same kind of validity for A-L. de Jussieu, Vicq d'Azyr, Lamarck, and Candolle.'[7] Nonetheless, the relations between visible and invisible structures changed in palpable ways during that time, insofar as one focused on 'the existence of functions essential to the living being' and made the 'notion of life ....indispensable to the ordering of natural beings.'[8] This process altered the very understanding of classification itself:

---

[7] Michel Foucault: *The Order of Things: An Archaeology of the Human Sciences*. New York: Vintage Books 1973, p. 226.
[8] Foucault: *The Order of Things*, p. 227–228.

To classify, therefore, will no longer mean to refer the visible back to itself, while allotting one of its elements the task of representing the others; it will mean, in a movement that makes analysis pivot on its axis, to relate the visible to the invisible, to its deeper cause, as it were, then to rise upwards once more from that hidden architecture towards the more obvious signs displayed on the surfaces of bodies.[9]

When the distinction between organic and inorganic became fundamental, so did the 'opposition of life and death,'[10] of living and non-living. For the 'life sciences' that were re-forming themselves from a post-natural history perspective, this opposition marks the beginning of a new ordering of disciplines and cultures, through which, around 1800, modernity constituted itself in epistemological differences, not exclusively natural-scientific but also, especially, cultural differences.[11] In his famous interpretation of Diego Velázquez' *Las Meninas*, Foucault emphasized the point where life, work, and language intersect to constitute modernity:

> When natural history becomes biology, when the analysis of wealth becomes economics, when, above all, reflection upon language becomes philology, and Classical *discourse*, in which being and representation found their common locus, is eclipsed, then, in the profound upheaval of such an archaeological mutation, man appears in his ambiguous position as an object of knowledge and as a subject that knows: enslaved sovereign, observed spectator, he appears in the place belonging to the king, which was assigned to him in advance by *las Meninas*, but from which his real presence has for so long been excluded.[12]

The systems of knowledge and the taxonomies of classification that Michel Foucault and Wolf Lepenies have examined illustrate that the differentiation between natural science, on the one hand, and culture, on the other, implies that life, in a bio-scientific sense, is the object of knowledge (and study) and that knowledge *about* life accumulates only *outside* of this object. We should keep this distinction in mind when we consider the admonitions Jürgen Habermas has advanced in the context of the public debates surrounding stem cell research. Habermas's rebuke to philosophers can also be applied to literary scholars, most especially to literary theorists: 'The new technologies make a public discourse on the right understanding of cultural forms of life in general

---

9 Foucault: *The Order of Things*, p. 229.
10 Foucault: *The Order of Things*, p. 232.
11 See Hansjörg Bay / Kai Mertens: Die Ordnung der Kulturen: *Zur Konstruktion ethnischer, nationaler und zivilisatorischer Differenzen 1750–1850*. Würzburg: Königshausen & Neumann 2006, and Ottmar Ette et al. (eds.): *Alexander von Humboldt: Aufbruch in die Moderne*. Berlin: Akademie Verlag 2001.
12 Foucault: *The Order of Things*, p. 312.

an urgent matter. And philosophers no longer have any good reasons for leaving such a dispute to biologists and engineers intoxicated by science-fiction.'[13]

In the early twenty-first century, systems of ordering knowledge production continue, as a rule, to prescribe clear distinctions between the natural sciences and the humanities and between the humanities and the social sciences.[14] The strange career of the so-called 'life sciences' is a case in point. Even before the German Minister for Education and Research, in cooperation with academic institutions, announced the 'year of the life sciences' in 2001, discussions of the human genome, stem cell research, the possibility for cloning animal or human life, and the engineering of genes or seeds had increasingly left the public with the impression that a few, highly specialized academic fields actually covered the entire spectrum of knowledge about human life. At least prior to September 11, 2001, a search for the 'key' to human life dominated feature pages, television shows, and political debates. The mystery of life now appeared to be decipherable: it was a code, a calculable and, in the end, predictable, chain.[15] The popularization of fascinating theories for comprehending life and of impressive natural-scientific research results changed how people conceived of everyday life and of a safe future. Both the mass media and sponsors of research invested the biosciences with extraordinary significance: the 'life sciences' became THE sciences of life.

But the genetic code of life is not the only thing we can *read*. Equally readable is the discursive code that places the biosciences at the center of a society's attention. Against their hegemonic claims to universality, Hans-Georg Gadamer offers a cautionary note about the relationship between the natural sciences and the humanities:

---

13 Jürgen Habermas: *The Future of Human Nature*. Cambridge MA: Polity, Blackwell 2003, p. 15.

14 But actual developments within academic scholarly practice over the last twenty years (see Frühwald et al) have been quite different: the crossing of disciplinary lines increasingly blurred these divisional distinctions. One need not be clairvoyant to predict that this tendency will gain momentum as transdisciplinary concepts of knowledge production mature and, in the process, develop in ways both parallel and complementary to other forms of academic specialization. The goal of a transdisciplinary structure is not the interdisciplinary exchange among conversation partners firmly anchored in a discipline but a continual crisscrossing of diverse disciplines. It goes without saying that the development and the results of this 'nomadic' practice, which is trans-disciplinary in the true sense, must be tested and secured through ongoing disciplinary and interdisciplinary contacts. In this way, it becomes possible to render dynamic radically different areas of knowledge and to join them together more strongly and flexibly.

15 For the genetic code's tantalizing history of metaphorizing and readability see Hans Blumenberg: *Die Lesbarkeit der Welt*. Frankfurt am Main: Suhrkamp 1981, p. 372–409.

One enjoys asking the humanities in which precise sense they want to be sciences, in light of the fact that there are no criteria for comprehending texts or words. For the natural sciences and various forms of technology, it is certainly true that a lack of ambiguity of their means of communication is guaranteed. But it is incontrovertible that even the apparatus of a civilization that is founded on science and technology by far does not cover all aspects of 'living together.'[16]

The phrase 'life sciences' is as ambiguous as it is radiant and all-encompassing. It vastly reduces the term 'life' when compared to the breadth of meaning it enjoyed in western Antiquity. Because of its possessive and repressive tendencies, and through the metaphors it borrows from literature and the humanities, the concept of 'life sciences' attempts to bar other branches of knowledge from accessing life.

Philosophy has long since reacted to the challenge of genetic technology. In the context of eugenics, for instance, philosophy has questioned what life would be like without, as Habermas puts it, 'the emotions roused by moral sentiments like obligation and guilt, reproach and forgiveness, without the liberating effect of moral respect, without the happiness felt through solidarity and without the depressing effect of moral failure, without the 'friendliness' of a civilized way of dealing with conflict and opposition.'[17] Yet, in a 2000 speech, Habermas also observes that philosophy is no longer confident enough to risk 'answers to questions regarding the personal, or even the collective, conduct of life.'[18] Criticizing the field of ethics for having been reduced to what Adorno had called 'a melancholy science,'[19] Habermas tellingly resorts to a literary text to point to the potential for disconcerting questions – and no less disconcerting answers – that literature has always held in store for its readers. Max Frisch's novel *Stiller* (1954) shows that literature never misses an opportunity to tell us about life and to show us the paradoxes and aporias of knowledge-for-living. Habermas uses *Stiller* to make this point: 'Frisch has Stiller, the public prosecutor, ask: "What does a human being do with the time he has to live?" I was hardly fully aware of the question; it was simply an irritation.'[20] Literary scholars, unlike philosophers, hardly react to such questions; they do not even register

---

[16] Hans-Georg Gadamer: 'Über das Hören.' In: Thomas Vogel (ed.): *Über das Hören: Einem Phänomen auf der Spur*. Tübingen: Attempto 1996, p. 202.
[17] Habermas: *The Future of Human Nature*, p. 73.
[18] Habermas: *The Future of Human Nature*, p. 1.
[19] Habermas: *The Future of Human Nature*, p. 15.
[20] Habermas: *The Future of Human Nature*, p. 1.

them anymore. In the end, is it not literary scholarship that has turned from a joyful, or at least pleasurable, pursuit into a melancholy one?

The speedy dissemination of the term 'life sciences' has provoked many reactions and complaints but, it seems to me, has not resulted in any new strategies in the fields that focus on literature. Literary scholars have hardly even begun to consider the impact of the biosciences' recourse to the life metaphor and all the confusion and perplexity that follow in its wake. Above all, literary scholars should know better than to risk relinquishing the term 'life' and allowing it to function in such a limited way.

The public's ready embrace of the term 'life science' indicates that people have an enormous interest in the systematic study of life, and this interest should open our eyes to the opportunities for the humanities if they were to conceive of themselves as part of the sciences for living. After all, life is not the loot of a single cluster of disciplines; it does not obey the logic of a simple code. Indeed, work in the natural sciences has gained much clarity from its varied encounters, for instance, with 'moral economies' and 'cognitive passions.' Historian of science Lorraine Daston sums it up succinctly:

> In our culture, academic knowledge production stands for rationality and factuality, which is why it almost sounds like a paradox when one advances the hypothesis that such work depends crucially on specific constellations of emotions and values. While emotions may affect academics by increasing their motivation and values can influence their research results in the form of ideologies or as institutionalized norms, neither feelings nor values can penetrate the innermost core of systematic knowledge production – at least according to the usual binary oppositions and borderlines they dictate. Our current ideal of scientific objectivity is predicated on the existence and impermeability of these borders. Nonetheless, I claim that.... [c]ertain forms of empiricism, of quantification, and of objectivity are not only compatible with moral economies; they actually require them.[21]

While it might be comforting to think that the 'life sciences' participate in life more than they would either know or care, this does not excuse humanists from the responsibility to protect life from the bio-scientific claim to represent it completely and exclusively. Especially in times of heated debates about pre-implantation diagnostics and stem cell research, literary scholarship stands a better chance than philosophy to propose models for life without arousing the suspicion of proffering, or even prescribing, normative concepts. This is particularly

---

21 Lorraine Daston / Katharine Park: *Wonders and the Order of Nature, 1150–1750*. New York: Zone Books 1998, p. 157 [The German translation, *Wunder, Beweise und Tatsachen zur Geschichte der Rationalität*. Frankfurt am Main: Fischer 2001, is only loosely based on Daston and Park's book. TN]

important because models for the 'right (way of) life,' both in literature and in philosophy, have an ever-shorter half-life in multicultural, intercultural, and transcultural contexts where life forms and situations rapidly pluralize.

If we perceive the 'life sciences' merely as a network of largely applied sciences while, at the same time, considering them as an experimental ensemble of biochemical, biophysical, biotechnological, and medical fields of research, then we inevitably run the risk of losing the broad cultural diversity inherent in *bios*. A culturally sound concept of life, one that is also oriented towards literature, can counteract such a potential danger by reclaiming the differentiation between *zoé*, 'the simple fact of living common to all living beings,' and *bios*, which denotes 'the form or way of living proper to an individual or group.'[22] Giorgio Agamben places this distinction at the center of his *Homo sacer* right from the very start. The Italian philosopher is in the tradition of great intellectuals whose thinking revolved, to a considerable degree, around the epistemological relevance of forms as well as concepts of life.

In an essay for the programmatic journal *Die Wandlung* (Transformation), Leo Spitzer defined literary scholarship as 'the science that seeks to comprehend the human being to the extent to which he expresses himself in words (speech) and linguistic creations.'[23] For this 'science,' following Auerbach's line of thought about a philology of *Weltliteratur*, to dare again 'what earlier periods dared to do – to designate man's place in the universe,'[24] it has to conceive of itself as a science-for-living and, as such, as part of the 'life sciences' in the broadest sense of that term. That such an idea is hardly foreign, at least to scholarship in Romance languages, is evident from the notable and yet unnoticed frequency of the lexeme 'life' at the end of Auerbach's foundational work *Mimesis*. Here, Auerbach grapples with a new orientation and a new conception of philology against the background of the catastrophes of World War II and the Shoah and in the midst of an acutely felt linguistic and cultural homogenization. It is no coincidence that the final chapter of *Mimesis*, in the German original, ends with the verb 'erleben,' which means 'to experience' or 'to live through.'

> The strata of societies and their different *ways of life* have become inextricably mingled. There are no longer even exotic peoples. A century ago (in Mérimée for example), Corsicans or Spaniards were still exotic; today, the term would be quite unsuitable for Pearl

---

22 Giorgio Agamben: *Homo sacer: Sovereign Power and Bare Life*. Stanford, MA: Stanford University Press 1998, p. 1.
23 Leo Spitzer: 'Das Eigene und das Fremde: Über Philologie und Nationalsozialismus.' In: *Lendemains* 18, 69–70 (1993), p. 179.
24 Erich Auerbach: 'Philology and Weltliteratur.' In: *Centennial Review* 13 (1969), p. 17.

> Buck's Chinese peasants. Beneath the conflicts, and through them, an economics and cultural leveling process is taking place. It is still a long way to a common life of *mankind* on earth, but the goal begins to be visible. And it is most concretely visible now in the unprejudiced, precise, interior and exterior representation of the random *moment in the lives* of different people. So the complicated process of dissolution, which led to fragmentation of the exterior action, to reflection of consciousness, and to stratification of time, seems to be tending toward a very simple solution. Perhaps it will be too simple to please those who, despite all its dangers and catastrophes, admire and love our epoch for the sake of its *abundance of life* and the incomparable historical vantage point which it affords. But they are few in number, and probably they will not *live to see* much more than the first forewarnings of the approaching unification and simplification (O.E. emphases).[25]

Today, we have a broader view than Auerbach did in the immediate post-WWII period of the process of cultural homogenization that he sketched and of the simultaneous process of cultural (re-)differentiation that was then underway. Yet, his insistence on a concept of life stands for an awareness of the need for literary scholars to *care about and for life* in the fullest sense.

To determine anew the place of humans in the universe, literary scholarship needs to reflect anew on its own place in a changed system of knowledge production. A concept of *knowledge-for-living*, understood as one of literary studies' tasks, would be able to deliver an important impetus for creating an academic landscape better, and more productively, attuned to the cultural diversity of human life. The conception of bio-sciences as 'life sciences,' in its turn, would greatly benefit from reclaiming the idea of life in a cultural and literary-theoretically grounded way that would return to the very idea of 'life science' its indispensable cultural dimension. At the same time, this return would make it possible to distinguish purely bio-scientific concerns from more comprehensive questions and analytical practices.

Knowledge-for-Living

Through the concept of *knowledge-for-living*, I want to suggest new perspectives on literature's, and literary scholarship's, relevance to human societies and their histories. To move the question of individual and collective life into literary scholars' immediate line of vision, we need to consider what exactly this new concept signifies. Terminologically, 'knowledge-for-living' opens our view onto the complex relationship between the compound phrase's two semantic

---

[25] Erich Auerbach: *Mimesis: The Representation of Reality in Western Literature*. Princeton: Princeton University Press 2003, p. 552–553.

poles. This relationship is multi-layered or multi-dimensional. For one, to combine 'living' with 'knowledge' implies knowledge *about*, or *of*, life. For another, it implies knowledge for the purpose or benefit of living. Further, these different aspects of knowledge exist in life and are inseparable for a living (and knowing) subject. Knowledge is a fundamental characteristic of both life processes and the practice of living. From this vantage, knowledge-for-living appears as a specific way of living one's life, which includes reflecting on how one lives. Knowledge for living can be gained both through concrete experiences in immediate life contexts *and* through the production and reception of symbolic goods. In this way, knowledge-for-living can also be understood as an *imagined* form of living and as a process of imagining life (and lives), in which self-referentiality and self-reflexivity are of critical importance. In other words, knowledge-for-living is bound up in specific life experiences but never tied to a single logic. Rather, the term implies the ability to think and act simultaneously according to different sets of logic.

Against this background, one may understand literature as an ever-changing and, at the same time, interactive storehouse of knowledge-for-living. In contrast to philosophy, which seeks to construct internally coherent systems of meaning, literature focuses on artistically enriching coherence with *in*coherence, a process that quantum theory knows as superposition. As a mutable and dynamic storehouse of knowledge-for-living, literature devises and aesthetically shapes blueprints for how to live. For this purpose, it draws on, and draws in, many different partial knowledges, including academic discourses. As Roland Barthes put it in 'From Scholarship to Literature' (1967):

> there is certainly no single academic matter [matière scientifique] that the literature of the world has not treated at some point: the world of the work is a total world, in which all knowledge (social, psychological, historical) takes place, so that, for us, literature has that grand cosmogenic unity which so delighted the ancient Greeks but which the compartmentalization of our academic fields [sciences] denies us today. Further, like academic scholarship [science], literature is methodological: it has its programs of research, which vary according to schools and periods (like those of scholarship), its rules of investigation, sometimes even its experimental pretensions.[26]

---

26 Roland Barthes: 'De la Science à la Literature.' In: *Roland Barthes: Le bruissement de la langue: Essais Critiques IV*. Paris: Seuil 1984, p. 13–14 [Richard Howard, in his translation of Barthes in *The Rustle of Language*. Berkeley: University of California Press 1989, p. 3–4, renders the French 'science' and 'scientifique' as 'science' and 'scientific,' which, though in keeping with the arguments in this article, is still confusing in English. Barthes's use of the French

Literature specializes in not being specialized, neither with respect to disciplines nor to lived realities and cultural differences. Because it neither negates nor cements the division between the humanities and the biosciences and has access to a multitude of codes from radically different traditions of thinking and writing, literature can be regarded as a medium for circulating the most diverse fragments of knowledge. Because of this characteristic, literature is singularly able to store a wide range of knowledge-for-living and keep it at its readers' disposal. It also shapes forms of life artistically, in Juri Lotman's sense of a secondary modeling system, enabling readers to experience them aesthetically. Unlike in the biosciences and biotechnologies, life and knowledge can be thought of together in specific forms, practices, and models in the realm of literature where life is *not* forced into disciplinary systems.[27] For literary criticism and critical theory, knowledge-for-living is intrinsic to the very process of knowing; it is part of the object of study and of the subject's (the scholar's) individual life contexts.

As it unfolds a complex understanding of life, literature is marvelously prepared to respond to the dilemma that, according to Habermas, the latest biotechnological developments have created: 'The boundary between the nature that we 'are' and the organic endowments that we 'give' to ourselves disappears.'[28] Literary acts of creation reside at this very boundary.

Literature or life

On January 11, 1896, at 9 a.m. on a Sunday, an eighteen-year-old woman opens her veins and writes with her own blood, 'this kind of ink that will suggest to you half of my thoughts,'[29] a desperate and, at once, determined letter to her lover, the Cuban modernist Carlos Pío Uhrbach.[30] A member of a large Cuban family of poets, Juana Borrero had written poems and painted since her early childhood. On this occasion, she first composed a poem in her own blood, followed by a long letter that presented the young man with the choice between life and love, between fighting in the island's War of Independence and herself:

---

noun 'science' corresponds much more closely to the German 'Wissenschaft' than to the English 'science,' which generally continues to exclude the humanities. TN]
27 It remains to be seen, however, to what extent genetics and stem cell research will develop new models of knowledge that can put into perspective, or even undermine, the supposed externality of knowledge to actual life processes that have no consciousness of themselves.
28 Habermas: *The Future of Human Nature*, p. 12.
29 Juana Borrero: *Epistolario*. Havana: Academia de Ciencias de Cuba, 1966–1967, p. 256.
30 For more on Borrero, see chapter 4 above.

Whichever way you want to look at it: is not the motherland [la patria] a rival in romance like any other woman? And a lucky rival at that, because you give yourself to her! To you, it seems dishonorable not to follow her call ... and it does not strike you as criminal to extinguish with a single blow all hopes of a soul like mine? If my tears cannot move you, and the certainty of my death does not touch you, of what is your heart made? ... Your *patria or your Juana*: you choose. If you go, you will lose me.[31]

Juana Borrero would die less than two months later in exile in Key West. She liquefied and *liquidated* her life, her reading, her love in a single tour de force, in an attempt to prevent Uhrbach from joining the fight for independence just as Borrero's father had done. The cooled writing of her heart, her own blood dried on the paper, mixes with the bodily fluid of the tears that left traces on so many of her letters to manifest the poet's physical presence on paper. Her demand for absolute devotion, along with her radically possessive claim toward this man, of whom, in another letter, she requested that he never love her physically even after their marriage, generates here a textual body in which a bare life cannot disengage from its cultural dimensions and from the literature that guides how this poet lived her life. Thousands of pages of letters illustrate to what extent it is impossible to separate Borrero's living, reading, and loving from literature. To her, writing had long been a threat to her life. Writing pushed the blood from her veins into a body of writing, and into a form of body writing, passed on to us as an early form of female *body art*. Art here enters the body, the body pushes itself into art: the body-as-art embodies in writing its own knowledge-for-living.

Few authors enact, in such an absolute sense, what Barthes described in *A Lover's Discourse* (1977): 'This is the condition of my survival; for if I did not forget, I should die. The lover who doesn't forget *sometimes* dies of excess, exhaustion, and tension of memory (like Werther)'[32]. The pathological dimension in Borrero's' work is as unmistakable as the artistic productivity of a love discourse that refuses to forget and that condemns to silence everything that might distract. Any knowledge of one's own possibilities and conditions of survival is thus negated. At the same time, Juana Borrero wanted to live out the poem 'La virgen triste,' in which the great love of her youth, the Cuban poet Julián Casal, predicts the premature death of this 'melancholy virgin,' turning her death into

---

31 Borrero: *Epistolario*, p. 257.
32 Roland Barthes: *A Lover's Discourse: Fragments*. New York: Hill and Wang 1977, p. 14.

a literary fait accompli.[33] As was so often the case with Borrero, literature charted her life's course.

Juana Borrero's writing inserts itself into both poetic and pathological (as in medical) discourses; remember that her father, Esteban Borrero, was both a physician and poet. The Cuban author chose between literature and life in a way very different from what the Spanish writer Jorge Semprún depicted in French in his 1994 fictional text 'Writing or life' (*L'écriture ou la vie*). Borrero's example shows that literature's knowledge-for-living is what I call survival knowledge, which can also turn on itself and lead to death. The example further illustrates that, in Borrero's writing, the body is where nature and culture inextricably intertwine, where pathological and poetic discourses suffuse each other. As it liquefies in the process of her writing, the poet's body forms a 'material body' in which the knowledge of 'being a body' and 'having a body' overlap in a way very different way from what happens during the sexual act. The blood-red writing to her beloved develops a knowledge-for-living rooted in the *in*ability to survive because Borrero knows that this kind of writing is the only way to open up one's own objectified body to a heightening of all sensual experience, all the pain and all the passion that goes into 'being a body.' Only in this way, in a state of intensity that literature has magnified to a monstrous degree, can one sacrifice one's own body to literature, as object and artifact, as a trace of and in writing. Literature or life: life for the sake of literature.

In Borrero's writing, literature's knowledge-for-living intersects with philosophical concepts of insight and perception in probably the closest and, at the same time, the most disturbing way.[34] Pushed to a literary extreme in thousands of pages, Borrero's lover's discourse rejects *in* life the medical, bio-scientific knowledge *of* life as energetically as it draws life's knowledge of itself into a more and more exhausting turbulence that also is literature. Juana Borrero: a life beyond life; a survival (within) literature that always knows the limits of the validity of its own staged life knowledge. Borrero's life and writing show the experimental character of literature in an unusual and spectacular way: literature becomes an experiment on one's own material body. Writing nourished by the

---

[33] For more details, see Ottmar Ette: 'Gender Trouble: José Martí and Juana Borrero'. In: Mauricio A. Font / Alfonso W. Quiroz (eds.): *The Cuban Republic and José Martí: Reception and Use of a National Symbol*. Lanham; Boulder: Lexington Books 2006, p. 230–33

[34] Helmuth Plessner has used these concepts to develop a philosophical anthropology that tries 'to recognize the specific ways in which the materialization of our own bodies is made concrete.' Helmut Plessner: *Gesammelte Schriften*, vol. 3. Edited by Günter Dux et al. Frankfurt am Main: Suhrkamp 1980–1985, vol. 3, p. 383.

poetic and the pathological turns the body into that place where the different areas, forms, and functions of knowledge about life, knowledge-for-living, and knowledge in life can be poeticized as part of life's processes.

The academic study of literature needs to counter the unreflected and uncritical exclusion of the concept of life and connect literature's experimental character with bio-scientific insights into the fundamental complexity of life processes, to make more apparent to what extent literature experiments and plays with the various aspects of life's irreversibility and unpredictability. For example, Honoré de Balzac's *Human Comedy* and Émile Zola's *roman experimentel* are both more than and *different* from bio-scientific models of knowledge, the concepts of which both authors claimed to be translating into literature. But literary creation hardly limits itself to staging prior academic discourses on life. Zola, in particular, gears his literary project toward simulating life in the novel's laboratory in order, in a second, extra-textual step, to try to change actual life practices on the part of individuals as well as entire social groups and nations. Temporal distance notwithstanding, one could easily relate this ambitious project to current ideas in molecular biology about biological machines and concepts of life implicit in them: 'On one level, molecular biology sees life as self-reproducing biological machines. On a second level, it reproduces some of these machines in the laboratory in, as one might say, slow motion, yet while rebuilding them it optimizes some of their parts and substitutes its own goals for those of the original.'[35]

Literary knowledge-for-living both contrasts with and complements these scientific discourses. Above all, it creates an experimental relationship among the different discourses on life, no matter if they are aesthetic and artistic, philosophical and socio-scientific, pathological or clinical, or medical and bio-scientific. In the process, the knowledge for survival that unfolds in this way within literature can turn into a life unto death, be it – as in Juana Borrero's case – through the author's leading her life according to art's principles, or – as in the case of the reception of Goethe's *Werther* – through suicidal life practices on the part of readers. As Flaubert's *Madame Bovary* shows, the collapsing of life into literature has fatal consequences. Even the result of the experiment – and literature always implies the experimental testing of knowledge-for-living – produces new knowledge of and in life. Literature mediates specific knowledge of how one lives, or might live, which becomes knowledge of how (not) to live, or survive. For literature, which can see, shape, and semanticize the totality of life far

---

[35] Karin Knorr-Cetina: *Epistemic Cultures: How the Sciences Make Knowledge*. Cambridge, MA: Harvard University Press 1999, p. 156.

beyond the death of a protagonist, death is only a relative reference point. Within the frame of its own historically established rules, literature can experiment with the irreversibility of all life processes.

Intratextual and extratextual dimensions of Knowledge-for-Living

Knowledge-for-living has behind it a long tradition in western European literary histories, in which, starting with Aristotle's concept of catharsis, the question of literature's performance of knowledge-for-living has been as central as the question of how to acquire such knowledge. In his essay on the act of reading[36] from a phenomenological point of view, originally published in English in 1972, Wolfgang Iser identifies three major aspects of the relationship between text and reader: 'the process of anticipation and retrospection, the consequent unfolding of the text as a living event, and the resultant impression of lifelikeness.'[37] Compelling the reader to 'seek continually for consistency' causes 'the reader to be entangled in the text 'gestalt' that he himself has produced;' this is what creates the impression of 'experiencing' as a form of imaginative living-through.[38] Insofar as the act of reading includes 'an element of our being of which we are not directly conscious,' literature offers us 'the chance to formulate the unformulated.'[39] Following Iser, we may say that fictionality creates a space of experimentation in which readers, in serious playfulness, can test out different life situations, where they can engage with those situations to collect experiences that they could not have in 'real life.'

Iser's observations that 'fictional texts [are] always ahead of our practice of life, of the way in which we live our lives'[40] touches on a problem that the field of reception aesthetics has introduced but never fully engaged: the interconnectedness of literature and life practice, which is implicit in the idea of knowledge-

---

36 See Wolfgang Iser: *The Act of Reading: A Theory of Aesthetic Response*. Baltimore: Johns Hopkins University Press 1978.
37 Iser: *The Act of Reading*, p. 142 [The article first appeared in *New Literary History* III (Winter 1971/72), p. 279–99. TN]
38 Iser: *The Act of Reading*, p. 142–143.
39 Iser: *The Act of Reading*, p. 145.
40 Wolfgang Iser: 'Die Apellstruktur der Texte: Unbestimmtheit als Wirkungsbedingung literarischer Prosa.' In: Rainer Warning (ed.): *Rezeptionsästhetik: Theorie und Praxis*. Munich: Fink 1975, p. 250.

for-living.[41] The extent to which literature integrates different fragments of knowledge-for-living and sets them in motion enables it to produce knowledge-for-living as knowledge of having imaginatively lived through an event or situation. In this way, literature translates into narrative models the discursive structures of what one might call, with a wink in Barthes' direction, fragments of a living discourse. Unlike philosophy, literature has the ability to translate life knowledge into experiential knowledge that is unfettered from the discipline-bound rules of academic discourse, allowing it to come into view more clearly. Along with being able *simultaneously* to integrate multiple sets of logic, this ability is one of literature's greatest trump cards. In the words of Rudolf zur Lippe, literature wants more than merely to 'collect knowledge *about* life'; it shows how 'experience' in life functions as 'the context that is being sought or desired.'[42] My brief recourse to the promise that Wolfgang Iser's reader response theories has yet to fulfill helps explain how the concept of knowledge-for-living applies to and functions in literary texts in at least two ways: intra-textually (for instance, in the narrative modeling of characters) and extra-textually (for example, in how people experience art in a given society).

On the *intratextual* level, the challenge is to understand the dynamic modeling of literary characters as complex *choreographies* of individuals who possess different kinds of life knowledge. For example, in Miguel de Cervantes's *Don Quixote,* the cradle of the modern European novel, there are two characters with vastly divergent knowledges for living. The novel juxtaposes their respective knowledges in ever-new twists and turns of the plot and experimentally tests, reflects, and modifies them in its fictional laboratory. Sancho Panza, on the one hand, inhabits the world of Spanish sayings, relying on knowledge that has been accumulated in the proverbs of Iberian popular culture, which Werner Krauss presented in such novel and entertaining ways.[43] Don Quixote's knowledge-for-living, on the other hand, represents the splendor and the peril, the creativity and the collapse of a fictional world that unexpectedly, and fatally, encroaches upon the practice of 'real' life. The novel sets in motion these anti-

---

41 [An English text that articulates some of these ideas is Iser's 'Indeterminacy and the Reader's Response in Prose Fiction.' In: J. Hillis Miller (ed.): *Aspects of Narrative: Selected Papers from the English Institute.* New York: Columbia 1971; see also Iser: *The Act of Reading.* TN].
42 Rudolf zur Lippe: *Sinnenbewusstsein: Grundlegung einer anthropologischen Ästhetik,* vol. 2. Baltmannsweiler: Schneider Verlag Hohengehren 2000, p. 2331.
43 See Werner Krauss: *Die Welt im spanischen Sprichwort.* Leipzig: Reclam 1946; and Werner Krauss: *Grundprobleme der Literaturwissenschaft: Zur Interpretation literarischer Werke.* Reinbeck bei Hamburg: Rowohlt 1968, p. 308–333.

thetical fragments of knowledge-for-living and charts the consequences of their movements and clashes.

For certain characters, the literary experiment can turn out to be very painful, as it does for Flaubert's Emma Bovary in her intratextual constellations with the country doctor Bovary, the pharmacist Homais, the merchant Lheureux, and the estate owner Rodolphe. Emma's life project is irrevocably wrecked through her contact with these differently located socio-cultural discourses of mediocrity and the characters' *idées reçues* that so fascinated Flaubert.

The world of the novel may thus be understood as a microcosm of very different types of knowledge-for-living, to the extent at least that the heteroglossia on which Bakhtin insisted so emphatically can mark the existence of an open dialogue within the 'feedback-linked multiparameter systems' of which knowledge-for-living consists.[44] At the same time, Bakhtin's considerations point to the important configuration of synopsis and crossfading, that is, to the totalizing claim with which the modern novel has burdened theories about it from the very start:

> In the novel, all socio-ideological voices, that is, all characteristic idioms of an age have to be represented. In short, the novel must be a microcosm of polyvocality. ..... A language shows its peculiarity only when it correlates with all other languages that are part of one and the same contradictory unity of social becoming. Each language in the novel is a standpoint, a socio-ideological horizon of real societal groups and their representatives.[45]

If we understand literature as an interactive storage medium for knowledge-for-living, then Bakhtin's cosmos of polyvocality, in its turn, can be said to refer to forms, norms, and ways of life that are as different as they are differently acquired. The self-referentiality and self-reflexivity of all processes of knowledge-for-living are embedded in the specific multi-, inter-, and transcultural contexts of literature as a whole, and most especially in the translingual literary forms that I have called Literatures without a fixed Abode. Literature offers forms of local knowledge-for-living (or what Clifford Geertz has termed 'local knowledge' from the perspective of anthropology) as well as forms of a worldwide circulation of knowledge, which, on the intra-textual level, represent specifically de-localized or trans-localized life practices.

---

44 Friedrich Cramer: *Chaos and Order: The Complex Structure of Living Systems*. Weinheim: VHC 1993, p. 168.
45 Mikhail M. Bakhtin and Rainer Grübel: *Die Ästhetik des Wortes*. Frankfurt am Main: Suhrkamp 1979, p. 290 [This text is excerpted in Pam Morris (ed.): *The Bakhtin Reader: Selected Writings of Bakhtin, Mededev, Voloshinov*. London: Arnold 2003, p. 114–20. TN].

On the *extratextual* level, attention to specific cultural and socio-historical ways of acquiring literary knowledge-for-living take center stage. Where 'closeness to life' and the testing of a 'life practice' through fiction is concerned, the question arises of how to translate the literary experiment into one's own ways of living, perhaps even into certain groups' practices of everyday life. Whatever the cultural specifics of such a translation, it never literally carries over from one situation to another. The history of Aristotle's concept of catharsis may prove the extent to which the translatability and transferability of knowledge-for-living have occupied and influenced western European literature and literary theory. Literature's problematic power to shape ideas of a 'good life' *and* to corrupt presumably innocent, yet receptive, readers registered in the nineteenth-century French immoralism trials against novels and poetry[46], the court proceedings against *Lady Chatterley's Lover*, the ostracism of 'deviant' authors in Cuba, and the *fatwa* against Salman Rushdie, among many examples. In the foreground of this long tradition always stood reflections of how intra-textual knowledge-for-living might be transformed into extratextual life practice or else of how this transformation, this acquisition of knowledge, might be prevented or at least slowed. Whether it wants to or not, literature taps into readers' knowledge-for-living and threatens to upend existing norms.

The reciprocal imbrications of intratextual and extratextual levels are particularly important for a literary work's paratextual apparatus: prefaces and afterwards, titles and subtitles, illustrations and interviews with authors. The literatures of the world bridge immense distances in time and place to facilitate transtemporal and trans-local acquisitions of life knowledge. Rather than being a rare occurrence, this diversity of culturally inflected patterns of interpretations and practices of knowledge acquisition is what fascinates contemporary authors and their worldwide audiences. As Amin Maalouf pointed out in a 2001 interview:

> Quite right, the fact that human beings from the most different cultures read the same stories, react to them, smile about the same texts or get excited by them, presents an opportunity to create passage ways between vastly different cultures. This is art's function... It is true: when I write, I am never in the mood to turn to a specific readership, to people who belong to a single culture.[47]

---

46 See Klaus Heitmann: *Der Immoralismus: Prozess gegen die französische Literatur im 19. Jahrhundert*. Bad Homburg: Gehlen 1970.
47 Amin Maalouf: 'Je parle du voyage comme d'autres parlent de leur maison (interview with David Babouin).' In: *Magazine littéraire* 394 (2001), p. 101.

Following Maalouf, who was born in Lebanon, lives in Paris, and whose novels, written in French, are available in many languages, we might say that reading literature in different cultural surrounds can create new connections between cultures, which can influence the behavior, even the life practices, of different groups of readers anywhere in the world. At the same time, it is safe to assume that national and monolingual narratives continue to dominate the scene. The one-hundred-year old reception history of Cuban poet, essayist, and revolutionary José Martí, which is unlikely to end even with Fidel Castro's demise, illustrates the degree to which certain discursive forms or political ideas remain accessible to later generations of readers.[48] This accessibility holds equally true for norms and forms of life and even extends to readers adopting certain patterns of action and ways of life. There are numerous examples of such extratextual processes from different regions and cultures. What they share is that they all respond to readers' specific needs for creating meaning at a particular point in time.

Also notable, on the extratextual level, are the ways in which writers dramatize their own lives in an attempt to influence readers. A writer who prefers to present himself either in the privacy of his study or in the library, as opposed to demonstrating out in the street, with or without a cigar, with or without companions from the present or the afterlife, projects a self-referential life knowledge that his readers can attain. Such staging of one's life practices and life styles can affect how we access the knowledge-for-living stored in such an author's texts and how we engage with a polysemousness that enables different processes of creating meaning.

Knowledge-for-living-together

Taken together, the intratextual and extratextual dimensions of the knowledge-for-living that literature stores comprise fundamental aspects of what I would like to call the *knowledge-for-living-together*. Literary scholarship ought to devote special attention to the ways in which novels, drama, and poetry render explicit different literary characters' knowledge-for-living. Of vital significance in this context are artistic representations of living spaces: a city, a house, and a

---

48 See Ottmar Ette: *José Martí: Eine Geschichte seiner Rezeption. Part 1: Apostel – Dichter – Revolutionär*. Tübingen: Niemeyer 1991; and Ottmar Ette, 'Europa als Bewegung: Zur literarischen Konstruktion eines Faszinosums.' In: Dieter Holtmann / Peter Riemer (eds.): *Europa: Einheit und Vielfalt. Eine interdisziplinäre Betrachtung*. Münster: LIT Verlag 2001, p. 15–44.

room are fractal patterns that may function like a *modèle réduit* (Claude Lévi-Strauss) or a *mise-en-abyme* (André Gide) to offer paradigms of knowledge-for-living and confer knowledge for how to live together in a given society. Examining representations of such spaces affords us the opportunity to tease out specific forms of living together as they manifest themselves in literary texts and to situate these forms culturally, historically, or societally. We can deduce from such studies highly dynamic forms of knowledge – highly dynamic because they are, by necessity, highly adaptable – that are most accurately described as knowledge-for-living together.

At core, knowledge-for-living together is knowledge of the conditions, possibilities, and limits of living together as the literatures of the world have shaped it aesthetically and have tested it experimentally from radically different cultural perspectives. The concept has not only social, political, and economical dimensions but also cultural and ethical ones. Although the literatures of the world have always been concerned with knowledge-for-living-together, literary scholars have yet to mine this resource in any extensive and systematic fashion. Nor have they contributed any of this knowledge to recent public debates on the subject of life. But literary criticism and critical theory should be at the forefront of such discussions as we face the most important and, at the same time, riskiest challenge of the twenty-first century: the search for paradigms of coexistence that would suggest ways in which humans might live together in peace and mutual respect for each other's differences.

Literary scholarship, as part of the sciences-for-living, is always acutely aware of itself, because it wants to produce knowledge-for-living-together. This self-reflexivity is perhaps the legacy of Roland Barthes' posthumously published lecture *Comment vivre ensemble* [How to live together]. In this lecture-seminar held at the Collège de France in 1976-77, Barthes focuses his intellectual attention and theoretical curiosity on the question of how people might live together in difference. He notes under the keyword 'closure' that the process of leaving the protective mother's womb might itself stand for life and its definition: 'to leave is to be exposed: life itself.'[49] Unsurprisingly, Barthes, as semiologist and sign theorist, concerns himself with the question of distance to the Other and to material objects, both in the novelistic sphere and in actual life. Barthes also addresses the significance of touching the other slightly (what he called *frôlage*),[50] which shows performatively that the other's body is not taboo, no matter what the reason for touching it. He also focuses on the significance of

---

49 Roland Barthes: *Comment vivre ensemble*. Paris: Seuil 2002, p. 96.
50 Barthes: *Comment vivre*, p. 112.

an immediate environment for living together, a certain *proxémie*, the concept of which the author of *The Pleasure of the Text* had taken from Edward Twitchell. 'Proximity' refers to a culturally shaped space that surrounds the subject at arm's length, so to speak, and whose perhaps most important objects – as 'créateurs de proxémie' – are the lamp and the bed.[51] Barthes also took important cues from Gaston Bachelard's *The Poetics of Space* (1958)[52] and developed Bachelard's spatial analysis as he addressed the question of living together.

Probing the very different forms and rhythms of cloistral and anchoretic coexistences, for instance, would bring to light a broad spectrum of historically accumulated knowledge of *vivre ensemble*, of which only parts have been passed on to later generations. Analyses of texts by Thomas Mann, Emile Zola, Daniel Defoe, or André Gide, in addition to the numerous autobiographemes of scholars themselves, can broaden this spectrum even further. Much like Iser, in the writings of his that I have quoted above, Barthes starts from the premise that literature is always ahead of everything else: 'toujours en avance sur tout.'[53] In other words, literature has in store for its readers areas of knowledge and questions that academic scholarship, notably psychology, would have to labor long and hard to bring to life.

Barthes' question, in *Comment vivre ensemble*, is, in many ways, intertwined with his *Lover's Discourse*, but it stretches the former text toward a new horizon. Barthes' inquiry into the topic of living together illustrates initial possibilities for how literary analysis might connect literature and life without collapsing one into the other. The realization of literature's own meaning and entelechy must not lead to a continued exiling of life from literary scholarship. The bracketing of one of the central questions that literature poses has inhibited literary theory's development, particularly since the second half of the twentieth century. We continue to feel this trend's negative repercussions today, when societies should instead recognize literature as an indispensable source of knowledge-for-living and knowledge-for-living-together. While this function should not replace other functions of literature, literary theory should finally accept it and take it seriously as a genuine research subject.

In thousands of years, the literatures of the world have accumulated a body of knowledge that has tremendous relevance for the knowledge-for-living-together. Literary scholarship would do well to devote much more, and more systematic, attention to analyzing exactly how literature stores such knowledge.

---

51 Barthes: *Comment vivre*, p. 155–156.
52 See Gaston Bachelard: *The Poetics of Space*. New York: Penguin 2014.
53 Barthes: *Comment vivre*, p. 167.

Exploring this storage function in detail is a foundation for reorienting literary theory and for precise and dynamic accounts of specific forms and ways of life. The different genres and sub-genres of the literatures of the world can provide us with knowledge of how to live (in the novel), of how people have lived (in biography), and of how one can try to transform one's own performed life into knowledge-for-living (in autobiography). The varieties of autobiographical life and survival writing, in particular, produce a knowledge whose analysis is indispensable for a comprehensive understanding of life. This knowledge will help inform the further development of our societies, challenging their historically grown self-conceptions and guiding meaningful agendas for the future.

The issue of how to live together better includes the question of how to approach knowledges-for-living with complete different cultural origins and inflections. Any knowledge-for-living together will consequently have to reflect on the limits and the validity of its 'own' ideas in the lived contexts of multicultural side-by-side-ness, intercultural togetherness, and transcultural mixedupness. Paradigms for producing knowledge-for-living together will also have to combine respect for others with an awareness of gender, social, and other cultural differences. Doing so is crucial for the peaceful coexistence of a humanity that, since the mid-twentieth century, has been in possession of nuclear and other means of its own destruction.

Literary Scholarship as a science-for-living-together

For Nietzsche, historicism was the dominant discipline that had to be relativized and brought back into dialogue with other branches of science and scholarship. Only in this way could one not just lament the disadvantages of history for life but actually determine its uses for life across the entire educational and academic spectrum. Today's dominant academic culture is no doubt that of the natural sciences, with the biotechnological 'life sciences' at the top and almost paradigmatically spearheading the trend. In order to lessen the perils of a one-sided understanding of knowledge production about life as an exclusively natural-scientific endeavor, we must pay closer attention to the limits of such an endeavor and create dialogical structures beyond a strict separation of 'the two cultures.'

I see it as inevitable that literary scholarship will develop in the direction of a science-for-living-together and that the humanities be incorporated into a broader conception of the sciences- for-living. Nevertheless, we should not fool ourselves: art and literature will not provide us with some higher form of knowledge about life. But literature is capable of simulating many different forms of life practice, making them accessible performatively, and offering readers ways of 're-living' them and an understanding of the limits of their own cultural knowledge(s).

The time is right to understand literary scholarship as a science-for-living-together and to embark on research collaborations that include literary studies as much as they do bioscientific research. Such collaborations might helpfully contribute to elaborating what Auerbach, in the above passage from the final chapter of *Mimesis*, calls the 'abundance of life.' Literary scholars need to rise to the challenge of using their analytical frameworks to emphasize the 'abundance of life' that literature holds in store for its readers, augment it, and carry the results of their critical analyses out into our various societies.

Complementary approaches and methods from the natural sciences, the social sciences, and the humanities, together within a broad-based understanding of the 'life sciences' as part of the sciences for living, can open up new perspectives for the systematic exploration of art and literature as experiential knowledge, as survival knowledge, and as knowledge-for-living-together. A decisive and *invigorating* application of literary scholarship's unique potential offers an untimely response to increasingly pressing questions about the uses that the study of literature has for life. If the humanities succeed in 'organiz[ing] the chaos within' themselves, then they may recognize – to invoke Nietzsche one last time – their 'real needs.'[54]

---

54 Nietzsche: 'On the Uses,' p. 123.

Note on the Text and Acknowledgments

Writing-between-Worlds: TransArea Studies and the Literatures-without-a-fixed-Abode differs from Ottmar Ette's *ZwischenWeltenSchreiben: Literatur ohne festen Wohnsitz* (Berlin: Kulturverlag Kadmos, 2005) in several respects. Author and translator agreed to omit chapters 2 and 9 of the German book because of their narrower relevance to readers in the field of Romance literatures. For Ette's original chapter 9, we substituted under the same heading ('Configurations') a composite text that combines portions of a polemic Ette published in 2007 in a special issue of the journal *Lendemains* – "Literaturwissenschaft als Lebenswissenschaft: Eine Programmschrift im Jahr der Geisteswissenschaften" – with parts of the first chapter of his 2004 book *ÜberLebenswissen: Die Aufgabe der Philologie*. The current chapter 9 is a revised version of a translation published in PMLA's 'Criticism in translation' section in 2010 (125.4). We also added a preface, excerpted from the first section of chapter 1 of Ette's *Transarea: Eine literarische Globalisierungsgeschichte* (Berlin: De Gruyter, 2012). Another excerpt from that same chapter made its way into the present chapter 1 ('Transit') under the section title 'Globalization and TransArea studies: What does globalization mean?'

Different English versions of two chapters by nameless translators were previously published in the following venues: chapter 3 ('Relations') as 'Islands, Borders and Vectors: The Fractal World of the Caribbean' (in Lieven D'hulst, Jean-Marc Moura, et al [eds], *Caribbean Interfaces*. Amsterdam: Rodopi, 2007, p. 110-151) and chapter 2 ('Figurations') as "Literatures without a Fixed Abode: Figures of Vectorial Imagination beyond the Dichotomies of National and World Literature' (in Ottmar and Friederike Pannewick [eds]: *ArabAmericas: Literary entanglements of the American hemisphere and the Arab world*. Madrid and Frankfurt amMain: Iberoamericana and Vervuert, 2006, p. 19-68.)

My thanks go to F. David T. Arens for his inexorable editorial counsel; Markus Lenz for his invaluable assistance in tracking down sources and troubleshooting the manuscript; and Ottmar Ette for so many stimulating and pleasurable conversations that they are really one long dialogue-in-progress.

Bibliography

Aciman, André: *Out of Egypt. A Memoir*. New York: Riverhead Books 1994.
Aciman, André (ed.): *Letters of Transit. Reflections on Exile, Identity, Language, and Loss*. New York: The New Press 1999.
Ackermann, Irmgard: *Emine Sevgi Özdamar*. 1999. In: Hermann Korte (ed.): *Kritisches Lexikon zur deutschsprachigen Gegenwartsliteratur,* 62nd Supplement. Munich: Edition text + kritik 1978–2015.
Adorno, Theodor W.: *Minima Moralia. Reflections from a Damaged Life*. Translated by E. F. N. Jephcott. London: New Left 1974.
Agamben, Giorgio: *Homo sacer. Sovereign Power and Bare Life*. Translated by Daniel Heller-Roazen. Stanford: Stanford University Press 1998.
Agamben, Giorgio: *Remnants of Auschwitz. The Witness and the Archive: Homo sacer III*. Translated by Daniel Heller-Roazen. New York: Zone Books 1999.
Agamben, Giorgio: *State of Exception*. Translated by Kevin Attell. Chicago: The University of Chicago Press 2005.
Agamben, Giorgo: *Stato die eccezione. Homo sacer, II*. Turin: Bollati Boringhieri 2003.
Albert, Matthias: *Zur Politik der Weltgesellschaft. Identität und Recht im Kontext internationaler Vergesellschaftung*. Weilerswist: Velbrück Wissenschaft 2002.
Albert, Matthias, and Lothar Brock: *Debordering in the World of States. New Spaces in International Relations*. Frankfurt am Main: World Society Research Group 1995.
Albert, Matthias, and Brock, Lothar: Debordering the World of States. New Spaces in International Relations. In: Matthias Albert; Lothar Brock, and Klaus Dieter Wolf (eds.): *Civilizing World Politics. Society and Community beyond the State*. Boston: Rowman & Littlefield 2000, p. 19–43.
Albert, Matthias, Lothar Brock, and Klaus Dieter Wolf (eds.): *Civilizing World Politics. Society and Community beyond the State*. Boston: Rowman & Littlefield 2000.
Anzaldúa, Gloria: *Borderlands / La Frontera. The New Mestiza*. San Francisco: Aunt Lute Books 1987.
Applemann Williams, William: *The Roots of the Modern American Empire. A Study of the Growth and Shaping of Social Consciousness in a Marketplace Society*. St. Helens: Wood Westworth & Co. 1970.
Apter, Emily: Global *Translatio*. The 'Invention' of Comparative Literature, Istanbul, 1933. In: Christopher Prendergast (ed.): *Debating World Literature*. London: Verso 2004, p. 77–109.
Arenas, Reinaldo: Hallucinations. Being an Account of the Life and Adventures of Friar Servando Teresa de Mier. Translated by Gordon Brotherston. London: Jonathan Cape 1971.
Arenas, Reinaldo: *El central poema*. Barcelona: Seix Barral 1981.
Arenas, Reinaldo: *El mundo alucinante*. Barcelona: Montesinos 1981.
Arenas, Reinaldo: *Arturo, la estrella más brillante*. Barcelona: Montesinos 1984.
Arenas, Reinaldo: *El Central. A Cuban Sugar Mill*. Translated by Anthony Kerrigan. New York: Avon 1984.
Arenas, Reinaldo: *'Old Rosa', and 'The Brightest Star'. Two novels*. Translated by Ann Tashi Slater and Andrew Hurley. New York: Grove/Atlantic 1989.
Arenas, Reinaldo: *Before Night Falls*. Translated by Dolores M. Koch. New York: Penguin 1993.
Arenas, Reinaldo: *Otra vez el mar*. Barcelona: Tusquets Editores Andanzas 2002.

Arenas, Reinaldo: *Autoepitaph. Selected poems*. Translated and edited by Camelly Cruz-Martes and R. Kelly Washbourne. Gainesville, FL: University Press of Florida 2014.
Arendt, Hannah: *On Revolution*. New York: Viking 1963.
Arendt, Hannah: *Macht und Gewalt*. Munich: Piper 1970.
Arendt, Hannah: *Elemente und Ursprünge totaler Herrschaft*. Complete edition. Munich: Piper 1991.
Arent, Hannah: *On Violence*. Boston MA: Houghton Mifflin Harcourt 1970.
Arnold, Heinz Ludwig (ed.): *Kritisches Lexikon zur fremdsprachigen Gegenwartsliteratur*. Munich: edition text+kritik 2001.
Asholt, Wolfgang, and Ottmar Ette (eds.): Literaturwissenschaft als Lebenswissenschaft. Programm – Projekte – Perspektiven. Tübingen: Narr 2010.
Aub, Max: *Manuscrito del Cuervo. Historia de Jacobo*. Introducción, edición y notas de José Antonio Pérez Bowie con un Epílogo de José María Naharro-Calderón. Segorbe, Castellón: Universidad de Alcalá de Henares Fundación Max Aub 1999.
Aub, Max: *Obra poética completa*. In: Joan Oleza Simó (ed.): *Max Aub: Obras completas. Edición crítica*. Estudio introductorio y notas Arcadio López Casanova et al., vol.1. Valencia: Biblioteca Valenciana 2001.
Aub, Max: *Hablo como hombre*. Edición, introducción y notas de Gonzalo Sobejano. Segorbe: Fundación Max Aub 2002.
Aub, Max, Bernhard J. Dotzler, and Barck Karlheinz (eds.): *Auerbach-Alphabet. Karlheinz Carlo Barck zum 70. Geburtstag. Trajekte* V.9. Berlin: Zentrum für Literaturforschung 2004.
Auerbach, Erich: Philology and Weltliteratur. Translated by Edward Said and Maire Said. In: *Centennial Review* 13 (1969), p. 1–17.
Auerbach, Erich: *Mimesis. The Representation of Reality in Western Literature*. Fiftieth anniversary edition. Princeton: Princeton University Press 2003.
Azougarh, Abdeslam: *Miguel Barnet. Rescate e invención de la memoria*. Geneva: Editions Slatkine 1996.
Bachelard, Gaston: *The Poetics of Space*. Foreword by Mark Z. Danielewski. Introduction by Richard Kearney. New York: Penguin Classics 2014.
Bade, Klaus: *Europa in Bewegung. Migration vom späten 18. Jahrhundert bis zur Gegenwart*. Munich: C. H. Beck 2000.
Bade, Klaus J.: *Migration in European History. The Making of Europe*. Translated by Allison Brown. Oxford: Blackwell 2003.
Bahner, Werner (ed.): *Cervantes und seine Zeit*. Berlin: Akademie Verlag 1990.
Bakhtin, Mikhail M.: *Die Ästhetik des Wortes*. Edited by Rainer Grübel. Translated by Rainer Grübel and Sabine Reese. Frankfurt am Main: Suhrkamp 1979.
Balutansky, Kathleen M. and Marie-Agnès Sourieau (eds.): *Caribbean Creolization. Reflections on the Cultural Dynamics of Language, Literature and Identity*. Miami: University Press of Florida 1998.
Bancarel, Gilles (ed.): *Raynal et ses réseaux*. Paris: Champion 2011.
Bandau, Anja: Strategien der Autorisierung. Projektionen der Chicana bei Gloria Anzaldúa und Cherrie Moraga. Hildesheim: Olms 2004.
Barnes, Julian: *Flaubert's parrot*. New York: Knopf 1985.
Barnet, Miguel: *Canción de Rachel*. Buenos Aires: Galerna 1969.
Barnet, Miguel: *Gallego*. Madrid: Alfaguara 1981.
Barnet, Miguel: *La vida real*. Madrid: Alfaguara 1986.
Barnet, Miguel: *Rachel's Song. A novel*. Willimantic, CT: Curbstone Press 1991.

Barnet, Miguel: *A True Story. A Cuban in New York*. Translated b Regina Galasso and José Manuel Prieto González. New York: Jorge Pinto Books 2010.
Barthes, Roland: *A Lover's Discourse. Fragments*. Translated by Richard Howard. New York: Hill and Wang 1977.
Barthes, Roland: De la science à la littérature. In: Roland Barthes: *Le bruissement de la langue. Essais Critiques IV*. Paris: Seuil 1984, p. 13–20.
Barthes, Roland: *Le bruissement de la langue*. Essais Critiques IV. Paris: Seuil 1984.
Barthes, Roland: *The Rustle of Language*. Translated by Richard Howard. Berkeley: University of California Press 1989.
Barthes, Roland: *Œuvres complètes*. Édition établie et présentée par Eric Marty. 3 vols. Paris: Seuil 1993–1995.
Barthes, Roland: Le dernier des écrivains heureux. In: Roland Barthes: *Œuvres complètes*. Édition établie et présentée par Eric Marty, vol.1. Paris: Seuil 1993–1995, p. 1235–1240.
Barthes, Roland: *Comment vivre ensemble. Simulations romanesques de quelques espaces quotidiens*. Notes de cours et de séminaires au Collège de France, 1976–1977. Paris: Seuil/IMEC 2002.
Baudelaire, Charles: *The Flowers of Evil*. Includes parallel French text. A new translation by James McGowan. Oxford: Oxford University Press Oxford World's Classics 2008.
Bay, Hansjörg: Der verrückte Blick. Schreibweisen der Migration in Özdamars Karawanserei-Roman. In: *Sprache und Literatur* 30.83 (1999, p. 29–46.
Bay, Hansjörg; Kai Mertens: Die Ordnung der Kulturen. Zur Konstruktion ethnischer, nationaler und zivilisatorischer Differenzen 1750–1850. Würzburg: Königshausen & Neumann 2006.
Benítez Rojo, Antonio: *The Repeating Island. The Caribbean and the Postmodern Perspective*. Translated by James E. Maraniss. 2nd ed. Durham N.C.: Duke University Press, Postcontemporary Interventions 1992.
Benítez-Rojo, Antonio: *La isla que se repite*. Barcelona: Editorial Casiopea 1998.
Benítez-Rojo, Antonio: Three Words toward Creolization. In: Kathleen M. Balutansky and Marie-Agnès Sourieau (eds.): *Caribbean Creolization. Reflections on the Cultural Dynamics of Language, Literature and Identity*. Miami: University Press of Florida 1998, p. 53–61.
Benjamin, Walter: *Illuminations. Essays and Reflections*. Translated by Harry Zohn. New York: Schocken Books 1955.
Benjamin, Walter: The Task of the Translator. In: Walter Benjamin: *Illuminations. Essays and Reflections*. Translated by Harry Zohn. New York: Schocken Books 1955, p. 70–82.
Benjamin, Walter: Die Aufgabe des Übersetzers. In: Rolf Tiedemann and Hermann Schweppenhäuer (eds.): *Walter Benjamin: Gesammelte Schriften*, 4/1. Frankfurt am Main: Suhrkamp 1977–1985, p. 9–21.
Benjamin, Walter: Notizen über ‚Objective Verlogenheit' I. In: Rolf Tiedemann and Hermann Schweppenhäuer (eds.): *Walter Benjamin: Gesammelte Schriften*, 6. Frankfurt am Main: Suhrkamp 1977-1985, p. 60–62.
Benjamin, Walter: Über den Begriff der Geschichte. In: Rolf Tiedemann and Hermann Schweppenhäuer (eds.): *Walter Benjamin: Gesammelte Schriften,* 1/2. Frankfurt am Main: Suhrkamp 1977–1985, p. 691–704.
Benjamin, Walter: On the Concept of History. In: Howard Eiland and Michael W. Jennings (eds.): *Walter Benjamin: Selected Writings*. Translated by Edmund Jephcott and Others, 4. Cambridge MA: Harvard University Press 2003, p. 389–400.
Benjamin, Walter and Hannah Arendt (eds.): *Illuminations. Essays and Reflections*. Translated by Harry Zohn. New York: Schocken Books 1969.

Bernabé, Jean; Patrick Chamoiseau; Raphaël Confiant; and Mohamed B. Taleb Khyar: *In Praise of Creoleness*. In: *Callaloo* 13.4 (1990, p. 886–909.
Bernecker, Walther L.: Staatliche Grenzen – kontinentale Dynamik. Zur Relativität von Grenzen in Lateinamerika. In: Marianne Braig; Ottmar Ette; and Dieter Ingenschay (eds.): *Grenzen der Macht - Macht der Grenzen. Lateinamerika im globalen Kontext*. Frankfurt am Main: Vervuert 2005, p. 7–37.
Bhabha, Homi: *The Location of Culture*. New York: Routledge 1994.
Birkenmaier, Anke, and Roberto González Echevarría (eds.): *Cuba, un siglo de literatura 1902-2002*. Madrid: Editorial Colibrí 2004. Online at https://books.google.com/books?id=t1V-lAAAAMAAJ.
Bitterli, Urs: *Die "Wilden" und die "Zivilisierten". Grundzüge einer Geistes- und Kulturgeschichte der europäisch-überseeischen Begegnung*. Munich: Deutscher Taschenbuch Verlag 1982.
Blumenberg, Hans: *Arbeit am Mythos*. Frankfurt am Main: Suhrkamp 1979.
Blumenberg, Hans: *Die Lesbarkeit der Welt*. Frankfurt am Main: Suhrkamp 1981.
Boa, Elizabeth: Sprachenverkehr. Hybrides Schreiben in Werken von Özdamar, Özakin und Demirkan. In: Mary Howard (ed.): *Interkulturelle Konfigurationen. Zur deutschsprachigen Erzählliteratur von Autoren nichtdeutscher Herkunft*. Munich: iudicium 1997, p. 115–138.
Boggs, Colleen Glenney: *Transnationalism and American literature*. Literary Translation 1773-1892. New York: Routledge 2007.
Bolívar, Simón: Contestación de un Americano Meridional a un caballero de esta isla. In: Simón Bolívar (ed.): *Obras completas*.1. Madrid: Maveco de Ediciones 1984, p. 160–171.
Bolívar, Simón: *El Libertador. Writings of Simón Bolívar*. New York: Oxford University Press 2003.
Bongie, Chris: *Islands and Exiles. The Creole Identities of Post/colonial Literature*. Stanford: Stanford University Press 1998.
Bongie, Chris: *Friends and Enemies. The Scribal Politics of Post/colonial Literature*. Liverpool: Liverpool University Press 2008.
Borchers, Elisabeth: Übersetzer und Lektor. In: Fritz Nies; Albert-Reiner Glaap, and Wilhelm Gössmann (eds.): *Ist Literaturübersetzen lehrbar? Beiträge zur Eröffnung des Studiengangs Literaturübersetzen an der Universität Düsseldorf*. Tübingen: Narr 1989, p. 45–62.
Borges, Jorge Luis: El escritor argentino y la tradición. In: *Sur* 232 (1955), p. 1–8.
Borges, Jorge Luis: The Argentine Writer and Tradition. In: *Odyssey* 1 (1961), p. 33–41.
Borges, Jorge Luis: *Labyrinths. Selected Stories and Other Writings*. Edited by Donald A. Yates and James E. Irby. New York: New Directions 1964.
Borgmann, Monika: Städte sind wie Geschichten. In: *Die Zeit* 45 (November 11, 1996), p. 80.
Borrero, Juana: *Epistolario*. 2 vols. Havana: Academia de Ciencias de Cuba, 1966–1967.
Börsenverein Deutscher Verleger-und Buchhändler-Verbände: *Buch und Buchhandel in Zahlen. 1952-2004*. Frankfurt am Main: MVB Marketing- und Verlagsservice des Deutschen Buchhandels, GmbH 2004.
Bourdieu, Pierre: *Homo academicus*. Stanford, CA: Stanford University Press 1984.
Braig, Marianne; Ottmar Ette, and Dieter Ingenschay (eds.): *Grenzen der Macht - Macht der Grenzen. Lateinamerika im globalen Kontext*. Frankfurt am Main: Vervuert Verlag 2005.
Brasilia Declaration 2005: *Declaración de Brasilia. Cumbre América del Sur. Países Arabes*. Online at http://www2.mre.gov.br/aspa/Decl/espanol.doc.
Brendecke, Arndt: *Imperium und Empirie. Funktionen des Wissens in der spanischen Kolonialherrschaft*. Cologne: Böhlau 2009.

Brittain, Victoria, and Gillian Slovo: *Guantanamo. Honor Bound to Defend Freedom. Taken from spoken evidence*. London: Oberon Books 2004.
Buck-Morss, Susan: *Hegel and Haiti*. In: *Critical Inquiry* (Chicago) 26 (2000), p. 821–865.
Buck-Morss, Susan: *Hegel, Haiti and Universal history*. Pittsburgh, Pa: University of Pittsburgh Press 2009.
Buschmann, Albrecht: *Die Macht und ihr Preis. Detektorisches Erzählen bei Leonardo Sciascia und Manuel Vázquez Montalbán*. Würzburg: Königshausen & Neumann 2005.
Calvino, Italo: *Saggi 1945–1985*. Milan: Arnoldo Mondadori Editore 1995.
Calvino, Italo: *Savona. Storia e natura*. In: Italo Calvino: *Saggi 1945–1985*. Milan: Arnoldo Mondadori Editore 1995, p. 2390–2402.
Caplan Jane and John Torpey (eds.): *Documenting Individual Identity. The Development of State Practices in the Modern World*. Princeton: Princeton University Press 2001.
Caproni, Giorgio: *L'opera in versi*. Critical edition by Luca Zuliani. Milan: Mondadori 1989.
Caproni, Giorgio: *Poesie 1932–1986*. Milan: Garzanti 1989.
Carpentier, Alejo: *War of Time*. Translated by Frances Partridge. London: Gollancz 1970.
Carpentier, Alejo: *La Ciudad de las Columnas*. Havana: Editorial Letras Cubanas 1982.
Casanova, Pascale: *La République mondiale des lettres*. Paris: Seuil 1999.
Cassin, Barbara; Steven Rendall, and Emily S. Apter (eds.): *Dictionary of Untranslatables. A Philosophical Lexicon*. Princeton: Princeton University Press 2014.
Castells, Manuel: *Das Informationszeitalter. Wirtschaft - Gesellschaft - Kultur*. Opladen: Leske & Budrich 2003.
Cavafy, Constantine P.: *Collected Poems*. Tanslated by Edmund Keeley and Philip Sherrard. Princeton, NJ: Princeton University Press 1992.
Clarfield, Gerard H.: *United States Diplomatic History*. Vol. 1: Readings for the eighteenth and nineteenth centuries. Boston: Houghton Mifflin 1973.
Cohen, Albert: Jour de mes dix ans. In: *La France libre* (July 16, 1945 and August 15, 1945), p. 193-200 (part 1) and 287-294 (part 2).
Cohen, Ralph (ed.): *New Directions in Literary History*. Baltimore: Johns Hopkins University Press 1974.
Colli, Giorgio, and Massimo Montinari (eds.): *Friedrich Nietzsche: Kritische Studienausgabe in 15 Einzelbänden*. Berlin: DTV, De Gruyter 1988.
Condé, Maryse: *Traversée de la mangrove*. Paris: Mercure de France 1992.
Condé, Maryse: *Crossing the Mangrove*. New York: Anchor Books / Doubleday 1995.
Cramer, Friedrich: *Chaos and Order. The Complex Structure of Living Systems*. Foreword by I. Prigonine. Translated by D. I. Loewus. Weinheim: VHC 1993.
Crosby, Alfred W.: The Columbian exchange. Biological and cultural consequences of 1492. Westport, Connecticut: Greenwood 1972.
Damrosch, David: *What is World Literature?* Princeton NJ: Princeton University Press 2003.
Daston, Lorraine: *Wunder, Beweise und Tatsachen. Zur Geschichte der Rationalität*. Translated by Gerhard Herrgott, Christa Krüger, and Susanne Scharnowski. Frankfurt am Main: Fischer 2001.
Daston, Lorraine; Katharine Park: *Wonders and the Order of Nature, 1150–1750*. New York: Zone Books 1998.
De la Nuez, Iván: *La balsa perpetua. Soledad y conexiones de la cultura cubana*. Barcelona: Editorial Casiopea 1998.
Díaz, Jesús: *Dime algo sobre Cuba*. Madrid: Espasa 1998.

Djebar, Assia 1998: Schreiben in Europa. Über den Roman Nächte in Strassburg. Haus der Kulturen der Welt. Berlin, 28.11.1998. Online at http://www.unionsverlag.com/info/link.asp?link_id=256&pers_id=12&pic=./%20portrait/DjebarAssia.jpg&t.

D'Oria Domenico: *Calvino traduit par Calvino*. In: *Lectures*.4–5 (1980), p. 177–193.

Dröscher, Barbara and Carlos Rincón (eds.): *La Malinche. Übersetzung, Interkulturalität und Geschlecht*. Berlin: Verlag Walter Frey – Edition tranvía 2001.

Durán, Manuel (ed.): *Octavio Paz: Obras completas*. México, Domino mexicano: Fondo de Cultura Económica 1994–1999.

Ecker, Gisela (ed.): *Kein Land in Sicht. Heimat - weiblich?* Munich: Fink 1997.

Eckermann, Johann Peter: *Gespräche mit Goethe in den letzten Jahren seines Lebens*. Frankfurt am Main: Insel 1981.

Eiland, Howard and Michael W. Jennings (eds.): *Walter Benjamin: Selected Writings*. Translated by Edmund Jephcott and Others. Cambridge MA: Harvard University Press 2003.

Eisenstadt; Shmuel N.: *Multiple Modernities*. New Brunswick, NJ: Transaction Publishers 2002.

Eisler, Colin: Who is Dürer's 'Syphilitic Man'? In: *Perspectives in Biology and Medicine* LII.1 (2009), p. 48–60.

Elsie, Robert (ed.): *Konstantinos Kavafis. Das Gesamtwerk, griechisch-deutsch*. Translated by Robert Elsie. Zurich: Ammann 1997.

Ette, Ottmar: *José Martí. Eine Geschichte seiner Rezeption*. Teil 1: Apostel – Dichter – Revolutionär. Tübingen: Niemeyer 1991.

Ette, Ottmar: Así habló Próspero. Nietzsche, Rodó y la modernidad filosófica de 'Ariel.' In: *Cuadernos Hispanoamericanos* 528 (1994), p. 48–62.

Ette, Ottmar: Los colores de la libertad. *Nueva York*, 14 de enero de 1990. Entrevista con Reinaldo Arenas. In: Ottmar Ette and Arenas Reinaldo (eds.): *La Escritura de la memoria. Reinaldo Arenas : textos, estudios y documentación*. Frankfurt am Main: Vervuert 1996, p. 75–91.

Ette, Ottmar: *Roland Barthes. Eine intellektuelle Biographie*. Frankfurt am Main: Suhrkamp 1998.

Ette, Ottmar: Albert Cohen – 'Jour de mes dix ans.' Räume und Bewegungen interkultureller Begegnung. In: Sybille Grosse and Axel Schönberger (eds.): *Dulce et decorum est philologiam colere. Festschrift für Dietrich Briesemeister zu seinem 65. Geburtstag*. Frankfurt am Main: Domus Editoria Europaea 1999, p. 1295–1322.

Ette, Ottmar: Europa als Bewegung. Zur literarischen Konstruktion eines Faszinosum. In: Dieter Holtmann and Peter Riemer (eds.): *Europa: Einheit und Vielfalt. Eine interdisziplinäre Betrachtung*. Münster: LIT Verlag 2001, p. 15–44.

Ette, Ottmar: Kuba. Insel der Inseln. In: Ottmar Ette and Martin Franzbach (eds.): *Kuba heute. Politik, Wirtschaft, Kultur*. Frankfurt am Main: Vervuert 2001, p. 9–25.

Ette, Ottmar: *Literatur in Bewegung. Raum und Dynamik grenzüberschreitenden Schreibens in Europa und Amerika*. Weilerswist: Velbrück Wissenschaft 2001.

Ette, Ottmar: Faire éclater la problématique d'une littérature nationale. Entretien avec la romancière haïtienne Yanick Lahens à Berlin, le 24 mars 2002. In: *Lendemains* 27.105-106 (2002), p. 221–235.

Ette, Ottmar: *Weltbewusstsein. Alexander von Humboldt und das unvollendete Project einer anderen Moderne*. Weilerwist: Velbrück Wissenschaft 2002.

Ette, Ottmar: Die Fremdheit in der Mutterzunge. Emine Sevgi Özdamar, Gabriela Mistral, Juana Borrero und die Krise der Sprache in Formen des weiblichen Schreibens zwischen Spätmoderne und Postmoderne. In: Kacianka Reinhard and Peter V. Zima (eds.): *Krise und Kri-*

tik der Sprache. Literatur zwischen Spätmoderne und Postmoderne. Tübingen: Francke 2004, p. 251–268.
Ette, Ottmar: *ÜberLebenswissen. Die Aufgabe der Philologie*. Berlin: Kulturverlag Kadmos 2004.
Ette, Ottmar: Una literatura sin fronteras. Ficciones y fricciones en la literatura cubana del siglo XX. In: Anke Birkenmaier and Roberto González Echevarría (eds.): *Cuba, un siglo de literatura 1902–2002*. Madrid: Editorial Colibrí 2004, p. 407–433.
Ette, Ottmar: Wege des Wissens. Fünf Thesen zum Weltbewusstsein und den Literaturen der Welt. In: Sabine Hoffmann and Monika Wehrheim (eds.): *Lateinamerika. Orte und Ordnungen des Wissens*. Festschrift für Birgit Scharlau. Tübingen: Narr 2004, p. 169–184.
Ette, Ottmar: Una literatura sin residencia fija. Insularidad, historia y dinámica sociocultural en la Cuba del siglo XX. In: *Revista de Indias* 65.235 2005, p. 729–753.
Ette, Ottmar: *ZwischenWeltenSchreiben. Literaturen ohne festen Wohnsitz*. ÜberLebenswissen II. Berlin: Kadmos 2005.
Ette, Ottmar: Gender Trouble. José Martí and Juana Borrero. In: Mauricio A. Font and Alfonso W. Quiroz (eds.): *The Cuban Republic and José Martí. Reception and Use of a National Symbol*. Lanham-Boulder: Lexington Books 2006, p. 180–193; 230–233.
Ette, Ottmar: Literatures without a Fixed Abode. Figures of Vectorial Imagination Beyond the Dichotomies of National and World Literature. In: Ottmar Ette and Friederike Pannewick (eds.): *ArabAmericas. Literary entanglements of the American hemisphere and the Arab world*. Madrid and Frankfurt am Main: Iberoamericana and Vervuert 2006, p. 19–68.
Ette, Ottmar: Unterwegs zu einer Weltwissenschaft? Alexander von Humboldts Weltbegriffe und die transarealen Studien. In: *HiN - Alexander von Humboldt im Netz. Internationale Zeitschrift für Humboldt-Studien Potsdam/Berlin* VII.13 (2006), p. 34–54.
Ette, Ottmar: Literaturwissenschaft als Lebenswissenschaft. Eine Programmschrift im Jahr der Geisteswissenschaften. In: *Lendemains* 32.125 (2007), p. 7–32.
Ette, Ottmar: *Alexander von Humboldt und die Globalisierung. Das Mobile des Wissens*. Frankfurt am Main: Insel 2009.
Ette, Ottmar: Le monde transarchipélien de la Caraibe colonial. In: Ottmar Ette and Gesine Müller (eds.): *Caleidoscopios coloniales. Transferencias culturales en el Caribe del siglo XIX / Kaléidoscopes coloniaux*. Madrid and Frankfurt am Main: Vervuert - Iberoamericana 2010, p. 23–64.
Ette, Ottmar: *ZusammenLebensWissen. List, Last und Lust literarischer Konvivenz im globalen Maßstab*. Berlin: Kulturverlag Kadmos Berlin ÜberLebenswissen, 3 2010.
Ette, Ottmar: *TransArea. Eine literarische Globalisierungsgeschichte*. Berlin: De Gruyter 2012.
Ette, Ottmar and Arenas Reinaldo (eds.): *La Escritura de la memoria. Reinaldo Arenas: textos, estudios y documentación*. Frankfurt am Main: Vervuert 1996.
Ette, Ottmar; Mercedes Figueras, and Joseph Jurt (eds.): *Max Aub - André Malraux. Guerrra civil, exilio y literatura*. Madrid: Iberoamericana Vervuert 2005.
Ette, Ottmar and Martin Franzbach (eds.): *Kuba heute. Politik, Wirtschaft, Kultur*. Frankfurt am Main: Vervuert 2001.
Ette, Ottmar; Ute Hermanns, Bernd M. Scherer et al. (eds.): *Alexander von Humboldt. Aufbruch in die Moderne*. Berlin: Akademie Verlag 2001.
Ette, Ottmar and Gesine Müller (eds.): *Caleidoscopios coloniales. Transferencias culturales en el Caribe del siglo XIX / Kaléidoscopes coloniaux*. Madrid, Frankfurt am Main: Vervuert - Iberoamericana 2010.

Ette, Ottmar and Friederike Pannewick (eds.): *ArabAmericas. Literary entanglements of the American hemisphere and the Arab world*. Madrid and Frankfurt am Main: Iberoamericana and Vervuert 2006.
Evans, Robert Charles: *A Critical Introduction to C.P. Cavafy*. Chapel Hill, NC: University of North Carolina 1988.
Ezrahi, Sidra deKoven: *Booking Passage. Exile and Homecoming in the Modern Jewish Imagination*. Berkeley: University of California Press 2000.
Fatah, Sherko: *Im Grenzland*. Berlin: btb – Verlag 2003.
Fatah, Sherko: Warum bleibt mein Onkel in Bagdad? Stimmungen in der Republik der Angst: Das große Hoffen auf Saddams Sturz. In: *Frankfurter Allgemeine Zeitung* 41 (February 18, 2003), p. 33.
Fayad, Luis: *La caída de los puntos cardinales*. Bogotá: Editorial Planeta Colombiana 2000.
Fernández de Lizardi, José Joaquín: *The itching parrot = El Periquillo Sarniento*. Garden City NY: Doubleday Doran 1942.
Fernández Retamar, Roberto: *Calibán y otros ensayos*. Havana: Editorial Arte y Literatura 1979.
Fernández Retamar, Roberto: *Caliban and other Essays*. Minneapolis: University of Minnesota Press 1989.
Finkielkraut, Alain: *Le juif imaginaire*. Paris: Seuil 1980.
Fischer, Sibylle: *Modernity Disavow(ed.) Haiti and the Cultures of Slavery in the Age of Revolution*. Durham N.C.: Duke University Press 2004.
Font, Mauricio A. and Alfonso W. Quiroz (eds.): *The Cuban Republic and José Martí. Reception and Use of a National Symbol*. Lanham-Boulder: Lexington Books 2006.
Foucault, Michel: *The Order of Things. An Archaeology of the Human Sciences*. New York: Vintage Books 1973.
Fraser, Nancy: *Justice Interruptus. Critical Reflections on the 'Postsocialist' Condition*. New York: Routledge 1997.
Frenzel, Elisabeth: *Stoffe der Weltliteratur. Ein Lexikon dichtungs–geschichtlicher Längsschnitte*. Sixth edition and with an added index. Stuttgart: Alfred Kröner 1983.
Freud, Sigmund: *The Uncanny*. Translated by David Mc Lintock. New York: Penguin 2003.
Fried, Erich: Übersetzen oder nachdichten? In: Fritz Nies; Albert-Reiner Glaap, and Wilhelm Gössmann (eds.): *Ist Literaturübersetzen lehrbar? Beiträge zur Eröffnung des Studiengangs Literaturübersetzen an der Universität Düsseldorf*. Tübingen: Narr 1989, p. 29–44.
Fröhlich, Margrit: Reinventions of Turkey. Emine Sevgi Özdamar's 'Life is a Caravanserai.' In: Karen Jankowsky and Carla Love (eds.): *Other Germanies. Questioning Identity in Women's Literature and Art*. New York: State University of New York 1997, p. 56–73.
Frühwald, Wolfgang; Hans-Robert Jauss; Reinhart Koselleck et al. (eds.): *Geisteswissenschaften heute. Eine Denkschrift*. Frankfurt am Main: Suhrkamp 1991.
Gadamer, Hans-Georg: Über das Hören. In: Thomas Vogel (ed.): *Über das Hören. Einem Phänomen auf der Spur*. Tübingen: Attempto 1996, p. 197–205.
Galeano, Eduardo: *Las venas abiertas de América Latina*. Mexico, D.F.: Siglo XXI Editores 1982.
Galeano, Eduardo: *The Open Veins of Latin America*. New York: Monthly Review Press 1997.
Ganten, Detlev; Thomas Deichmann, and Thilo Spah (eds.): *Leben, Natur, Wissenschaft. Alles was man wissen muss*. Frankfurt am Main: Eichborn 2003.
García Márquez, Gabriel: *Crónica de una muerte anunciada*. Barcelona: Editorial Bruguera 1981.
García Márquez, Gabriel: *Chronicle of a Death Foretold*. Translated by Gregory Rabassa. New York: Knopf - Vintage 2003.

García Usta, Jorge: Arabes en Macondo. In: *Deslinde* 21 (1997), p. 122–139.
Garscha, Karsten: Zum Phänomen der fingierten Mündlichkeit in der lateinamerikanischen Erzählliteratur. In: Birgit Scharlau (ed.): *Bild – Wort – Schrift. Beiträge zur Lateinamerika-Sektion des Freiburger Romanistentages*. Tübingen: Narr 1989, p. 121–130.
Gauss, Karl-Markus: Fremde Welt, so nah. Der kurdisch deutsche Autor Sherko Fatah schreibt seinen ersten Roman. In: *Die Zeit* 13 (2001).
Geertz, Clifford: *Local Knowledge. Further Essays in Interpretatory Anthropology*. New York: Basic Books 1983.
Genette, Gérard: *Palimpsestes. La littérature au second degré*. Paris: Seuil 1982.
Gerbi, Antonello: *The Dispute of the New World. The History of a Polemic, 1750-1900*. Revised and enlarged edition. Translated by Jeremy Moyle. Pittsburgh, Pa: University of Pittsburgh Press 1973.
Gerbi, Antonello: *La disputa del nuovo mondo. Storia di una polemica, 1750-1900*. Milan: Riccardo Ricciardi editore 1983.
Giles, Paul: *Virtual Americas. Transnational Fictions and the Transatlantic Imaginary*. Durham, NC: Duke University Press 2002.
Gilroy, Paul: *The Black Atlantic. Modernity and Double Consciousness*. London: Verso 1993.
Glissant, Édouard: *Le discours antillais*. Paris: Seuil 1981.
Glissant, Édouard: *Poétique de la Relation*. Paris: Gallimard 1990.
Glissant, Édouard: *Caribbean Discourse. Selected essays*. Translated and with an introduction by J. Michael Dash. Charlottesville: University Press of Virginia 1999.
Glissant, Édouard: *Poetics of Relations*. Translated by Betsy Wing. Ann Arbor: University of Michigan Press 2000.
Goethe, Johann Wolfgang von: *The Maxims and Reflections of Goethe*. Translated by Thomas Bailey Saunders. New York: MacMillan and Company 1906.
Gómez de Avellaneda, Gertrudis: *Autobiografía y cartas. Estudio y notas de Lorenzo Cruz-Fuentes*. Huelva: Diputación Provincial 1996.
Gómez de Avellaneda, Gertrudis: *Sab and Autobiography*. Translated and edited by Nina M. Scott. Austin: University of Texas Press 2003.
González Echevarría, Roberto: *Alejo Carpentier, the pilgrim at home*. Ithaca, NY: Cornell University Press 1977.
González Echevarría, Roberto: Cuban. In: *Encuentro de la Cultura Cubana* 15 (1999–2000), p. 103–112.
González Echevarría, Roberto: *The Pride of Havana. A History of Cuban Baseball*. New York: Oxford University Press 1999.
Goytisolo, Juan: On Emine Sevgi Özdamar. In: *New York Times Literary Supplement* 12 (1994).
Graf, Karin (ed.): *Übersetzerwerkstatt 1900. Ein Brevier und Materialien*. Berlin: Literarisches Colloquium 1991.
Greenblatt, Stephen: *Marvelous Possessions. The Wonder of the New World*. Chicago: University of Chicago Press 1991.
Grosse, Sybille, and Axel Schönberger (eds.): *Dulce et decorum est philologiam colere. Festschrift für Dietrich Briesemeister zu seinem 65. Geburtstag*. 2 vols. Frankfurt am Main: Domus Editoria Europaea 1999.
Gruzinski, Serge: *Les quatre parties du monde. Histoire d'une mondialisation*. Paris: La Martinière 2004.
Guille, Martine and Reinhard Kiesler (eds.): *Romania una et diversa. Philologische Studien für Theodor Berchem zum 65. Geburtstag*. Tübingen: Narr 2000.

Guillén, Nicolás: *El libro de los sones*. Havana: Editorial Letras Cubanas 1982.
Guillén, Nicolás: *Páginas vueltas. Memorias*. Edición homenaje al 80 aniversario de su nacimiento 1982. Havana: Unión de Escritores y Artistas de Cuba 1982.
Gumbrecht, Hans Ulrich: *Production of Presence. What Meaning Cannot Convey*. Stanford CA: Stanford University Press 2004.
Habermas, Jürgen: Die Moderne. Ein unvollendetes Projekt. In: Jürgen Habermas: *Kleine politische Schriften I-IV*. Frankfurt am Main: Suhrkamp 1981, p. 444–464.
Habermas, Jürgen: Nachwort. In: Horkheimer Max und Theodor W. Adorno: *Dialektik der Aufklärung. Philosophische Fragmente*. Frankfurt am Main: Fischer 1986, p. 277–294.
Habermas, Jürgen: *Faktizität und Geltung. Beiträge zur Diskurstheorie des Rechts und des demokratischen Rechtsstaats*. Frankfurt am Main: Suhrkamp 1992.
Habermas, Jürgen: Staatsbürgerschaft und nationale Identität. In: Jürgen Habermas: *Faktizität und Geltung. Beiträge zur Diskurstheorie des Rechts und des demokratischen Rechtsstaats*. Frankfurt am Main: Suhrkamp 1992, p. 632–660.
Habermas, Jürgen: *The Future of Human Nature*. Cambridge, MA: Polity; Blackwell 2003.
Hartmann, Geoffrey: *The Longest Shadow. In the Aftermath of the Holocaust*. Bloomington: Indiana University Press 1996.
Hayakawa, S. I., and Alan R. Hayakawa: *Language in Thought and Action*. 5th ed. San Diego Calif.: Harcourt Brace Jovanovich 1990.
Hayakawa, Samuel: *Language in Action*. New York: Harcourt, Brace & Co. 1939.
Hearn, Lafcadio: *A Japanese Miscellany*. Boston, MA: Little, Brown, and Company 1901.
Hearn, Lafcadio: *In ghostly Japan. 1899*. London: Kegan Paul 1907.
Hearn, Lafcadio: *Two Years in the French West Indies*. Oxford: Signal 2001.
Hearn, Lafcadio, and Christopher E. G. Benfey: *American Writings*. New York: Library of America 2009.
Heitmann, Klaus: *Der Immoralismus. Prozess gegen die französische Literatur im 19. Jahrhundert*. Bad Homburg: Gehlen 1970.
Hermann Korte (ed.): *Kritisches Lexikon zur deutschsprachigen Gegenwartsliteratur*. Munich: Edition text + kritik 1978–2015.
Höffe, Otfried von: *Demokratie im Zeitalter der Globalisierung*. Munich: Beck 1999.
Hoffmann, Sabine and Monika Wehrheim (eds.): Lateinamerika. Orte und Ordnungen des Wissens. Festschrift für Birgit Scharlau. Tübingen: Narr 2004.
Hofmeister, Wilhelm: Ein Gipfel der falschen Erwartungen und des falschen Zungenschlages. Das 1. Gipfeltreffen Südamerika – Arabische Liga. In: *Focus Brasilien* 4 (2005), p. 1–7.
Holtmann, Dieter, and Peter Riemer (eds.): *Europa: Einheit und Vielfalt. Eine interdisziplinäre Betrachtung*. Münster: LIT Verlag 2001.
Horkheimer Max; Theodor W. Adorno: *Dialectic of Enlightenment. Philosophical Fragments*. Translated by John Cumming. New York: Continuum 1972.
Horkheimer Max; Adorno, Theodor W.: *Dialektik der Aufklärung. Philosophische Fragmente*. Frankfurt am Main: Fischer Verlag 1986.
Horn, Eva; Stefan Kaufmann and Ulrich Bröckling (eds.): *Grenzverletzer. Von Schmugglern, Spionen und anderen subversiven Gestalten*. Berlin: Kulturverlag Kadmos 2002.
Howard, Mary (ed.): *Interkulturelle Konfigurationen. Zur deutschsprachigen Erzählliteratur von Autoren nichtdeutscher Herkunft*. Munich: iudicium 1997.
Humboldt, Alexander von: *Examen critique de l'histoire de la géographie du nouveau continent et des progrès de l'astronomie nautique aux quinzième et seizième siècles*. Paris: Librairie de Gide 4 1838.

Humboldt, Alexander von: *Ensayo Político sobre la Isla de Cuba*. Introducción por Fernando Ortiz. Havana: Cultural S. A. 1930.
Humboldt, Alexander von: *Ansichten der Natur*. Mit wissenschaftlichen Erläuterungen. Nördlingen: Greno 1986.
Humboldt, Alexander von: *Views of nature*. Translated by Mark W. Person. Edited by Jackson, Stephen T. Jackson and Laura Dassow Walls. Chicago: University of Chicago Press 2014.
Humboldt, Alexander von; John S. Thrasher: *The Island of Cuba, by Alexander Humboldt*. Translated from the Spanish, with notes and a preliminary essay by John S. Thrasher. New York: Derby & Jackson 1856.
Huntington, Samuel P.: *The Clash of Civilizations*. New York: Simon & Schuster 1996.
Iser, Wolfgang: Indeterminacy and the Reader's Response in Prose Fiction. In: J. Hillis Miller (ed.): *Aspects of Narrative. Selected Papers from the English Institute*. New York: Columbia University Press 1971, p. 1–45.
Iser, Wolfgang: The Reading Process. A Phenomenological Approach. In: Ralph Cohen (ed.): *New Directions in Literary History*. Baltimore: Johns Hopkins University Press 1974, p. 125–146.
Iser, Wolfgang: Die Apellstruktur der Texte. Unbestimmtheit als Wirkungsbedingung literarischer Prosa. In: Rainer Warning (ed.): *Rezeptionsästhetik. Theorie und Praxis*. Munich: Fink 1975, p. 228–252.
Iser, Wolfgang: *The Act of Reading. A Theory of Aesthetic Response*. Baltimore: Johns Hopkins University Press 1978.
Jahn, Bernhard: *Raumkonzepte in der Frühen Neuzeit. Zur Konstruktion van Wirklichkeit in Pilgerberichten, Amerikareisebeschreibungen und Prosaerzählungen*. Frankfurt am Main: Peter Lang 1993.
Jakobson, Roman: On Linguistic Aspects of Translation. In: Stephen Rudy (ed.): *Roman Jakobson: Selected Writings*, 2. Paris: De Gruyter Mouton 1971-1985, p. 260–266.
Jakobson, Roman: Word and Language. 1971. In: Stephen Rudy (ed.): *Roman Jakobson: Selected Writings* 2. Paris: De Gruyter Mouton 1971-1985.
Jankowsky, Karen and Carla Love (eds.): *Other Germanies. Questioning Identity in Women's Literature and Art*. New York: State University of New York 1997.
Joan Oleza Simó (ed.): *Max Aub: Obras completas. Edición crítica*. Estudio introductorio y notas Arcadio López Casanova et al. Valencia: Biblioteca Valenciana 2001.
Joseph, Anne M.: Anthropometry, the Police Expert, and the Deptford Murders. The Contested Introduction of Fingerprinting for the Identification of Criminals in Late Victorian and Edwardian Britain. In: Caplan Jane and John Torpey (eds.): *Documenting Individual Identity. The Development of State Practices in the Modern World*. Princeton: Princeton University Press 2001, p. 164–183.
Jurt, Joseph: Entstehung und Entwicklung der LATEINamerika Idee. In: *Lendemains* 27 (1982), p. 17–26.
Jurt, Joseph: *Das literarische Feld. Das Konzept Pierre Bourdieus in Theorie und Praxis*. Darmstadt: Wissenschaftliche Buchgesellschaft 1995.
Jusdanis, Gregory: *The Poetics of Cavafy. Textuality, Eroticism, History*. Princeton, NJ: Princeton University Press 2014.
Kacianka Reinhard and Peter V. Zima (eds.): *Krise und Kritik der Sprache. Literatur zwischen Spätmoderne und Postmoderne*. Tübingen: Francke 2004.
Kann, Emma: Biographische Notizen. In: *Exil: Forschung, Erkenntnisse, Ergebnisse* VI.1 (1986), p. 66–77.

Kann, Emma: Der Vagabund. In: *Mnemosyne* 15 (1998), p. 15.
Kant, Immanuel: *Kritik der reinen Vernunft* 1. Frankfurt am Main: Suhrkamp 1974.
Kant, Immanuel: *Critique of Pure Reason*. Translated by Werner S. Pluhar. Introduction by Patricia W. Kitcher. Indianapolis, Indiana: Hackett 1996.
Kavafis, Konstantinos: *Das Gesamtwerk. Griechisch und Deutsch*. Translated by Robert Elsie. Zurich: Ammann 1997.
Khoury, Elias (ed.): *Little Mountain*. Manchester: Carcanet Press Limited 1989.
Khoury, Elias: *The Kingdom of Strangers. A novel*. Translated by Paula Haydar. Fayetteville: University of Arkansas Press 1996.
Khoury, Elias: *Der geheimnisvolle Brief*. Translated by Leila Chammaa. Munich: C.H. Beck 2000.
Khoury, Elias: Wie der Westen Araber produziert. Erfahrungen eines libanesischen Schriftstellers mit der französischen Polizei – und drei Gründe, nicht zu reisen. In: *Die Zeit* 47 (November 15, 2001).
Kimminich, Eva and Claudia Krülls-Hepermann (eds.): *Zunge und Zeichen*. Berlin: Peter Lang 1999.
Kittler, Friedrich A. (ed.): *Austreibung des Geistes aus den Geisteswissenschaften. Programme des Poststrukturalismus*. Paderborn: Schöningh 1980.
Kittler, Friedrich A.: Autorschaft und Liebe. In: Friedrich A. Kittler (ed.): *Austreibung des Geistes aus den Geisteswissenschaften. Programme des Poststrukturalismus*. Paderborn: Schöningh 1980, p. 142–73.
Kleist, Heinrich von: Kurze Geschichte des gelben Fiebers in Europa. In: *Berliner Abendblätter* 19 and 20 (January 23 and 24, 1811), p. 73–75 and 77–79.
Kloepfer, Albrecht; Matsunaga, Miho: Yoko Tawada. 2000. In: Hermann Korte (ed.): *Kritisches Lexikon zur deutschsprachigen Gegenwartsliteratur,* 64th Supplement. Munich: Edition text + kritik 1978–2015.
Knorr-Cetina, Karin: *Epistemic Cultures. How the Sciences Make Knowledge*. Cambridge MA: Harvard University Press 1999.
Kohl, Karl-Heinz; Berliner Festspiele GmhH Berlin, and Martin-Gropius-Bau Berlin (eds.): *Mythen der neuen Welt. Zur Entdeckungsgeschichte Lateinamerikas*. Katalog Ausstellung des 2. Festivals der Weltkulturen Horizonte 1982, Lateinamerika vom 13. Juni - 29. Aug. 1982 im Martin-Gropius-Bau, Berlin. Berlin: Frölich & Kaufmann 1982.
Konuk, Kader: Das Leben ist eine Karawanserei. Heimat bei Emine Sevgi Özdamar. In: Gisela Ecker (ed.): *Kein Land in Sicht. Heimat - weiblich?* Munich: Fink 1997, p. 143–157.
Koselleck, Reinhart: *Futures past. On the semantics of historical time*. New York: Columbia University Press 2004.
Krauss, Werner: *Die Welt im spanischen Sprichwort*. Leipzig: Reclam 1946.
Krauss, Werner: *Grundprobleme der Literaturwissenschaft. Zur Interpretation literarischer Werke*. Reinbeck bei Hamburg: Rowohlt 1968.
Krauss, Werner: Das Problem der Übersetzung. In: Fritz Nies; Albert-Reiner Glaap and Wilhelm Gössmann (eds.): *Ist Literaturübersetzen lehrbar? Beiträge zur Eröffnung des Studiengangs Literaturübersetzen an der Universität Düsseldorf*. Tübingen: Narr 1989, p. 131–139.
Kutzinski, Vera M. (ed.): *Alexander von Humboldt's Translantic Personae*. London: Routledge 2012.
Kutzinski, Vera M.: 'Humboldt's Translator in the Context of Cuban History' by Fernando Ortiz. Translated from the Cuban. In: Vera M. Kutzinski (ed.): *Alexander von Humboldt's Translantic Personae*. London: Routledge 2012, p. 93-110.

Laabs, Klaus: Traducir a Reinaldo Arenas. In: *Apuntes Postmodernos / Postmodern Notes* Miami 6.1 (1995), p. 53–55.
Lahens, Yanick: *L'Exil: entre l'ancrage et la fuite. L'écrivain haïtien*. Port-au-Prince: Éditions Henri Deschamps 1990.
Lahens, Yanick: *Dans la maison du père*. Paris: Le Serpent à Plumes 2000.
Laitenberger, Hugo: William Julius Mickle und seine Übersetzung der 'Lusiaden'. In: Martine Guille and Reinhard Kiesler (eds.): *Romania una et diversa. Philologische Studien für Theodor Berchem zum 65. Geburtstag*. Tübingen: Narr 2000, p. 739–760.
Lamming, George: *The Pleasures of Exile*. Ann Arbor: University of Michigan Press 1992.
Lasker-Schüler, Else: *Sämtliche Gedichte*. Munich: Kösel-Verlag 1966.
Leddy Phelan, John: Pan-Latinism, French Intervention in Mexico 1861–1867 and the Genesis of the Idea of Latin America. In: Ortega y Medina, Juan Antonio (ed.): *Conciencia y autenticidad históricas. Escritos en homenaje a Edmundo O'Gorman*. México D.F.: UNAM 1968, p. 279–298.
Leitner, Claudia: Zunge des Eroberers. Markenzeichen kultureller Alteritäten: La Malinche. In: Eva Kimminich and Claudia Krülls-Hepermann (eds.): *Zunge und Zeichen*. Berlin: Peter Lang 1999, p. 41–70.
Lejeune, Philippe: *Je est un autre. L'autobiographie de la littérature aux médias*. Paris: Seuil 1980.
Lepenies, Wolf: *The End of Natural History*. New York: The Confucian Press 1980.
Lezama Lima, José: El romanticismo y el hecho americano. In: José Lezama Lima: *La expresión americana*. Madrid: Alianza Editorial 1969, p. 116.
Lezama Lima, José: *Poesía completa*. Havana: Editorial Letras Cubanas 1985.
Liu, Lydia: *Translingual Practice. Literature, National Culture, and Translated Modernity – China, 1900-1937*. Stanford, CA: Stanford University Press 1995.
Lotman, Jurij M.: *The Structure of the Artistic Text*. Translated by Gail Lenhoff and Ronald Vroon. Ann Arbort: University of Michigan Press 1977.
Lowell, Robert: *Life Studies*. New York: Farrar 1959; 1968.
Ludwig, Ralph (ed.): *Écrire la 'parole de nuit': la nouvelle littérature antillaise. Nouvelles, poèmes et réflexions poétiques de Patrick Chamoiseau, Raphael Confiant, René Depestre, Édouard Glissant, Bertène Juminer, Ernest Pépin, Gisèle Pineau, Hector Poullet et Sylviane Telchid*. Paris: Gallimard 1994.
Lüsebrink, Hans-Jürgen, and Manfred Tietz (eds.): *Lectures de Raynal. L'Histoire de deux Indes en Europe et en Amérique au XVIIIe siècle*. Oxford: The Voltaire Foundation 1991.
Maalouf, Amin: Je parle du voyage comme d'autres parlent de leur maison. Interview with David Babouiin. In: *Magazine littéraire* 394 (2001), p. 98–103.
Maalouf, Amin: *Disordered World. Setting a New Course for the Twenty-first Century*. Translated from the French by George Miller. London: Bloomsbury 2011.
Macheiner, Judith: *Übersetzen. Ein Vademecum*. Frankfurt am Main: Eichborn 1995.
Maihold, Günther: Die neue Ohn-Macht der Grenze. Mexiko USA. In: Marianne Braig; Ottmar Ette; Dieter Ingenschay et al. (eds.): *Grenzen der Macht – Macht der Grenzen. Lateinamerika im globalen Kontext*. Frankfurt am Main: Vervuert 2005, p. 39–76.
Mañach, Jorge: *Historia y estilo*. Havana: Minerva 1944.
Mandelbrot, Benoit B.: *The Fractal Geometry of Nature*. Rev. Ed. New York: W.H. Freeman and Company 1983.
Marinello, Juan: Americanismo y cubanismo literarios. In: Juan Marinello: *Ensayos*. Havana: Editorial Arte y Literatura 1977, p. 48–49.

Marinello, Juan: Sobre la interpretación y el entendimiento de la obra de José Martí. In: *Anuario del Centro de Estudios Martianos* 1 (1978), p. 7–10.
Martí, José: *Abdala. Escrito expresamente para la Patria.* In: José Martí: *Obras Completas* 18. Havana: Editorial de Ciencias Sociales 1975, p. 11–24.
Martí, José: Diario de Cabo Haitiano a Dos Ríos. In: José Martí: *Obras Completas* 19. Havana: Editorial de Ciencias Sociales 1975, p. 213–246.
Martí, José: Nuestra América. In: José Martí: *Obras Completas* 6. Havana: Editorial de Ciencias Sociales 1975, p. 15–23.
Martí, José: *Obras Completas*. 24 vols. Havana: Editorial de Ciencias Sociales 1975.
Martí, José: *Atlas histórico biográfico José Martí*. Havana: Instituto Cubano de Geodesia y Cartografía - Centro de Estudios Martianos 1983.
Martí, José: El Diablo Cojuelo. In: José Martí: *Obras Completas. Edición crítica* 1. Havana: Centro de Estudios Martianos 1983, p. 22.
Martí, José: *Obras Completas. Edición crítica*. 24 vols. Havana: Centro de Estudios Martianos 1983.
Martí, José: Dos patrias. In: José Martí: *Poesía completa. Edición crítica*.1. Havana: Editorial Letras Cubanas 1985, p. 127.
Martí, José: *Poesía completa. Edición crítica*. 2 vols. Havana: Editorial Letras Cubanas 1985.
Martí, José: Our America. In: Mari Carmen Ramírez; Tomás Ybarra-Frausto, and Hector Olea (eds.): *Critical Documents of 20th Century Latin American and Latino Art. Resisting Categories: Latin American and/or Latino?* New Haven: Yale University Press 2012, p. 208–215.
Meier-Braun, Karl-Heinz and Reinhold Weber (eds.): *Kulturelle Vielfalt. Baden-Württemberg als Einwanderungsland*. Stuttgart: W. Kohlhammer 2005.
Mejcher, Sonja: *Geschichten über Geschichten. Erinnerung im Romanwerk von Ilyas Huri*. Wiesbaden: Reichert 2001.
Meyer, Stefan G. (ed.): *The Experimental Arabic Novel. Postcolonial Literary Modernism in the Levant*. New York: SUNY Press 2001.
Meyer, Stefan G.: The patchwork novel: Elias Khoury. The Experimental Arabic Novel. Postcolonial Literary Modernism in the Levant. In: Stefan G. Meyer (ed.): *The Experimental Arabic Novel. Postcolonial Literary Modernism in the Levant*. New York: SUNY Press 2001, p. 129-14.
Meyer-Clason, Curt: Vom Übersetzen. In: Karin Graf (ed.): *Übersetzerwerkstatt 1900. Ein Brevier und Materialien*. Berlin: Literarisches Colloquium 1991.
Michaux, Henri: Lieux lointains. In: *Mercure de France* 1109 (1956), p. 52.
Miller, J. Hillis (ed.): *Aspects of Narrative. Selected Papers from the English Institute*. New York: Columbia University Press 1971.
Montejo, Esteban; Miguel Barnet: *The Autobiography of a Runaway Slave, by Esteban Montejo; edited by Miguel Barnet;.* Translated by Jocasta Innes. London: Bodley Head 1968.
Montejo, Esteban; Miguel Barnet: *Biography of a Runaway Slave*. Translated by Nick Hill. Willimantic, CT: Curbstone Press 1994.
Mora, Terezia, Imran Ayata, Wladimir Kaminer, and Navid Kermani: Ich bin ein Teil der deutschen Literatur, so deutsch wie Kafka. Interview. Berlin, April 2005. In: *Literaturen* 4 (2005), p. 26–31.
Moretti, Franco: Conjectures on World Literature. In: Christopher Prendergast (ed.): *Debating World Literature*. London: Verso 2004, p. 148–162.
Morris, Pam (ed.): *The Bakhtin Reader. Selected Writings of Bakhtin, Mededev, Voloshinov*. London: Arnold 2003.

Müller, Gesine: *Die koloniale Karibik. Transferprozesse in hispanophonen und frankophonen Literaturen*. Berlin: De Gruyter 2012.
Naipaul, V. S.: *A House for Mr. Biswas*. London: André Deutsch 1961.
Nies, Fritz: Probieren statt studieren? Kurzpräsentation des Studiengangs. In: Fritz Nies; Albert-Reiner Glaap, and Wilhelm Gössmann (eds.): *Ist Literaturübersetzen lehrbar? Beiträge zur Eröffnung des Studiengangs Literaturübersetzen an der Universität Düsseldorf*. Tübingen: Narr 1989, p. 23–28.
Nies, Fritz; Albert-Reiner Glaap, and Wilhelm Gössmann (eds.): *Ist Literaturübersetzen lehrbar? Beiträge zur Eröffnung des Studiengangs Literaturübersetzen an der Universität Düsseldorf*. Tübingen: Narr 1989.
Nietzsche, Friedrich: Die fröhliche Wissenschaft. In: Giorgio Colli and Massimo Montinari (eds.): *Friedrich Nietzsche: Kritische Studienausgabe* 3. Berlin: DTV, De Gruyter 1988.
Nietzsche, Friedrich: On the Uses and Disadvantages of History for Life. In: Friedrich Nietzsche: *Untimely Meditations*. Translated by R. J. Hollingdale. Cambridge MA: Cambridge University Press 1997, p. 57–123.
Nietzsche, Friedrich: *The Gay Science*. Translated by Thomas Common. New York: Dover Philosophical Classics 2006.
O'Gorman, Edmundo: *La invención de América*. México D.F.: Fondo de Cultura Económica 1958.
O'Gorman, Edmundo: *The Invention of America. An Inquiry into the historical Nature of the New World and the Meaning of its History*. Bloomington: Indiana University Press 1961.
Oliver, José F. A.: *finnischer wintervorrat. Gedichte*. Frankfurt am Main: Suhrkamp 2005.
Oliver, José F. A.: *Mein andalusisches Schwarzwalddorf. Essays*. Frankfurt am Main: Suhrkamp 2007.
Oliver, José F. A.: *wortaus, wortein*. In: Oliver, José F. A.: *Mein andalusisches Schwarzwalddorf. Essays*. Frankfurt am Main: Suhrkamp 2007, p. 17–31.
Ortega y Medina, Juan Antonio (ed.): Conciencia y autenticidad históricas. Escritos en homenaje a Edmundo O'Gorman. México D.F.: UNAM 1968.
Ortiz, Fernando: *Cuban counterpoint. Tobacco and sugar*. Translated by Harriet de Onís. New York: Knopf 1947.
Ortiz, Fernando: *Contrapunteo cubano del tabaco y el azúcar*. Caracas: Biblioteca Ayacucho 1978.
Ortiz Fernández, Fernandu: *Principi y Pròstes. Culecció d'aguiats menurquins que s'espéra cauran bé á n'es ventrey*. Ciutadélla: Cuina d'en Salvadó Fábregues 1895.
Osterhammel, Jürgen and Niels P. Petersson: *Geschichte der Globalisierung. Dimensionen, Prozesse, Epochen*. Munich: Beck 2003.
Osterhammel, Jürgen., and Niels P. Petersson: *Globalization. A short history*. Translated by Dona Geyer. Princeton, NJ: Princeton University Press 2005.
Özdamar, Emine Sevgi: *Mother Tongue*. Translated by Craig Thomas and Alberto Manguel. Toronto: Coach House Press 1994.
Özdamar, Emine Sevgi: *Die Brücke vom Goldenen Horn*. Cologne: Kiepenheuer & Witsch 1998.
Özdamar, Emine Sevgi: *Mutterzunge. Erzählungen*. Cologne: Kiepenheuer & Witsch 1998.
Özdamar, Emine Sevgi: *Das Leben ist eine Karawanserei hat zwei Türen aus einer kam ich rein aus der anderen ging ich raus*. Cologne: Kiepenheuer & Witsch 1999.
Özdamar, Emine Sevgi: *Life is a Caravanserai, Has Two Doors, I Came in One, I Went Out the Other*. Translated by Luise von Flotow. London: Middlesex University Press 2000.
Özdamar, Emine Sevgi (ed.): *Der Hof im Spiegel. Erzählungen*. Cologne: Kiepenheuer & Witsch 2001.

Özdamar, Emine Sevgi: Mein Istanbul. In: Emine Sevgi Özdamar: *Der Hof im Spiegel. Erzählungen*. Cologne: Kiepenheuer & Witsch 2001, p. 67–76. First published in: *Die Weltwoche*, August 6, 1998.
Özdamar, Emine Sevgi: *Seltsame Sterne starren zur Erde. Wedding - Pankow 1976/77*. Cologne: Kiepenheuer & Witsch 2003.
Özdamar, Emine Sevgi: Wir wohnen in einer weiten Hölle. Interview with Nils Minkmar. In: *Frankfurter Allgemeine Sonntagszeitung*, December 21, 2004, p. 23.
Özdamar, Emine Sevgi: *Sonne auf halbem Weg. Die Istanbul-Berlin Trilogie*. Cologne: Kiepenheuer & Witsch 2006.
Özdamar, Emine Sevgi: *The Bridge of the Golden Horn*. Translated by Martin Chalmers. London: Serpent's Tail 2007.
Pannewick, Friederike: Elias Khoury. In: Heinz Ludwig Arnold (ed.): *Kritisches Lexikon zur fremdsprachigen Gegenwartsliteratur*. Munich: edition text+kritik 2001.
Patai, Daphne; Will H. Corral (eds.): *Theory's Empire. An Anthology of Dissent*. New York: Columbia University Press 2005.
Paul, Bettina; Michael Lindenberg; and Henning Schmidt-Semisch: Der Schmuggler. In: Eva Horn; Stefan Kaufmann, and Ulrich Bröckling (eds.): *Grenzverletzer. Von Schmugglern, Spionen und anderen subversiven Gestalten*. Berlin: Kulturverlag Kadmos 2002, p. 98–113.
Paz, Octavio: 'La paloma azul'. Generaciones y semblanzas. Domino mexicano. In: Manuel Durán (ed.): *Octavio Paz: Obras completas* 4. México: Fondo de Cultura Económica 1994–1999.
Pelayo, Rubén: Chronicle of a Death Foretold 1981. In: Rubén Pelayo (ed.): *Gabriel García Márquez. A Critical Companion*. Westport, Connecticut: Greenwood Press 2001, p. 111–113.
Pérez Firmat, Gustavo: *The Cuban Condition. Translation and Identity in Modern Cuban Literature*. Cambridge, UK: Cambridge University Press 1989, 2006.
Pérez Firmat, Gustavo: *Life on the Hyphen. The Cuban-American Way*. Austin: University of Texas Press 1994.
Pflitsch, Andreas: Literatur, grenzenlos. Aspekte transnationalen Schreibens. In: Christian Szyska and Friederike Pannewick (eds.): *Crossings and Passages in Genre and Culture*. Wiesbaden: Reichert 2003, p. 87–120.
Pineau, Gisèle: Tourment d'amour. In: Ralph Ludwig (ed.): *Écrire la 'parole de nuit': la nouvelle littérature antillaise. Nouvelles, poèmes et réflexions poétiques de Patrick Chamoiseau, Raphael Confiant, René Depestre, Édouard Glissant, Bertène Juminer, Ernest Pépin, Gisèle Pineau, Hector Poullet et Sylviane Telchid*. Paris: Gallimard 1994, p. 79–87.
Pizarro, Ana: *El archipiélago de fronteras externas. Culturas del Caribe hoy*. Santiago de Chile: Editorial de la Universidad de Santiago de Chile 2002.
Plessner, Helmuth: *Gesammelte Schriften. Anthropologie der Sinne*. 10 vols. Frankfurt am Main: Suhrkamp 1980–1985.
Plumb, J. H. (ed.): *Crisis in the Humanities*. Harmondsworth: Penguin 1964.
Pöppel, Hubert: Elementos del género policíaco en la obra de Gabriel García Márquez. In: *Estudios de Literatura Colombiana* 4 (1999), p. 23–46.
Prendergast, Christopher (ed.): *Debating World Literature*. London: Verso 2004.
Rahona, Elena; Sieburth Stephanie: Keeping Crime Unsolv(ed.) Characters' and Critics' Responses to Incest in García Márquez' 'Crónica de una muerte anunciada.' In: *Revista de Estudios Hispánicos* 30 (1996), p. 433–459.

Ramírez, Mari Carmen; Tomás Ybarra-Frausto, and Hector Olea (eds.): *Critical Documents of 20th Century Latin American and Latino Art. Resisting Categories: Latin American and/or Latino?* New Haven: Yale UP 2012.
Raynal, Guillaume-Thomas: *A Philosophical and Political History of the Settlements and Trade of the Europeans in the East and West Indies*. Translated by J.O. Justamond. London: Routledge 2007.
Reinhardt, Ulfried: *Globalisierung. Literaturen und Kulturen des Globalen*. Berlin: Akademie Verlag 2010.
Reinstädler, Janett, and Ottmar Ette (eds.): *Todas las islas la isla. Nuevas y novísimas tendencias en la literatura y cultura de Cuba*. Frankfurt am Main: Vervuert - Iberoamericana 2000.
Ribeiro, Darcy: Does Latin America exist? In: Mari Carmen Ramírez; Tomás Ybarra-Frausto, and Hector Olea (eds.): *Critical Documents of 20th Century Latin American and Latino Art. Resisting Categories: Latin American And/or Latino?* New Haven: Yale University Press 2012, p. 155–163.
Rinner, Susanne: *The German Student Movement and the Literary Imagination*. New York: Berghahn Books 2013.
Rojas Mix, Miguel: Bilbao y el hallazgo de América latina. Unión continental, socialista y libertaria. In: *Caravelle Toulouse*.46 1986, p. 35–47.
Rousso, Henry: *Le syndrome de Vichy. De 1944 à nos jours*. Paris: Seuil 1990.
Said, Edward W.: Foreword. In: Elias Khoury (ed.): *Little Mountain*. Manchester: Carcanet Press Limited 1989, p. ix–xxi.
Said, Edward W.: No Reconciliation Allow(ed.) In: André Aciman (ed.): *Letters of Transit. Reflections on Exile, Identity, Language, and Loss*. Edited by André Aciman. New York: The New Press 1999, p. 87–114.
Sartorius, Joachim: *Alexandria. Ein Zyklus / Alejandria. Un ciclo 1999–2000*. Translated by José F. A. Oliver. Huelva: Deputación Provincial de Huelva 1999.
Sauer, Carl Ortwin: *The Early Spanish Main*. Cambridge, UK: Cambridge University Press 1969.
Sauer, Carl Ortwin: *Descubrimiento y dominación española del Caribe*. Translated by Stella Mastrangelo. Mexico D.F.: Fondo de Cultura Económica 1984.
Saussy, Haun (ed.): *Comparative Literature in an Age of Globalization*. Baltimore, MD: Johns Hopkins University Press 2006.
Schalk, Fritz and Gustav Konrad (eds.): *Erich Auerbach: Gesammelte Aufsätze zur romanischen Philologie*. Berne: Franke 1967.
Scharlau, Birgit: Beschreiben und beherrschen. Die Informationspolitik der spanischen Krone im 15. und 16. Jahrhundert. In: Karl-Heinz Kohl; Berliner Festspiele GmbH Berlin, and Martin-Gropius-Bau Berlin (eds.): *Mythen der neuen Welt. Zur Entdeckungsgeschichte Lateinamerikas*. Katalog Ausstellung des 2. Festivals der Weltkulturen Horizonte 1982, Lateinamerika vom 13. Juni – 29. Aug. 1982 im Martin-Gropius-Bau, Berlin. Berlin: Fröhlich & Kaufmann 1982, p. 92–100.
Scharlau, Birgit (ed.): *Bild-Wort-Schrift. Beiträge zur Lateinamerika-Sektion des Freiburger Romanistentages*. Tübingen: Narr 1989.
Scharlau, Birgit: Nuevas tendencias en los estudios de crónicas y documentos del periodo colonial latinoamericano. In: *Revista de crítica latinoamericana* (Lima) 31–32 (1990), p. 365–375.
Scharlau, Birgit (ed.): *Übersetzen in Lateinamerika*. Tübingen: Narr 2002.

Schlickers, Sabine: *Verfilmtes Erzählen. Narratologisch-komparative Untersuchung zu "El beso de la mujer araña" Manuel Puig / Héctor Babenco und "Crónica de una muerte anunciada" Gabriel García Márquez / Francesco Rosi*. Frankfurt am Main: Vervuert 1997.

Schlögel, Karl: *Im Raum lesen wir die Zeit. Über Zivilisationsgschichte und Geopolitik*. Munich: Carl Hanser 2003.

Segler-Messer, Silke: *Archive der Erinnerung. Literarische Zeugnisse des Überlebens nach der Shoah in Frankreich*. Köln: Böhlau 2005.

Seyhan, Azade: Lost in Translation. Re-Membering the Mother Tongue in Emine Sevgi Özdamar's *Das Leben ist eine Karawanserei*. In: *German Quarterly* 69 (1996), p. 414–426.

Silva, Armando: Encuadre y punto de vista. Saber y goce en 'Crónica de una muerte anunciada'. In: Universidad Nacional de Colombia and Instituto Caro y Cuervo (eds.): *XX Congreso nacional de Literatura, Lingüística y Semiótica. Memorias. "Cien años de Soledad," treinta años después*. Bogotá: Universidad Nacional de Colombia 1998, p. 19–30.

Singer, Wolf: *Ein neues Menschenbild? Gespräche über Hirnforschung*. Frankfurt am Main: Suhrkamp 2003.

Singh, Vandana: *The Woman who Thought She was a Planet. And Other Stories*. New Delhi: Zubaan 2013.

Snell-Hornby, Mary: Übersetzen, Sprache, Kultur. In: Mary Snell-Hornby (ed.): *Übersetzungswissenschaft – Eine Neuorientierung. Zur Integrierung von Theorie und Praxis*. Tübingen: Francke 1994, p. 9–29.

Soja, Edward: *Postmodern Geographies. The Reassertion of Space in Critical Social Theory*. London: Verso 1989.

Soldevila Durante, Ignacio: *El compromiso de la imaginación. Vida y obra de Max Aub*. Segorbe, Castellon: Fundación Max Aub 1999.

Sousanis, Nick: *Unflattening*. Cambridge, MA: Harvard University Press 2015.

Spitzer, Leo: Das Eigene und das Fremde. Über Philologie und Nationalsozialismus. In: *Lendemains* 18.69–70 (1993), p. 179–191.

Steiner, George: *After Babel. Aspects of Language and Translation*. Oxford: Oxford University Press 1975.

Stephen Rudy (ed.): *Roman Jakobson: Selected Writings*. 9 vols. Paris: De Gruyter Mouton 1971-1985.

Strauss, Botho: *Beginnlosigkeit. Reflexionen über Fleck und Linie*. Munich: Carl Hanser 1992.

Strutz, Johann and Peter V. Zima (eds.): *Literarische Polyphonie. Übersetzung und Mehrsprachigkeit in der Literatur*. Tübingen: Narr 1996.

Szyska, Christian and Friederike Pannewick (eds.): *Crossings and Passages in Genre and Culture*. Wiesbaden: Reichert 2003.

Tawada, Yoko: Fragebogen. In: *Deutschland* (Frankfurt am Main) August 1996, p. 54.

Tawada, Yoko: *Talisman. Literarische Essays*. Tübingen: Konkursbuch Verlag Claudia Gehrke 1996.

Tawada, Yoko: *Überseezungen. Literarische Essays*. Tübingen: Konkursbuch Verlag Claudia Gehrke 2002.

Tawada, Yoko, and Chantal Wright: *Portrait of a Tongue. An Experimental Translation*. Ottawa, Ontario: University of Ottawa Press 2013.

Tiedemann, Rolf, and Hermann Schweppenhäuer (eds.): *Walter Benjamin: Gesammelte Schriften*. Frankfurt am Main: Suhrkamp 1977-1985.

Tietz, Manfred: L'Espagne et l' "Histoire des deux Indes" de l'abbé Raynal. In: Hans-Jürgen Lüsebrink and Manfred Tietz (eds.): *Lectures de Raynal. L'Histoire de deux Indes en Europe et en Amérique au XVIIIe siècle*. Oxford: The Voltaire Foundation 1991, p. 99–130.
Todorov, Tzvetan: *The Conquest of America. The Question of the Other*. Translated by Richard Howard. New Zork: Harper Perennial 1992.
Todorov, Tzvetan: *Le nouveau désordre mondial. Réflexions d'un Européen*. Paris: Robert Laffont 2003.
Todorov, Tzvetan: *The New World Disorder*. Cambridge, UK: Polity 2005.
Twain, M.: *The Writings of Mark Twain*: P. F. Collier & Son Company 1907.
UNAIDS 2010: *Global Report. UNAIDS Report on the Global AIDS Epidemic: 2010*. Joint United Nations Programme on HIV/AIDS UNAIDS. Geneva.
Universidad Nacional de Colombia and Instituto Caro y Cuervo (eds.): *XX Congreso nacional de Literatura, Lingüística y Semiótica. Memorias. "Cien años de Soledad," treinta años después*. Bogotá: Universidad Nacional de Colombia 1998.
Utz, Peter: Transgressionen der Traduction. Robert Musils 'Mann ohne Eigenschaften' und Philippe Jaccottets 'L'Homme sans qualités'. In: Rainer Warning and Neumann Gerhard (eds.): *Transgressionen. Literatur als Ethnographie*. Freiburg im Breisgau: Rombach 2003, p. 151–172.
Vainio, Jari; Felicity Cutts: Yellow Fever. Division of Emerging and Other Communicable Diseases, Surveillance and Control. Geneva: World Health Organization 1998.
Valbert, Gérard: *Albert Cohen, le seigneur*. Paris: Grasset 1990.
Valdés, Zoé: Café Nostalgia. La turbulenta y hermosa corazonada de un abismo de que ne se podra volver. Barcelona: Planeta Colección Autores españoles e hispanoamericanos 1997.
Vera-León, Antonio: Hacer hablar. La transcripción testimonial. In: *Revista de crítica literaria latinoamericana* XVIII (1992), p. 181–199.
Vespucci, Amerigo: Letter on his Third Voyage from Amerigo Vespucci to Lorenzo Pietro Francesco Di Medici. In: *Amerigo Vespucci: The Letters of Amerigo Vespucci and Other Documents illustrative of his Career*. Translated with notes and an introduction. Edited and translated by Clements R. Markham. London: Printed for the Hakluyt Society 1894, p. 42–56.
Villaverde, Cirilo: *Cecilia Valdez or El Angel Hill. A Novel of 19th Century Cuba*. Translated from the Spanisch by Helen Lane. Oxford: Oxford University Press 2005.
Vogel, Thomas (ed.): *Über das Hören. Einem Phänomen auf der Spur*. Tübingen: Attempto 1996.
Wajsbrot, Cécile: *Pour la littérature*. Paris: Zulma 1999.
Wajsbrot, Cécile: *Beaune-la-Rolande*. Paris: Zulma 2004.
Wajsbrot, Cécile: *Le Tour du Lac*. Paris: Zulma 2004.
Wajsbrot, Cécile: *Mémorial*. Paris: Zulma 2005.
Walcott, Derek: The Antilles. Fragments of Epic Memory. In: Derek Walcott: *What the Twilight Says. Essays*. London: faber & faber 1998, p. 65–84.
Walter, Monica: Testimonio y melodrama. En torno a un debate actual sobre 'Biografía de un cimarrón' y sus consecuencias posibles. In: Janett Reinstädler and Ottmar Ette (eds.): *Todas las islas la isla. Nuevas y novísimas tendencias en la literatura y cultura de Cuba*. Frankfurt am Main: Vervuert – Iberoamericana 2000, p. 25–38.
Warning, Rainer (ed.): *Rezeptionsästhetik. Theorie und Praxis*. Munich: Fink 1975.
Warning, Rainer and Neumann Gerhard (eds.): *Transgressionen. Literatur als Ethnographie*. Freiburg im Breisgau: Rombach 2003.

Wasserstein, Bernard: *Europa ohne Juden. Das europäische Judentum seit 1945*. Cologne: Kiepenheuer & Witsch 1999.
Wehler, Hans-Ulrich: *Imperialismus. Studien zur Entwicklung des Imperium Americanum, 1865-1900*. Göttingen: Vandenhoeck & Ruprecht 1974.
Werner, Michael; Zimmermann, Bénédicte: Vergleich, Transfer, Verflechtung. Der Ansatz der 'histoire croisée' und die Herausforderung des Transnationalen. In: *Geschichte und Gesellschaft. Zeitschrift für historische Sozialwissenschaften* (Göttingen) 28 (2002), p. 607–636.
Winkle, Stefan: *Geisseln der Menschheit. Kulturgeschichte der Seuchen*. Düsseldorf: Artemis & Winkler 1997.
Wurm, Carmen: *Doña Marina, la Malinche. Eine historische Figur und ihre literarische Rezeption*. Frankfurt am Main: Vervuert 1996.
Young-Bruehl, Elisabeth: *Hannah Arendt. Leben, Werk und Zeit*. Frankfurt am Main: Fischer 2000.
Yourcenar, Marguerite: Konstantinos Kavafis. Eine Einführung. In: Robert Elsie (ed.): *Konstantinos Kavafis. Das Gesamtwerk, griechisch-deutsch*. Translated and edited by Robert Elsie. Zurich: Ammann 1997, p. 5–49.
Zeuske, Michael: The 'Cimarrón' in the Archives. A Re-Reading of Miguel Barnet's Biography of Esteban Montejo. In: *New West Indian Guide / Nieuwe West-Indische Gids* LXXI.3-4 (1997), p. 265–279.
Zilly, Berthold: Dankrede. In: *Der Übersetzer* (Munich) 30 (1996), p. 3–5.
Zilly, Berthold: O traductor implícito. Considerações acerca da translingualidade de 'Os Sertões'. In: *Revista da Universidade de São Paulo* 45 (2000), p. 85–105.
Zima, Peter V.: *Ideologie und Theorie. Eine Diskurskritik*. Tübingen: Francke 1989.
Zima, Peter V.: Der unfassbare Rest. Die Theorie der Übersetzung zwischen Dekonstruktion und Semiotik. In: Johann Strutz and Peter V. Zima (eds.): *Literarische Polyphonie. Übersetzung und Mehrsprachigkeit in der Literatur*. Tübingen: Narr 1996, p. 19–34.
Zimic, Stanislav: Pundonor calderoniano en Hispanoamérica con ilustración en "Crónica de una muerte anunciada" de García Márquez. In: *Acta Neophilologica* XXXIV.1-2 (2001), p. 87–103.
Zur Lippe, Rudolf: *Sinnenbewusstsein. Grundlegung einer anthropologischen Ästhetik*. Band II: Leben in Übergängen – Transzendenz. Baltmannsweiler: Schneider-Verlag Hohengehren 2000.
Zweig, Stefan: Amerigo. Die Geschichte eines historischen Irrtums. In: Stefan Zweig: *Zeiten und Schicksale. Aufsätze und Vorträge aus den Jahren 1902–1942*. Frankfurt am Main: Fischer 1990, p. 387–467.
Zweig, Stefan: *Zeiten und Schicksale. Aufsätze und Vorträge aus den Jahren 1902–1942*. Frankfurt am Main: Fischer 1990.

Name Index

Aciman, André 2, 3, 4, 5, 7, 8
Adanson, Michel 292
Adorno, Theodor W. 46, 47, 48, 49, 50, 51, 52, 59
Agamben, Giorgio 49, 50, 51, 54, 61, 62, 116, 119, 120, 297
Alemán, Mateo 174
Alighieri, Dante 5
Al-Rawi, Bisher 214, 215, 216
Anzaldúa, Gloria 211, 212
Arenas, Reinaldo 112, 114, 115, 116, 117, 119, 147, 148, 149, 151
Arendt, Hannah 20, 47, 52, 54, 60, 61, 116, 181, 182, X
Aristotle 304, 307
Asturias, Miguel Ángel 253
Atatürk, Mustafa Kemal 190, 195, 206
Aub, Max 45, 70, 71, 72, 73, 74, 75, 139, 259, 270, X
Auerbach, Erich 40, 41, 42, 43, 44, 45, 46, 47, 48, 50, 51, 52, 58, 60, 67, 83, 103, 297, 298, 312, X
Ayata, Imran 9

Bachelard, Gaston 310
Bakhtin, Mikhail 306, XXII
Balzac, Honoré de 75, 303
Baranczak, Stanislaw 80
Barcha, Mercedes 224, 237
Barnes, Julian 169
Barnet, Miguel 146, 147, 148, 159
Barthes, Roland 86, 115, 121, 162, 166, 167, 299, 301, 305, 309, 310, X
Baudelaire, Charles 144, 177
Beckett, Samuel 182
Benítez Rojo, Antonio 106, 114, 121, 122, 124, 139, 141, 142, 145, 151, 152, 153
Benjamin, Walter 32, 47, 48, 50, 51, 52, 53, 58, 74, 81, 98, 99, 129, 130, 131, 138, 141, 164, 176, 177, 179
Bernabé, Jean 107
Besson, Benno 196, 202
Bhabha, Homi 9, 208

Boggs, Colleen XIII
Bolívar, Simón 101, 102, 103, 140
Borges, Jorge Luis 135, 139, 159, 169, 170, 176, 248
Borrero Echeverría, Esteban 128, 302
Borrero, Juana 108, 128, 129, 130, 131, 133, 138, 300, 301, 302, 303
Bougainville, Louis-Antoine de 18
Bourdieu, Pierre 290
Brecht, Berthold 196, 197, 198, 200, 201, 202
Breton, André 75
Brittain, Victoria 214
Bush, George Walker 216
Butor, Michel 159

Calvino, Italo 131, 136, 165, 166
Camões, Luís de 163
Camus, Albert 245
Candolle, Augustin-Pyrame de 292
Caproni, Giorgio 6
Carpentier, Alejo 136, 144, 145
Casal, Julián 301
Casanova, Pascale 44
Cassin, Barbara XVI
Castro, Fidel 115, 147, 150, 209, 308
Cavafy, Constantine 5, 6, 46, 286, 288
Celan, Paul 61, 252
Cendrars, Blaise 182
Cervantes, Miguel de 135, 305
Césaire, Aimé 124
Chamisso, Adelbert von 193, 196
Chamoiseau, Patrick 107, 111, 124, 159
Charles V. 162
Ché Guevara, Ernesto 209
Cohen, Albert 62, 63, 64, 65, 66, 81
Colón, Bartolomé 94
Columbus, Christopher 13, 14, 16, 91, 92, 93, 94, 132, 136, 145, 215
Condé, Maryse 109, 112
Confiant, Raphaël 107, 111, 124
Conrad, Joseph 182
Cook, James 18

Cortázar, Julio 138
Cortés, Hernán 14, 162, 163
Cramer, Friedrich 44, 84, 85, 87, 97, 106

Da Silva, Lula 37
Damrosch, David XIV
Danticat, Edwidge 113
Darío, Rubén 25
Daston, Lorraine 296
De Acosta, José 15
De Galaup, Jean-François 18
De la Cosa, Juan 94, 95, 99
De la Nuez, Iván 119, 124, 151, 152
De la Vega el Inca, Garcilaso 15
De las Casas, Bartolomé 15
De Mier, Servando Teresa 140, 147, 148
De Pauw, Cornelius 21
De Sahagún, Bernardino 15
Defoe, Daniel 310
Del Casal, Julián 128, 133
Deleuze, Gilles 100, IX
Depestre, René 111, 124
Díaz del Castillo, Bernal 15
Díaz, Jesús 117, 154
Díaz, Ruy 16
Didérot, Denis 21
Djebar, Assia 56, 57, X
Dreyfus, Alfred 64, 65
Dürer, Albrecht 17, 18

Eco, Umberto 159
Euclid of Alexandria 88, 105

Fanon, Frantz 124
Faruq I. of Egypt 1
Fatah, Sherko 37, 270, 271, 272, 273, 274, 275, 276, 277, 278, 279, 280, 281, 282, 283
Fayad, Luis 219, 220, 221, 222, 223, 224, 227, 252, 254
Fernández de Lizardi, José Joaquín 125
Fernández de Oviedo, Gonzalo 15
Fernández Retamar, Roberto 124, 150
Finkielkraut, Alain 64
Flaubert, Gustave 75, 303, 306

Foucault, Michel 19, 292, 293
Franco, Francisco 72, 196
Frisch, Max 295
Fuentes, Carlos 150, 253
Funes, Reinaldo 108, 109

Gadamer, Hans-Georg 294, 295
Galeano, Eduardo 90, 91, 95, 114
García Márquez, Gabriel 223, 224, 225, 226, 227, 228, 229, 230, 231, 232, 233, 234, 235, 236, 237, 238, 239, 240, 241, 243, 245, 249, 250, 252, 253, 254
Gauss, Karl-Markus 271
Geertz, Clifford 306
Genette, Gérard 130, 185
George, Stefan 161, 170, 171
Gide, André 88, 93, 309, 310
Glissant, Édouard 99, 100, 108, 111, 124, IX, X
Goethe, Johann Wolfgang 40, 55, 57, 58, 176, 177, 178, 196, 289, 291, 303
Gómez de Avellaneda, Gertrudis 132
Gómez, Máximo 126
González Echevarría, Roberto 144, 151, 152, 153, 154
Goytisolo, Juan 55, 56, 57
Guattari, Félix 100, IX
Guillén, Nicolás 136, 142, 143

Habermas, Jürgen 28, 293, 294, 295, 300
Hall, Stuart 124
Hartman, Geoffrey 76
Hayakawa, Samuel Ichiye XVIII
Hearn, Lafcadio 25
Heine, Heinrich 196, 198
Heredia, José María 108, 132
Hikmet, Nazim 195
Homer 5, 46, 48, 49, 59
Horkheimer, Max 46, 47, 48, 49, 50, 51, 52, 59
Hugo von St. Viktor 45, 50
Humboldt, Alexander von 11, 21, 22, 92, 93, 136, 138, 139, 144, 145, 163, 164, X
Huntington, Samuel Phillips 26, 216

Iser, Wolfgang 304, 305, 310

Jakobson, Roman 34, 160, 162, 179
James, Henry 170
Jaspers, Karl 181
Jussieu, Antoine-Laurent de 292

Kafka, Franz 9
Kaminer, Wladimir 9
Kann, Emma 66, 67, 68, 69, 70
Kant, Immanuel 84, 85, 86, 87
Kent, Nicolas 214
Kermani, Navid 9
Khoury, Elias 38, 233, 238, 239, 240, 241, 242, 243, 244, 245, 246, 247, 248, 249, 250, 251, 252, 253, 254
Klee, Paul 51, 52
Kleist, Heinrich von 21, 22, 56
Klemperer, Victor 52
Koselleck, Reinhart 19
Krauss, Werner 52, 161, 162, 305

Lahens, Yanick 112, 113, 114
Lamarck, Jean Baptiste de 292
Lamming, George 107, 124
Lasker-Schüler, Else 196, 197, 198, 201, 202
Lenin 209
Leo Africanus 16
Lepenies, Wolf 19, 293
Lesage, Alain-René 173, 174
Lévi-Strauss, Claude 88, 309
Lezama Lima, José 140, 141, 143, 144, 147
Linnaeus, Carl 292
Llosa, Mario Vargas X
López de Gómara, Francisco 15
Lotman, Juri 300
Lowell, Robert XI

Maalouf, Amin 12, 28, 29, 307, 308, XXI, X
Macheiner, Judith 175
Malinowski, Bronislav 136
Mañach, Jorge 151
Mandelbrot, Benoît 87, 88, 89, 96

Mann, Thomas 310
Mao Zedong 209
Marinello, Juan 134, 135, 136, 145, 146, 149
Márquez, Gabriel García 38, X
Martí, José 23, 25, 103, 108, 126, 127, 128, 129, 130, 131, 133, 134, 138, 139, 140, 141, 142, 143, 149, 150, 154, 215, 302, 308, X
May, Karl 272, 288
Medici, Lorenzo di Pier Francesco de' 92
Mercado, Manuel 150
Mercator, Gerardus 93
Mérimée, Prosper 297
Meyer-Clason, Curt 157, 158, 160
Michaux, Henri 55
Mickle, William Julius 163, 164
Miranda, Francisco 140
Molière 195, 196
Montejo, Esteban 146, 147
Mora, Terézia 9
More, Thomas 18, 85
Moretti, Franco XIV, XV
Mukherjee, Bharati 35
Müller, Heiner 196
Muñoz, Juan Bautista 21

Nabokov, Vladimir 182
Naipaul, Vidiadhar Surajprasad 110, 111, 112
Nasser, Gamal Abdel 2
Newton, Isaac 105
Nies, Fritz 160, 171, 177
Nietzsche, Friedrich 49, 50, 289, 290, 291, 311, 312

O'Gorman, Edmundo 94
Odysseus 4, 6
Ohnesorg, Benno 206
Oliver, José Francisco Agüera 3, 4, 57, 179, 284, 285, 286, 287
Ortiz, Fernando 33, 132, 136, 137, 138, 139, 140, 141, 146, 154, 155
Özdamar, Emine Sevgi 10, 36, 55, 56, 57, 179, 187, 189, 190, 191, 192, 193, 194, 195, 196, 197, 198, 199, 200, 201,

202, 203, 204, 205, 206, 207, 208, 209, 210, 211, 212, 213

Paz, Octavio 181, 182, 213
Pérez Firmat, Gustavo 124, 134, 137, 151, 152
Perse, Saint-John 97
Pineau, Gisèle 111, 112
Pinochet, Augusto 225
Plessner, Helmut 302
Polo, Marco 92
Proust, Marcel 155, 161

Quevedo, Francisco de 169

Rabelais, François 81, 82, 260
Raynal, Guillaume-Thomas 21, 163, 164
Reyes, Rafael 224
Ribeiro, Darcy 89, 90, 95
Rilke, Rainer Maria 161
Rizal, José 25
Robbe-Grillet, Alain 75
Robertson, William 21
Rodó, José Enrique 23
Rodríguez, Luis Felipe 134, 140
Rodríguez, Simón 140
Rousso, Henry 76
Rumsfeld, Donald 215
Rushdie, Salman 247, 307

Said, Edward 7, 243, 248, 253
Sanguily, Manuel 114
Sarduy, Severo 150
Sartre, Jean-Paul 64, 150, 172
Saussy, Haun XV, XVI
Schlögel, Karl 30, 31, 32
Segler-Messner, Silke 49, 61, 76
Segovia, Tomás 181, 182
Semprún, Jorge X
Seward, William Henry 102
Seyhan, Azade 194
Shah of Iran, Mohammad Reza Pahlavi 206
Shakespeare, William 161, 169, 177
Singer, Wolf 42

Singh, Vandana IX
Slovo, Gillian 214
Snow, Charles Percy 292
Spitzer, Leo 297, X
Stalin 209
Stein, Gertrude 184
Strauss, Botho 6, 7, XIII
Straw, Jack 215

Tawada, Yoko 10, 179, 182, 183, 184, 185, 186, 187, 188, 189, 190, 191, 193, 194, 195, 202, 203, 211, 212, 213
Taylor, Rod 204
Thrasher, John Sidney 163, 164
Tocqueville, Alexis de 102
Todorov, Tzvetan 163
Touraine, Alain 243
Tournefort, Joseph Pitton de 292
Trotsky, Leo 209
Twain, Mark XVI

Uhrbach, Carlos Pío 128, 129, 133, 300, 301
Unamuno, Miguel de 135

Valdés, Zoé 132, 149, 154, 155
Vargas Llosa, Mario 150
Velázquez, Diego 293
Veli, Orhan 195
Vera-León, Antonio 146
Vespucci, Amerigo 92, 93, 94
Vicq d'Azyr, Félix 292
Villaverde, Cirilo 108, 132, 133, 149
Voltaire 161, 162, 164

Wajsbrot, Cécile 37, 75, 76, 77, 78, 79, 80, 81, 82, 83, 255, 256, 257, 258, 259, 260, 261, 262, 263, 264, 265, 266, 267, 268, 269, 270, 271, 273, 279
Walcott, Derek 97, 98, 99, 123, 124, 184
Wares, Sacha 214
Wasserstein, Bernard 76
Weigel, Helene 196
Weill, Kurt 196

Weiss, Peter 196, 198
Wieland, Christoph Martin 161, 173
Williams, William Carlos IX

Xirau, Ramón 181, 182

Zárate, Raúl de 117

Zeuske, Michael 147
Zilly, Berthold 173, 178, 179
Zima, Peter 175
Zola, Émile 303, 310
Zorzi, Alessandro 94
Zur Lippe, Rudolf 305
Zweig, Stefan 2

www.ingramcontent.com/pod-product-compliance
Lightning Source LLC
Chambersburg PA
CBHW050101170426
43198CB00014B/2415